PLUTO

URASAWA × TEZUKA

A NEW VISION BASED ON ASTRO BOY – 'THE GREATEST ROBOT ON EARTH'
BY NAOKI URASAWA AND OSAMU TEZUKA

005

...ED WITH **TAKASHI NAGASAKI**
...RVISED BY **MACOTO TEZKA**
...COOPERATION OF **TEZUKA PRODUCTIONS**

ACT 40 SAGE OF THE SANDS 3

ACT 41 SAHAD 27

ACT 42 A HOME IN HADES 51

ACT 43 AN ENCOUNTER WITH DEATH 75

ACT 44 I AM PLUTO 99

ACT 45 NEGOTIATION AND REPARATION 123

ACT 46 END OF THE DREAM 147

ACT 47 REAL TEARS 171

Act 40 Sage of the Sands

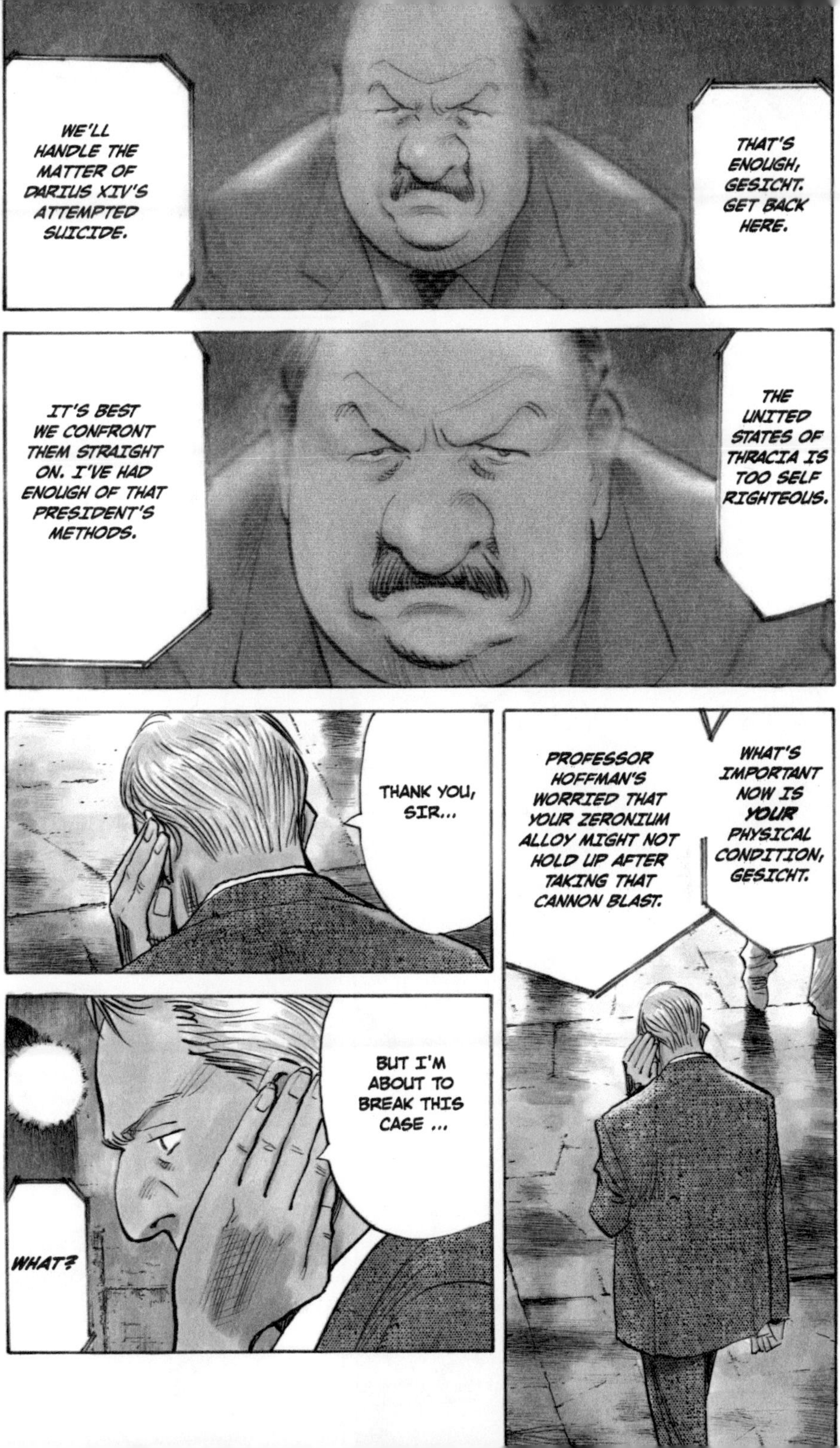
THAT'S ENOUGH, GESICHT. GET BACK HERE.
WE'LL HANDLE THE MATTER OF DARIUS XIV'S ATTEMPTED SUICIDE.
THE UNITED STATES OF THRACIA IS TOO SELF RIGHTEOUS.
IT'S BEST WE CONFRONT THEM STRAIGHT ON. I'VE HAD ENOUGH OF THAT PRESIDENT'S METHODS.
WHAT'S IMPORTANT NOW IS YOUR PHYSICAL CONDITION, GESICHT.
PROFESSOR HOFFMAN'S WORRIED THAT YOUR ZERONIUM ALLOY MIGHT NOT HOLD UP AFTER TAKING THAT CANNON BLAST.
THANK YOU, SIR...
BUT I'M ABOUT TO BREAK THIS CASE ...
WHAT?

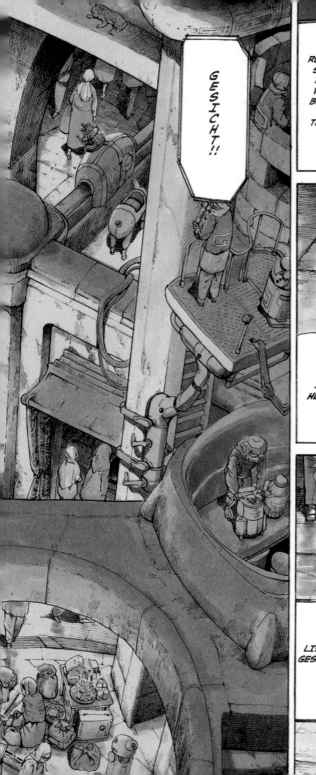

GESICHT!!

REALLY? SO YOU KNOW WHO'S BEHIND ALL THIS...?

THAT'S RIGHT. BUT I'M SURE THAT HUMANS WOULD CALL THIS...

...A HUNCH.

A... HUNCH? HOW DOES A ROBOT HAVE A HUNCH?

LISTEN, GESICHT!!

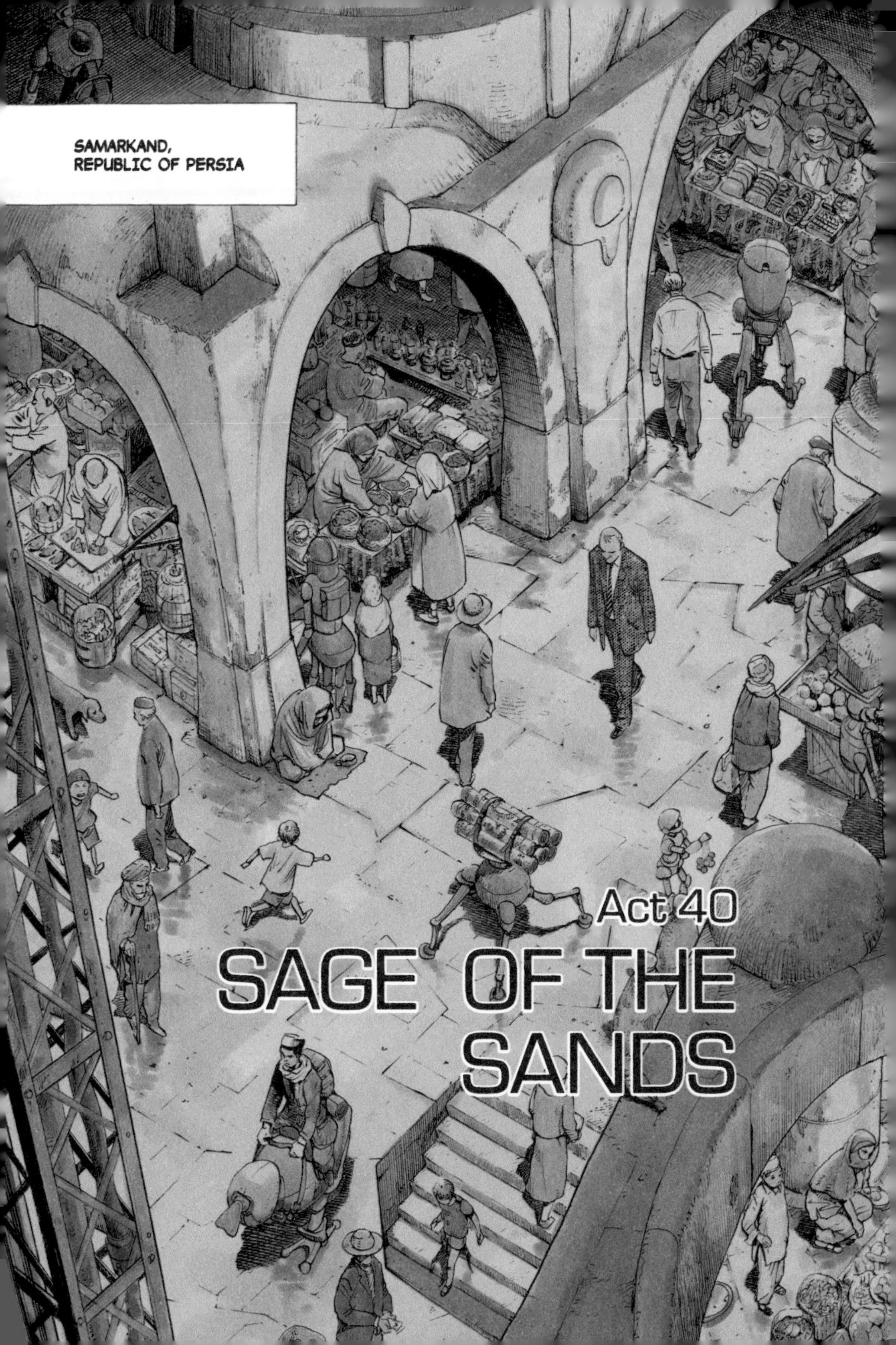
SAMARKAND,
REPUBLIC OF PERSIA
Act 40
SAGE OF THE SANDS

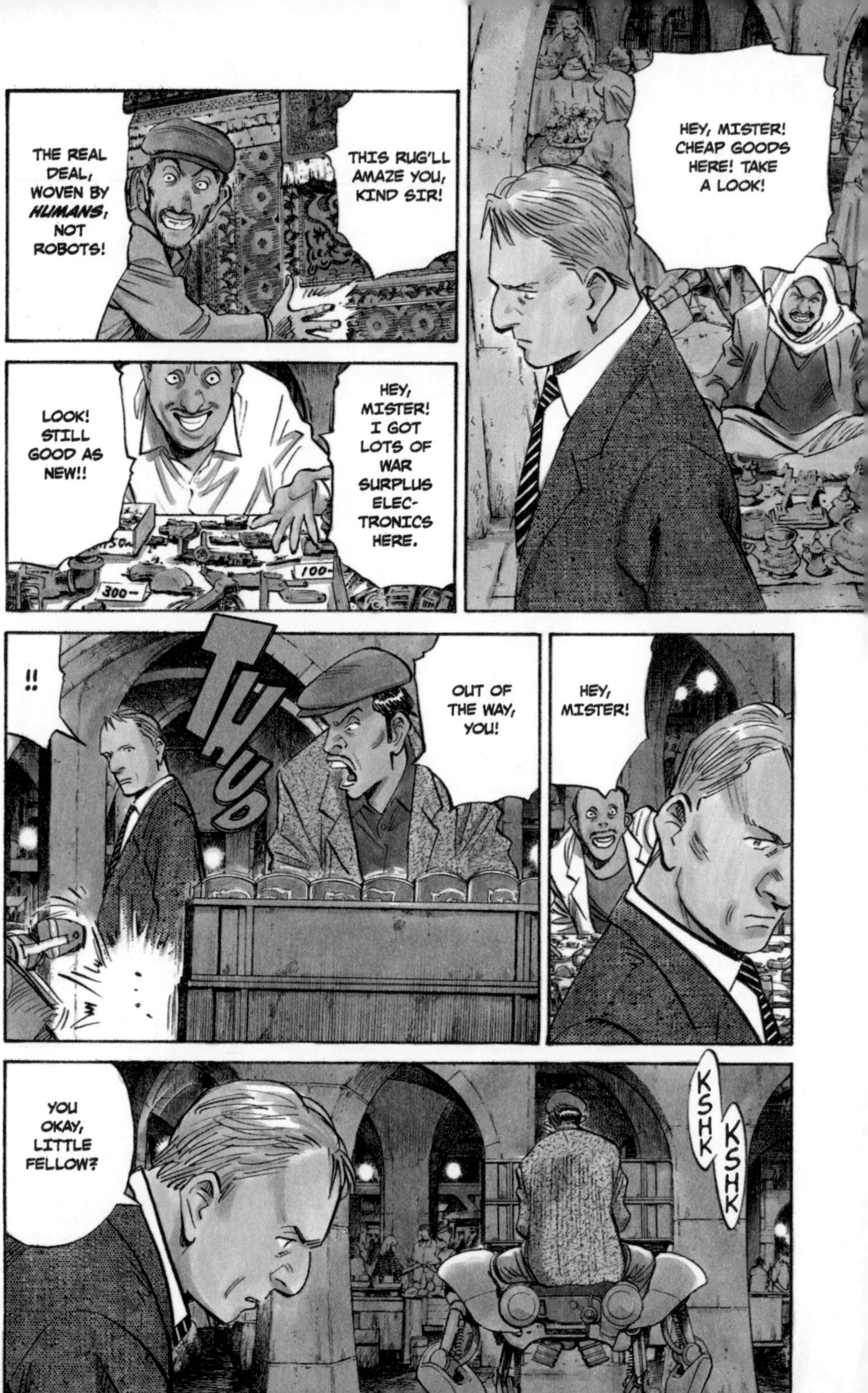
HEY, MISTER! CHEAP GOODS HERE! TAKE A LOOK!
THIS RUG'LL AMAZE YOU, KIND SIR!
THE REAL DEAL, WOVEN BY ***HUMANS***, NOT ROBOTS!
HEY, MISTER! I GOT LOTS OF WAR SURPLUS ELEC-TRONICS HERE.
LOOK! STILL GOOD AS NEW!!
300-
100-
HEY, MISTER!
OUT OF THE WAY, YOU!
THUD
!!
KSHK KSHK
YOU OKAY, LITTLE FELLOW?

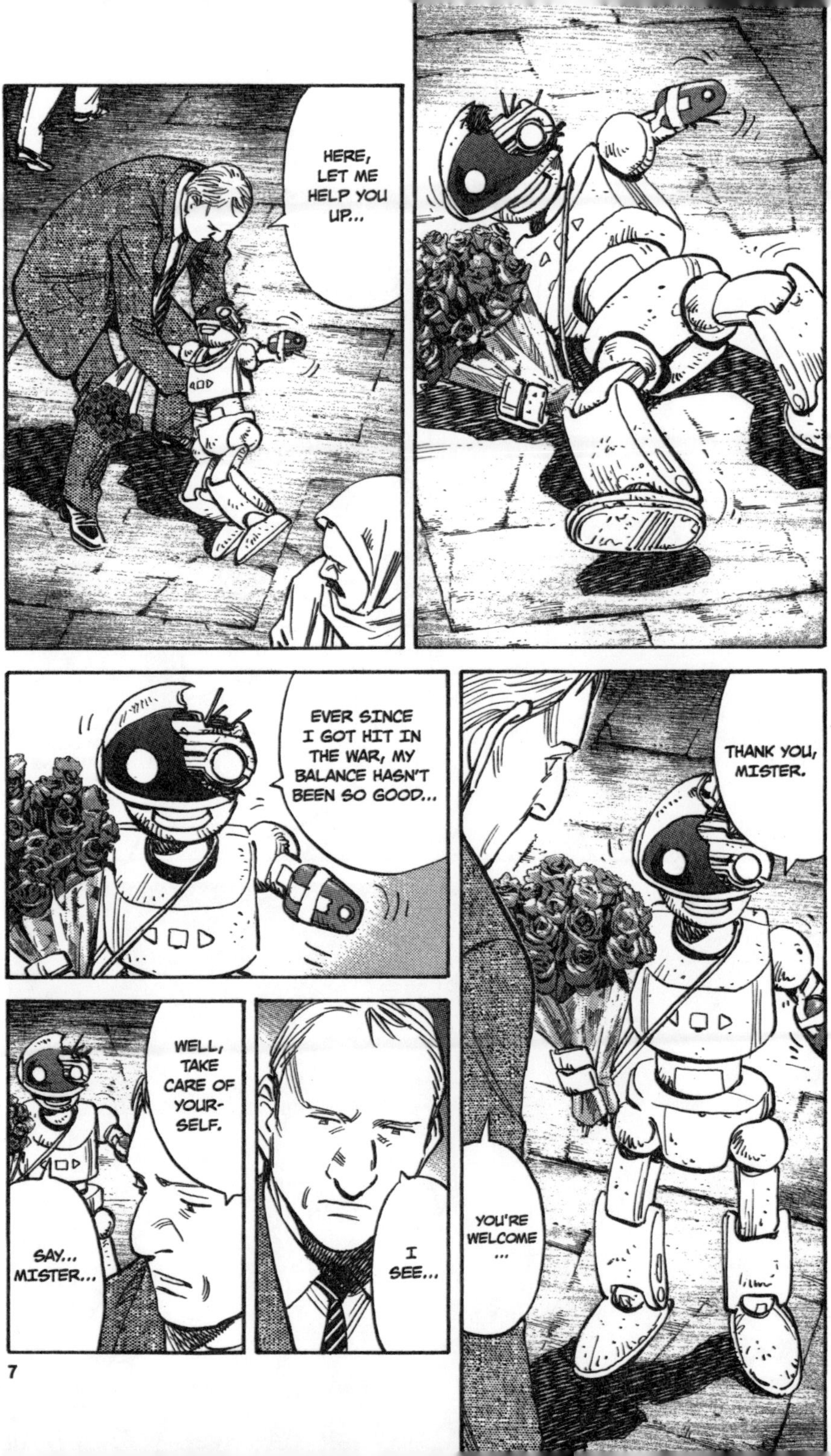
HERE, LET ME HELP YOU UP...
THANK YOU, MISTER.
YOU'RE WELCOME ...
EVER SINCE I GOT HIT IN THE WAR, MY BALANCE HASN'T BEEN SO GOOD...
I SEE...
WELL, TAKE CARE OF YOUR-SELF.
SAY... MISTER...

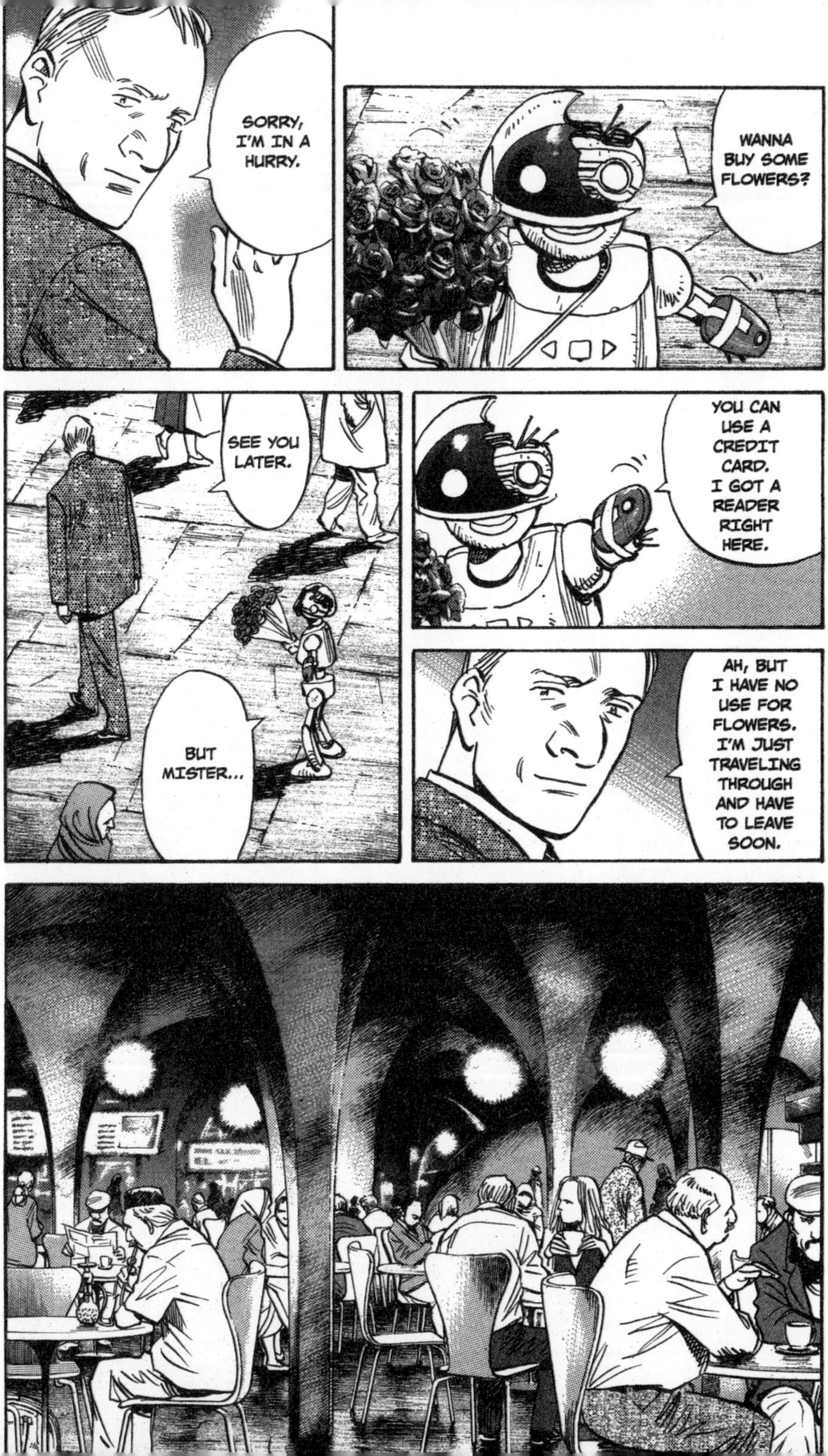
WANNA BUY SOME FLOWERS?
SORRY, I'M IN A HURRY.
YOU CAN USE A CREDIT CARD. I GOT A READER RIGHT HERE.
AH, BUT I HAVE NO USE FOR FLOWERS. I'M JUST TRAVELING THROUGH AND HAVE TO LEAVE SOON.
SEE YOU LATER.
BUT MISTER...

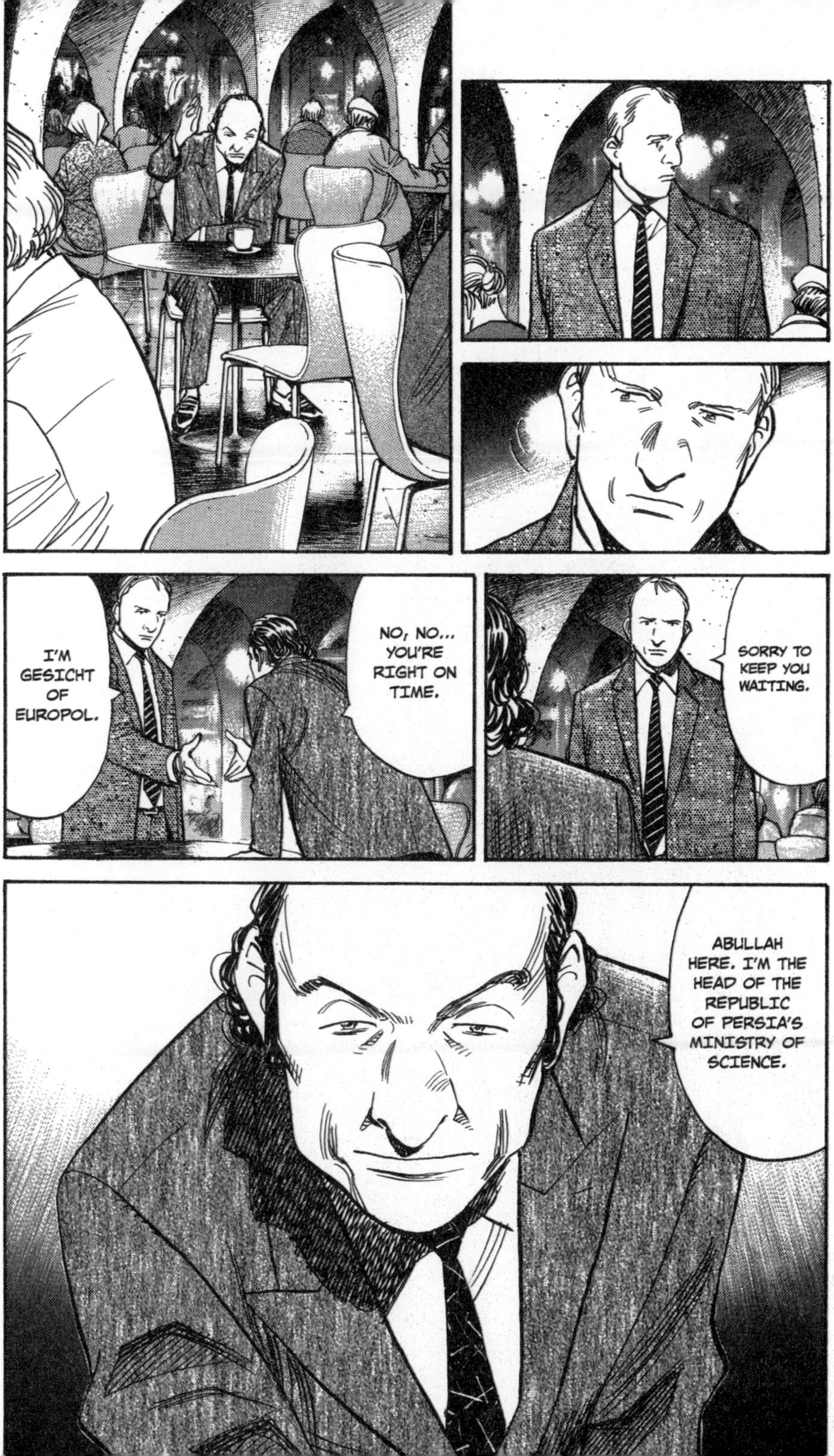
SORRY TO KEEP YOU WAITING.
NO, NO... YOU'RE RIGHT ON TIME.
I'M GESICHT OF EUROPOL.
ABULLAH HERE. I'M THE HEAD OF THE REPUBLIC OF PERSIA'S MINISTRY OF SCIENCE.

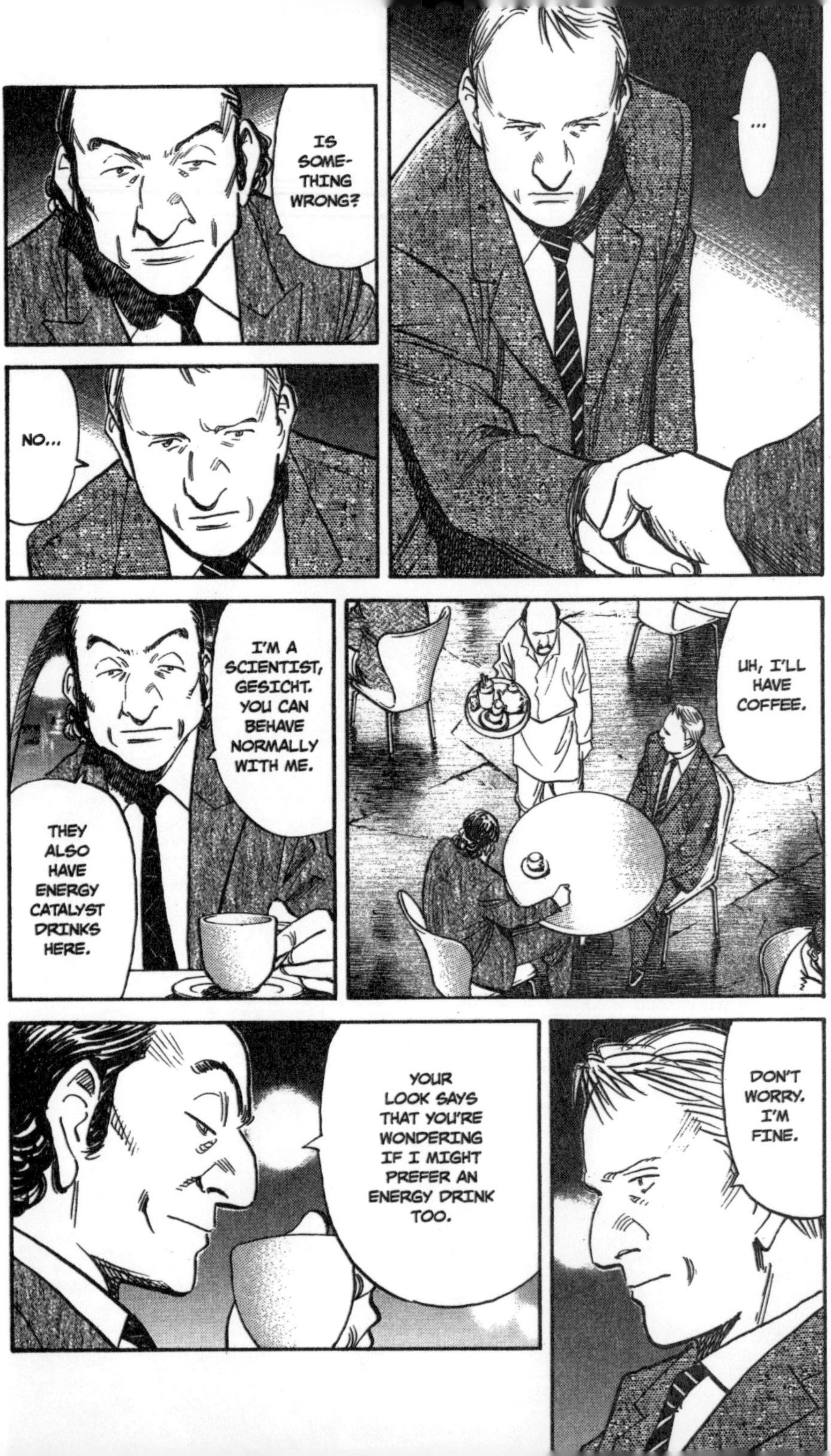
...
IS SOME-THING WRONG?
NO...
UH, I'LL HAVE COFFEE.
I'M A SCIENTIST, GESICHT. YOU CAN BEHAVE NORMALLY WITH ME.
THEY ALSO HAVE ENERGY CATALYST DRINKS HERE.
DON'T WORRY. I'M FINE.
YOUR LOOK SAYS THAT YOU'RE WONDERING IF I MIGHT PREFER AN ENERGY DRINK TOO.

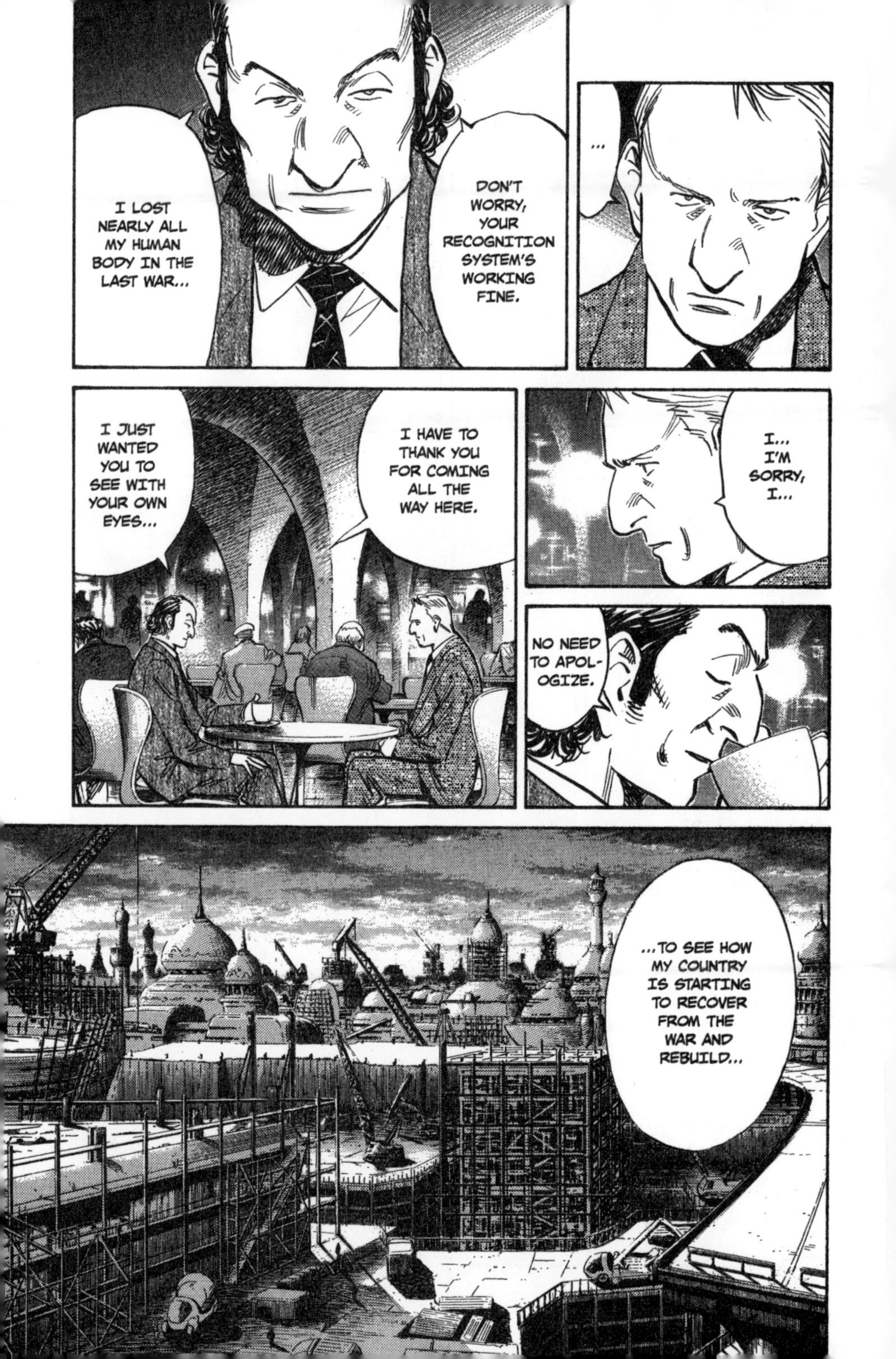
...
DON'T WORRY, YOUR RECOGNITION SYSTEM'S WORKING FINE.
I LOST NEARLY ALL MY HUMAN BODY IN THE LAST WAR...
I... I'M SORRY, I...
NO NEED TO APOLOGIZE.
I HAVE TO THANK YOU FOR COMING ALL THE WAY HERE.
I JUST WANTED YOU TO SEE WITH YOUR OWN EYES...
...TO SEE HOW MY COUNTRY IS STARTING TO RECOVER FROM THE WAR AND REBUILD...

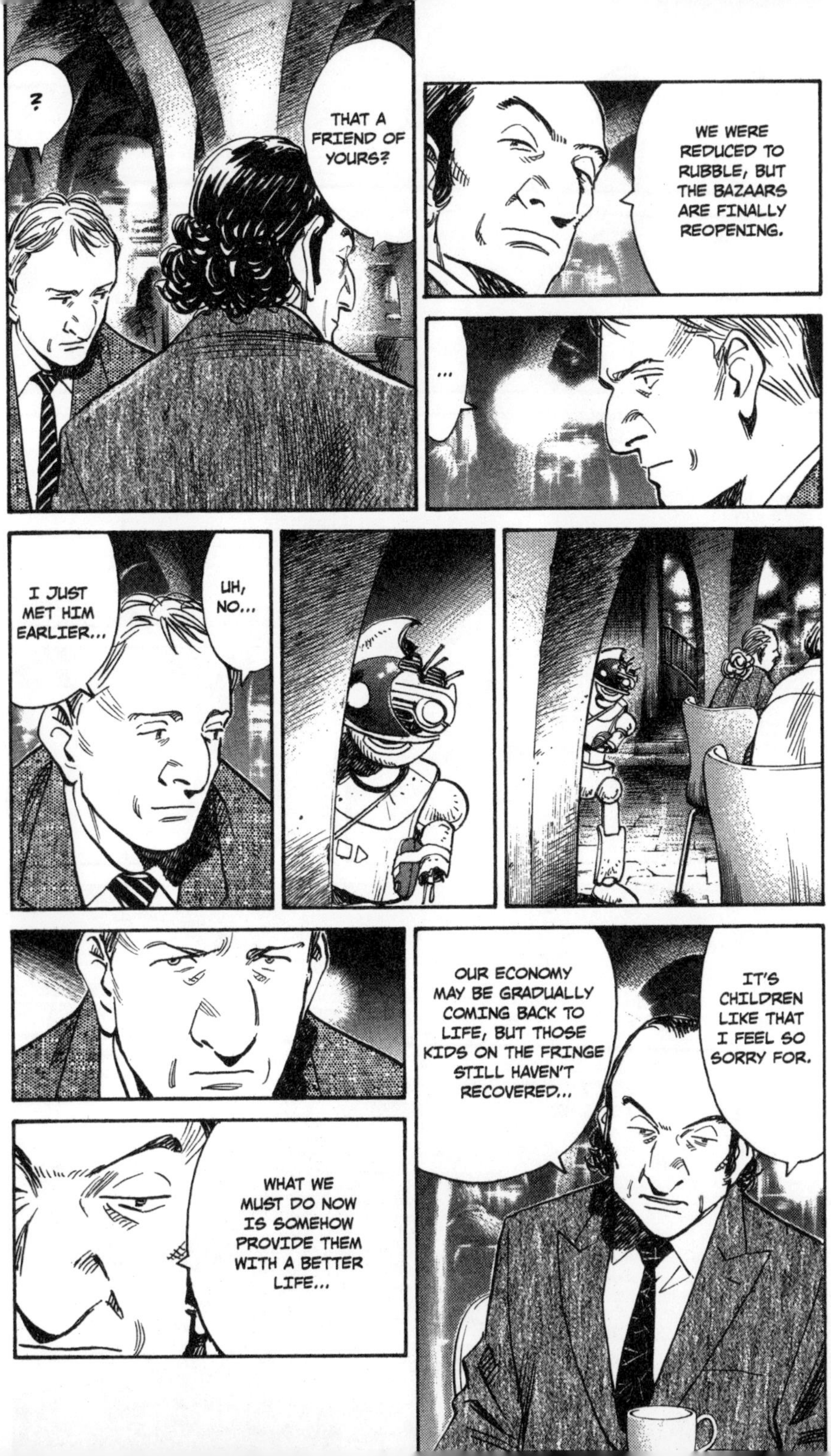
WE WERE REDUCED TO RUBBLE, BUT THE BAZAARS ARE FINALLY REOPENING.
...
THAT A FRIEND OF YOURS?
?
UH, NO...
I JUST MET HIM EARLIER...
IT'S CHILDREN LIKE THAT I FEEL SO SORRY FOR.
OUR ECONOMY MAY BE GRADUALLY COMING BACK TO LIFE, BUT THOSE KIDS ON THE FRINGE STILL HAVEN'T RECOVERED...
WHAT WE MUST DO NOW IS SOMEHOW PROVIDE THEM WITH A BETTER LIFE...

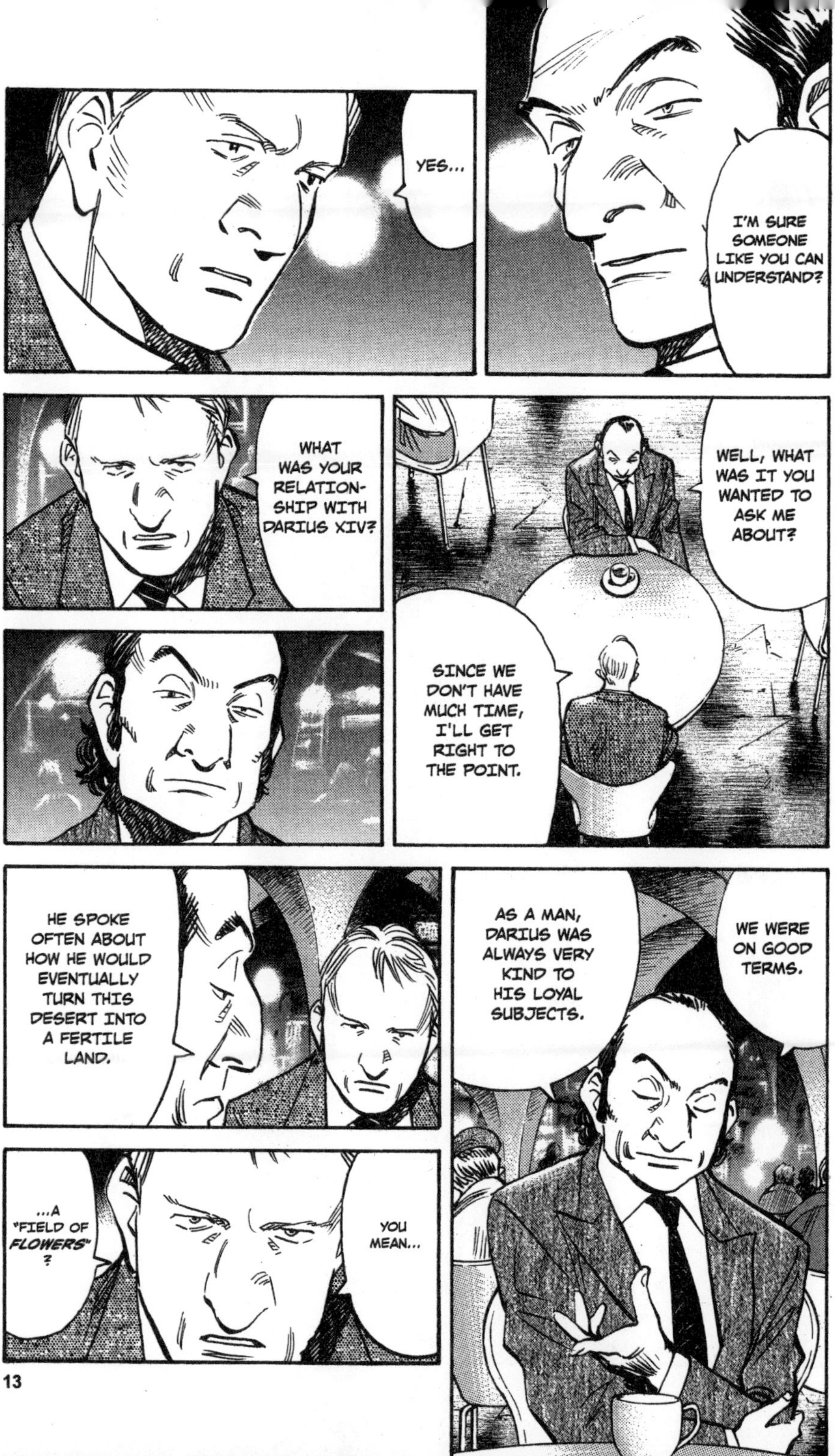
I'M SURE SOMEONE LIKE YOU CAN UNDERSTAND?
YES...
WELL, WHAT WAS IT YOU WANTED TO ASK ME ABOUT?
SINCE WE DON'T HAVE MUCH TIME, I'LL GET RIGHT TO THE POINT.
WHAT WAS YOUR RELATIONSHIP WITH DARIUS XIV?
WE WERE ON GOOD TERMS.
AS A MAN, DARIUS WAS ALWAYS VERY KIND TO HIS LOYAL SUBJECTS.
HE SPOKE OFTEN ABOUT HOW HE WOULD EVENTUALLY TURN THIS DESERT INTO A FERTILE LAND.
YOU MEAN...
...A "FIELD OF *FLOWERS*"?

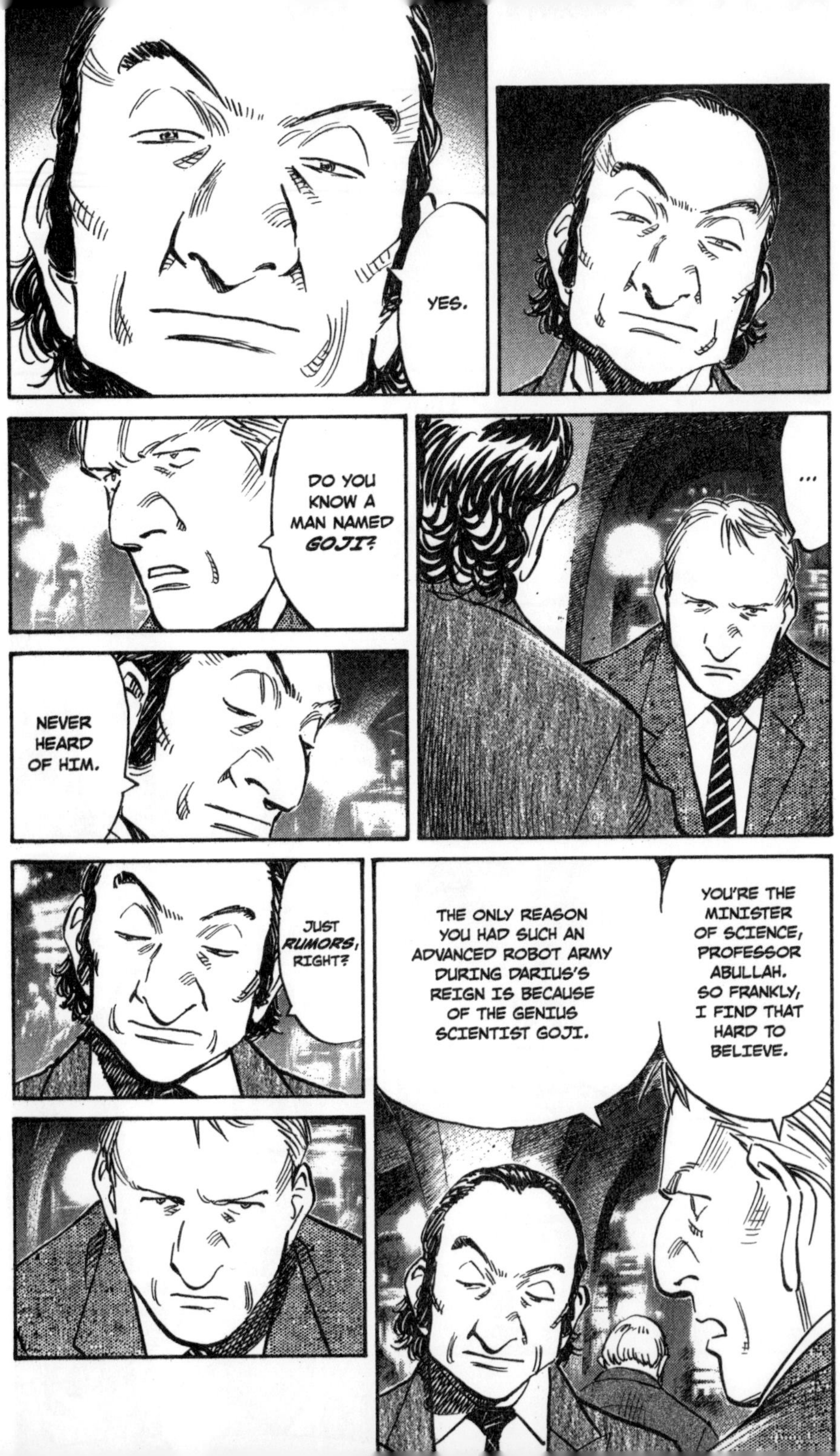
YES.
...
DO YOU KNOW A MAN NAMED GOJI?
NEVER HEARD OF HIM.
YOU'RE THE MINISTER OF SCIENCE, PROFESSOR ABULLAH. SO FRANKLY, I FIND THAT HARD TO BELIEVE.
THE ONLY REASON YOU HAD SUCH AN ADVANCED ROBOT ARMY DURING DARIUS'S REIGN IS BECAUSE OF THE GENIUS SCIENTIST GOJI.
JUST RUMORS, RIGHT?

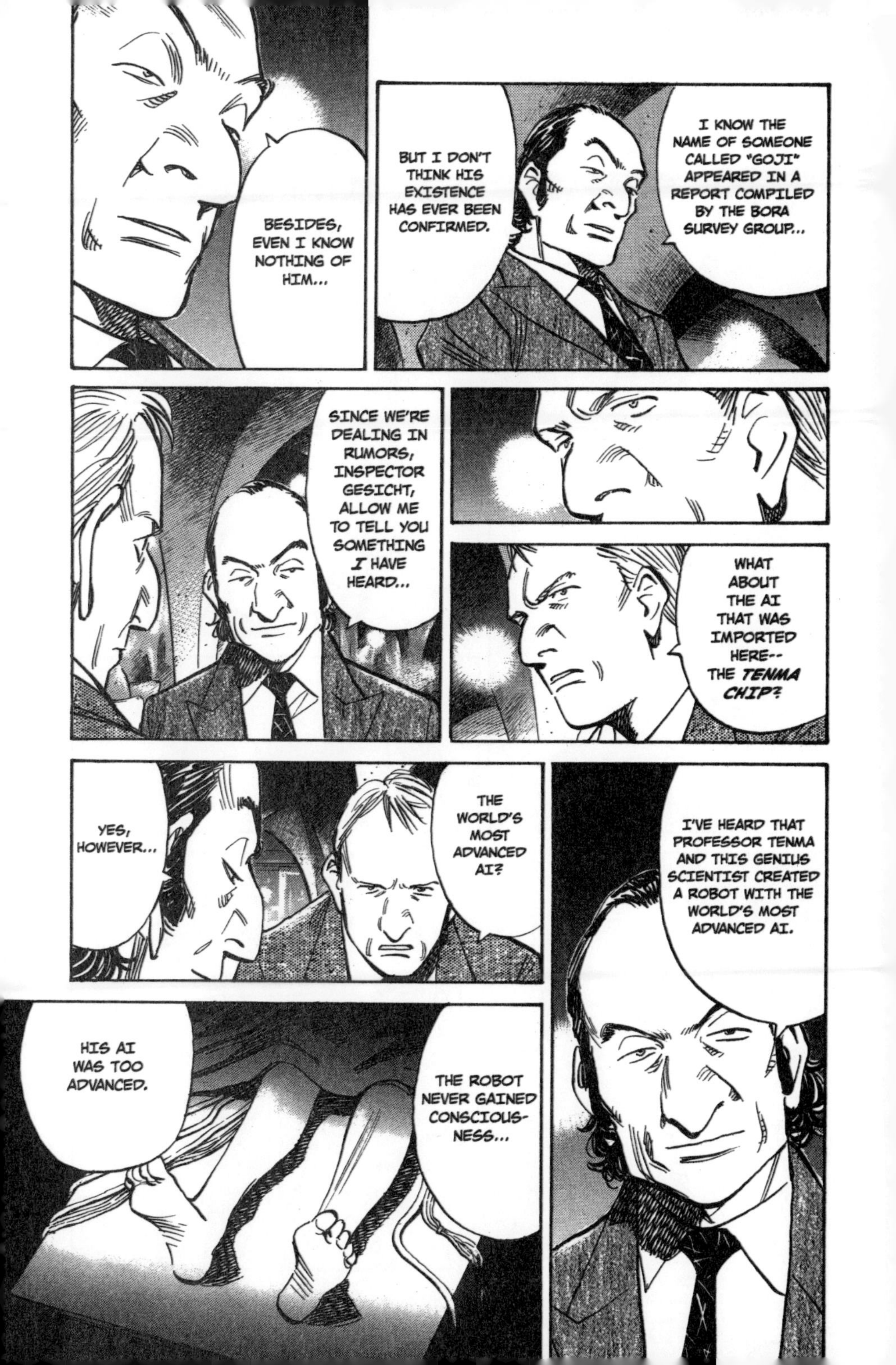
I KNOW THE NAME OF SOMEONE CALLED "GOJI" APPEARED IN A REPORT COMPILED BY THE BORA SURVEY GROUP...
BUT I DON'T THINK HIS EXISTENCE HAS EVER BEEN CONFIRMED.
BESIDES, EVEN I KNOW NOTHING OF HIM...
WHAT ABOUT THE AI THAT WAS IMPORTED HERE-- THE *TENMA CHIP*?
SINCE WE'RE DEALING IN RUMORS, INSPECTOR GESICHT, ALLOW ME TO TELL YOU SOMETHING *I* HAVE HEARD...
I'VE HEARD THAT PROFESSOR TENMA AND THIS GENIUS SCIENTIST CREATED A ROBOT WITH THE WORLD'S MOST ADVANCED AI.
THE WORLD'S MOST ADVANCED AI?
YES, HOWEVER...
HIS AI WAS TOO ADVANCED.
THE ROBOT NEVER GAINED CONSCIOUS-NESS...

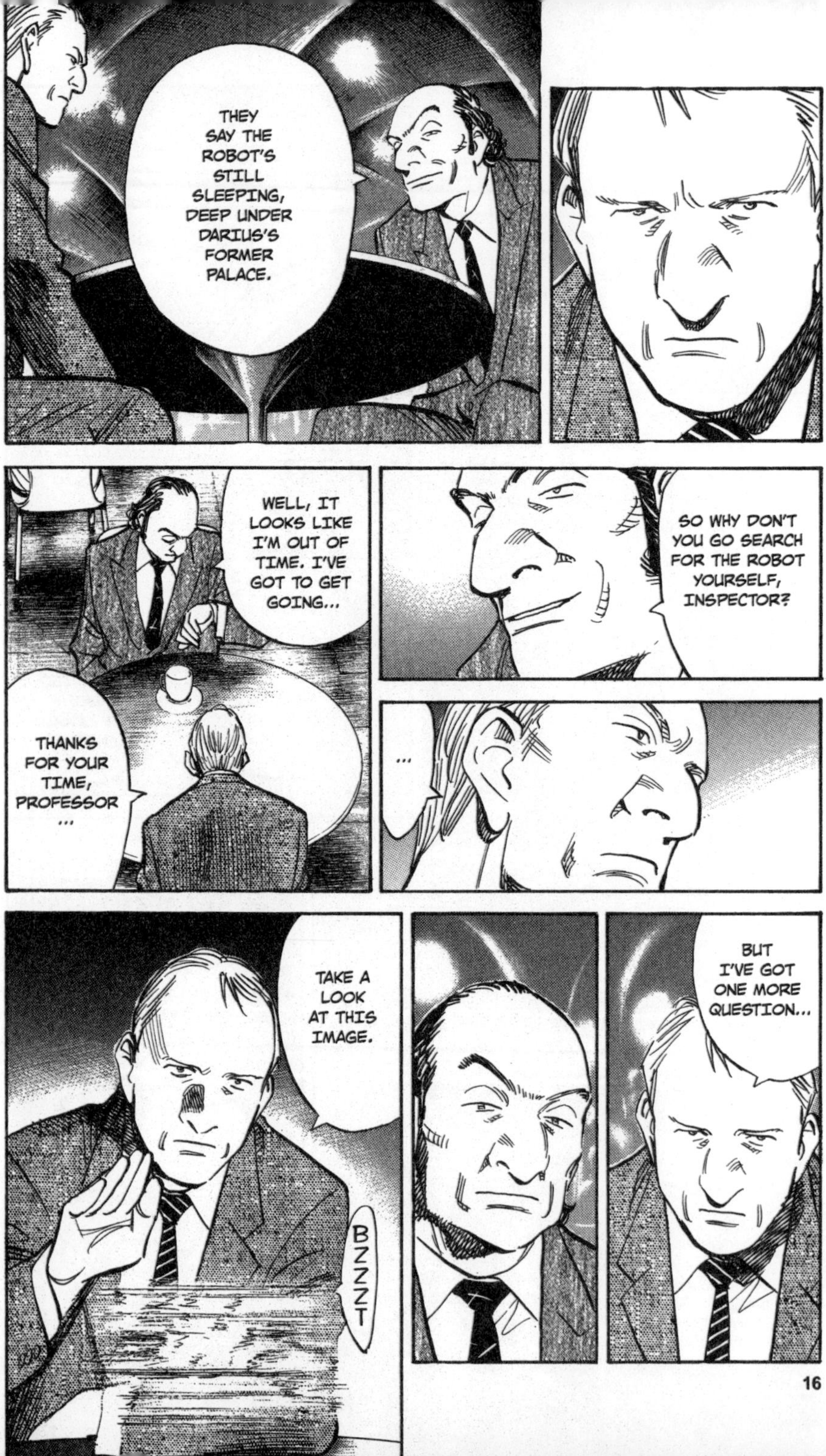
THEY SAY THE ROBOT'S STILL SLEEPING, DEEP UNDER DARIUS'S FORMER PALACE.
SO WHY DON'T YOU GO SEARCH FOR THE ROBOT YOURSELF, INSPECTOR?
...
WELL, IT LOOKS LIKE I'M OUT OF TIME. I'VE GOT TO GET GOING...
THANKS FOR YOUR TIME, PROFESSOR...
BUT I'VE GOT ONE MORE QUESTION...
TAKE A LOOK AT THIS IMAGE.
BZZZT

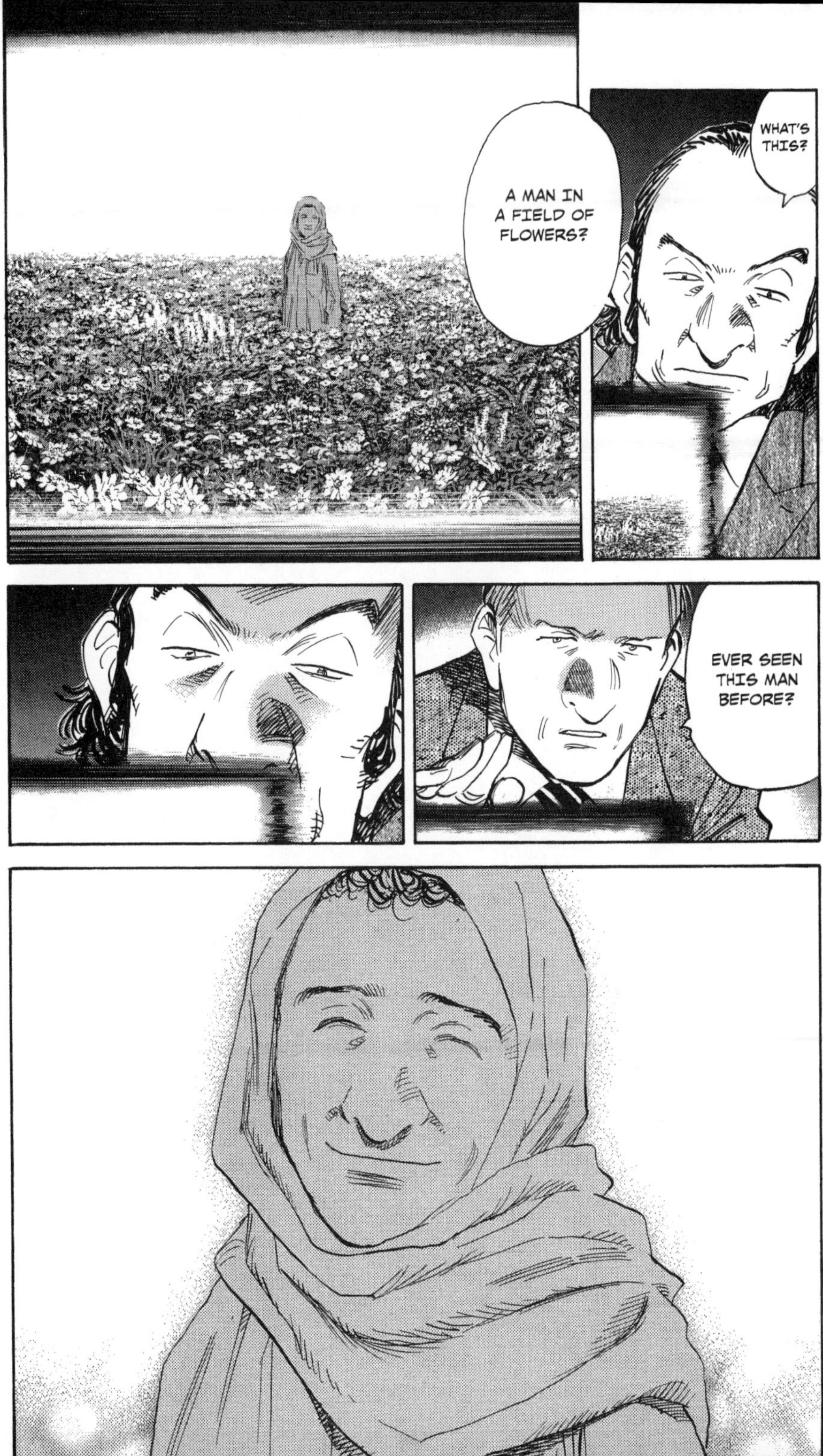
WHAT'S THIS?
A MAN IN A FIELD OF FLOWERS?
EVER SEEN THIS MAN BEFORE?

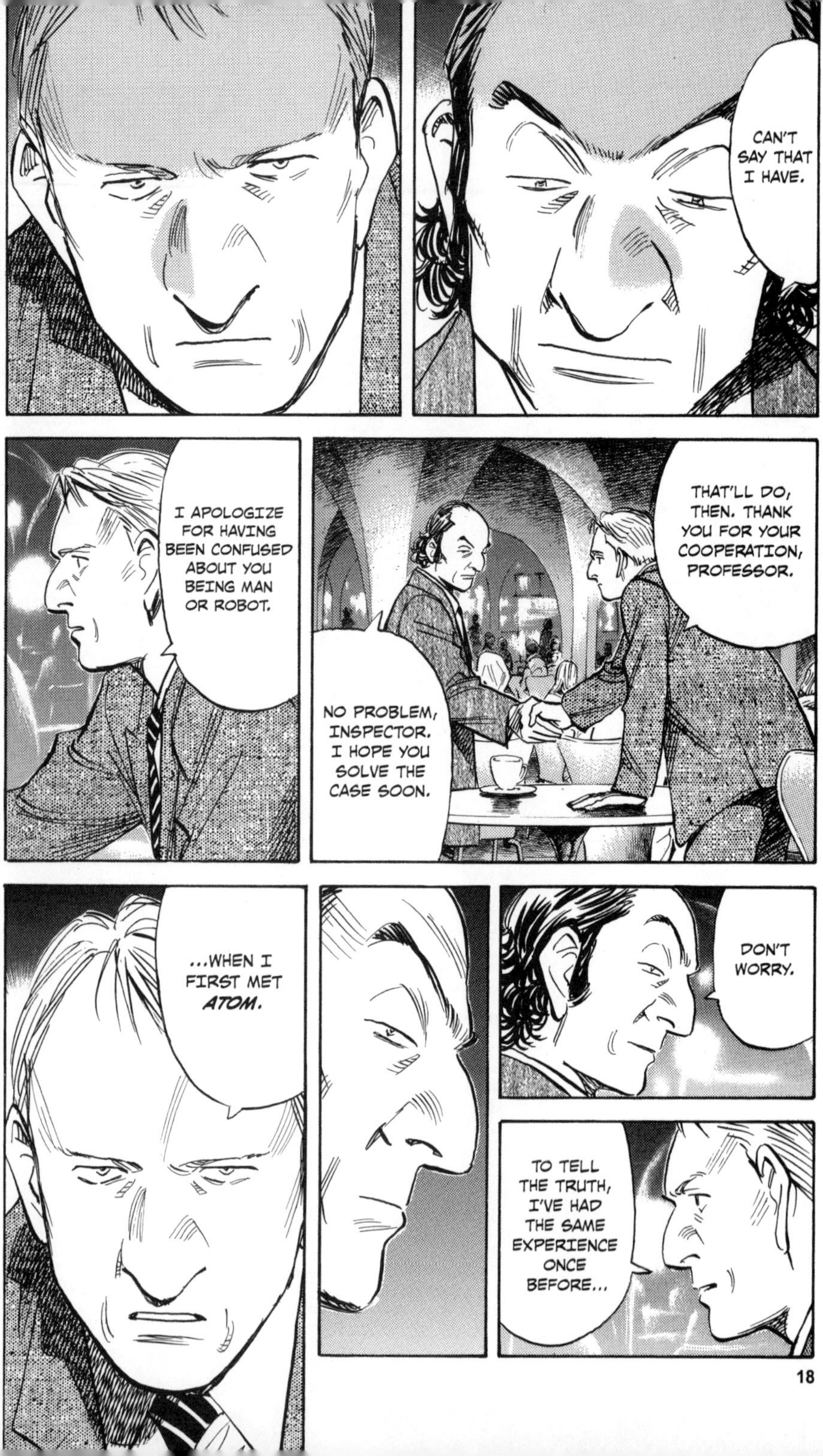
CAN'T SAY THAT I HAVE.
THAT'LL DO, THEN. THANK YOU FOR YOUR COOPERATION, PROFESSOR.
NO PROBLEM, INSPECTOR. I HOPE YOU SOLVE THE CASE SOON.
I APOLOGIZE FOR HAVING BEEN CONFUSED ABOUT YOU BEING MAN OR ROBOT.
DON'T WORRY.
TO TELL THE TRUTH, I'VE HAD THE SAME EXPERIENCE ONCE BEFORE...
...WHEN I FIRST MET *ATOM*.

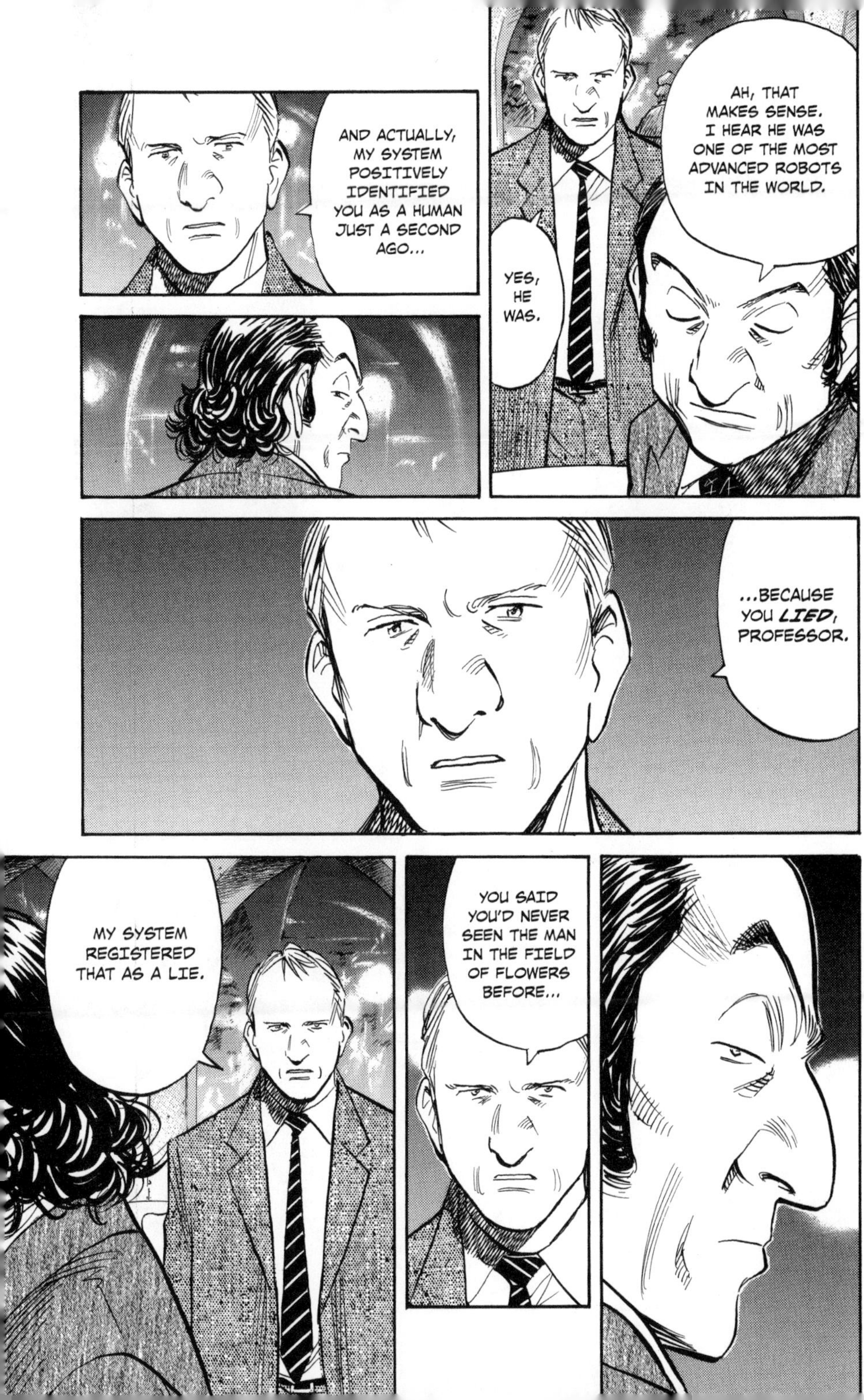
AH, THAT MAKES SENSE. I HEAR HE WAS ONE OF THE MOST ADVANCED ROBOTS IN THE WORLD.
YES, HE WAS.
AND ACTUALLY, MY SYSTEM POSITIVELY IDENTIFIED YOU AS A HUMAN JUST A SECOND AGO...
...BECAUSE YOU ***LIED***, PROFESSOR.
YOU SAID YOU'D NEVER SEEN THE MAN IN THE FIELD OF FLOWERS BEFORE...
MY SYSTEM REGISTERED THAT AS A LIE.

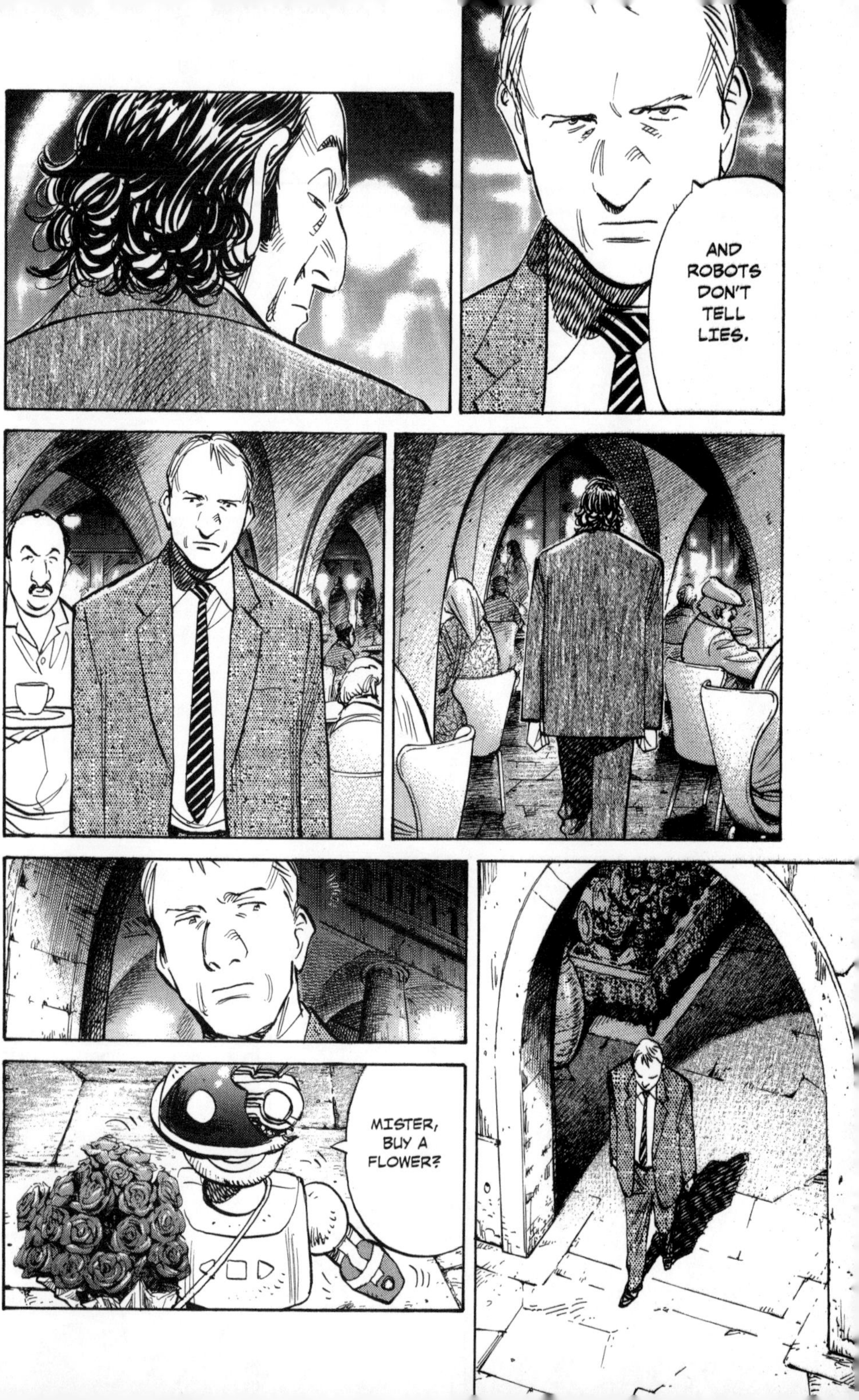
AND ROBOTS DON'T TELL LIES.
MISTER, BUY A FLOWER?

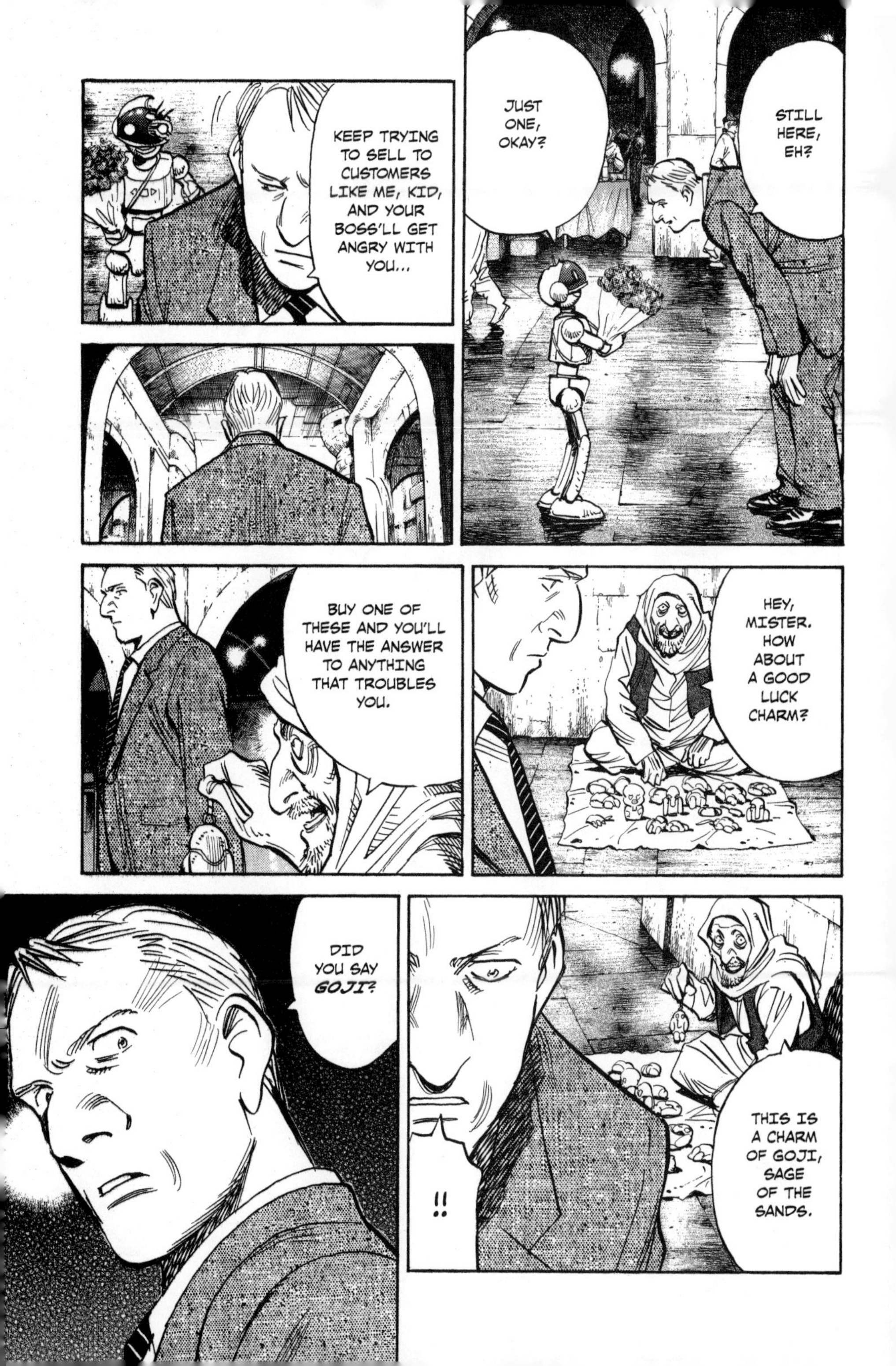
STILL HERE, EH?
JUST ONE, OKAY?
KEEP TRYING TO SELL TO CUSTOMERS LIKE ME, KID, AND YOUR BOSS'LL GET ANGRY WITH YOU...
HEY, MISTER. HOW ABOUT A GOOD LUCK CHARM?
BUY ONE OF THESE AND YOU'LL HAVE THE ANSWER TO ANYTHING THAT TROUBLES YOU.
THIS IS A CHARM OF GOJI, SAGE OF THE SANDS.
!!
DID YOU SAY *GOJI*?

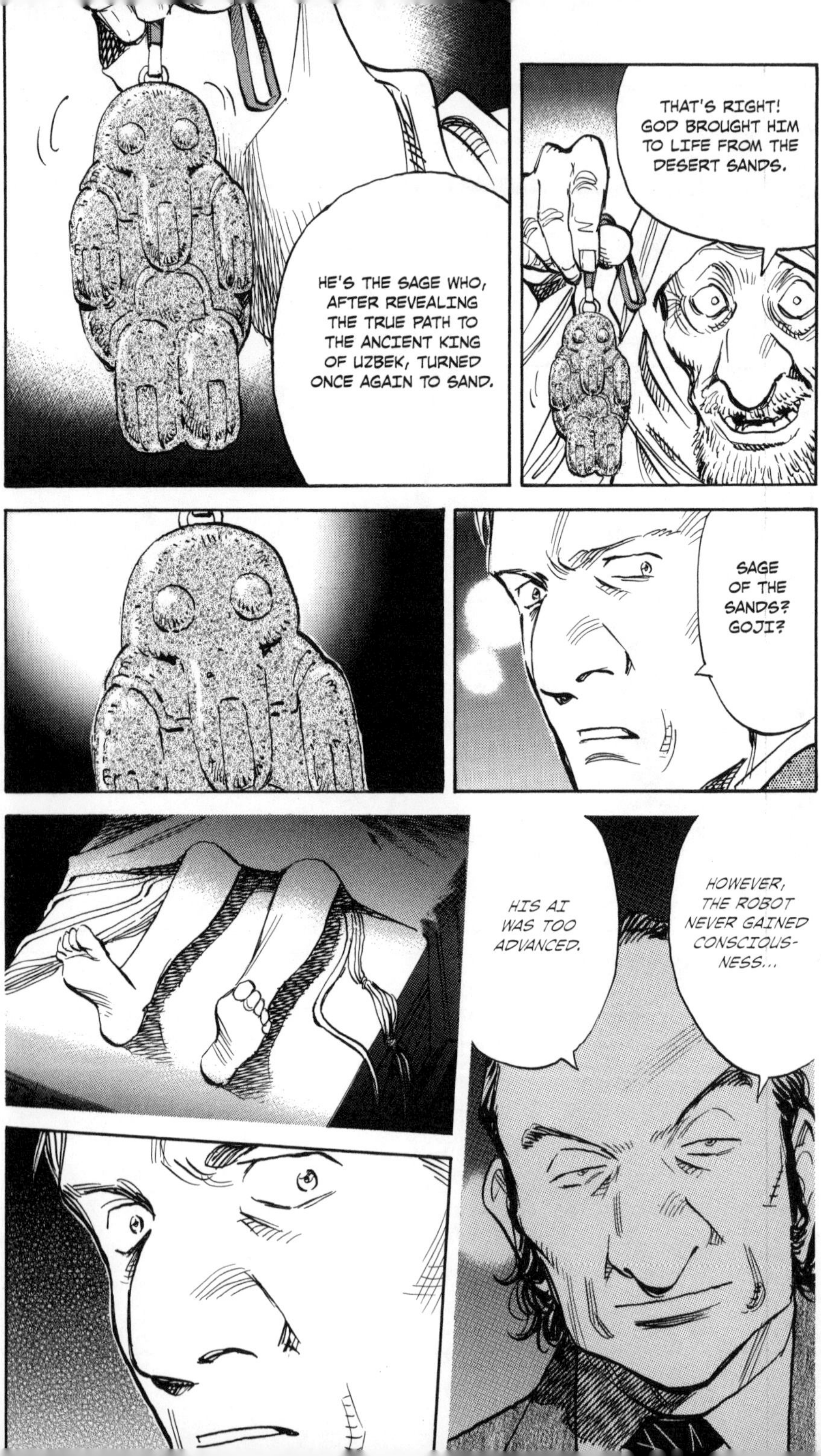
THAT'S RIGHT! GOD BROUGHT HIM TO LIFE FROM THE DESERT SANDS.
HE'S THE SAGE WHO, AFTER REVEALING THE TRUE PATH TO THE ANCIENT KING OF UZBEK, TURNED ONCE AGAIN TO SAND.
SAGE OF THE SANDS? GOJI?
HOWEVER, THE ROBOT NEVER GAINED CONSCIOUS-NESS...
HIS AI WAS TOO ADVANCED.

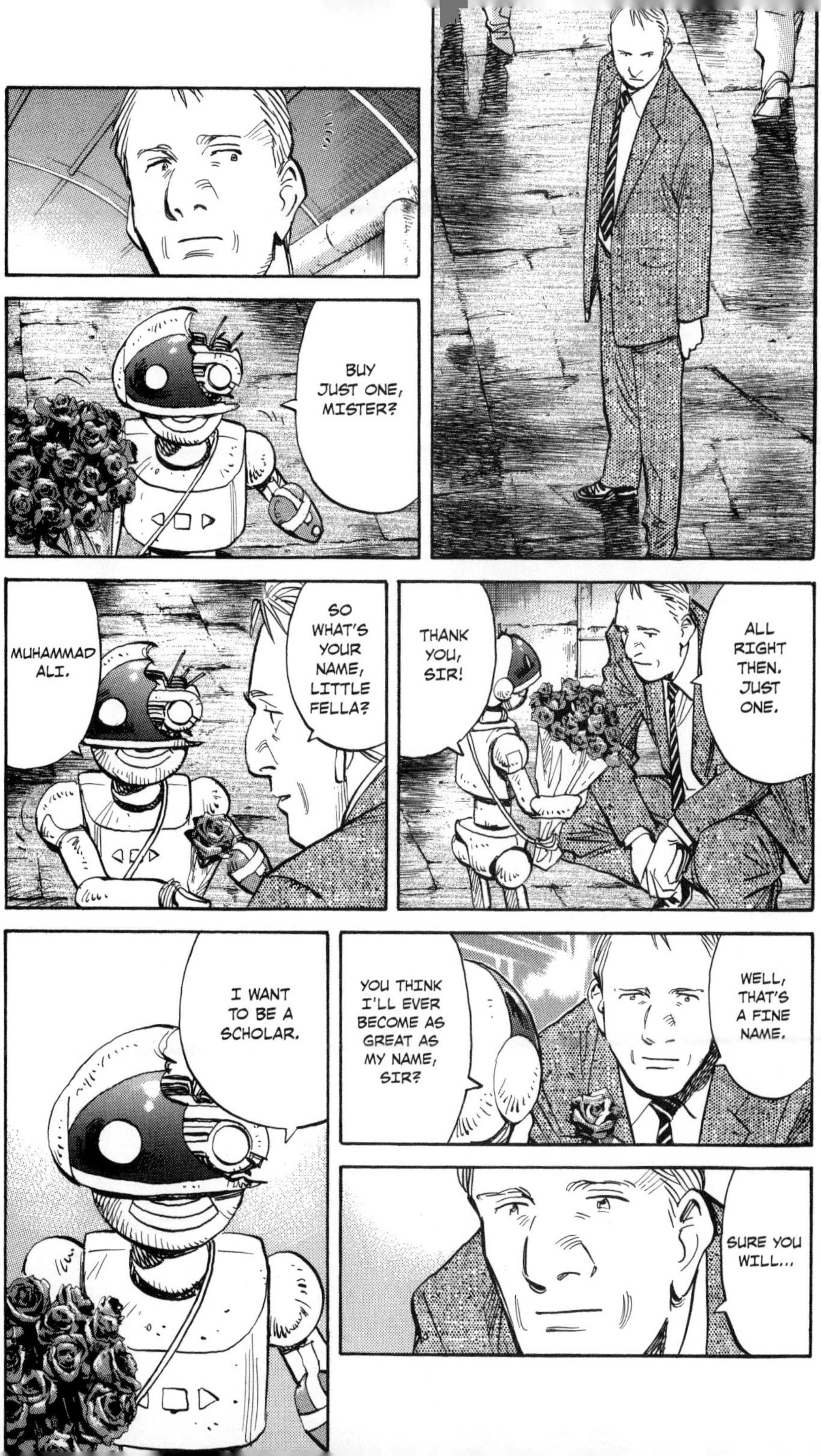
BUY JUST ONE, MISTER?
ALL RIGHT THEN. JUST ONE.
THANK YOU, SIR!
SO WHAT'S YOUR NAME, LITTLE FELLA?
MUHAMMAD ALI.
WELL, THAT'S A FINE NAME.
YOU THINK I'LL EVER BECOME AS GREAT AS MY NAME, SIR?
SURE YOU WILL...
I WANT TO BE A SCHOLAR.

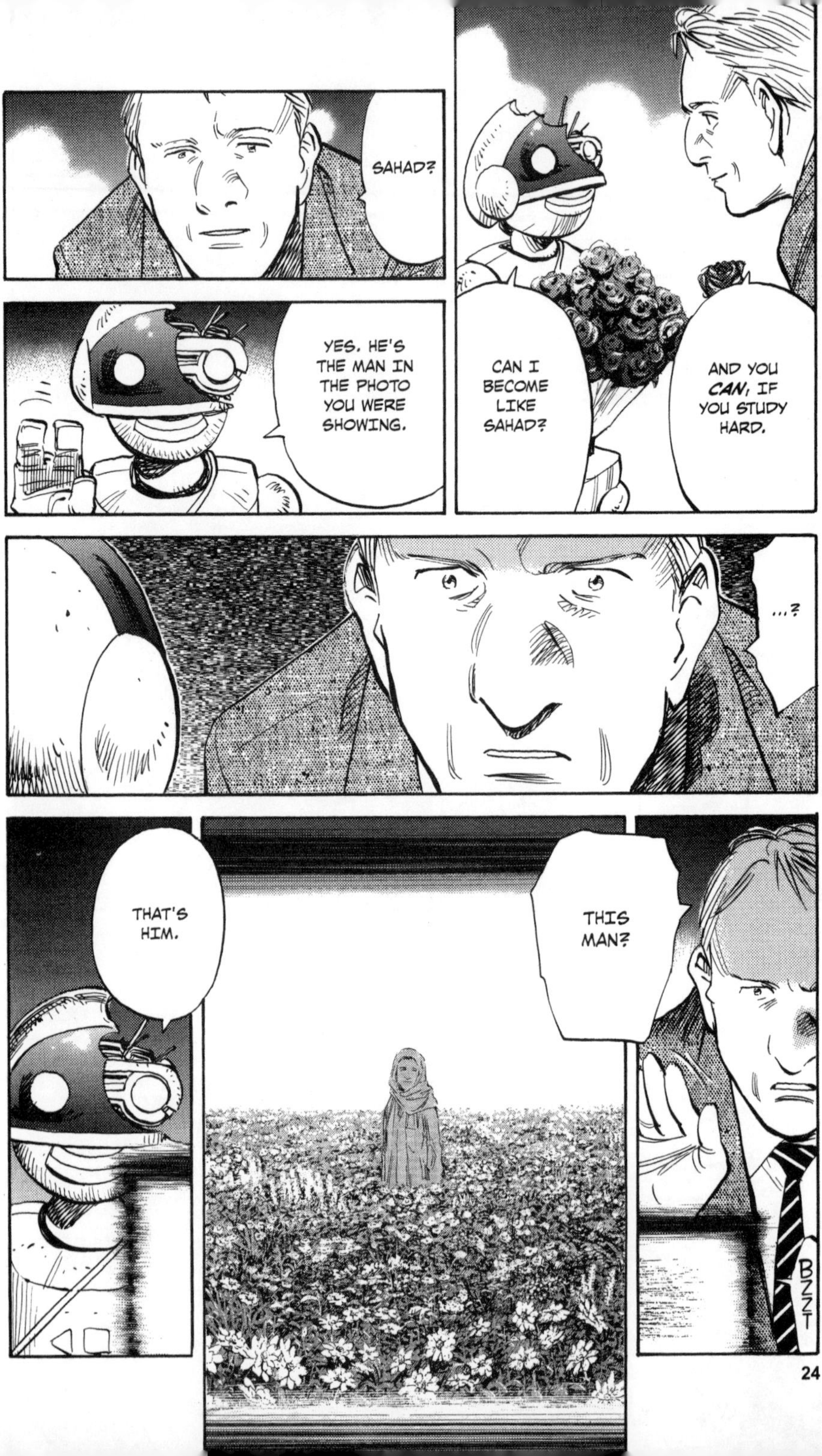
AND YOU CAN, IF YOU STUDY HARD.
CAN I BECOME LIKE SAHAD?
SAHAD?
YES. HE'S THE MAN IN THE PHOTO YOU WERE SHOWING.
...?
THIS MAN?
BZZT
THAT'S HIM.

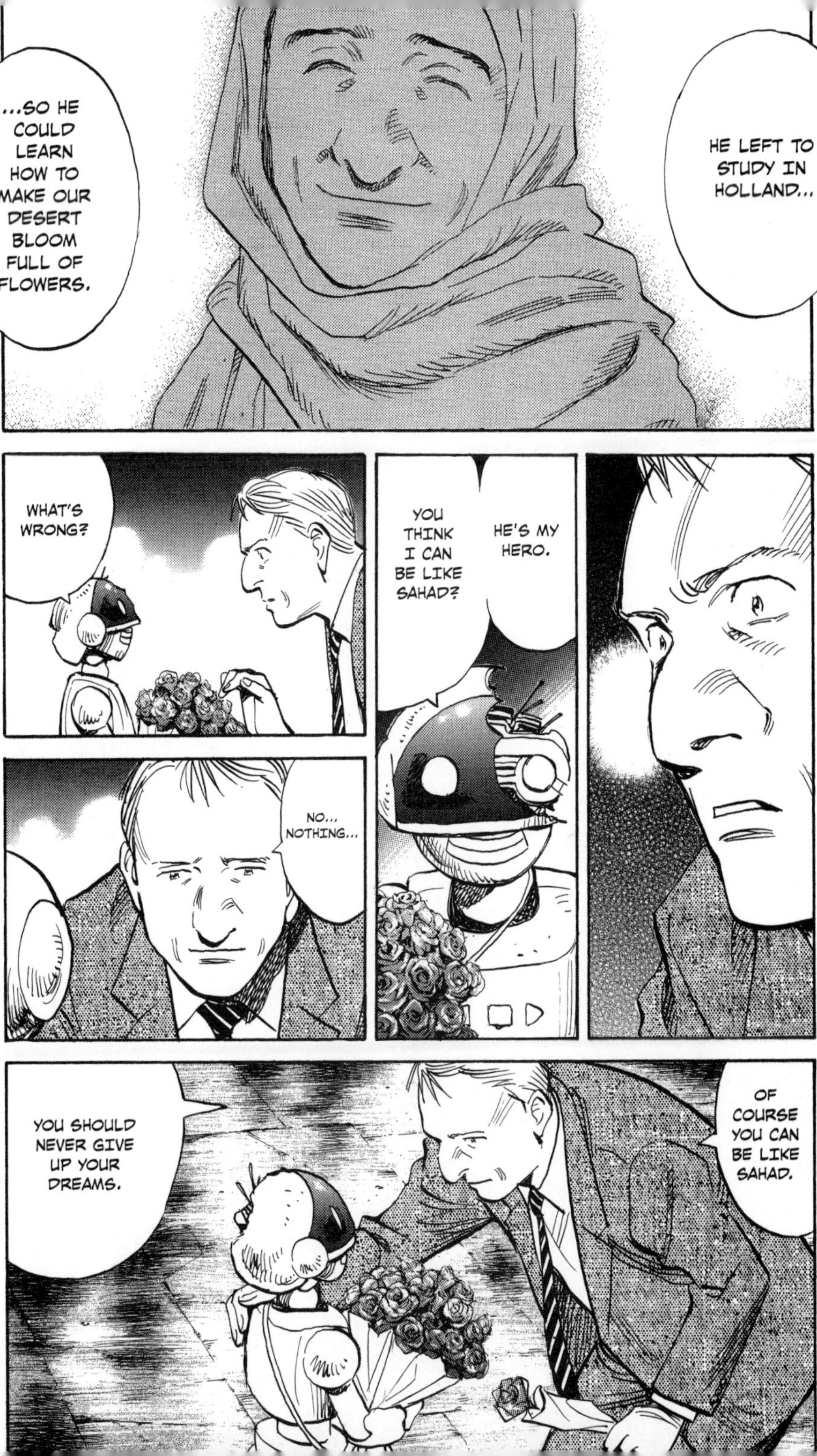
HE LEFT TO STUDY IN HOLLAND...
...SO HE COULD LEARN HOW TO MAKE OUR DESERT BLOOM FULL OF FLOWERS.
HE'S MY HERO.
YOU THINK I CAN BE LIKE SAHAD?
WHAT'S WRONG?
NO... NOTHING...
OF COURSE YOU CAN BE LIKE SAHAD.
YOU SHOULD NEVER GIVE UP YOUR DREAMS.

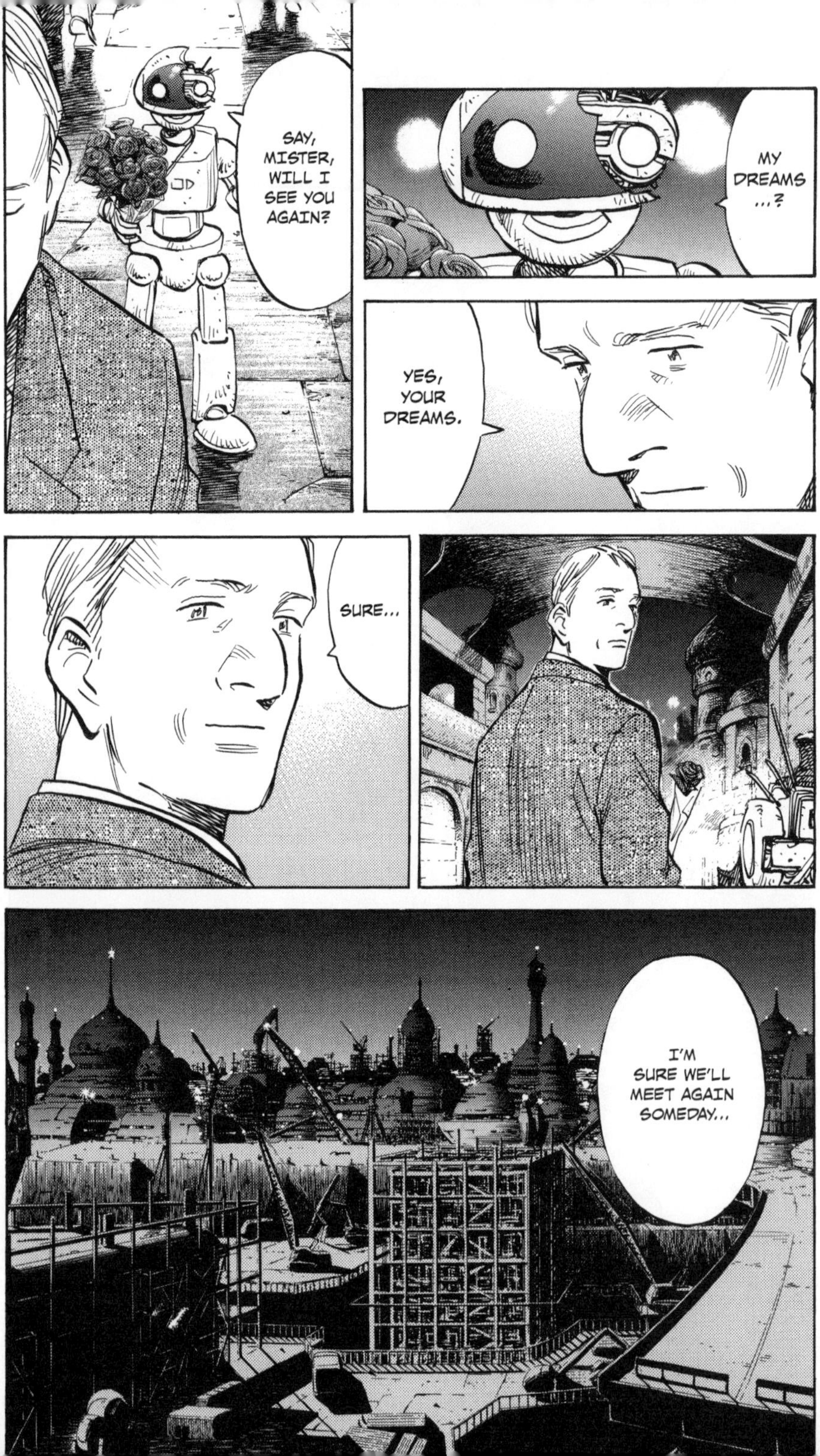
MY DREAMS ...?
YES, YOUR DREAMS.
SAY, MISTER, WILL I SEE YOU AGAIN?
SURE...
I'M SURE WE'LL MEET AGAIN SOMEDAY...

Act 41 SAHAD

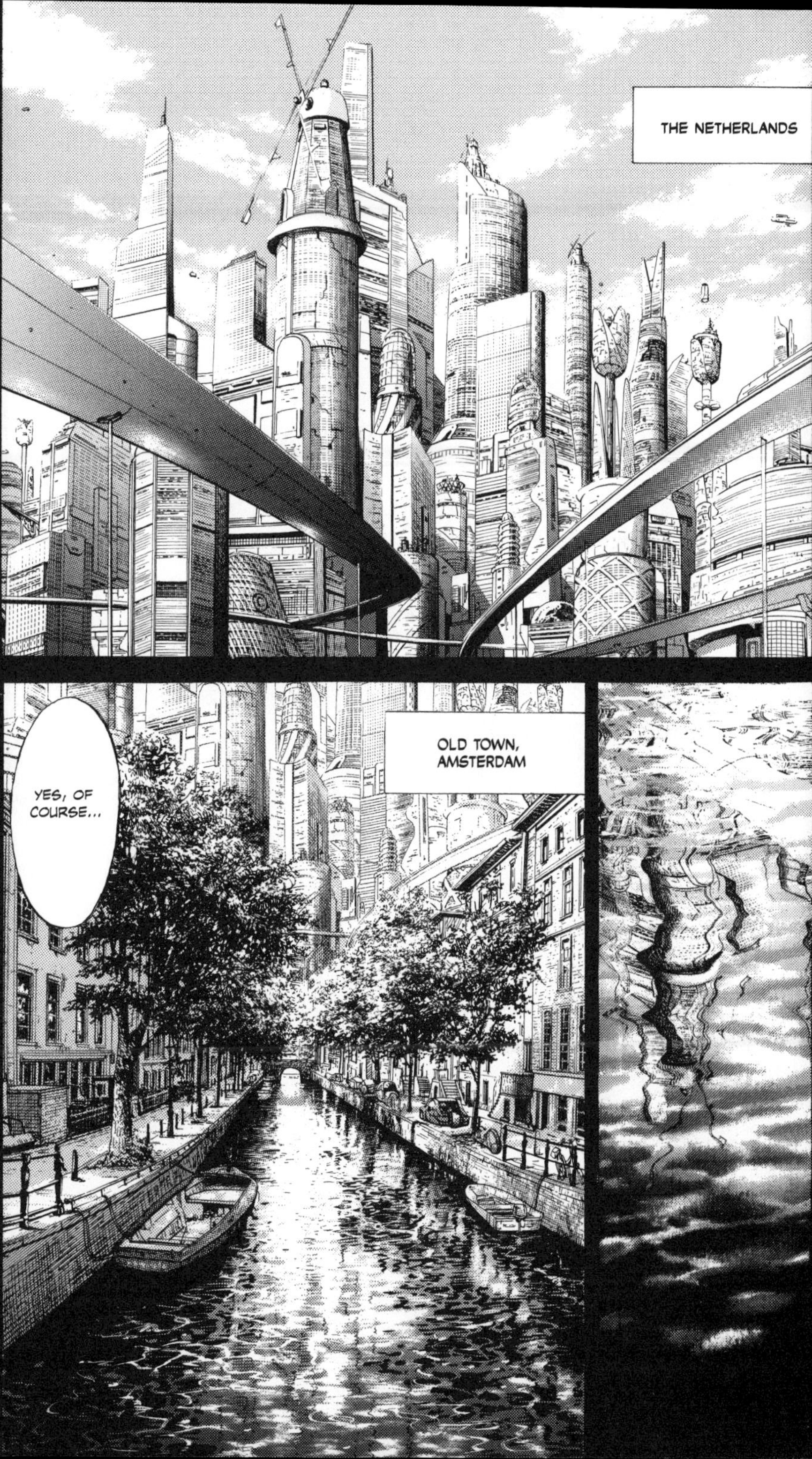

THE NETHERLANDS
OLD TOWN, AMSTERDAM
YES, OF COURSE...

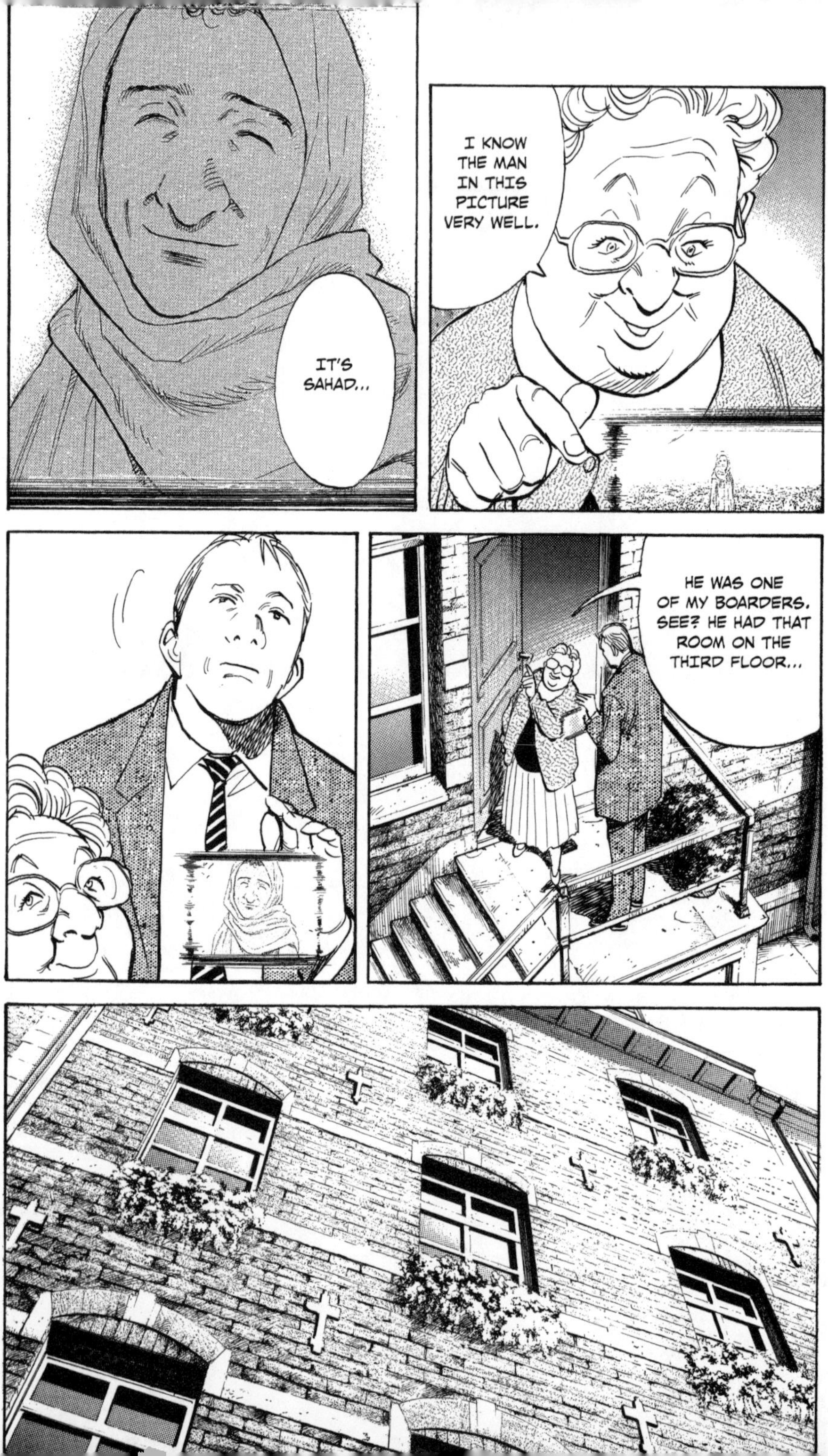
I KNOW THE MAN IN THIS PICTURE VERY WELL.
IT'S SAHAD...
HE WAS ONE OF MY BOARDERS. SEE? HE HAD THAT ROOM ON THE THIRD FLOOR...

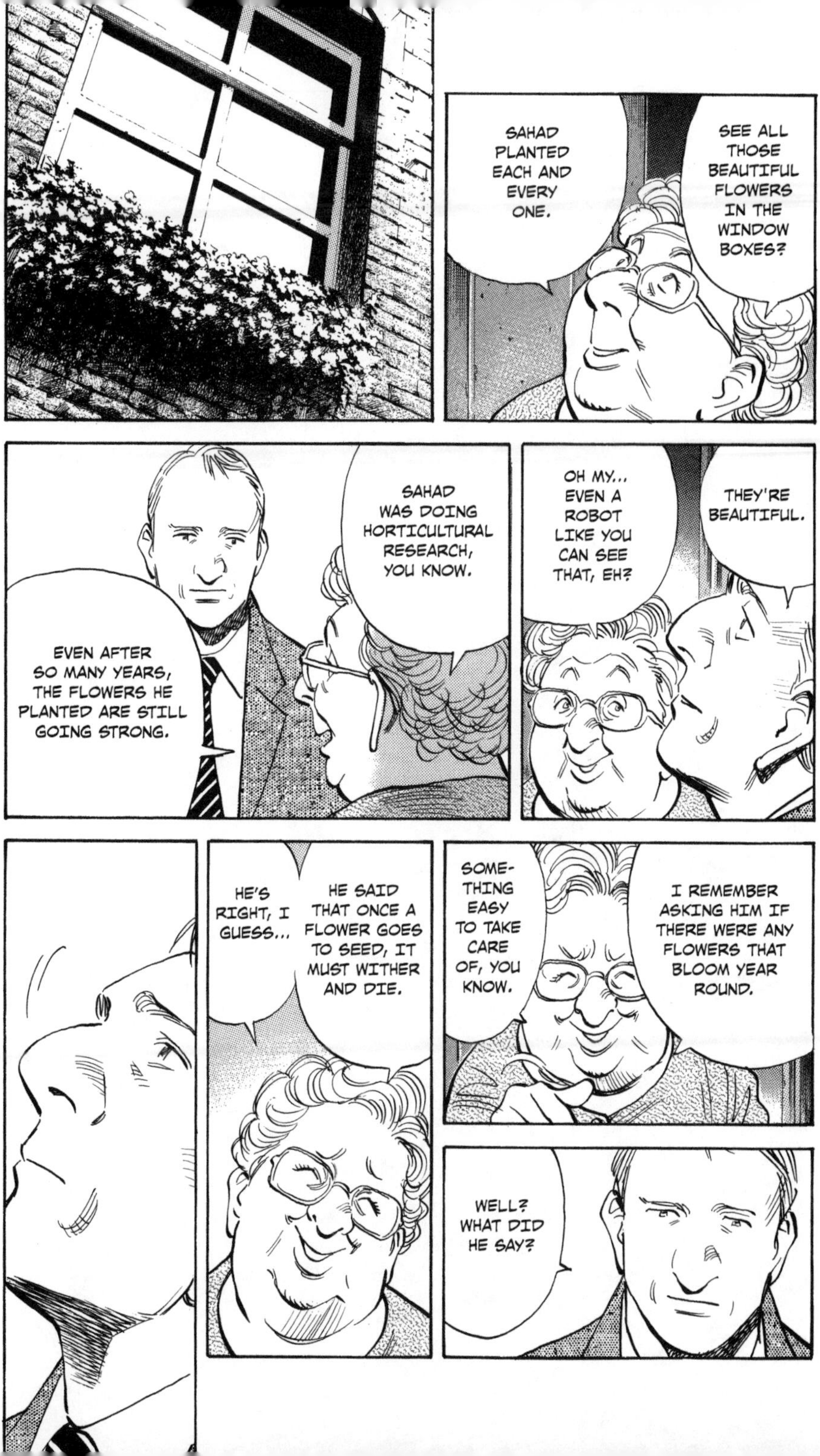
SEE ALL THOSE BEAUTIFUL FLOWERS IN THE WINDOW BOXES?
SAHAD PLANTED EACH AND EVERY ONE.
THEY'RE BEAUTIFUL.
OH MY... EVEN A ROBOT LIKE YOU CAN SEE THAT, EH?
SAHAD WAS DOING HORTICULTURAL RESEARCH, YOU KNOW.
EVEN AFTER SO MANY YEARS, THE FLOWERS HE PLANTED ARE STILL GOING STRONG.
I REMEMBER ASKING HIM IF THERE WERE ANY FLOWERS THAT BLOOM YEAR ROUND.
SOME-THING EASY TO TAKE CARE OF, YOU KNOW.
WELL? WHAT DID HE SAY?
HE SAID THAT ONCE A FLOWER GOES TO SEED, IT MUST WITHER AND DIE.
HE'S RIGHT, I GUESS...

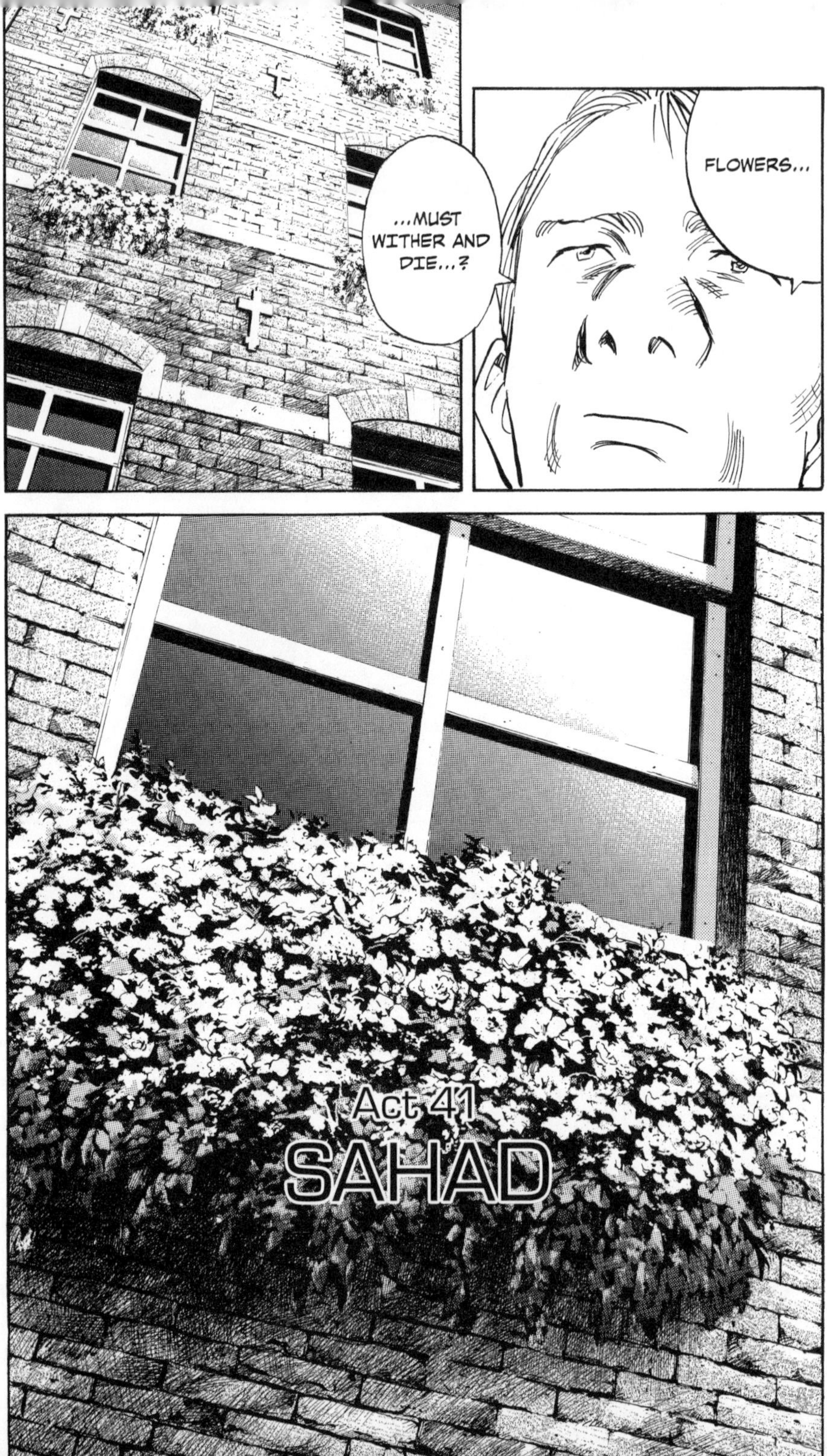
FLOWERS...
...MUST WITHER AND DIE...?
Act 41
SAHAD

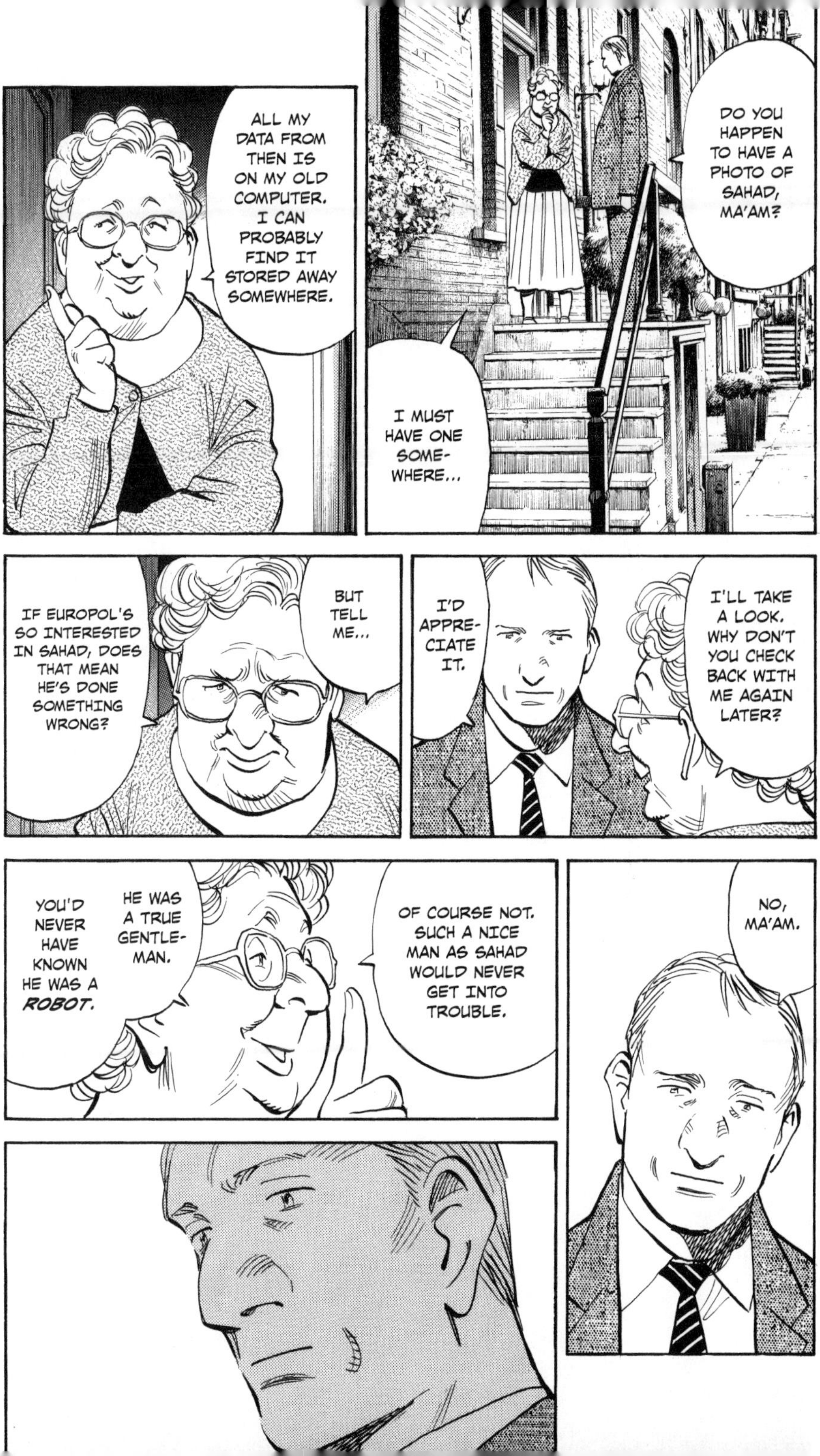

DO YOU HAPPEN TO HAVE A PHOTO OF SAHAD, MA'AM?
I MUST HAVE ONE SOME-WHERE...
ALL MY DATA FROM THEN IS ON MY OLD COMPUTER. I CAN PROBABLY FIND IT STORED AWAY SOMEWHERE.
I'LL TAKE A LOOK. WHY DON'T YOU CHECK BACK WITH ME AGAIN LATER?
I'D APPRE-CIATE IT.
BUT TELL ME...
IF EUROPOL'S SO INTERESTED IN SAHAD, DOES THAT MEAN HE'S DONE SOMETHING WRONG?
NO, MA'AM.
OF COURSE NOT. SUCH A NICE MAN AS SAHAD WOULD NEVER GET INTO TROUBLE.
HE WAS A TRUE GENTLE-MAN.
YOU'D NEVER HAVE KNOWN HE WAS A ***ROBOT***.

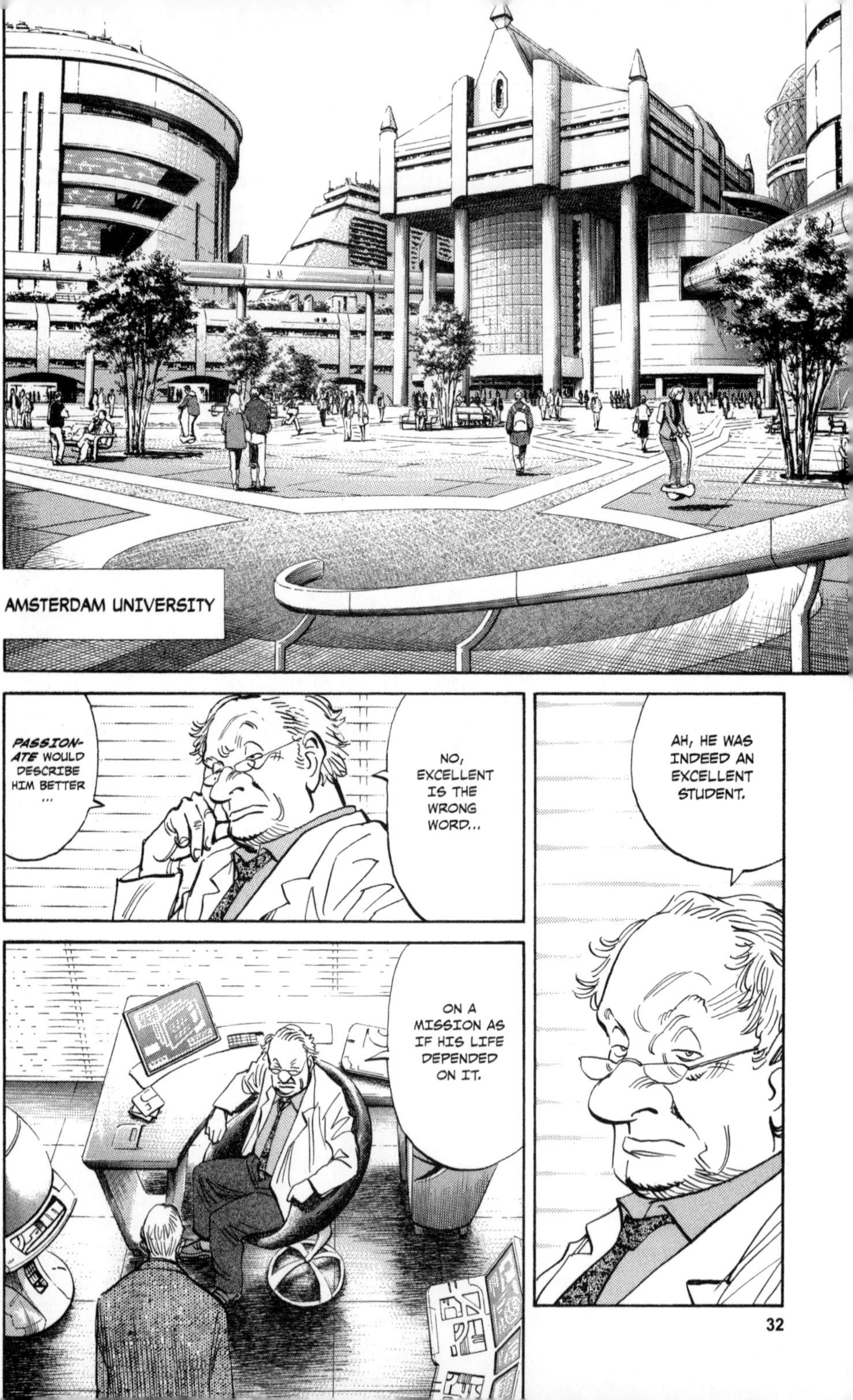
AMSTERDAM UNIVERSITY
AH, HE WAS INDEED AN EXCELLENT STUDENT.
NO, EXCELLENT IS THE WRONG WORD...
PASSIONATE WOULD DESCRIBE HIM BETTER ...
ON A MISSION AS IF HIS LIFE DEPENDED ON IT.

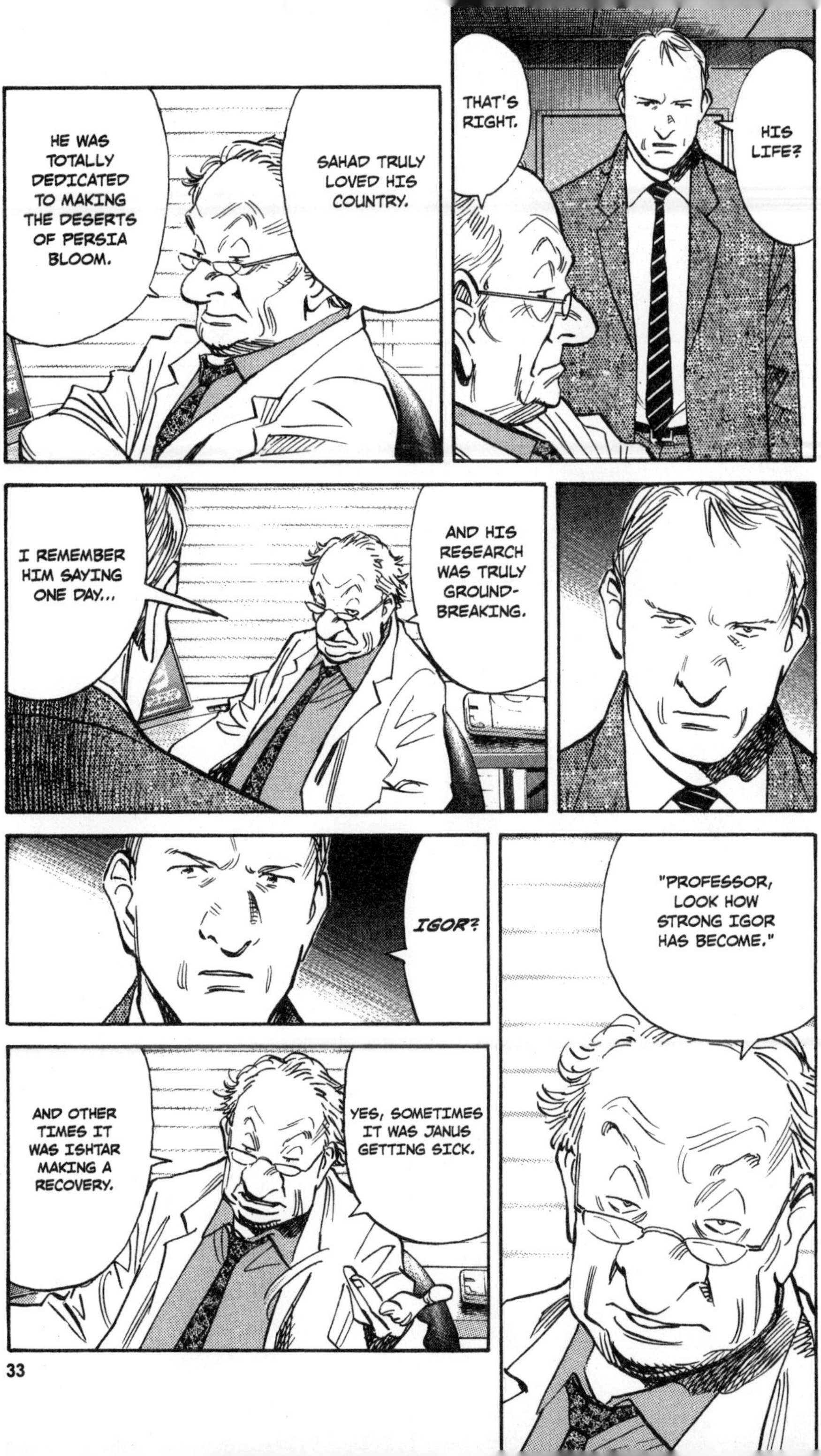
HIS LIFE?
THAT'S RIGHT.
SAHAD TRULY LOVED HIS COUNTRY.
HE WAS TOTALLY DEDICATED TO MAKING THE DESERTS OF PERSIA BLOOM.
AND HIS RESEARCH WAS TRULY GROUND-BREAKING.
I REMEMBER HIM SAYING ONE DAY...
"PROFESSOR, LOOK HOW STRONG IGOR HAS BECOME."
IGOR?
YES, SOMETIMES IT WAS JANUS GETTING SICK.
AND OTHER TIMES IT WAS ISHTAR MAKING A RECOVERY.

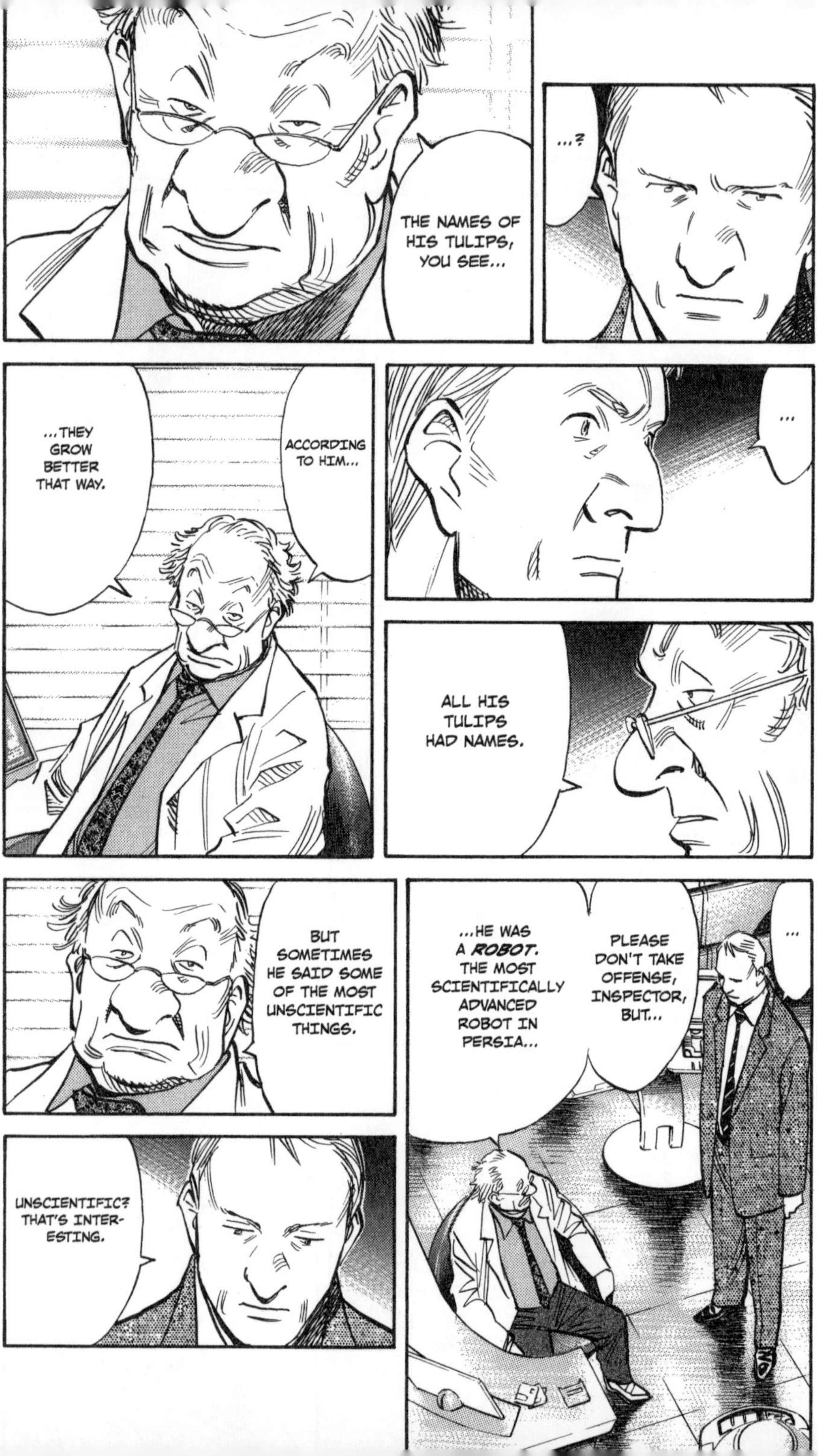
...?
THE NAMES OF HIS TULIPS, YOU SEE...
...
ALL HIS TULIPS HAD NAMES.
ACCORDING TO HIM...
...THEY GROW BETTER THAT WAY.
...
PLEASE DON'T TAKE OFFENSE, INSPECTOR, BUT...
...HE WAS A *ROBOT*. THE MOST SCIENTIFICALLY ADVANCED ROBOT IN PERSIA...
BUT SOMETIMES HE SAID SOME OF THE MOST UNSCIENTIFIC THINGS.
UNSCIENTIFIC? THAT'S INTER-ESTING.

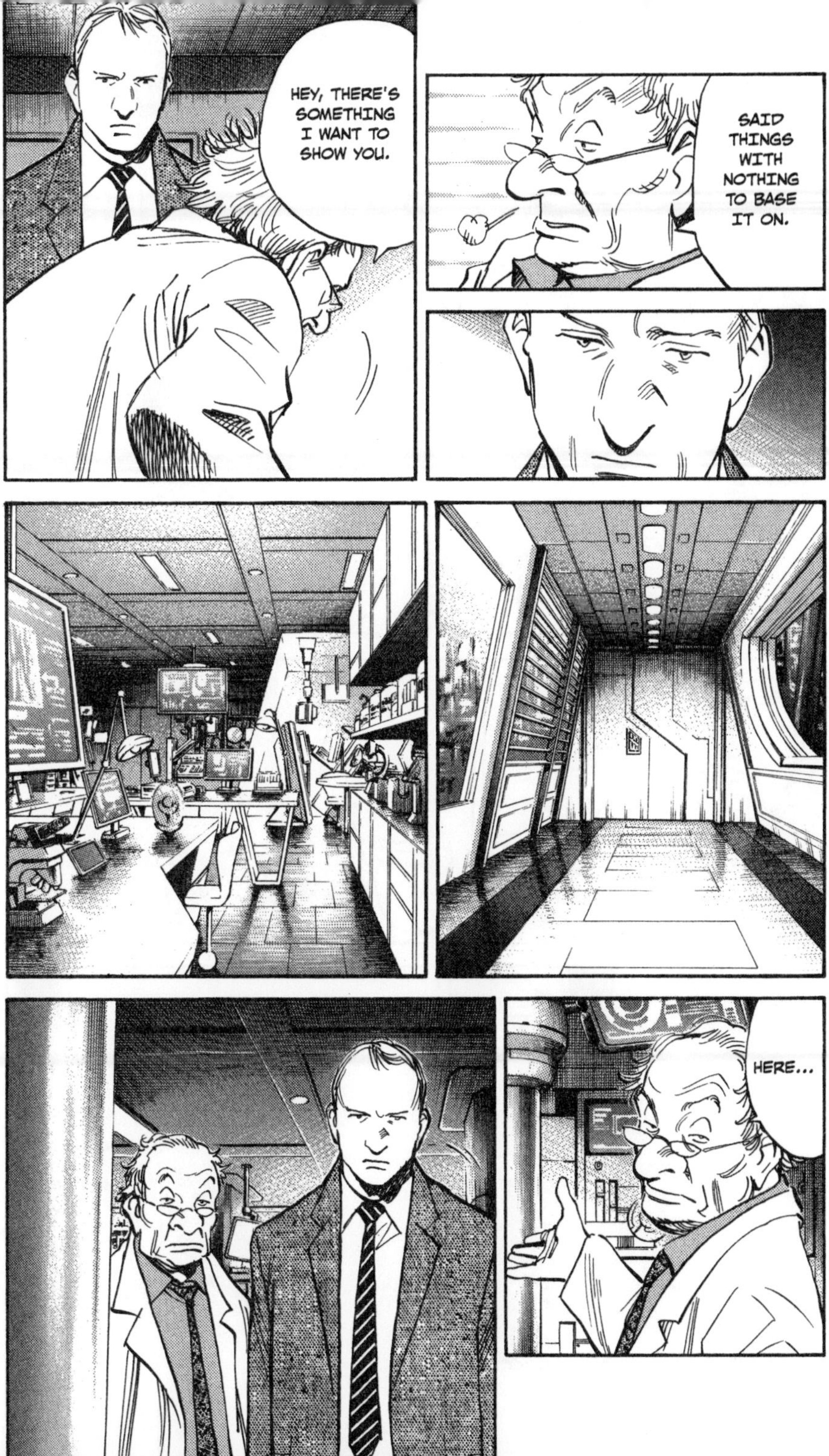
SAID THINGS WITH NOTHING TO BASE IT ON.
HEY, THERE'S SOMETHING I WANT TO SHOW YOU.
HERE...

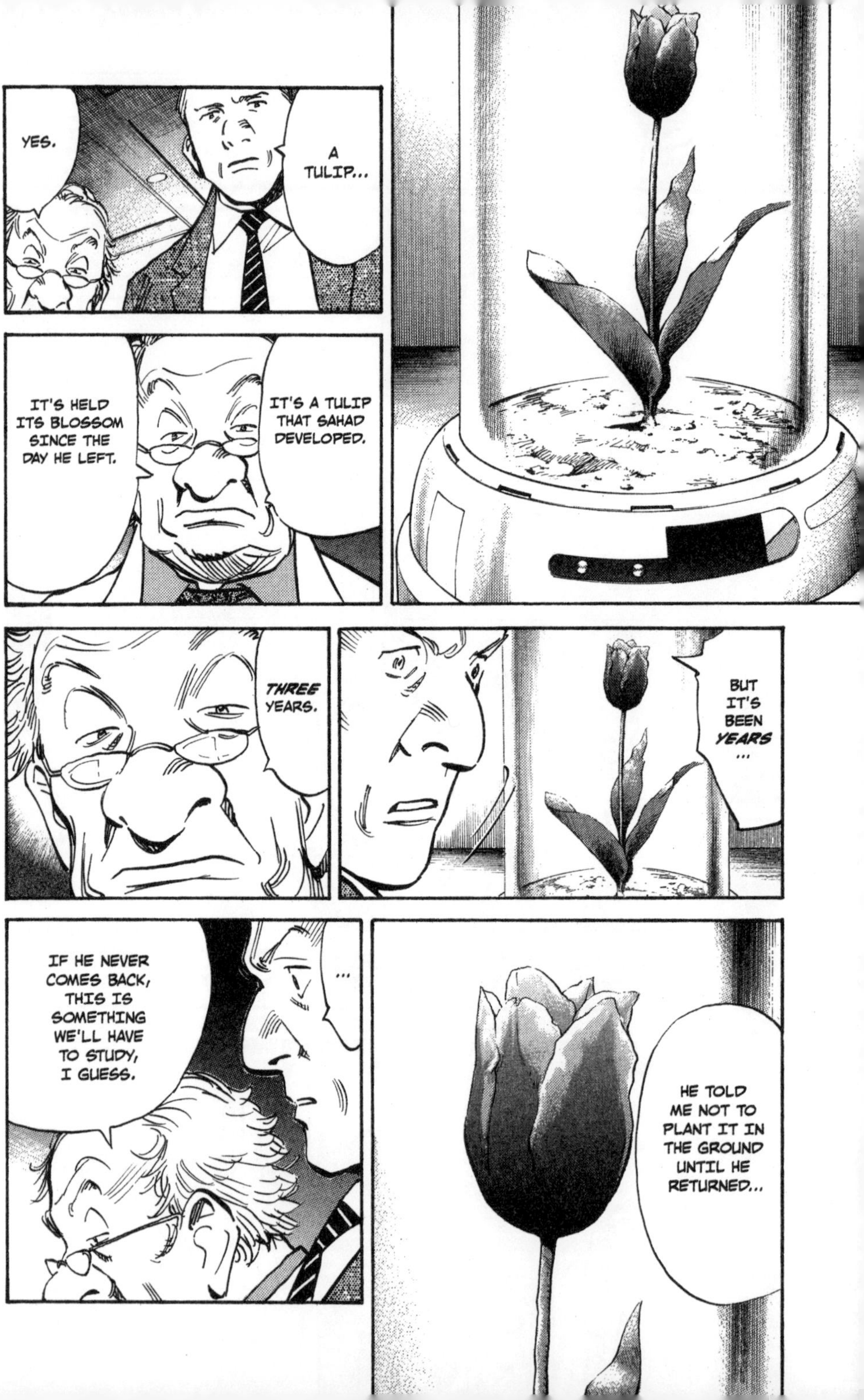
A TULIP...
YES.
IT'S A TULIP THAT SAHAD DEVELOPED.
IT'S HELD ITS BLOSSOM SINCE THE DAY HE LEFT.
BUT IT'S BEEN *YEARS* ...
THREE YEARS.
HE TOLD ME NOT TO PLANT IT IN THE GROUND UNTIL HE RETURNED...
IF HE NEVER COMES BACK, THIS IS SOMETHING WE'LL HAVE TO STUDY, I GUESS.
...

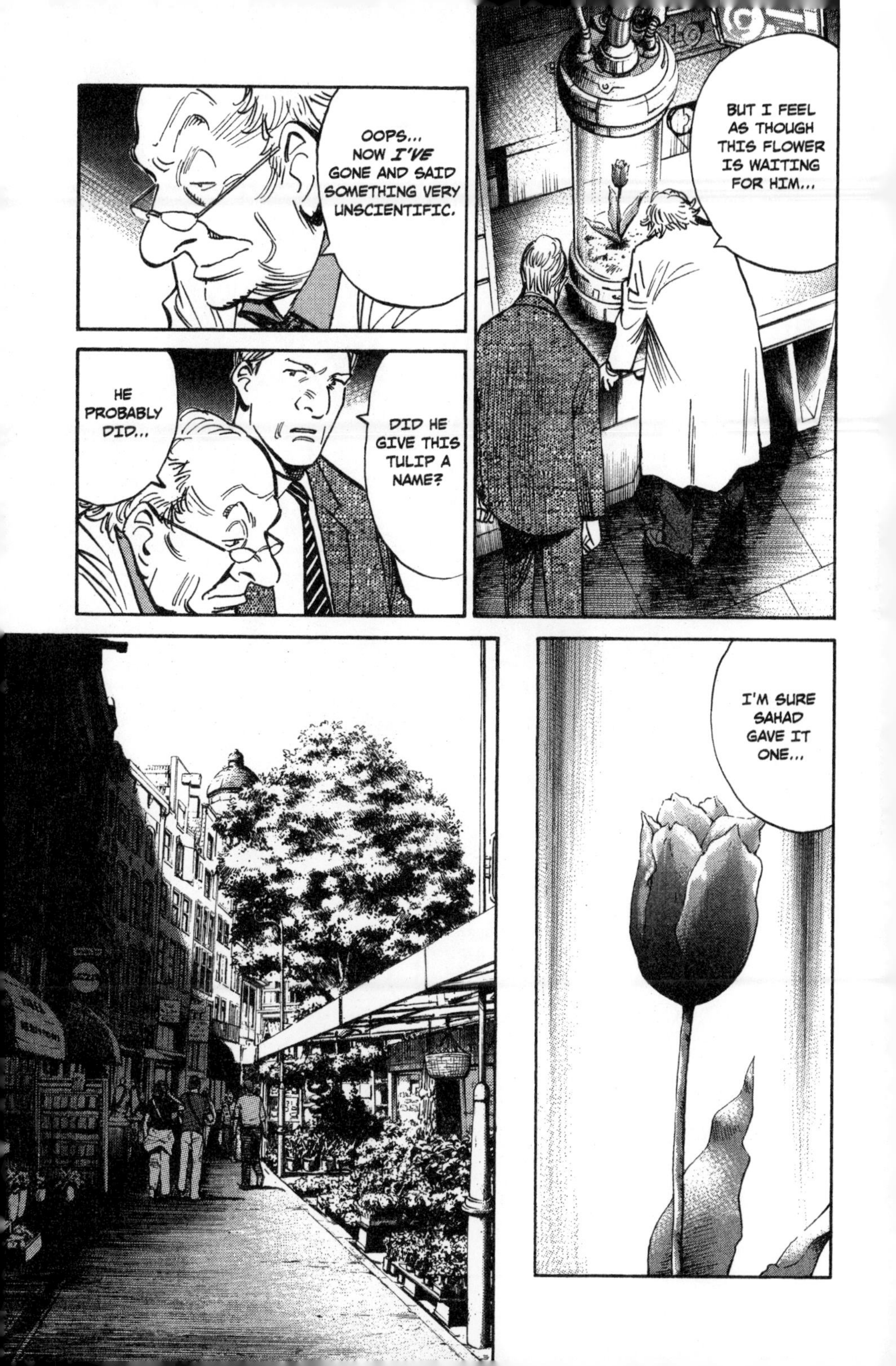
BUT I FEEL AS THOUGH THIS FLOWER IS WAITING FOR HIM...
OOPS... NOW *I'VE* GONE AND SAID SOMETHING VERY UNSCIENTIFIC.
DID HE GIVE THIS TULIP A NAME?
HE PROBABLY DID...
I'M SURE SAHAD GAVE IT ONE...

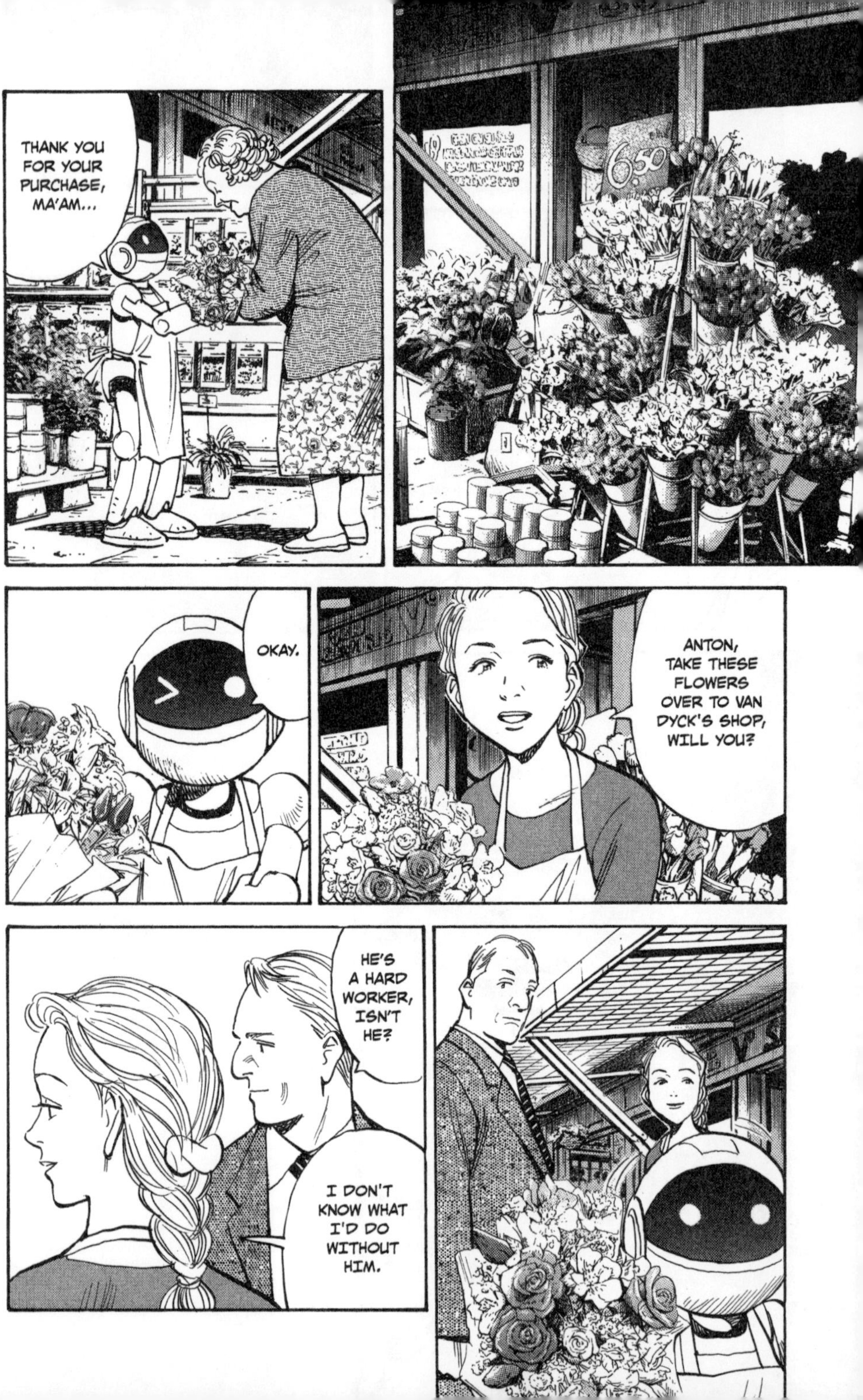
THANK YOU FOR YOUR PURCHASE, MA'AM...
ANTON, TAKE THESE FLOWERS OVER TO VAN DYCK'S SHOP, WILL YOU?
OKAY.
HE'S A HARD WORKER, ISN'T HE?
I DON'T KNOW WHAT I'D DO WITHOUT HIM.

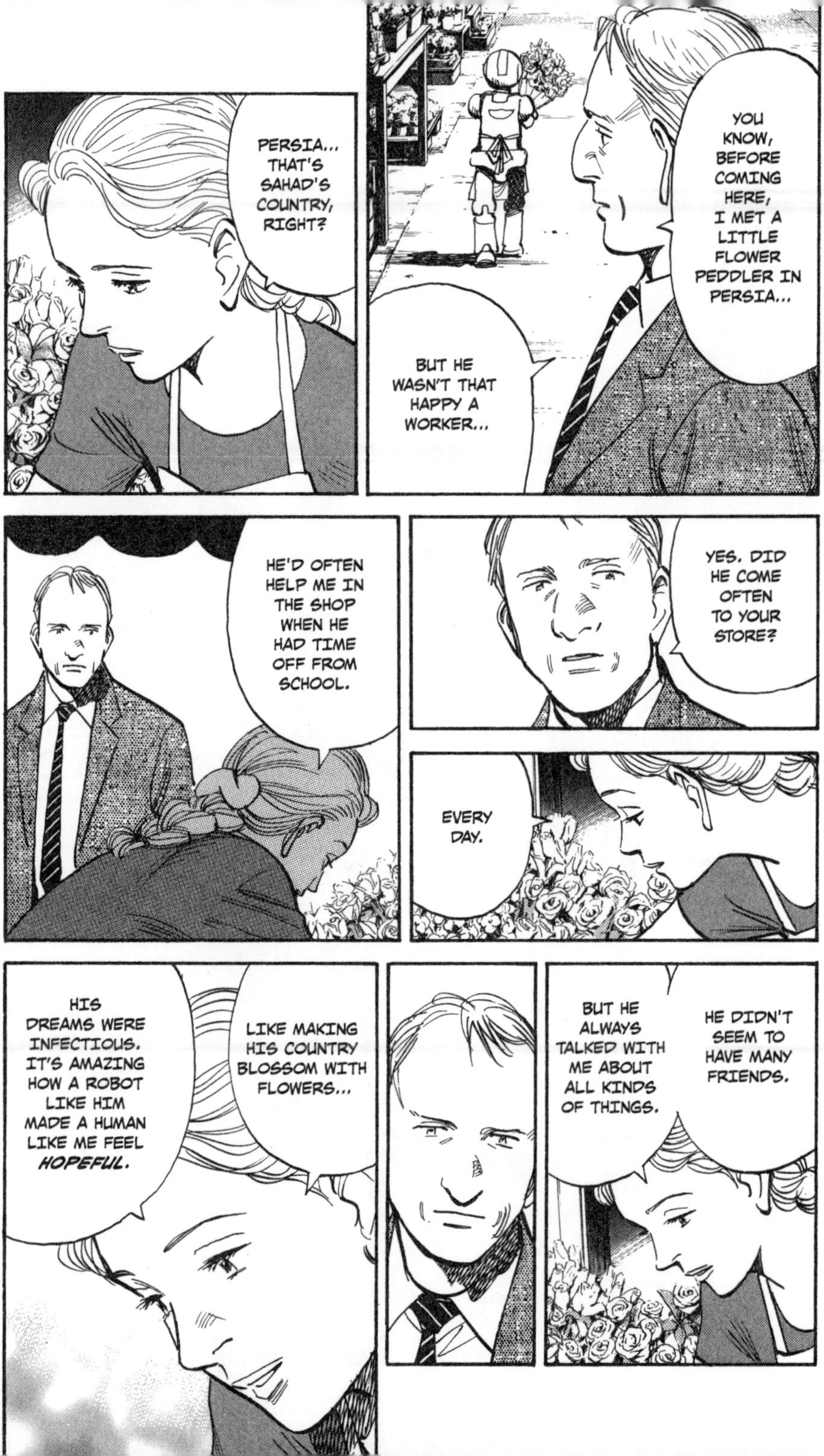
YOU KNOW, BEFORE COMING HERE, I MET A LITTLE FLOWER PEDDLER IN PERSIA...
BUT HE WASN'T THAT HAPPY A WORKER...
PERSIA... THAT'S SAHAD'S COUNTRY, RIGHT?
YES. DID HE COME OFTEN TO YOUR STORE?
EVERY DAY.
HE'D OFTEN HELP ME IN THE SHOP WHEN HE HAD TIME OFF FROM SCHOOL.
HE DIDN'T SEEM TO HAVE MANY FRIENDS.
BUT HE ALWAYS TALKED WITH ME ABOUT ALL KINDS OF THINGS.
LIKE MAKING HIS COUNTRY BLOSSOM WITH FLOWERS...
HIS DREAMS WERE INFECTIOUS. IT'S AMAZING HOW A ROBOT LIKE HIM MADE A HUMAN LIKE ME FEEL ***HOPEFUL***.

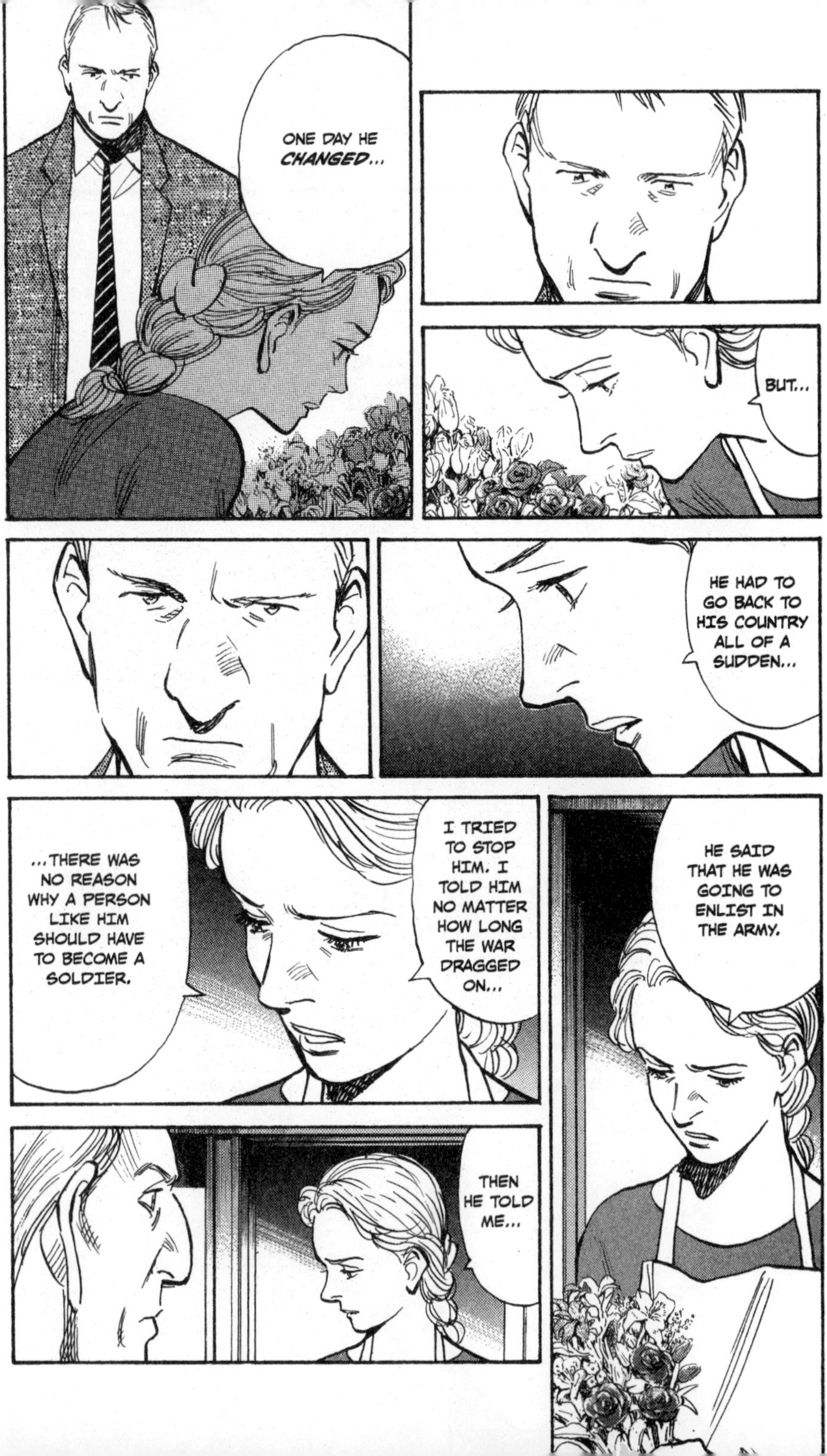
BUT...
ONE DAY HE CHANGED...
HE HAD TO GO BACK TO HIS COUNTRY ALL OF A SUDDEN...
HE SAID THAT HE WAS GOING TO ENLIST IN THE ARMY.
I TRIED TO STOP HIM. I TOLD HIM NO MATTER HOW LONG THE WAR DRAGGED ON...
...THERE WAS NO REASON WHY A PERSON LIKE HIM SHOULD HAVE TO BECOME A SOLDIER.
THEN HE TOLD ME...

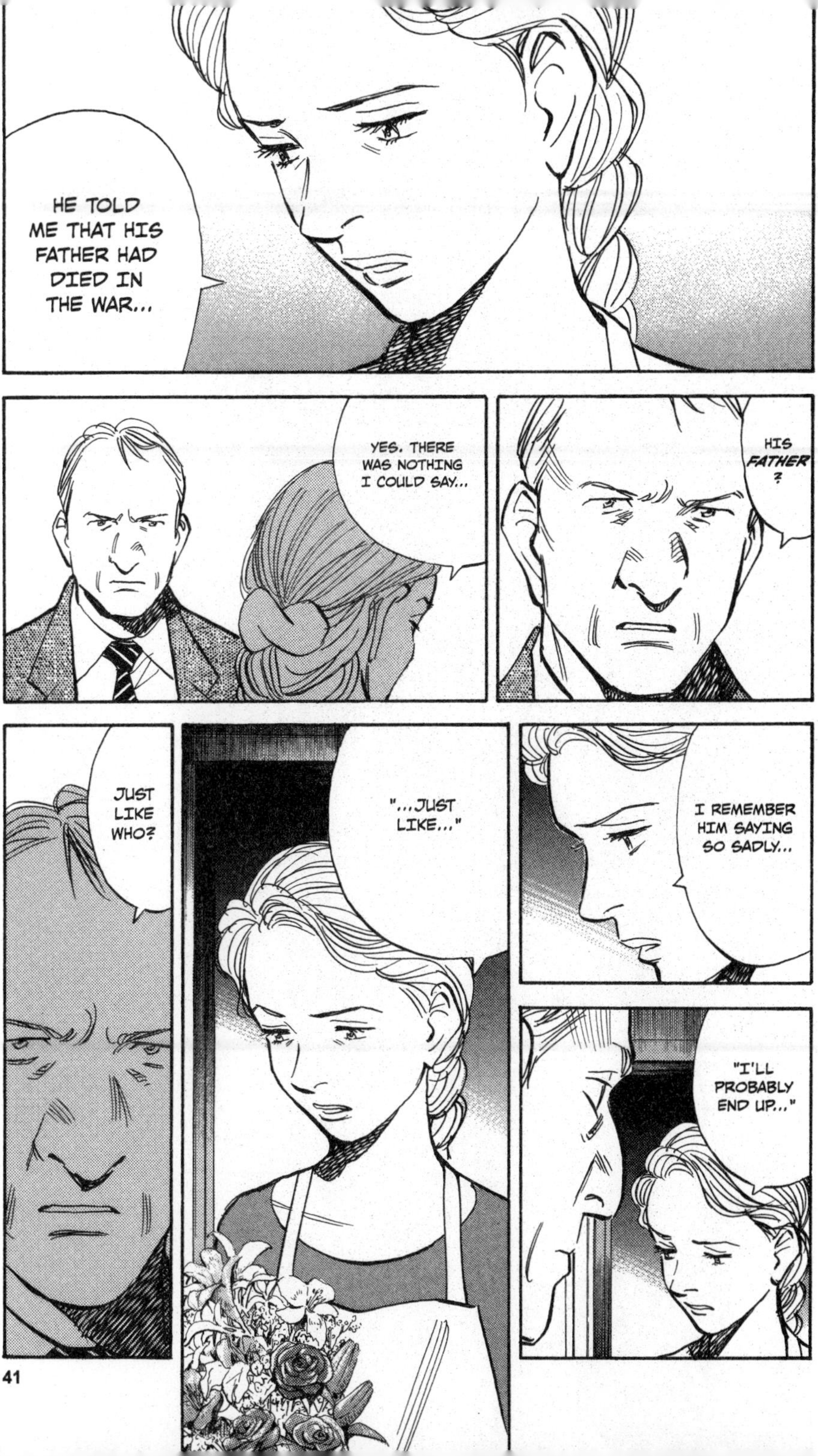
HE TOLD ME THAT HIS FATHER HAD DIED IN THE WAR...
HIS *FATHER*?
YES. THERE WAS NOTHING I COULD SAY...
I REMEMBER HIM SAYING SO SADLY...
"...JUST LIKE..."
JUST LIKE WHO?
"I'LL PROBABLY END UP..."

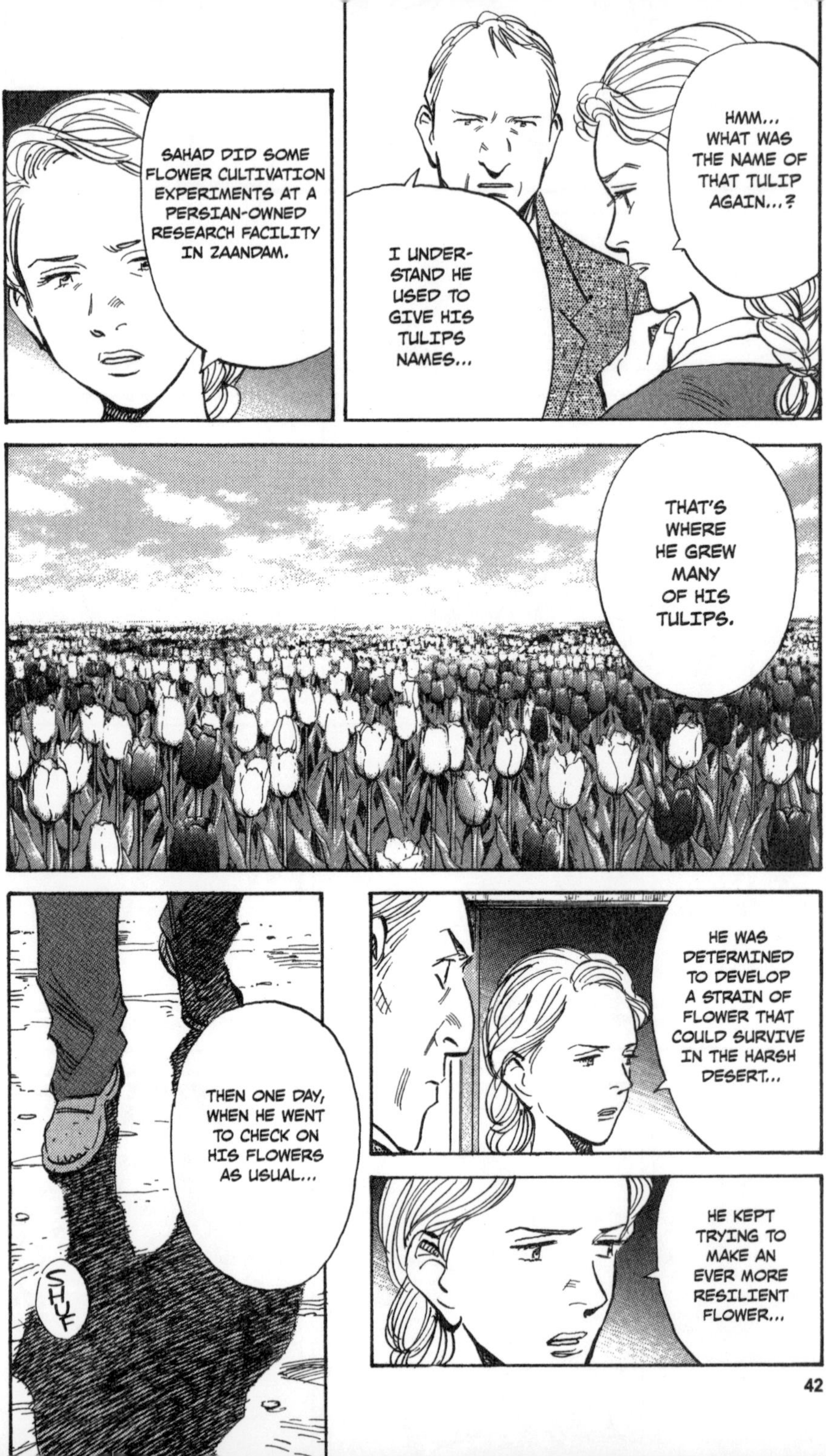
HMM... WHAT WAS THE NAME OF THAT TULIP AGAIN...?
I UNDER-STAND HE USED TO GIVE HIS TULIPS NAMES...
SAHAD DID SOME FLOWER CULTIVATION EXPERIMENTS AT A PERSIAN-OWNED RESEARCH FACILITY IN ZAANDAM.
THAT'S WHERE HE GREW MANY OF HIS TULIPS.
HE WAS DETERMINED TO DEVELOP A STRAIN OF FLOWER THAT COULD SURVIVE IN THE HARSH DESERT...
HE KEPT TRYING TO MAKE AN EVER MORE RESILIENT FLOWER...
THEN ONE DAY, WHEN HE WENT TO CHECK ON HIS FLOWERS AS USUAL...
SHUF

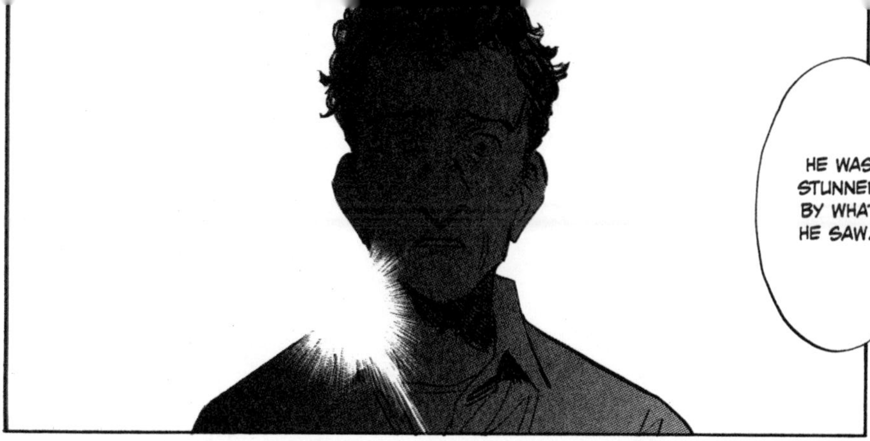
HE WAS STUNNED BY WHAT HE SAW...
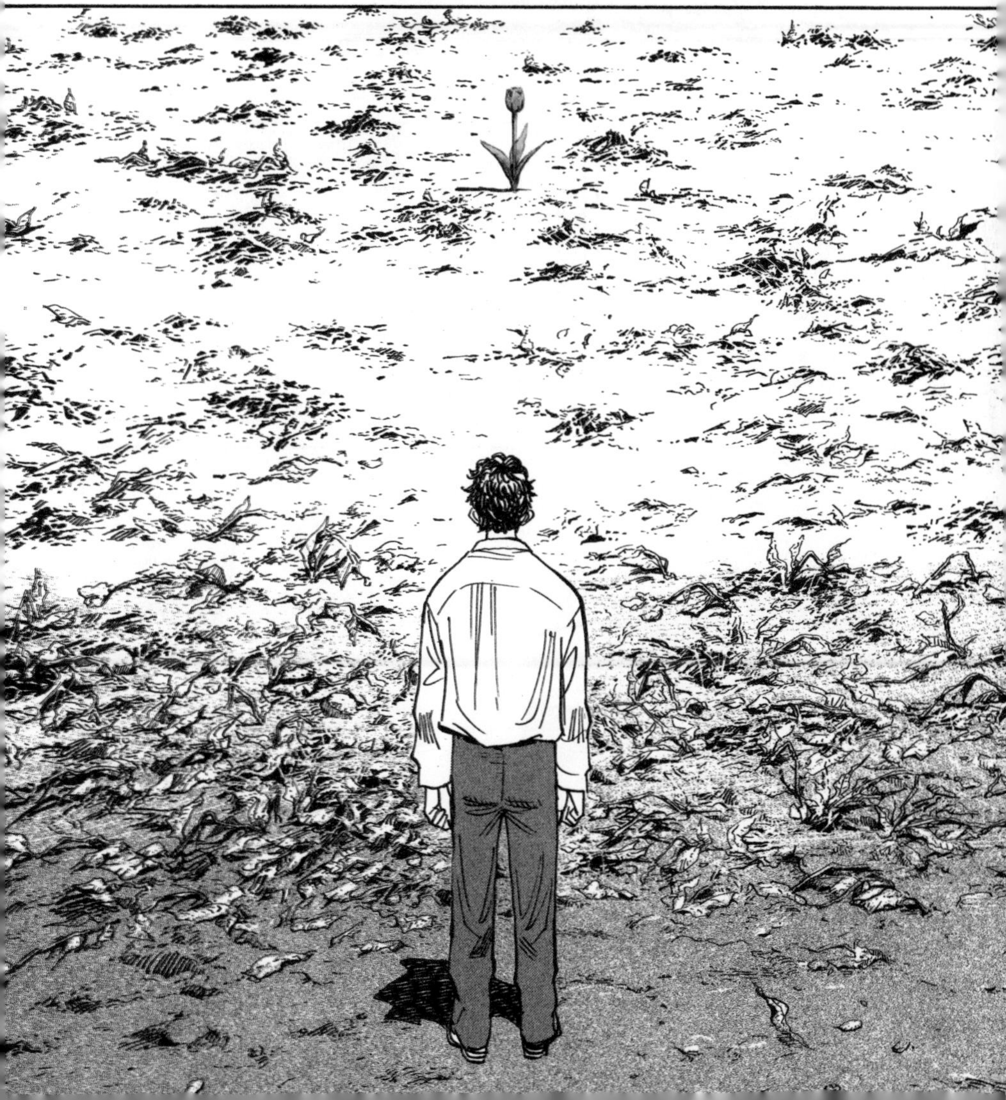

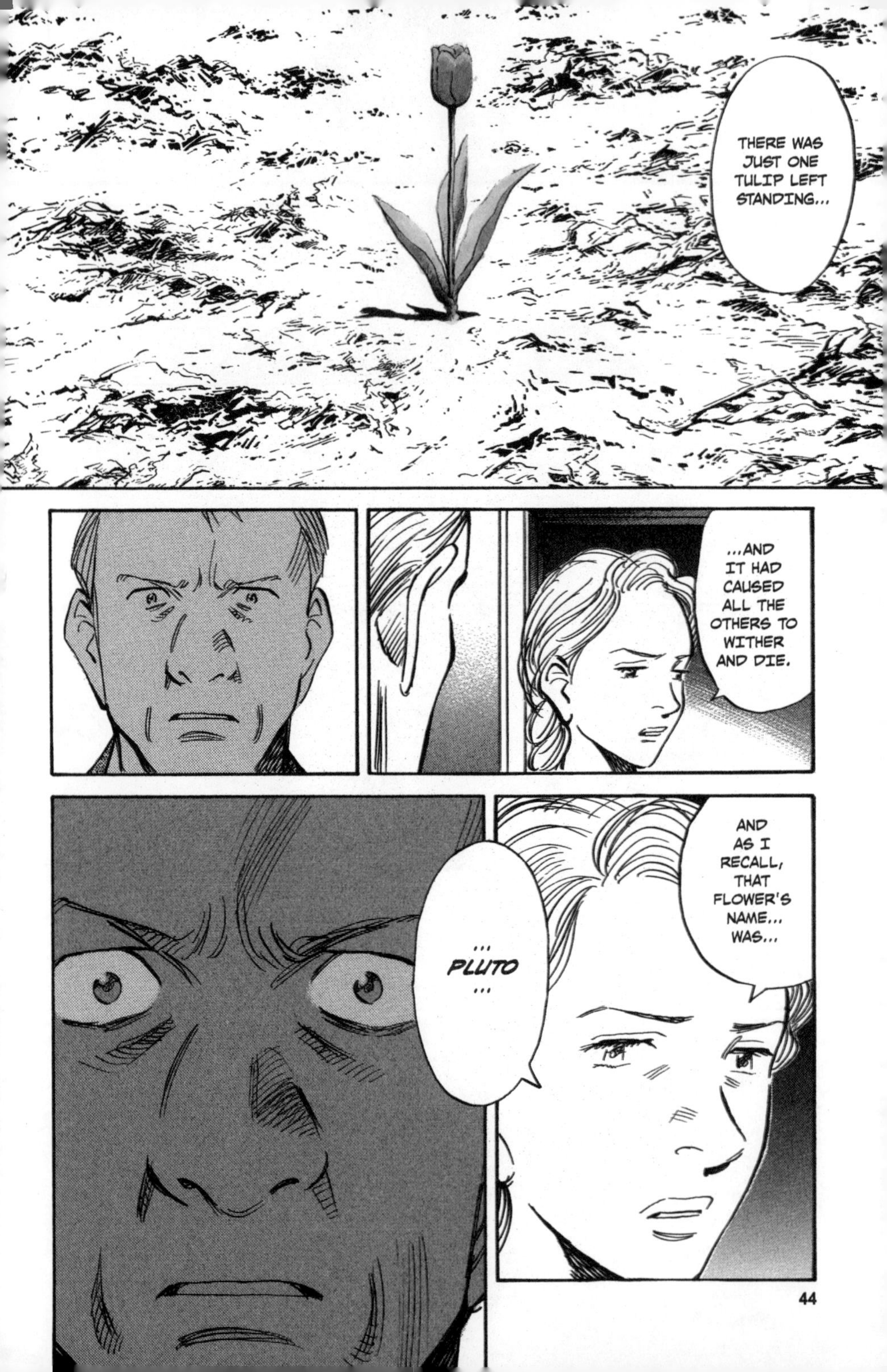
THERE WAS JUST ONE TULIP LEFT STANDING...
...AND IT HAD CAUSED ALL THE OTHERS TO WITHER AND DIE.
AND AS I RECALL, THAT FLOWER'S NAME... WAS...
... PLUTO ...

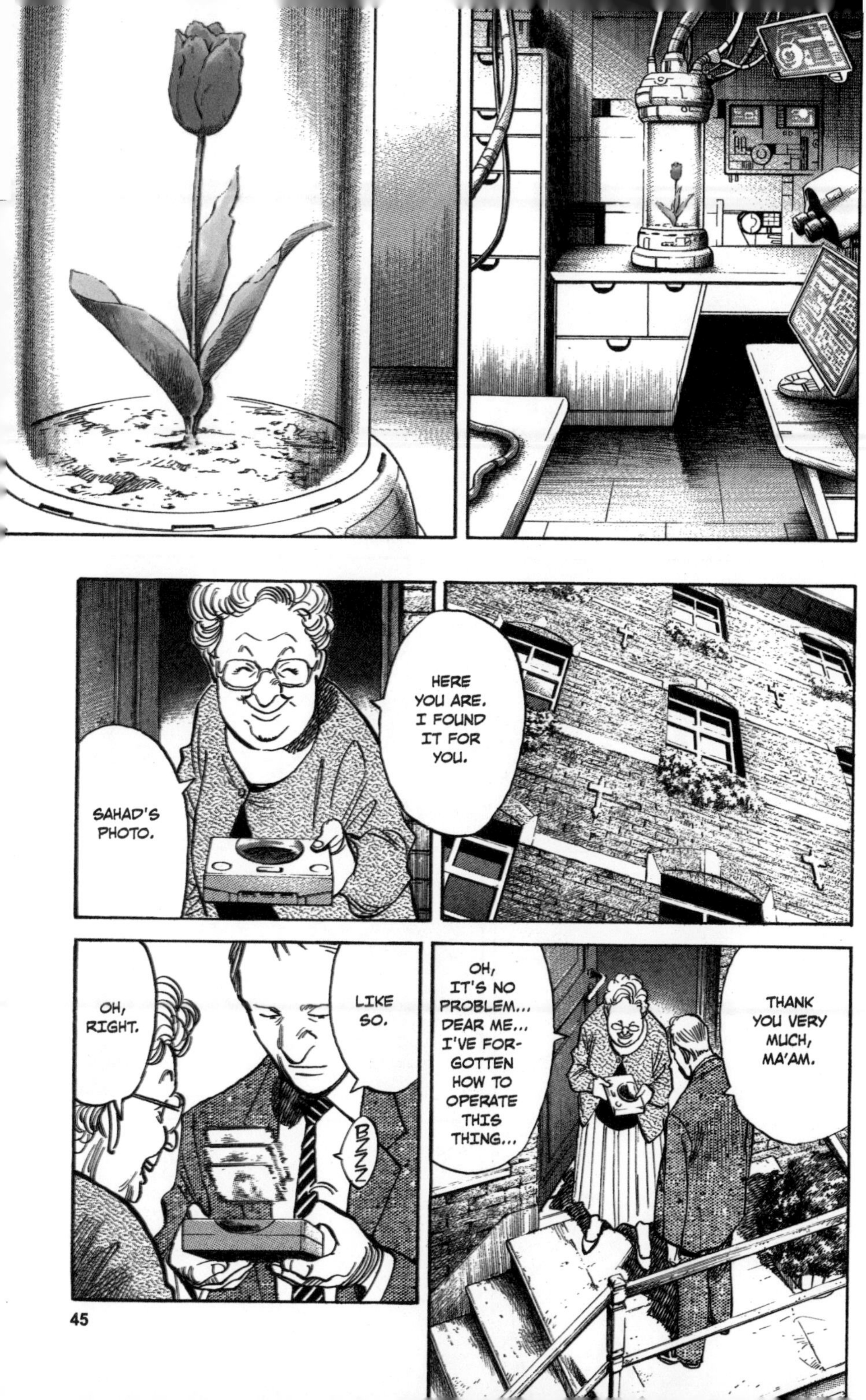

HERE YOU ARE. I FOUND IT FOR YOU.
SAHAD'S PHOTO.
THANK YOU VERY MUCH, MA'AM.
OH, IT'S NO PROBLEM... DEAR ME... I'VE FOR-GOTTEN HOW TO OPERATE THIS THING...
LIKE SO.
BZZZ
OH, RIGHT.

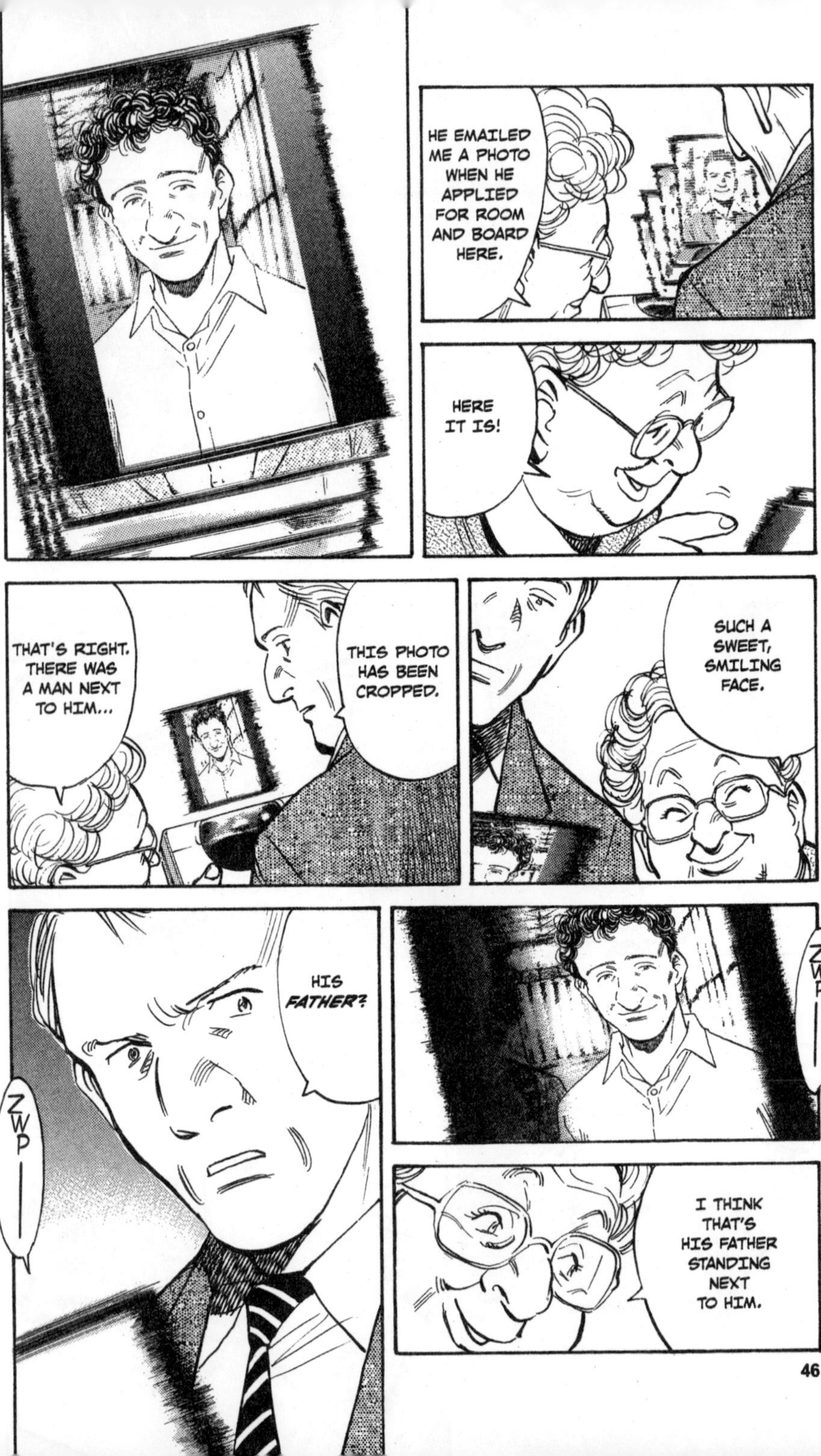
HE EMAILED ME A PHOTO WHEN HE APPLIED FOR ROOM AND BOARD HERE.
HERE IT IS!
SUCH A SWEET, SMILING FACE.
THIS PHOTO HAS BEEN CROPPED.
THAT'S RIGHT. THERE WAS A MAN NEXT TO HIM...
ZWP
I THINK THAT'S HIS FATHER STANDING NEXT TO HIM.
HIS *FATHER?*
ZWP

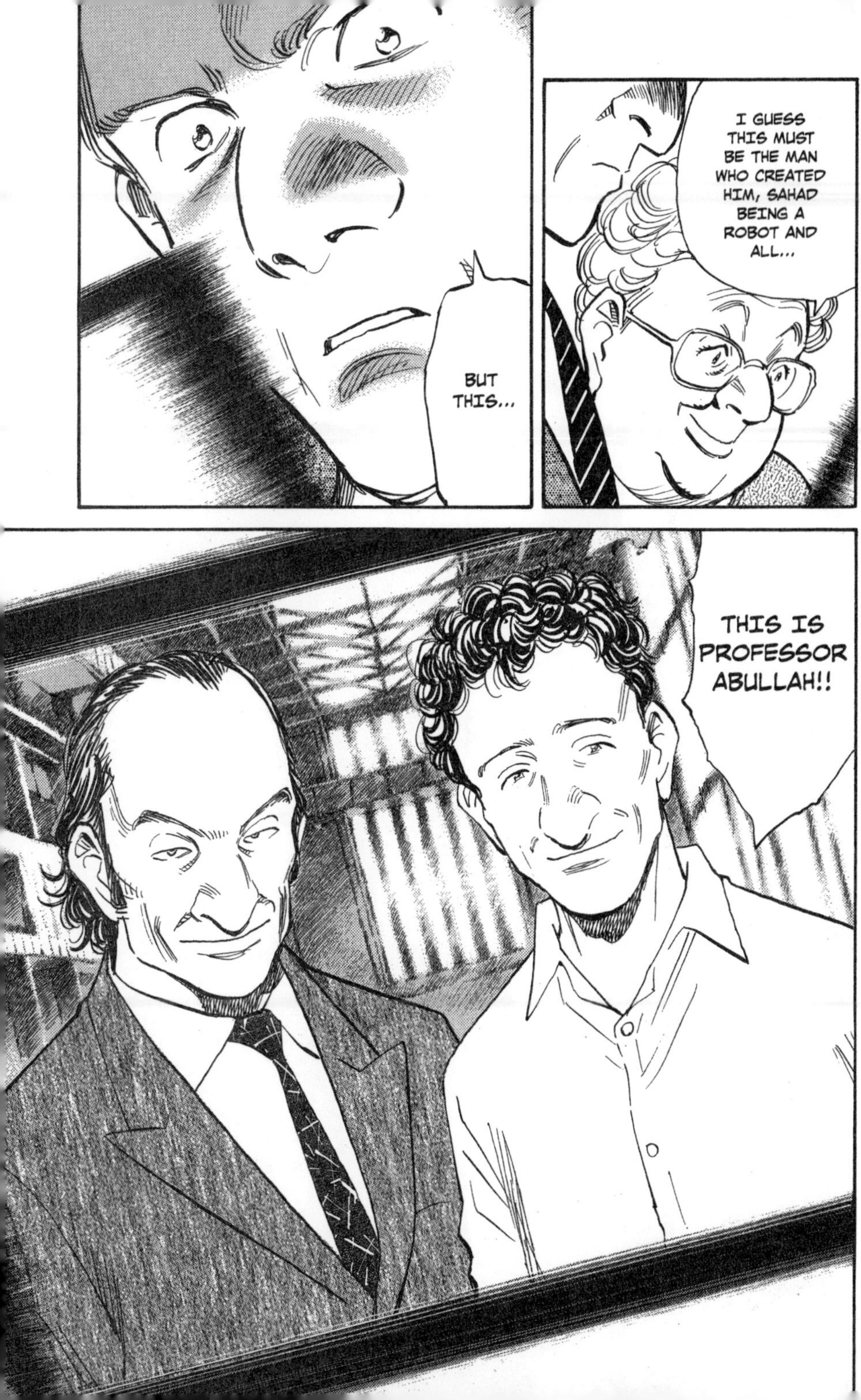
I GUESS THIS MUST BE THE MAN WHO CREATED HIM, SAHAD BEING A ROBOT AND ALL...
BUT THIS...
THIS IS PROFESSOR ABULLAH!!

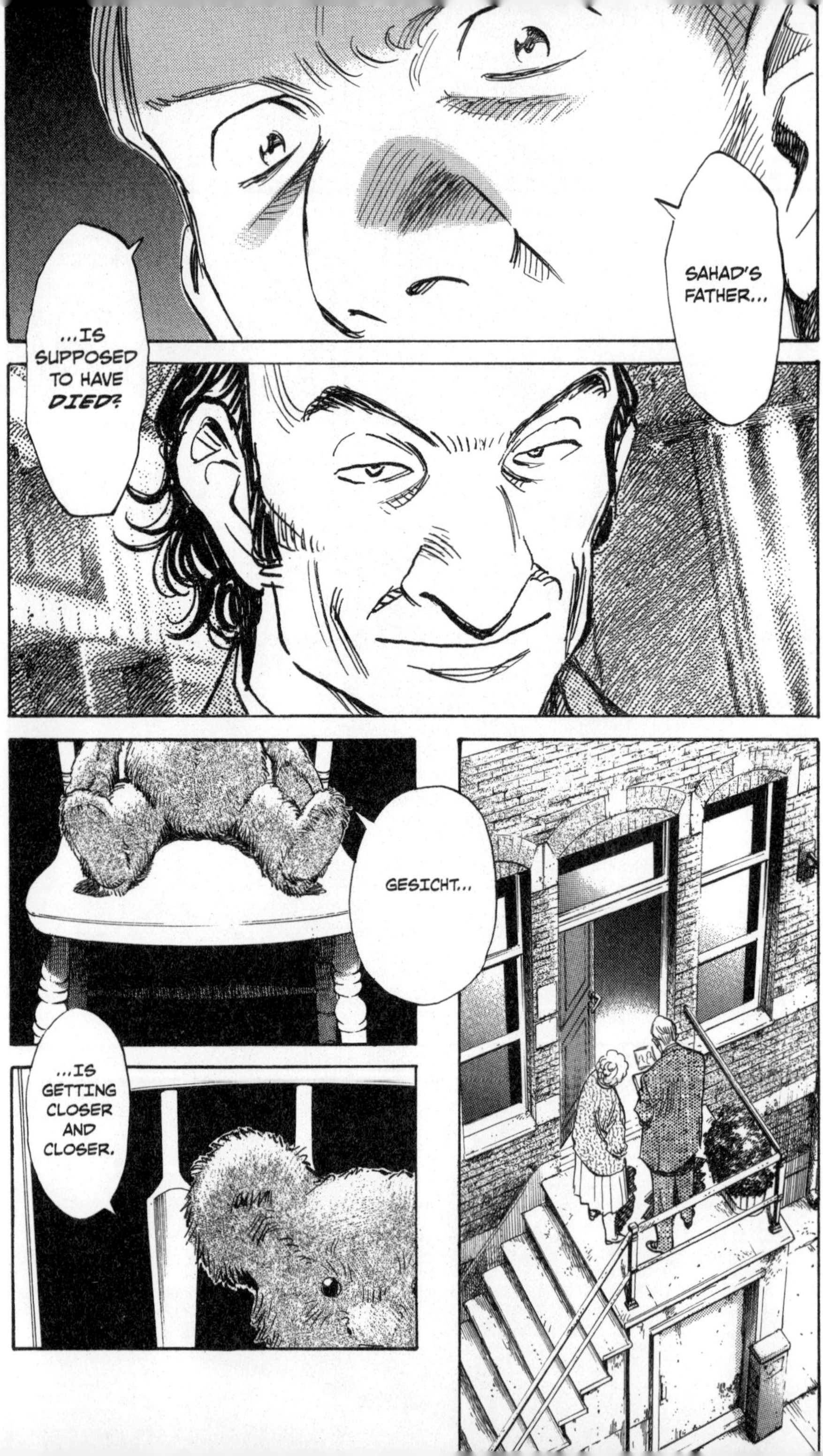
SAHAD'S FATHER...
...IS SUPPOSED TO HAVE DIED?
GESICHT...
...IS GETTING CLOSER AND CLOSER.

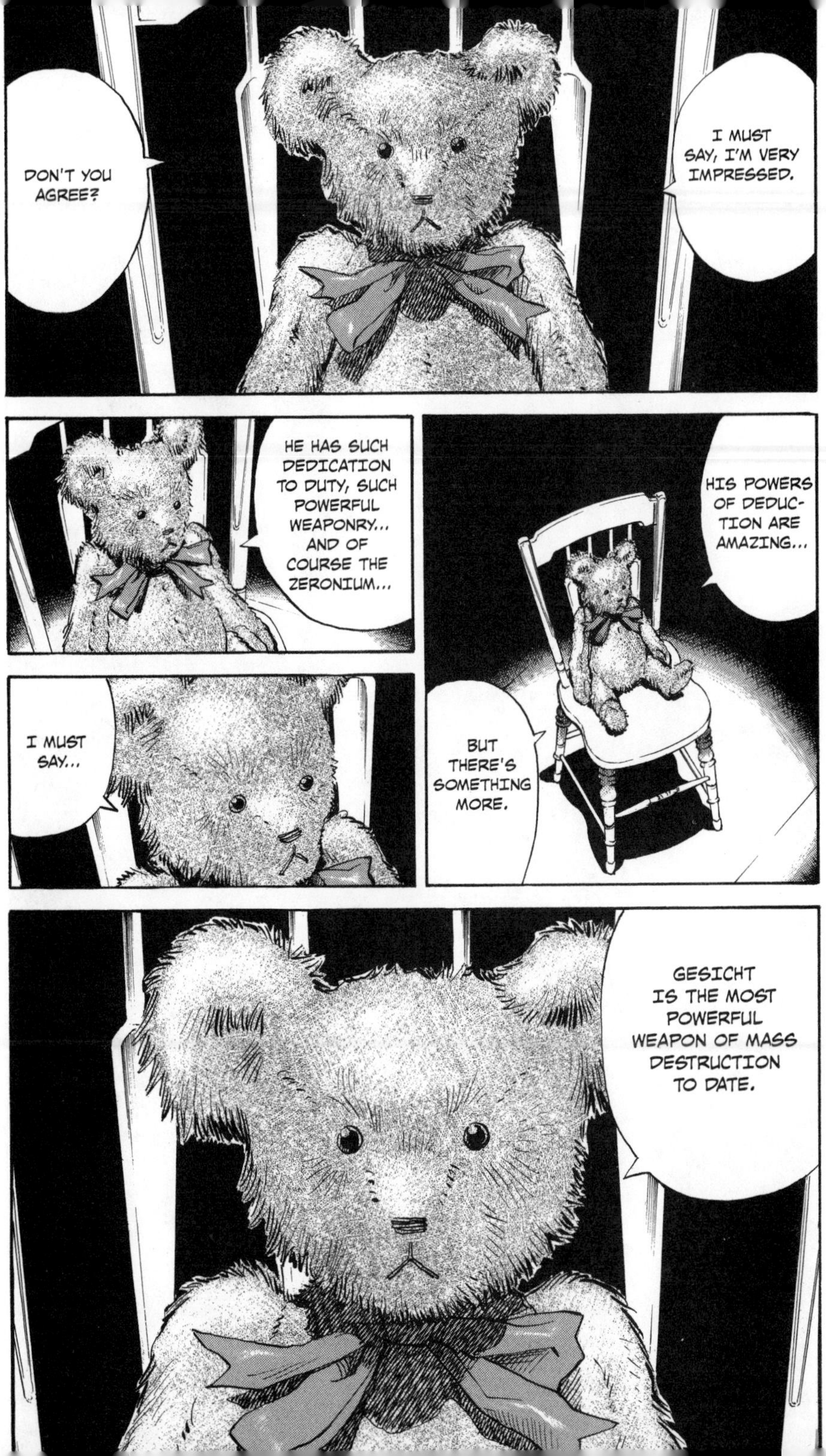
I MUST SAY, I'M VERY IMPRESSED.
DON'T YOU AGREE?
HIS POWERS OF DEDUC-TION ARE AMAZING...
BUT THERE'S SOMETHING MORE.
HE HAS SUCH DEDICATION TO DUTY, SUCH POWERFUL WEAPONRY... AND OF COURSE THE ZERONIUM...
I MUST SAY...
GESICHT IS THE MOST POWERFUL WEAPON OF MASS DESTRUCTION TO DATE.

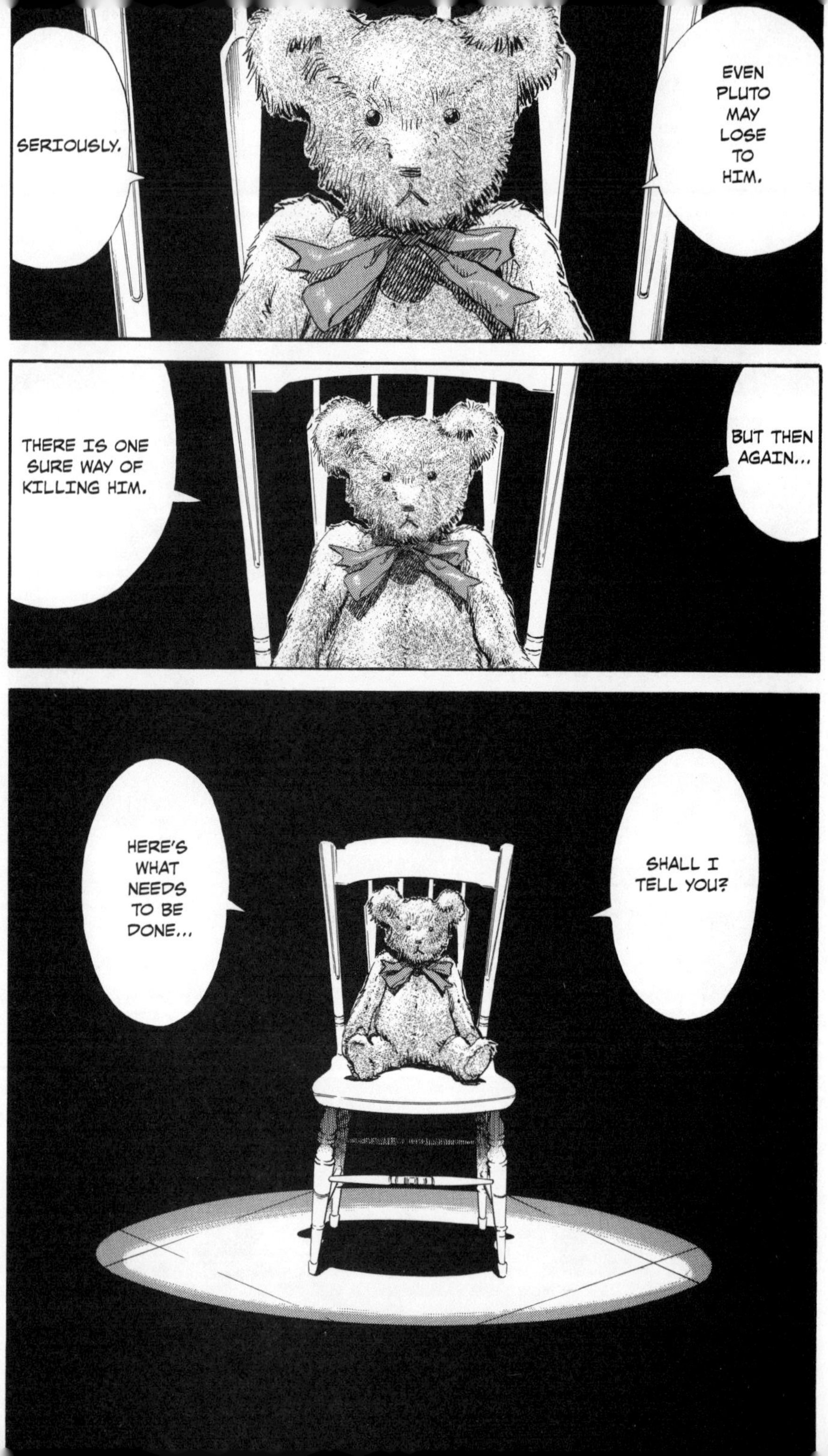
EVEN PLUTO MAY LOSE TO HIM.
SERIOUSLY.
BUT THEN AGAIN...
THERE IS ONE SURE WAY OF KILLING HIM.
SHALL I TELL YOU?
HERE'S WHAT NEEDS TO BE DONE...

Act 42 A Home in Hades

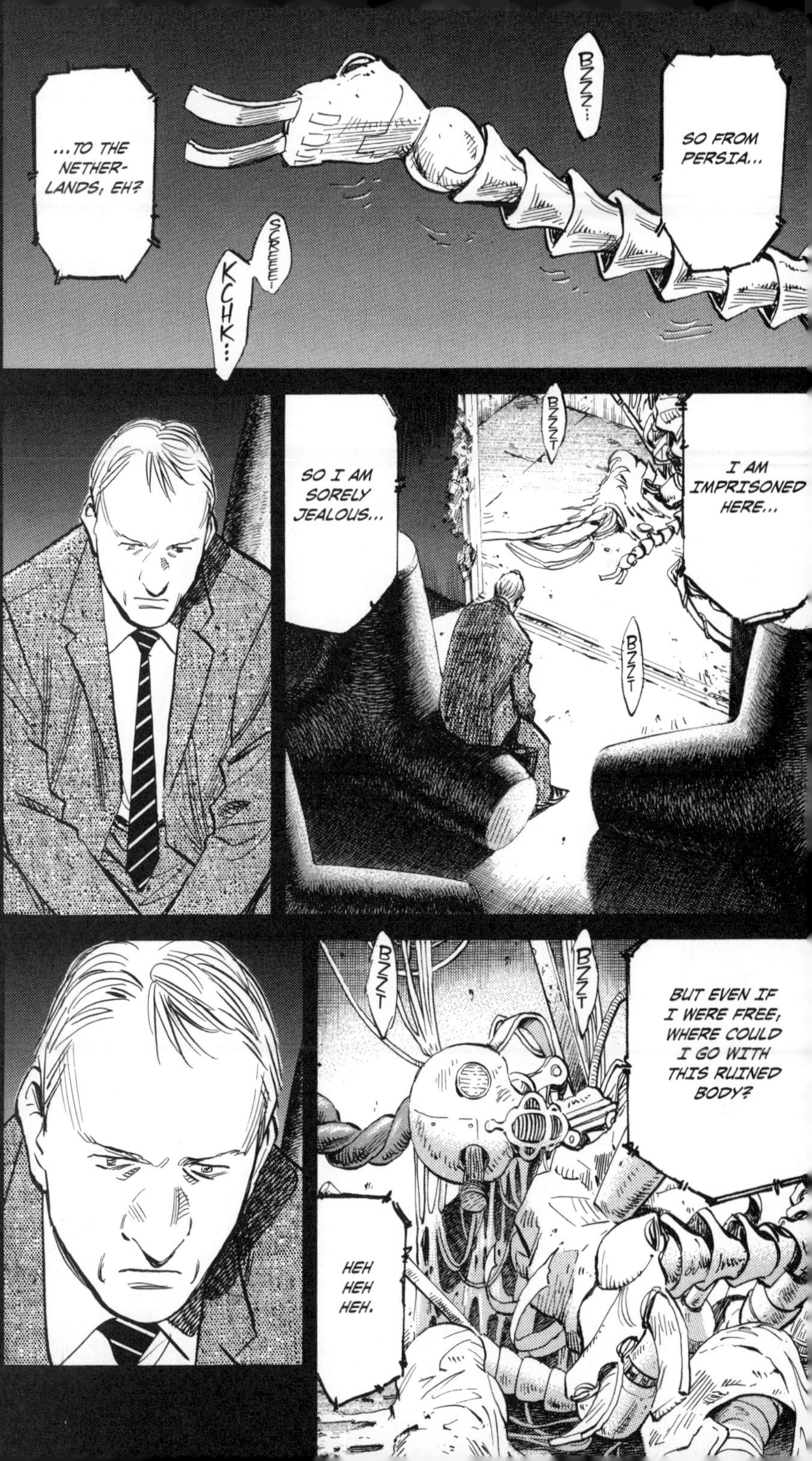
SO FROM PERSIA...
BZZZ...
...TO THE NETHER-LANDS, EH?
SCREEE...
KCHK...
I AM IMPRISONED HERE...
BZZT
BZZT
SO I AM SORELY JEALOUS...
BUT EVEN IF I WERE FREE, WHERE COULD I GO WITH THIS RUINED BODY?
BZZT
BZZT
HEH HEH HEH.

YES...

DID YOU FIGURE OUT WHO'S BEHIND THIS?

BZZT

WELL ...?

BZZT

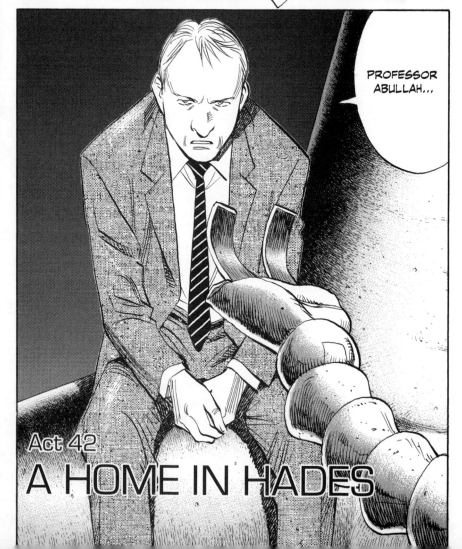

PROFESSOR ABULLAH...

Act 42
A HOME IN HADES

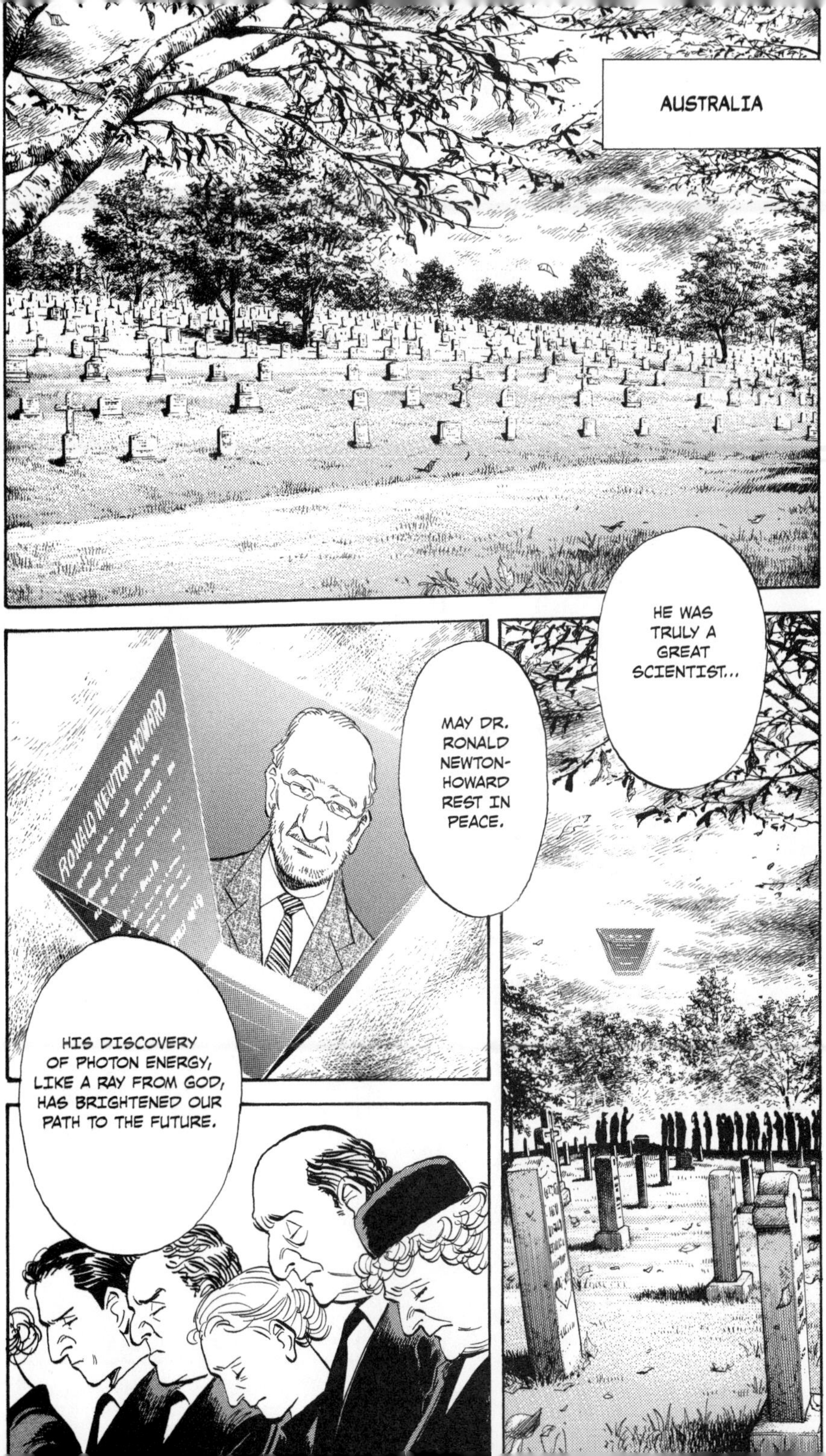
AUSTRALIA
HE WAS TRULY A GREAT SCIENTIST...
MAY DR. RONALD NEWTON-HOWARD REST IN PEACE.
RONALD NEWTON HOWARD
HIS DISCOVERY OF PHOTON ENERGY, LIKE A RAY FROM GOD, HAS BRIGHTENED OUR PATH TO THE FUTURE.

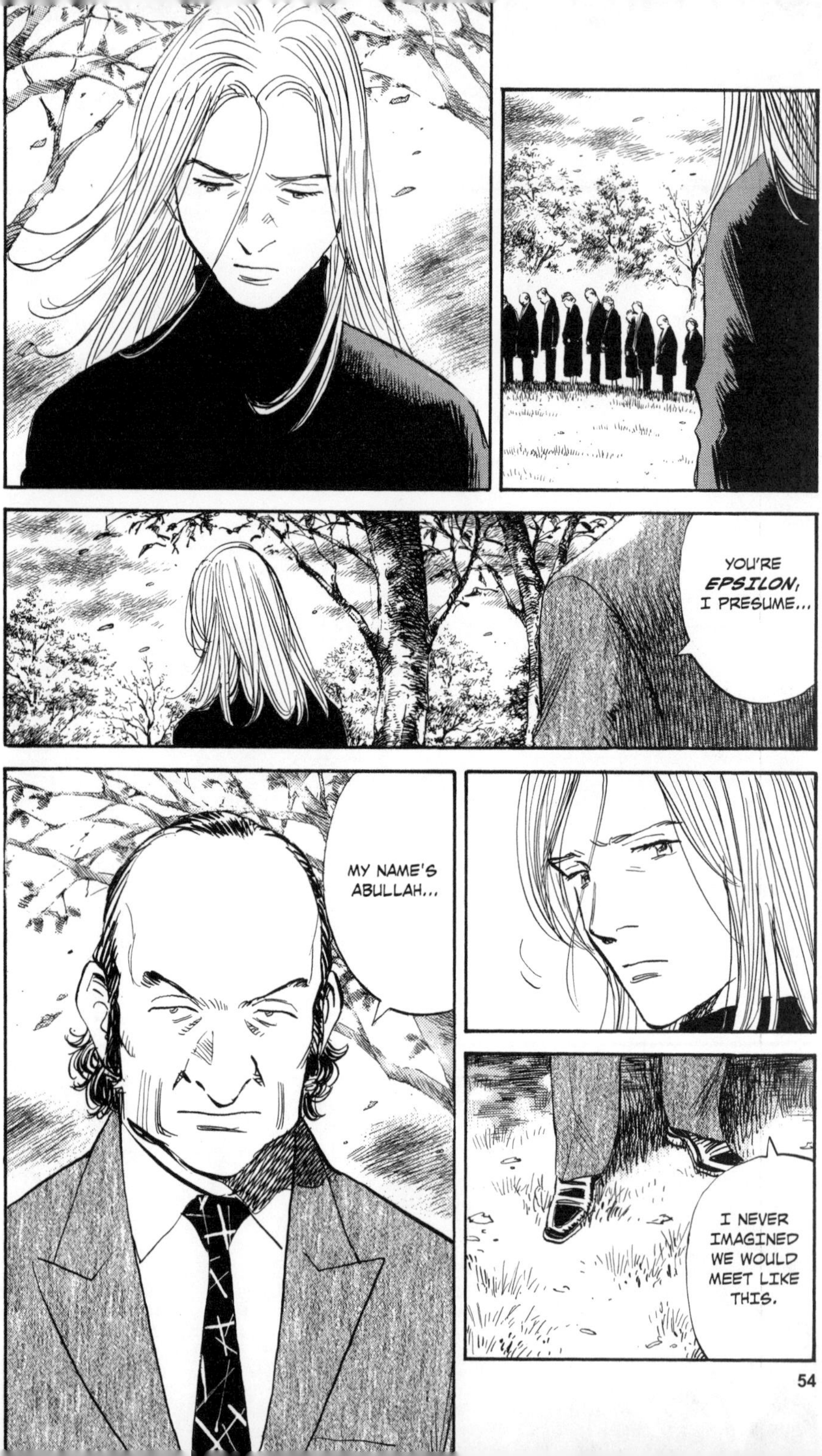
YOU'RE *EPSILON*, I PRESUME...
MY NAME'S ABULLAH...
I NEVER IMAGINED WE WOULD MEET LIKE THIS.

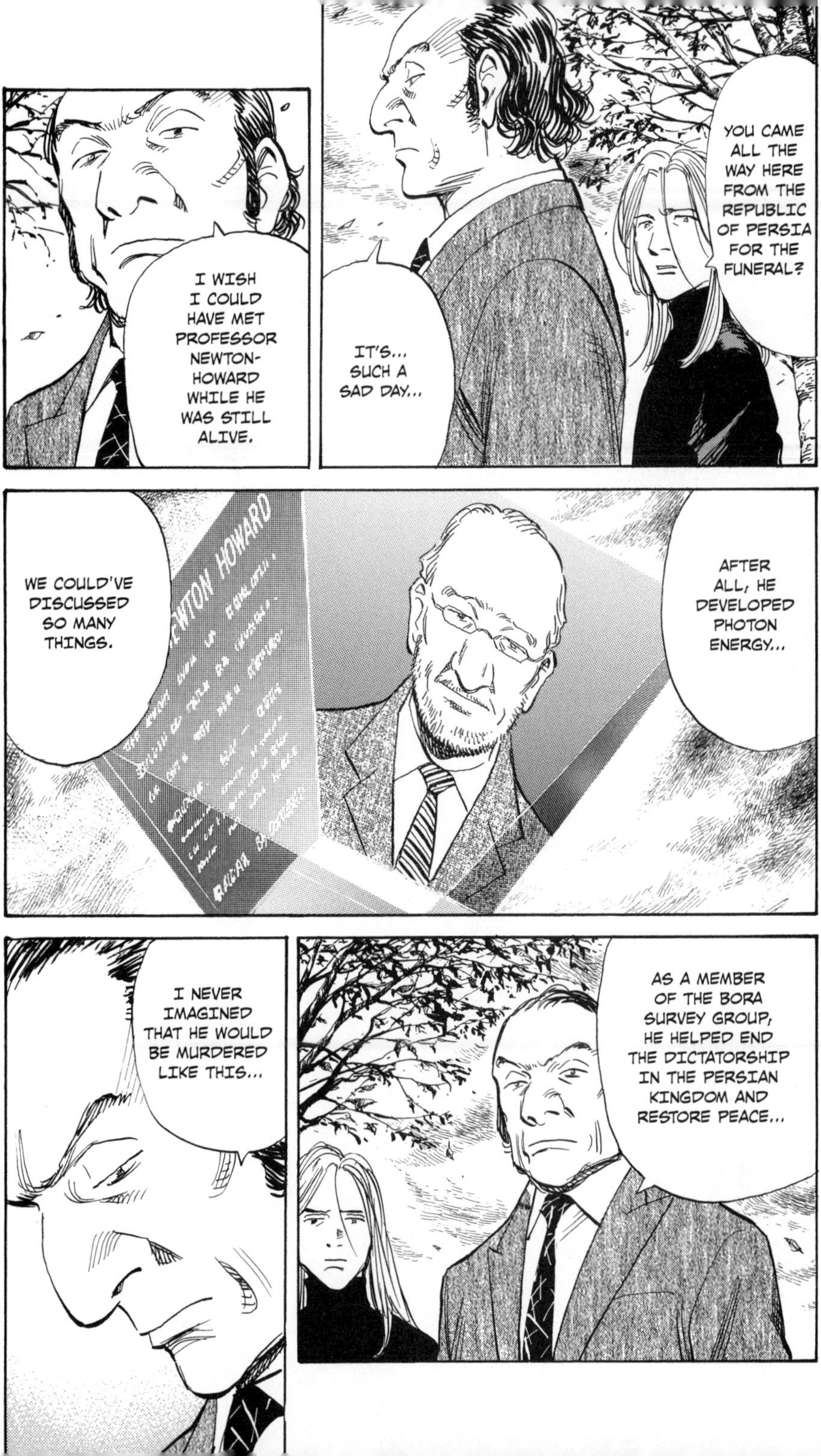

YOU CAME ALL THE WAY HERE FROM THE REPUBLIC OF PERSIA FOR THE FUNERAL?
IT'S... SUCH A SAD DAY...
I WISH I COULD HAVE MET PROFESSOR NEWTON-HOWARD WHILE HE WAS STILL ALIVE.
AFTER ALL, HE DEVELOPED PHOTON ENERGY...
WE COULD'VE DISCUSSED SO MANY THINGS.
AS A MEMBER OF THE BORA SURVEY GROUP, HE HELPED END THE DICTATORSHIP IN THE PERSIAN KINGDOM AND RESTORE PEACE...
I NEVER IMAGINED THAT HE WOULD BE MURDERED LIKE THIS...

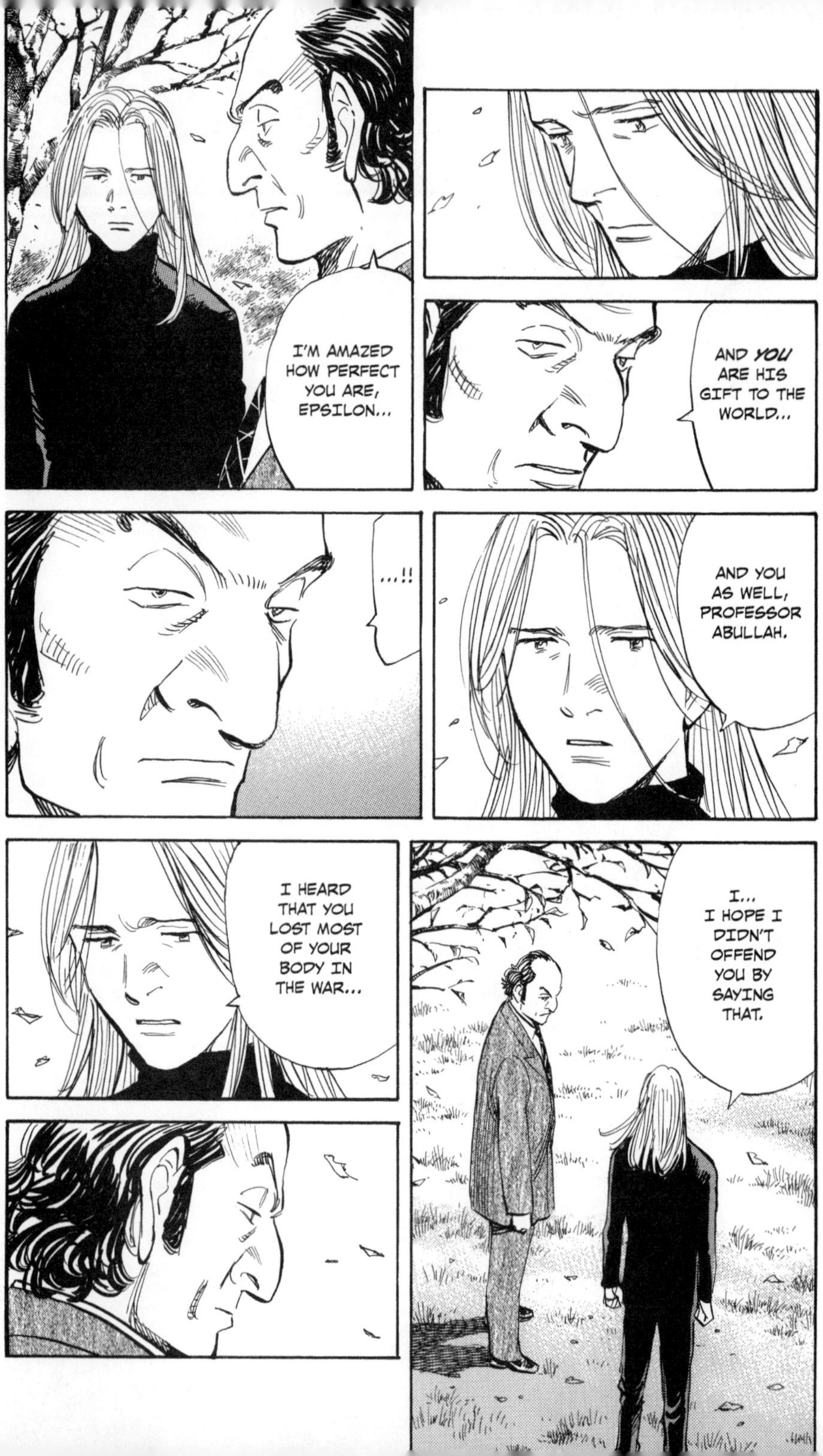
I'M AMAZED HOW PERFECT YOU ARE, EPSILON...
AND *YOU* ARE HIS GIFT TO THE WORLD...
...!!
AND YOU AS WELL, PROFESSOR ABULLAH.
I HEARD THAT YOU LOST MOST OF YOUR BODY IN THE WAR...
I... I HOPE I DIDN'T OFFEND YOU BY SAYING THAT.

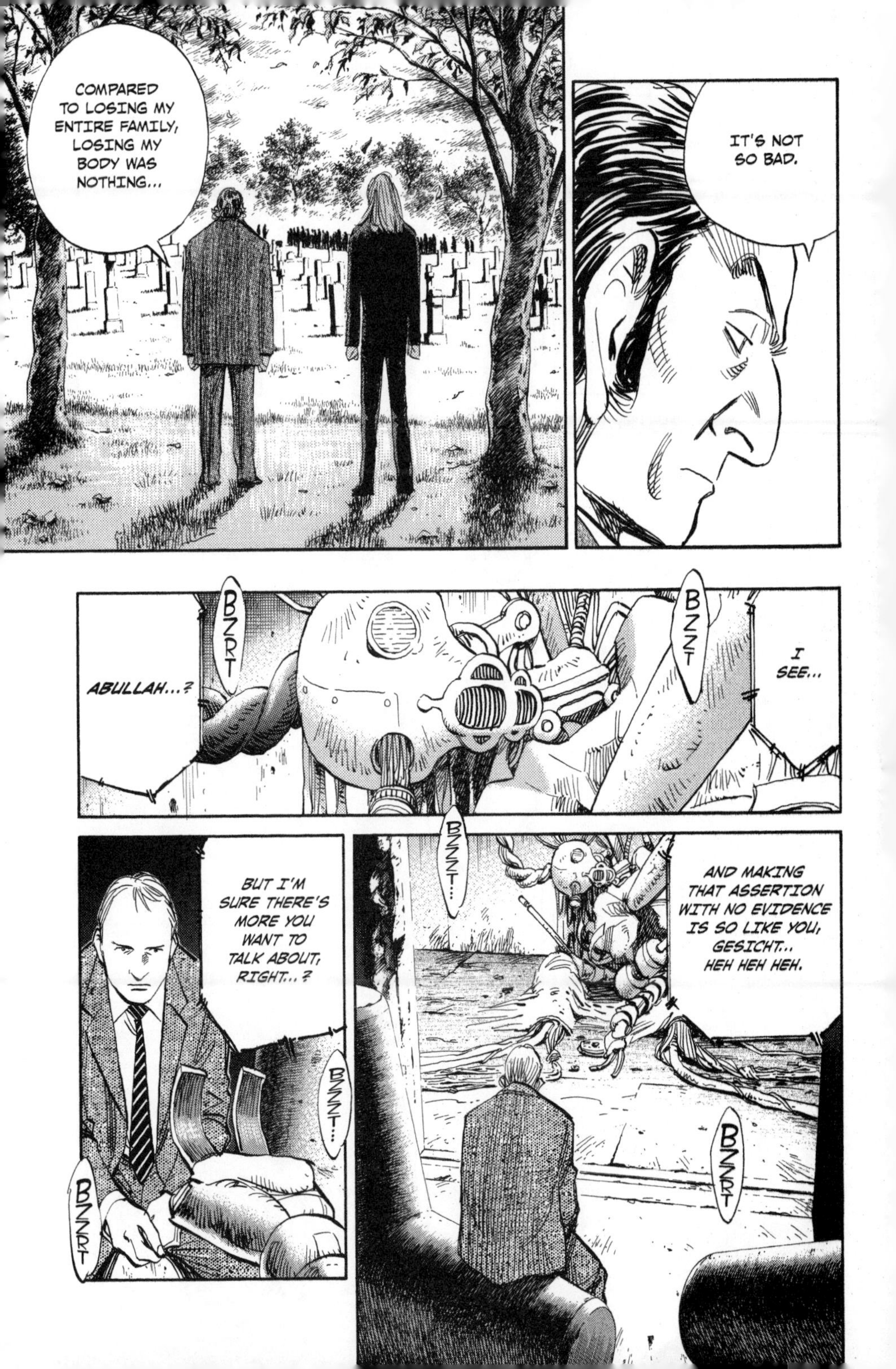
IT'S NOT SO BAD.
COMPARED TO LOSING MY ENTIRE FAMILY, LOSING MY BODY WAS NOTHING...
BZZT
I SEE...
BZRT
ABULLAH...?
BZZZT...
AND MAKING THAT ASSERTION WITH NO EVIDENCE IS SO LIKE YOU, GESICHT... HEH HEH HEH.
BZZRT
BUT I'M SURE THERE'S MORE YOU WANT TO TALK ABOUT, RIGHT...?
BZZZT...
BZZRT

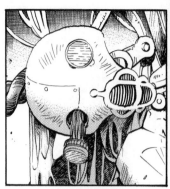

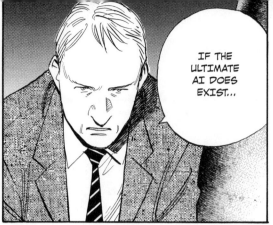

IF THE ULTIMATE AI DOES EXIST...
AND IF A ROBOT WERE EQUIPPED WITH SUCH AN AI-- ONE TOO ADVANCED FOR ITS SYSTEM...
WHAT WOULD HAPPEN?
BZZT
THE ROBOT WOULD NEVER GAIN CONSCIOUSNESS ...
BZZRT
BUT WHY?
HE'D BE CONFUSED. WOULDN'T KNOW WHO HE IS.

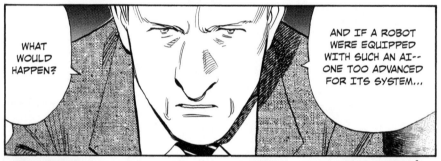

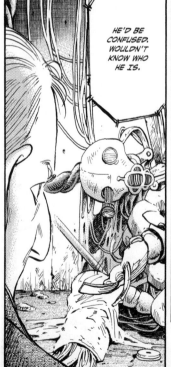

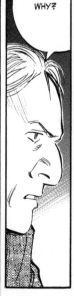

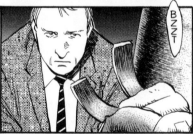

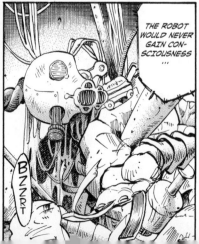

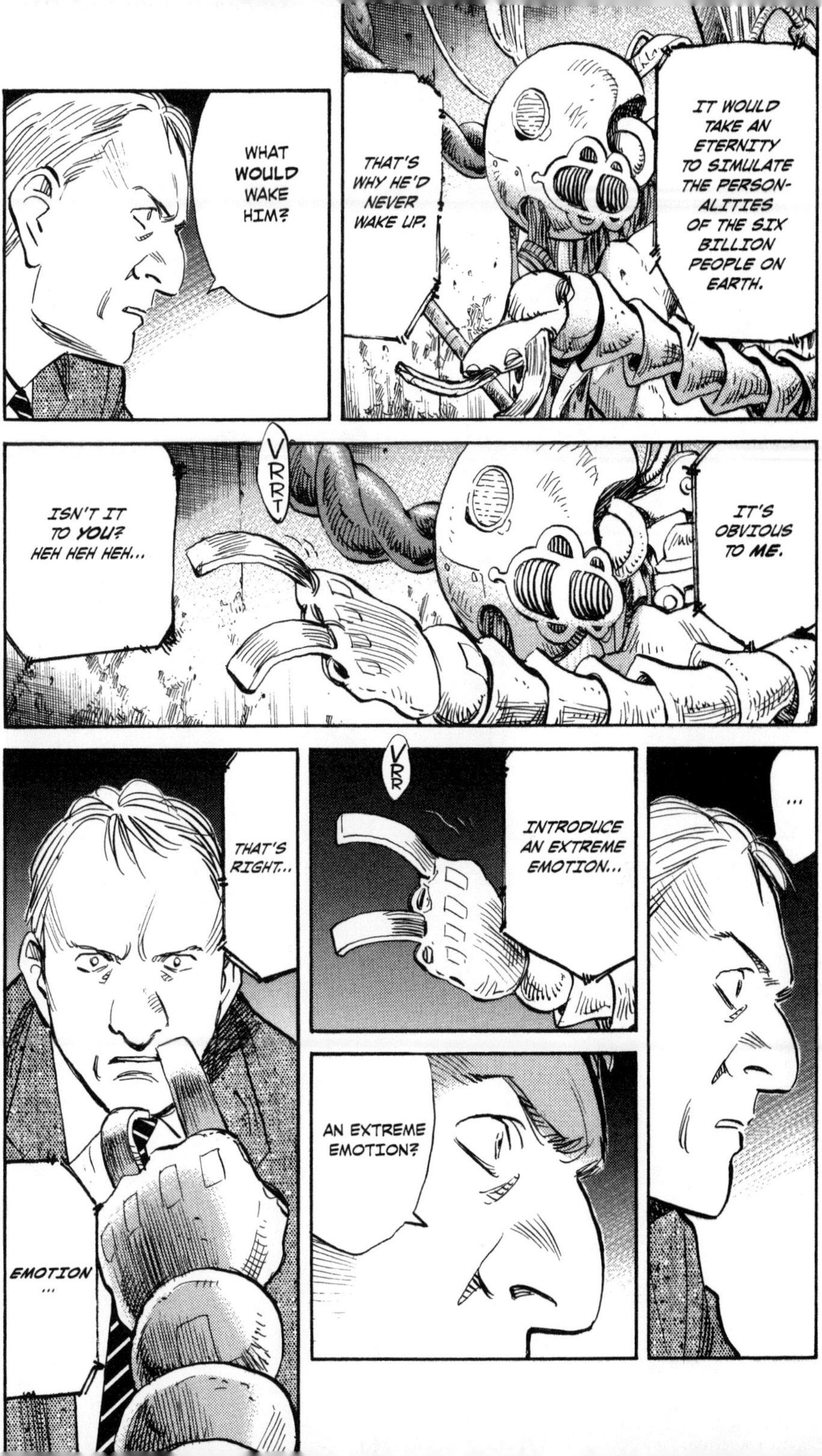
IT WOULD TAKE AN ETERNITY TO SIMULATE THE PERSON-ALITIES OF THE SIX BILLION PEOPLE ON EARTH.
THAT'S WHY HE'D NEVER WAKE UP.
WHAT WOULD WAKE HIM?
IT'S OBVIOUS TO ME.
VRRT
ISN'T IT TO YOU? HEH HEH HEH...
...
VRR
INTRODUCE AN EXTREME EMOTION...
AN EXTREME EMOTION?
THAT'S RIGHT...
EMOTION ...

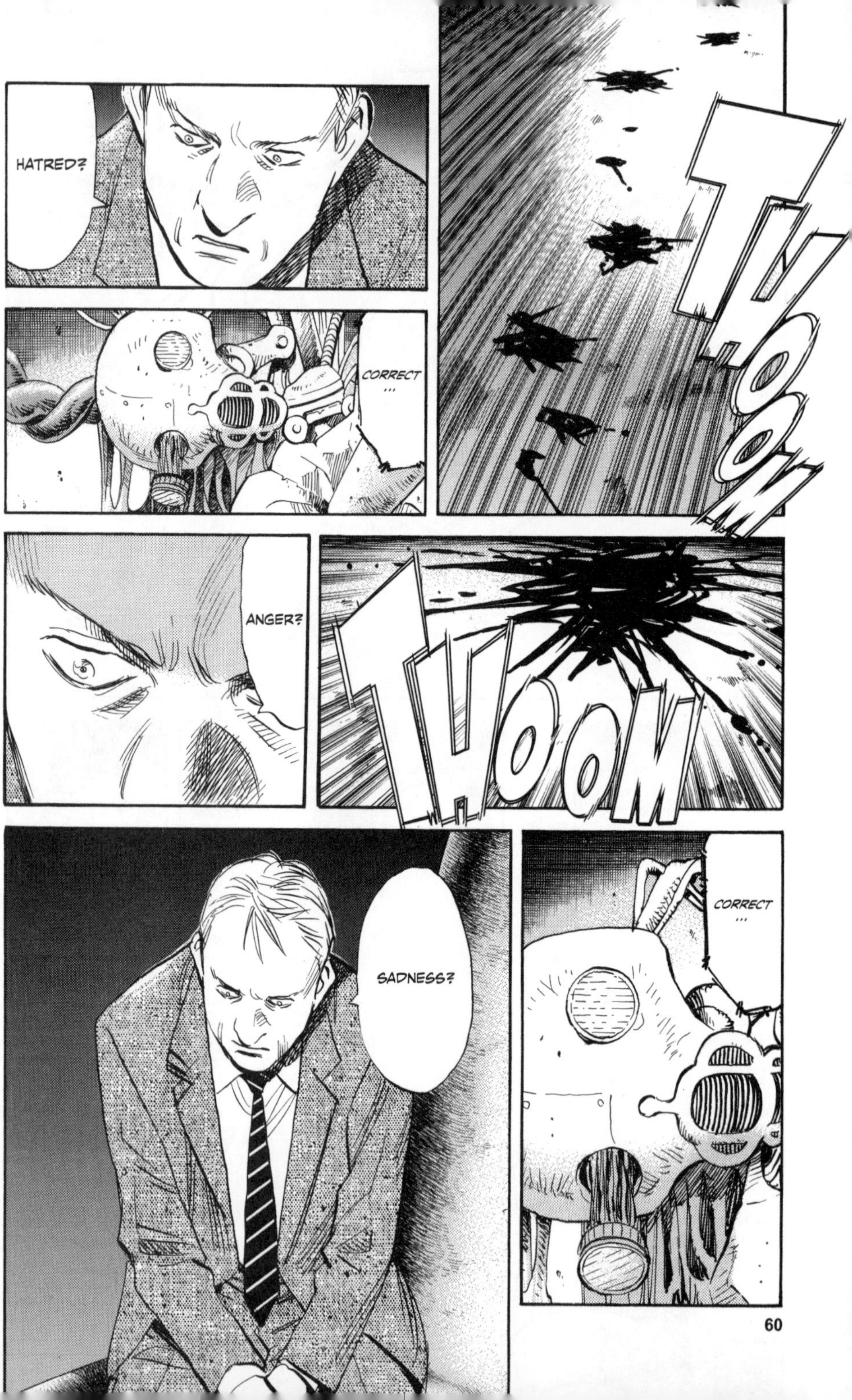
THOOOM
HATRED?
CORRECT ...
THOOM
ANGER?
CORRECT ...
SADNESS?

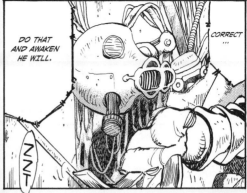

CORRECT...

DO THAT AND AWAKEN HE WILL.

ZZT

BZZT

HEH HEH HEH...

BRZZT

NOW WHAT KIND OF A ROBOT WILL HE BE ONCE HE'S CONSCIOUS?

IT COULD RAIN AT ANY MOMENT, JUDGING FROM THESE CLOUDS.

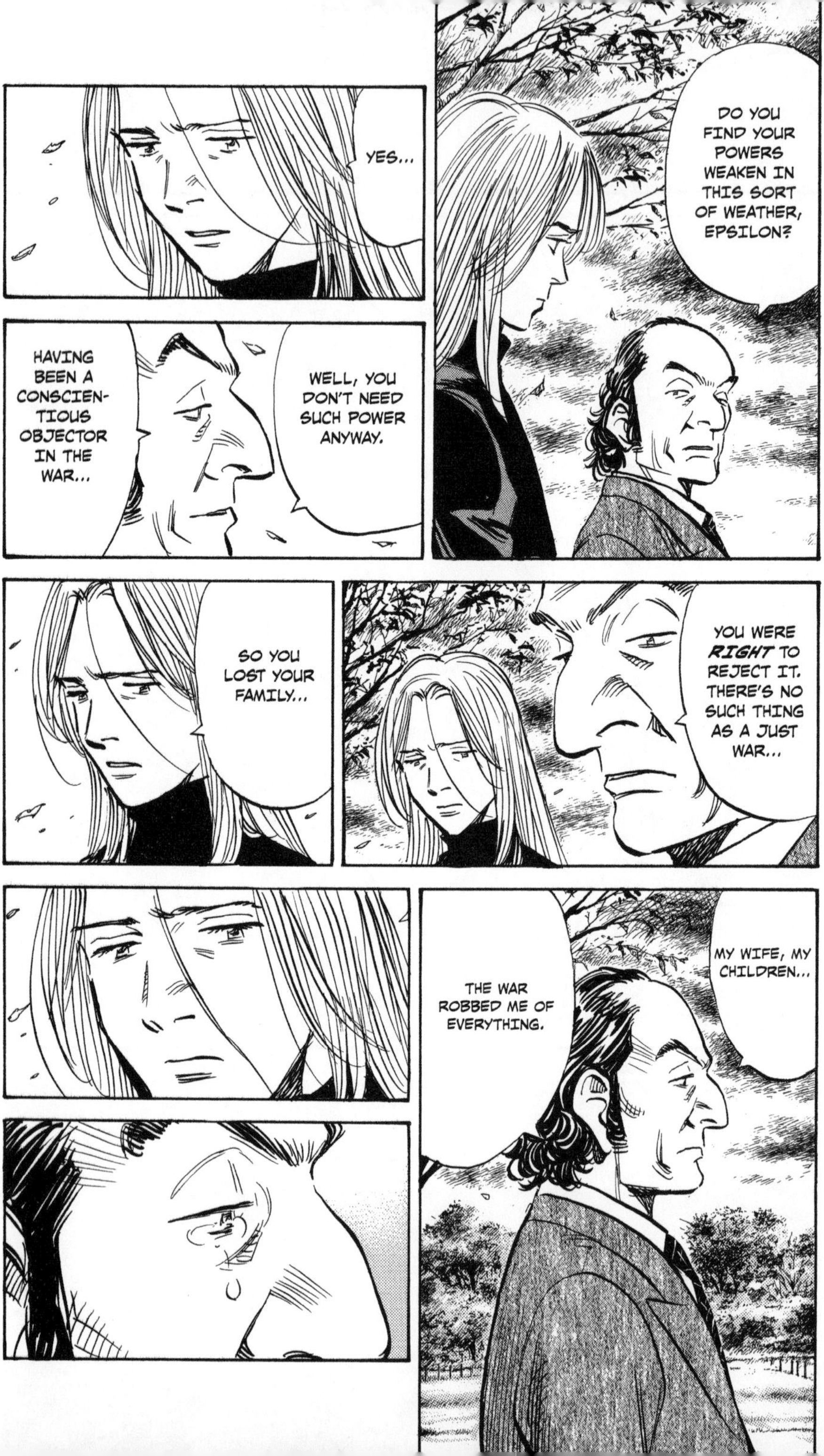
DO YOU FIND YOUR POWERS WEAKEN IN THIS SORT OF WEATHER, EPSILON?
YES...
WELL, YOU DON'T NEED SUCH POWER ANYWAY.
HAVING BEEN A CONSCIENTIOUS OBJECTOR IN THE WAR...
YOU WERE *RIGHT* TO REJECT IT. THERE'S NO SUCH THING AS A JUST WAR...
SO YOU LOST YOUR FAMILY...
MY WIFE, MY CHILDREN...
THE WAR ROBBED ME OF EVERYTHING.

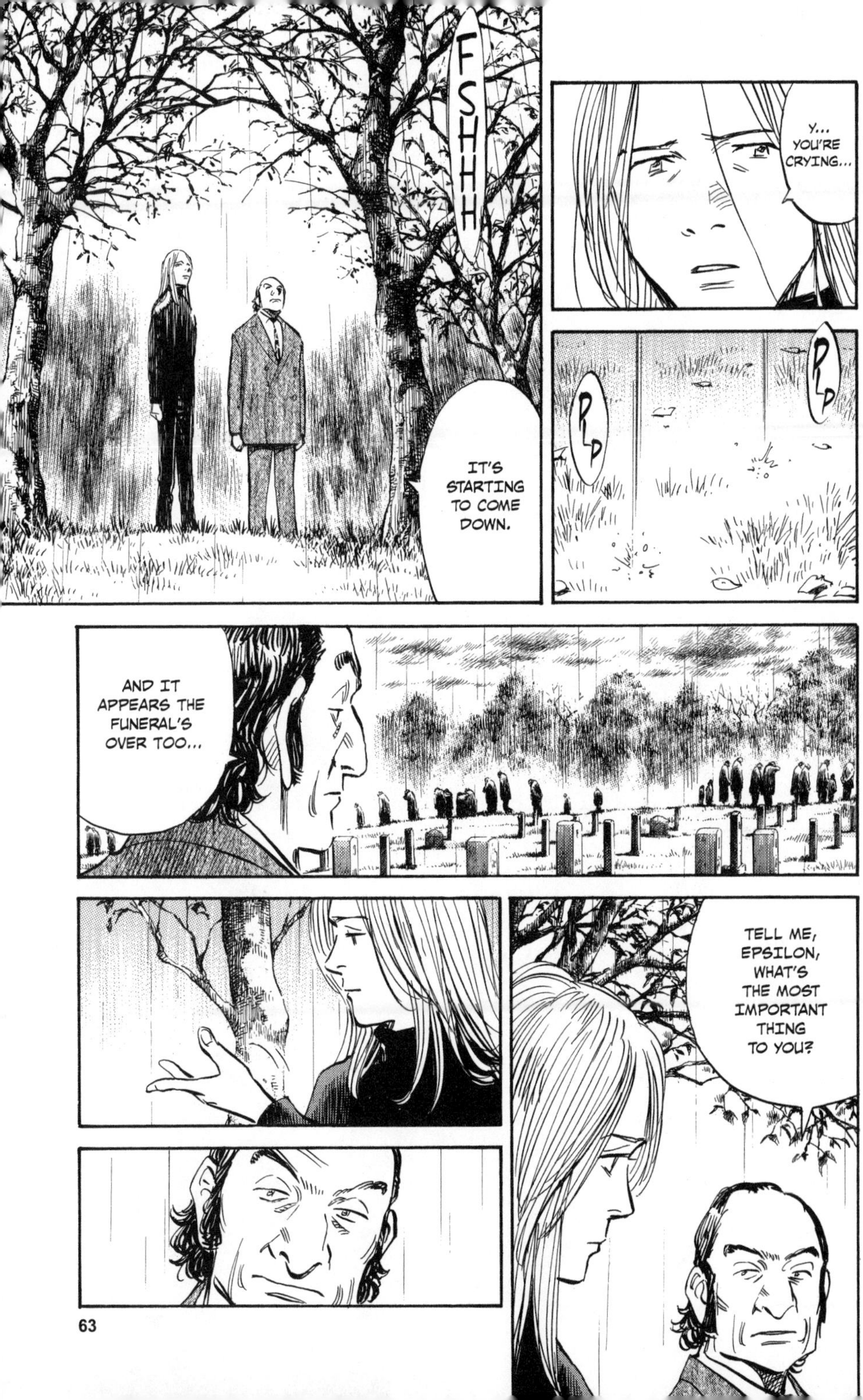
Y... YOU'RE CRYING...
PLP
PLP
FSHHH
IT'S STARTING TO COME DOWN.
AND IT APPEARS THE FUNERAL'S OVER TOO...
TELL ME, EPSILON, WHAT'S THE MOST IMPORTANT THING TO YOU?

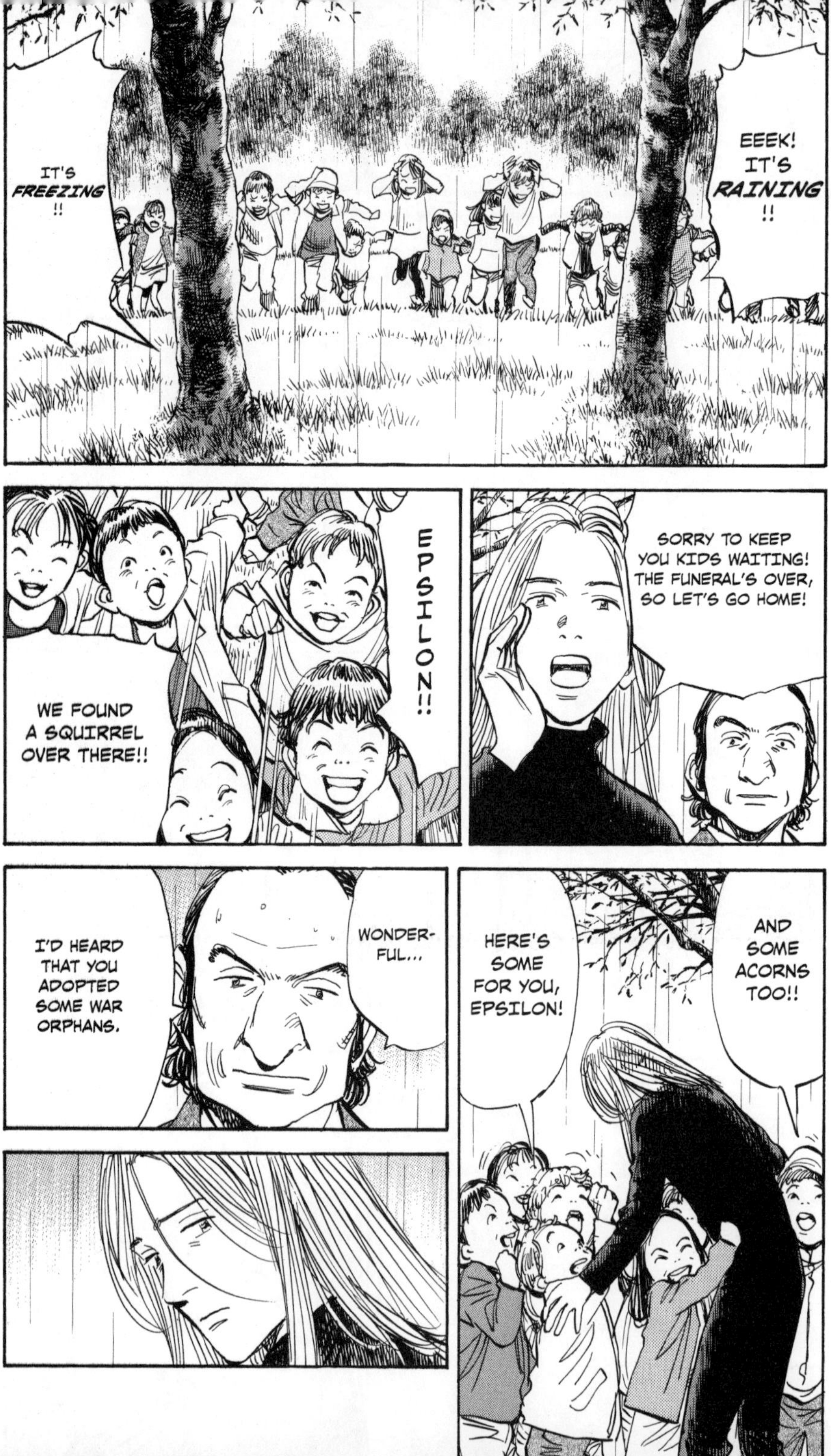
EEEK! IT'S *RAINING*!!
IT'S *FREEZING*!!
SORRY TO KEEP YOU KIDS WAITING! THE FUNERAL'S OVER, SO LET'S GO HOME!
EPSILON!!
WE FOUND A SQUIRREL OVER THERE!!
AND SOME ACORNS TOO!!
HERE'S SOME FOR YOU, EPSILON!
WONDERFUL...
I'D HEARD THAT YOU ADOPTED SOME WAR ORPHANS.

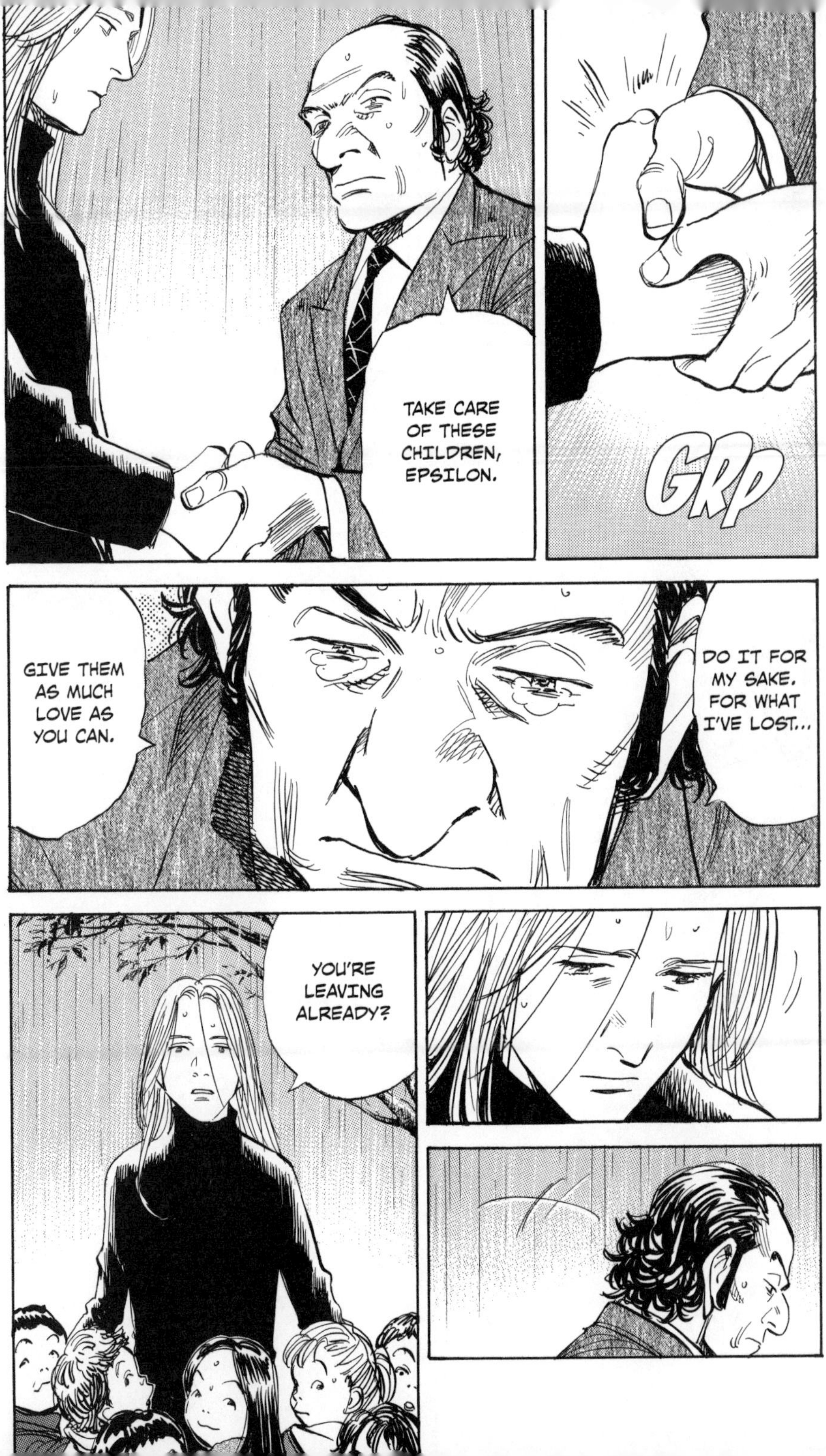
GRP
TAKE CARE OF THESE CHILDREN, EPSILON.
DO IT FOR MY SAKE. FOR WHAT I'VE LOST...
GIVE THEM AS MUCH LOVE AS YOU CAN.
YOU'RE LEAVING ALREADY?

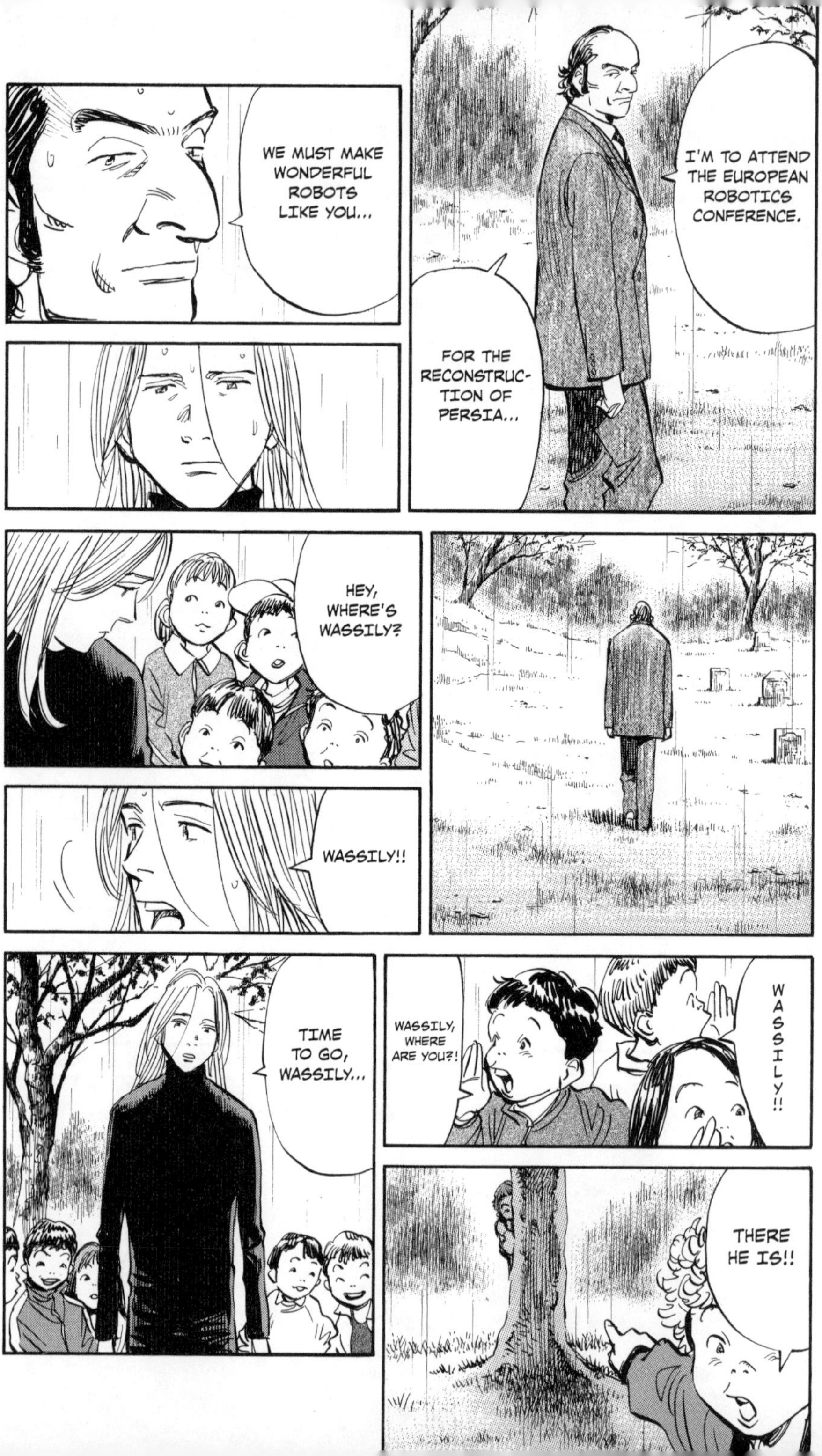
I'M TO ATTEND THE EUROPEAN ROBOTICS CONFERENCE.
FOR THE RECONSTRUCTION OF PERSIA...
WE MUST MAKE WONDERFUL ROBOTS LIKE YOU...
HEY, WHERE'S WASSILY?
WASSILY!!
WASSILY!!
WASSILY, WHERE ARE YOU?!
THERE HE IS!!
TIME TO GO, WASSILY...

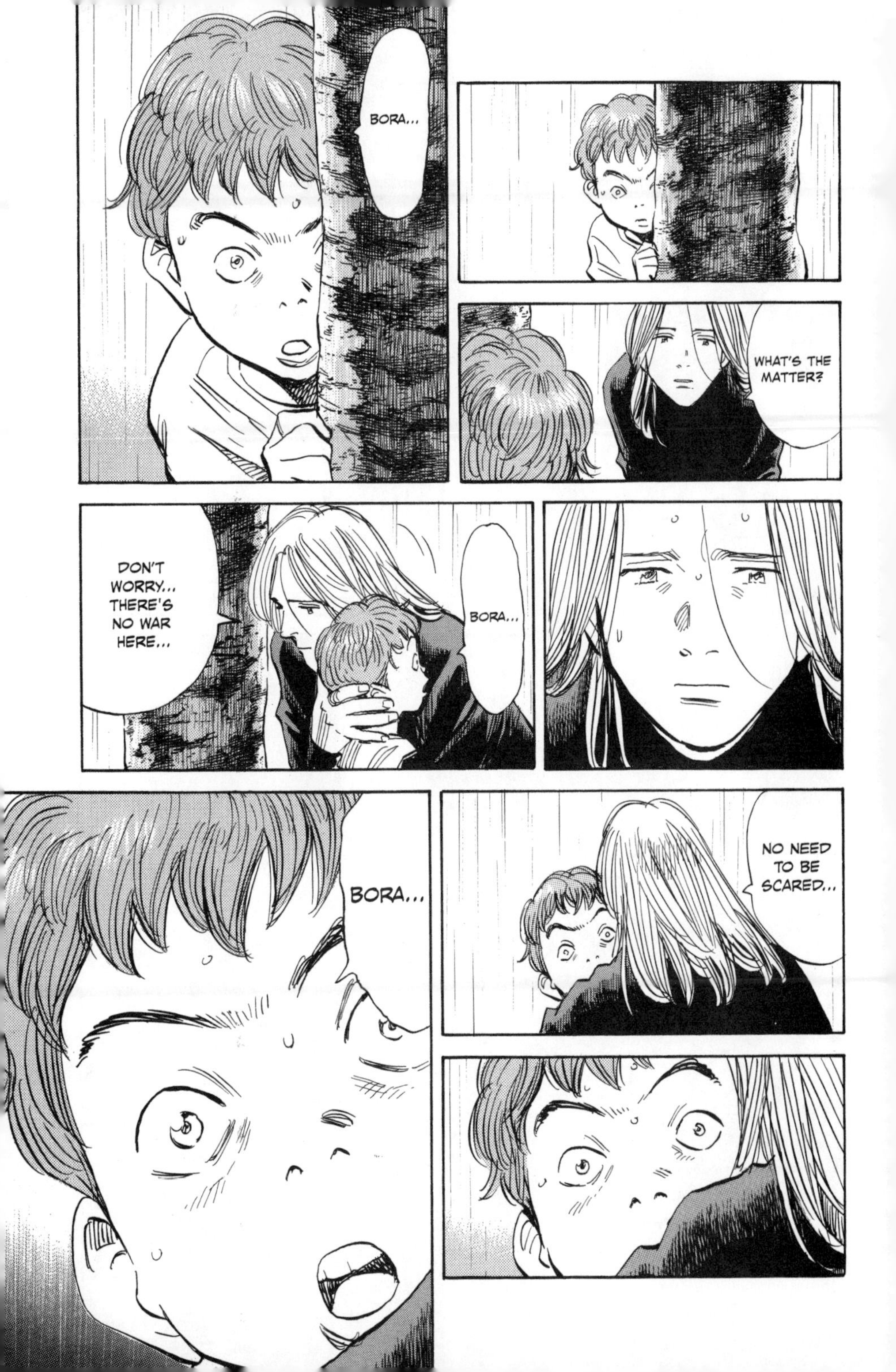
WHAT'S THE MATTER?
BORA...
BORA...
DON'T WORRY... THERE'S NO WAR HERE...
NO NEED TO BE SCARED...
BORA...

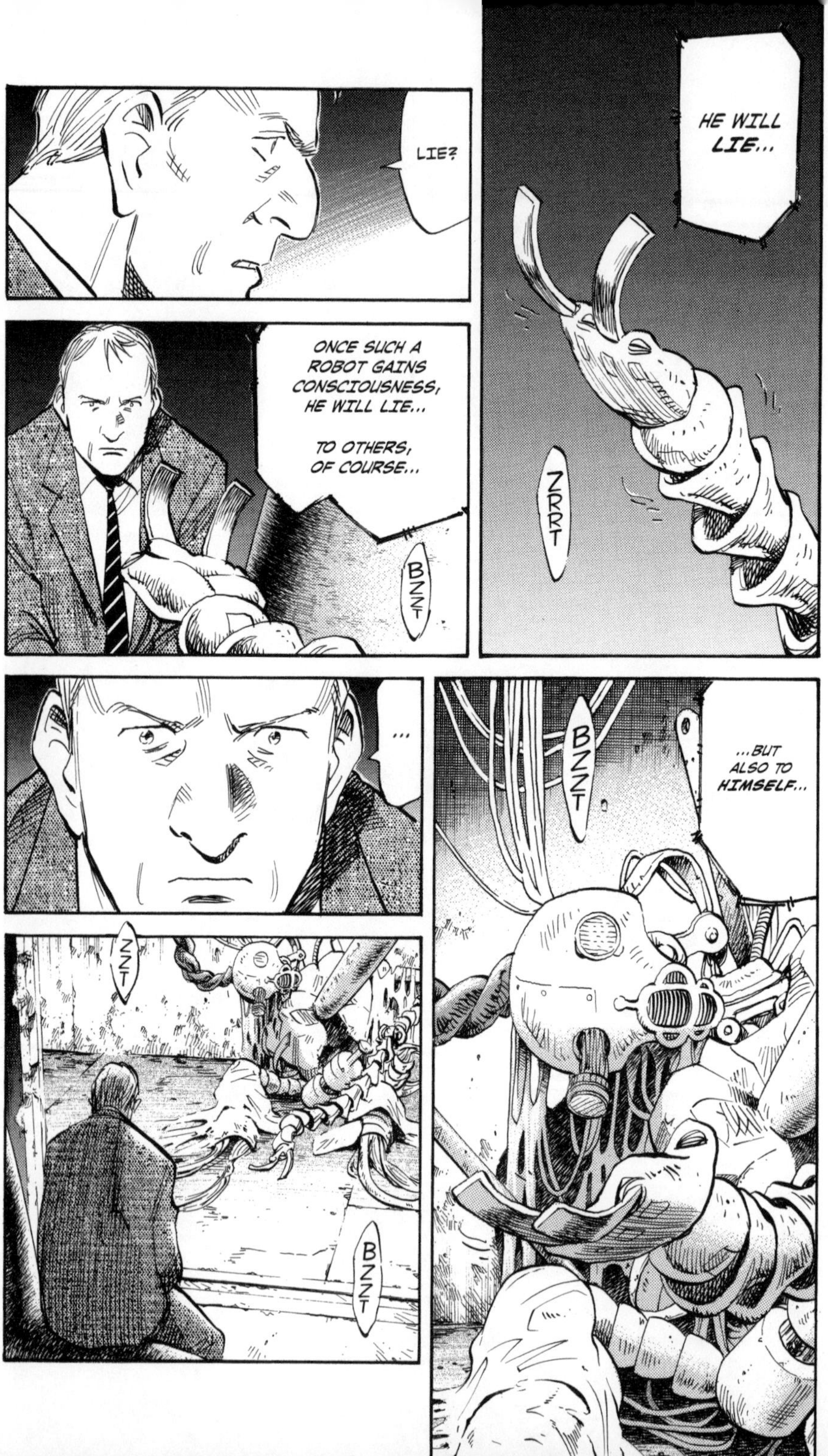
HE WILL LIE...
ZRRT
LIE?
ONCE SUCH A ROBOT GAINS CONSCIOUSNESS, HE WILL LIE...
TO OTHERS, OF COURSE...
BZZT
BZZT
...BUT ALSO TO HIMSELF...
...
ZZT
BZZT

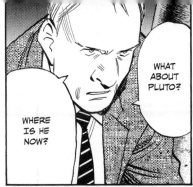

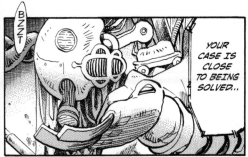

BZZT
YOUR CASE IS CLOSE TO BEING SOLVED...
WHAT ABOUT PLUTO?
WHERE IS HE NOW?
BZZT
HAVING BEEN SEVERELY INJURED IN HIS FIGHT WITH HERCULES, HE'S PROBABLY UNDERGOING MAINTENANCE...
HE'S PROBABLY BACK HOME...
VRR
BACK HOME?
WHERE SAHAD LIVES? IN PERSIA?
NO, PLUTO'S HOME...
THE TULIPS...

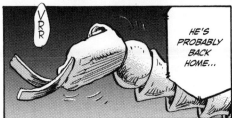

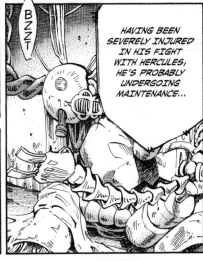

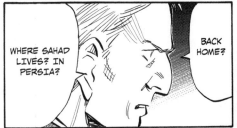

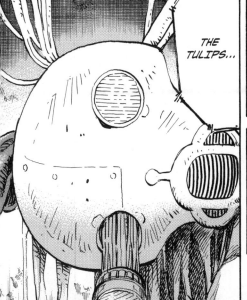

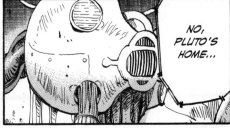

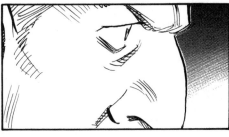

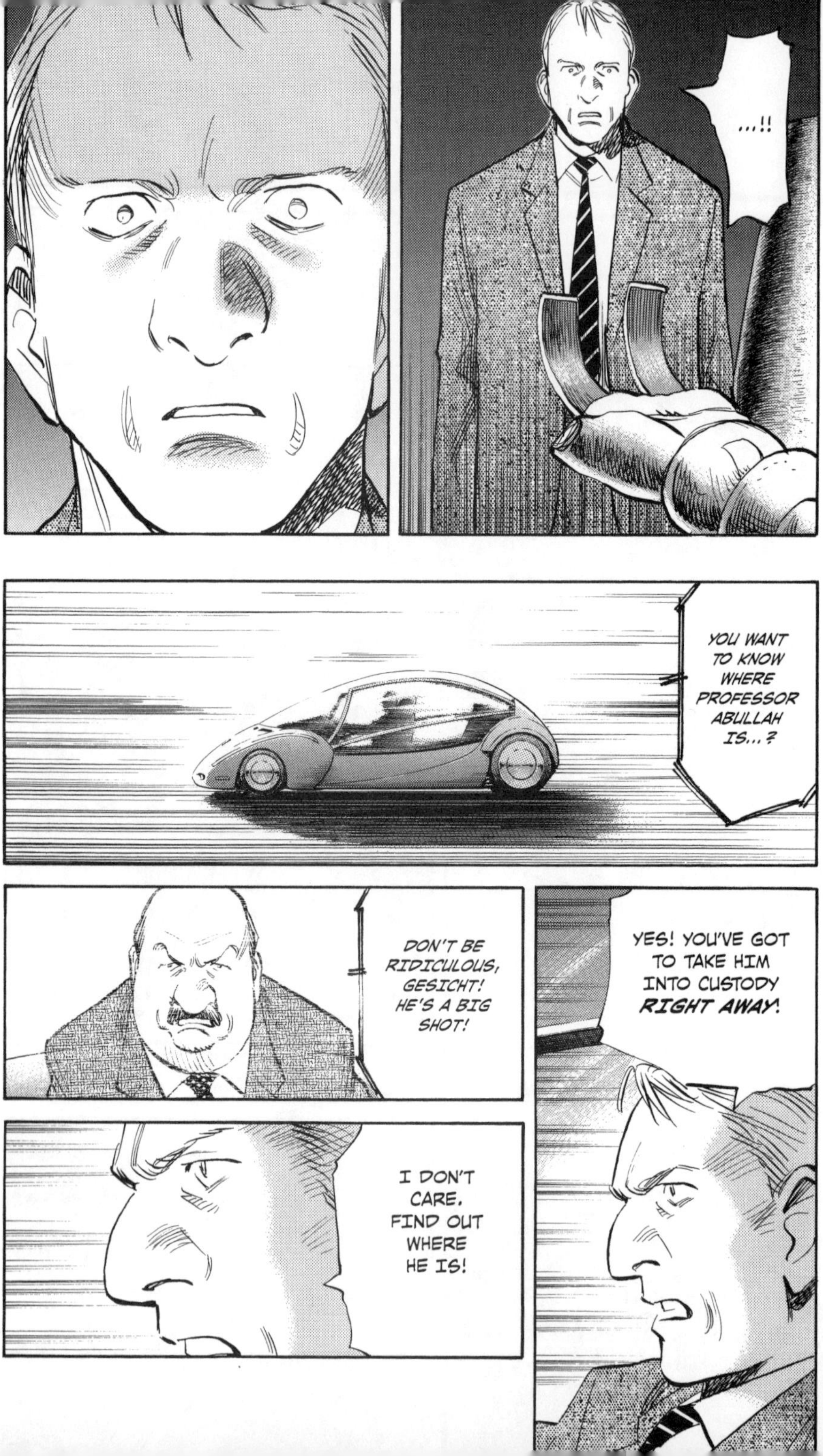

...!!
YOU WANT TO KNOW WHERE PROFESSOR ABULLAH IS...?
YES! YOU'VE GOT TO TAKE HIM INTO CUSTODY **RIGHT AWAY**!
DON'T BE RIDICULOUS, GESICHT! HE'S A BIG SHOT!
I DON'T CARE. FIND OUT WHERE HE IS!

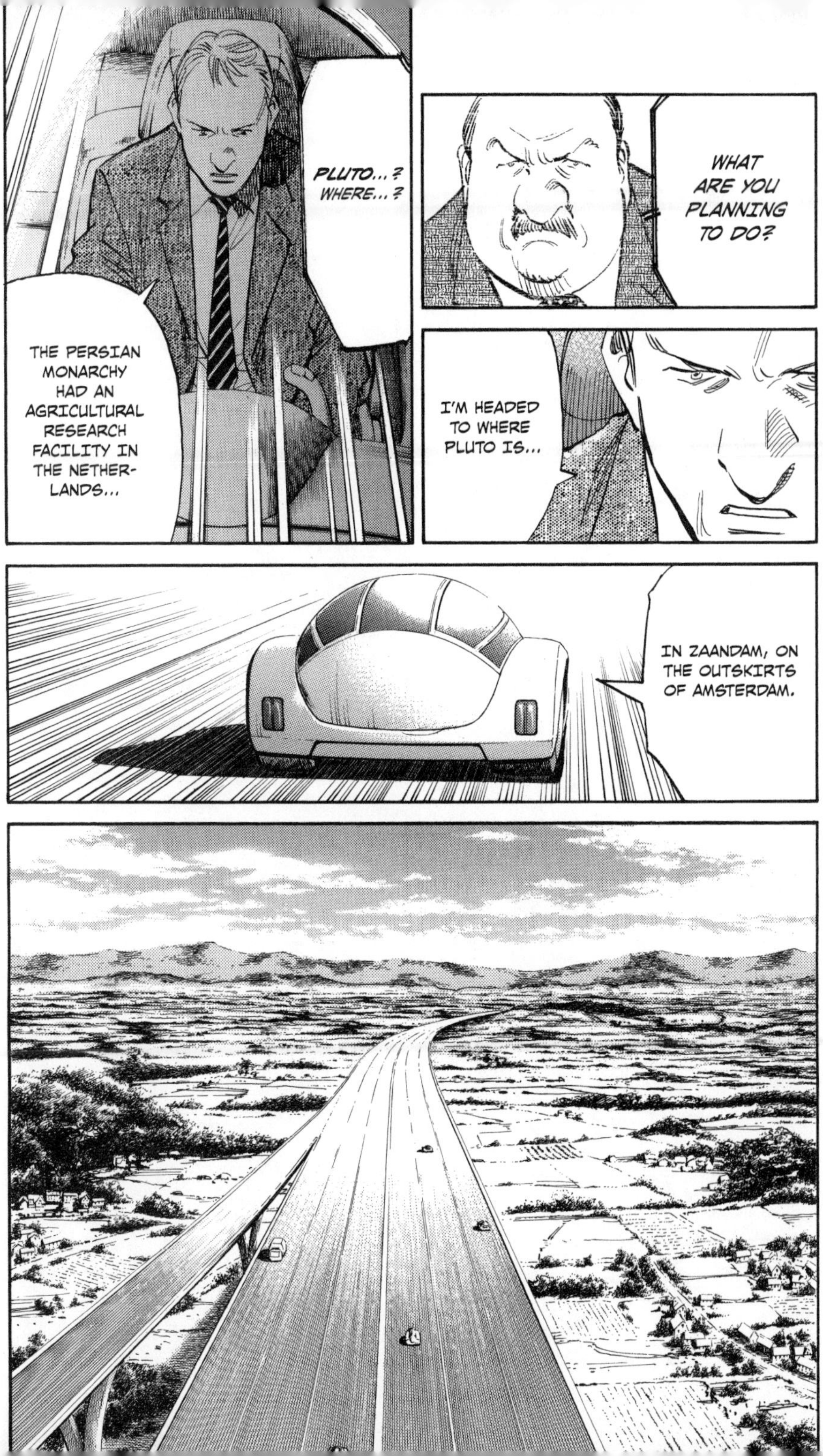
WHAT ARE YOU PLANNING TO DO?
I'M HEADED TO WHERE PLUTO IS...
PLUTO...? WHERE...?
THE PERSIAN MONARCHY HAD AN AGRICULTURAL RESEARCH FACILITY IN THE NETHER-LANDS...
IN ZAANDAM, ON THE OUTSKIRTS OF AMSTERDAM.

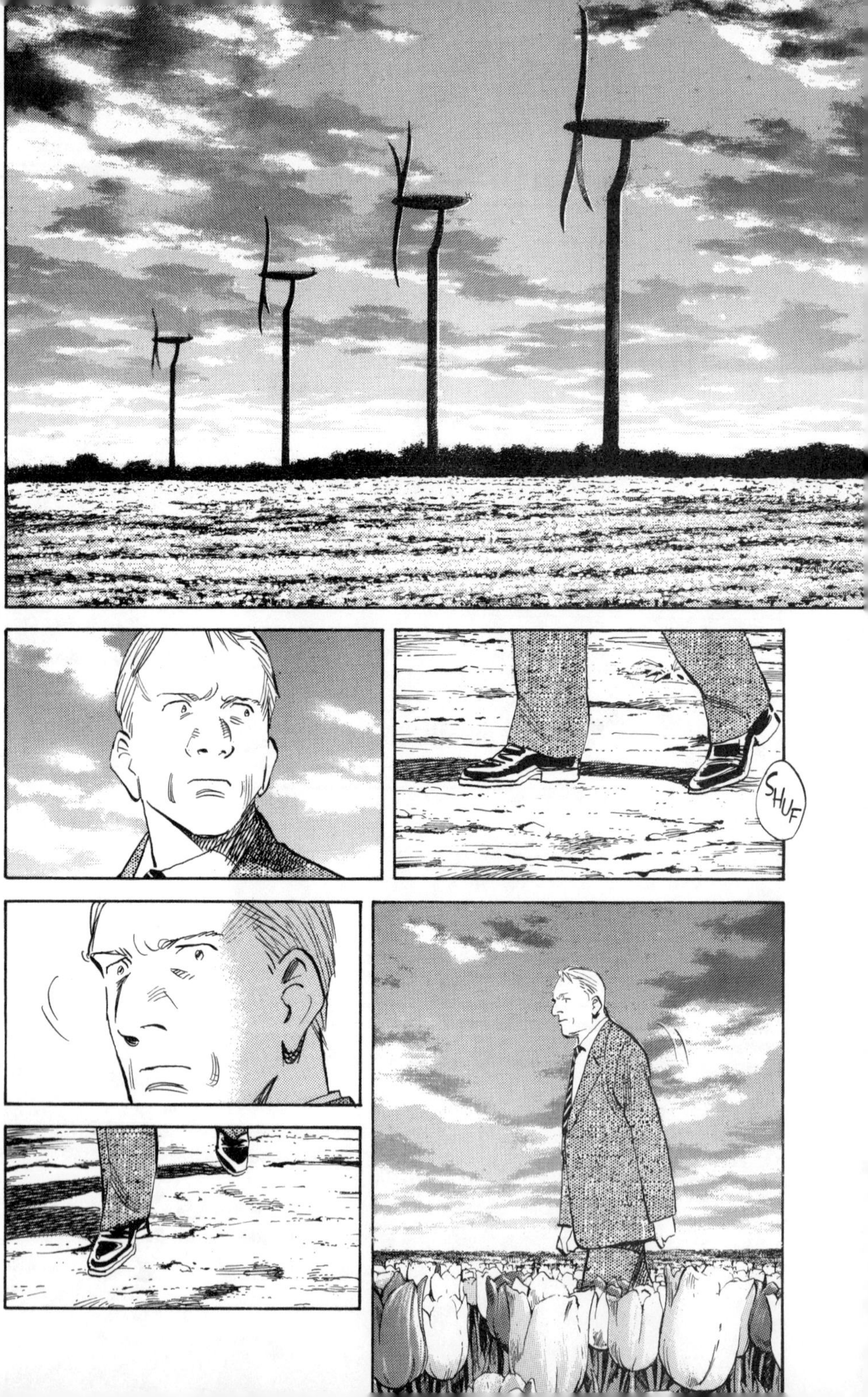
SHUF

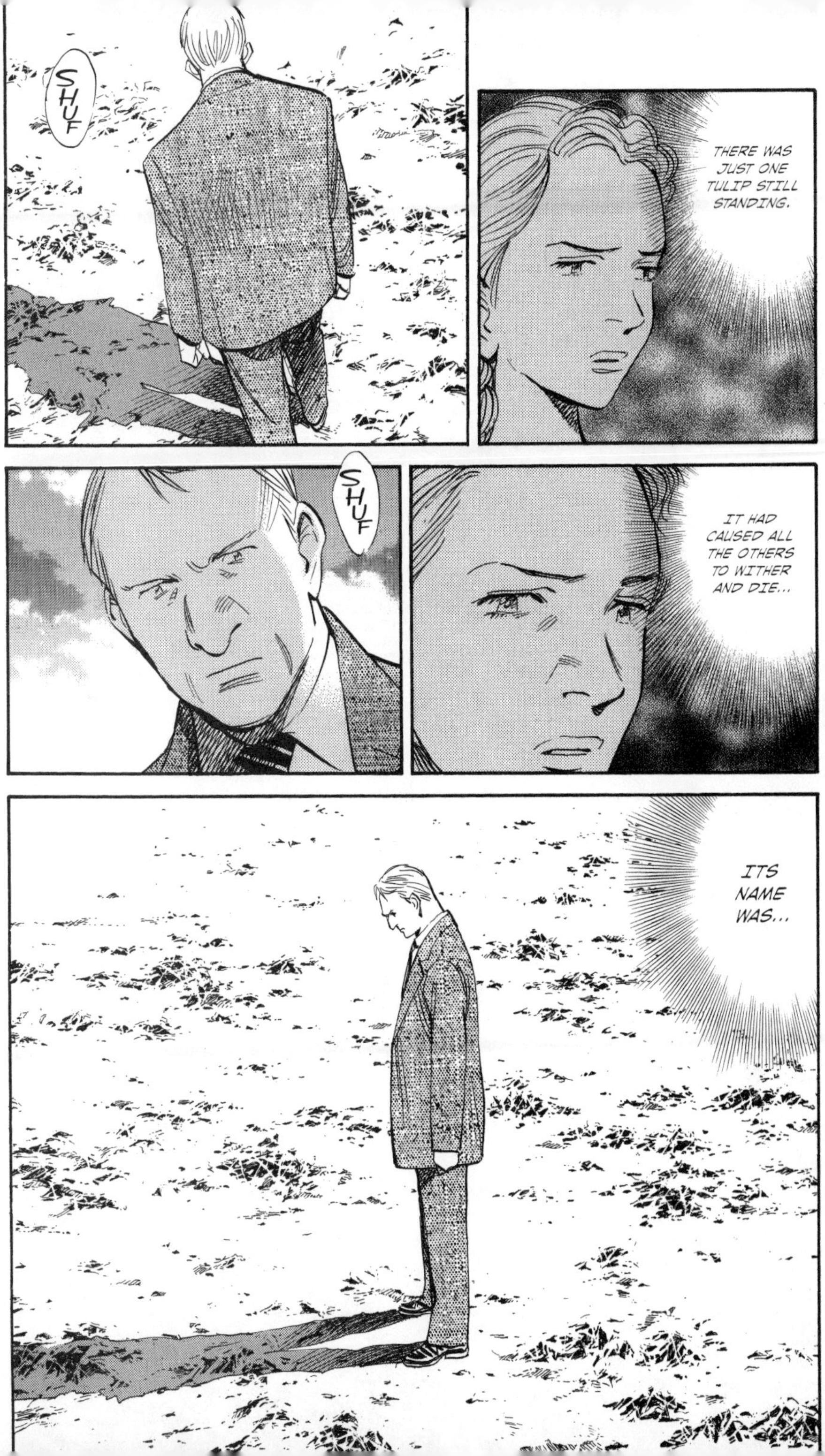
THERE WAS JUST ONE TULIP STILL STANDING.
SHUF
IT HAD CAUSED ALL THE OTHERS TO WITHER AND DIE...
SHUF
ITS NAME WAS...

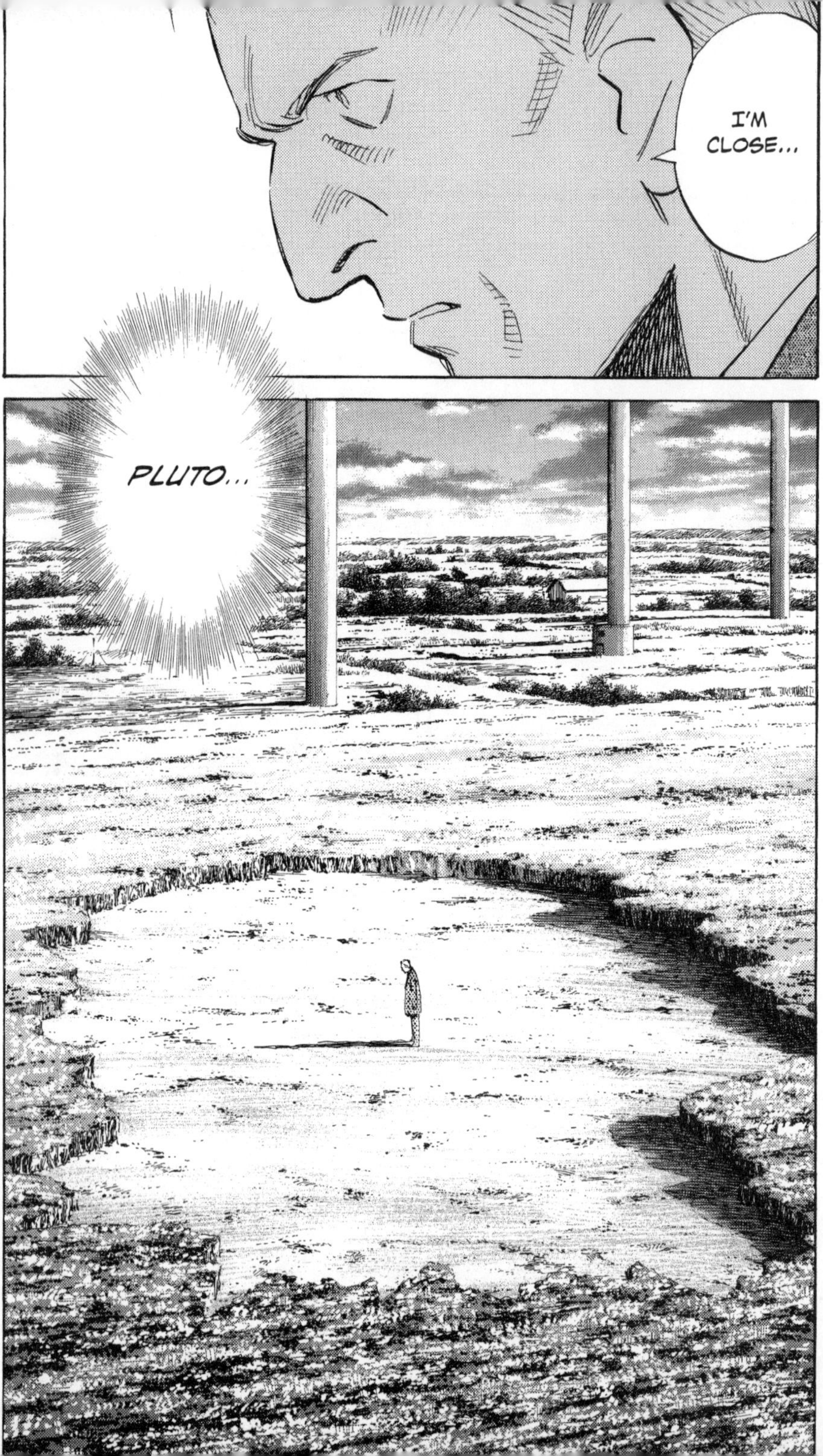
I'M CLOSE...
PLUTO...

Act 43 An Encounter with Death

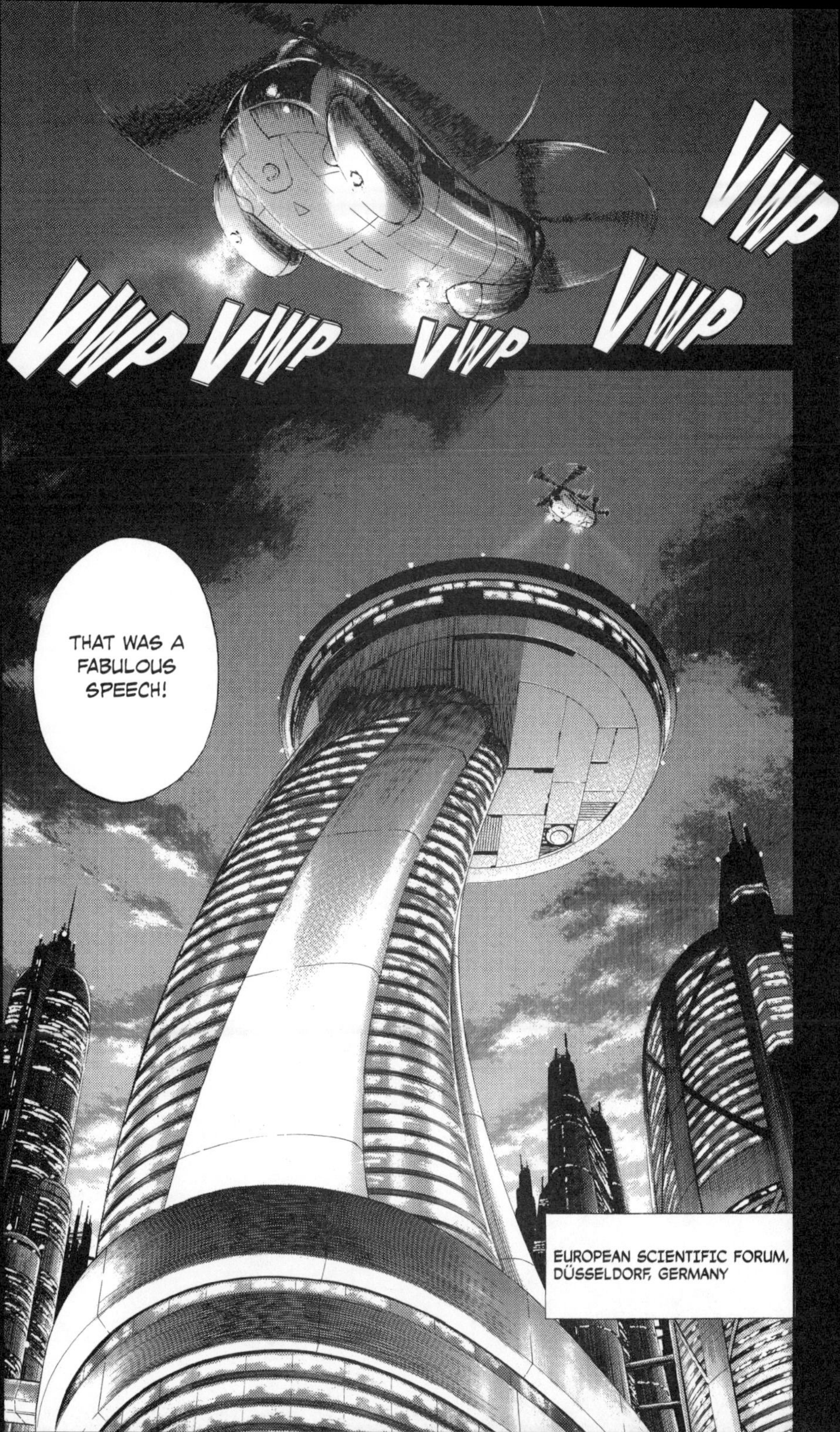
VWP
VWP
VWP
VWP
VWP
EUROPEAN SCIENTIFIC FORUM, DÜSSELDORF, GERMANY
THAT WAS A FABULOUS SPEECH!

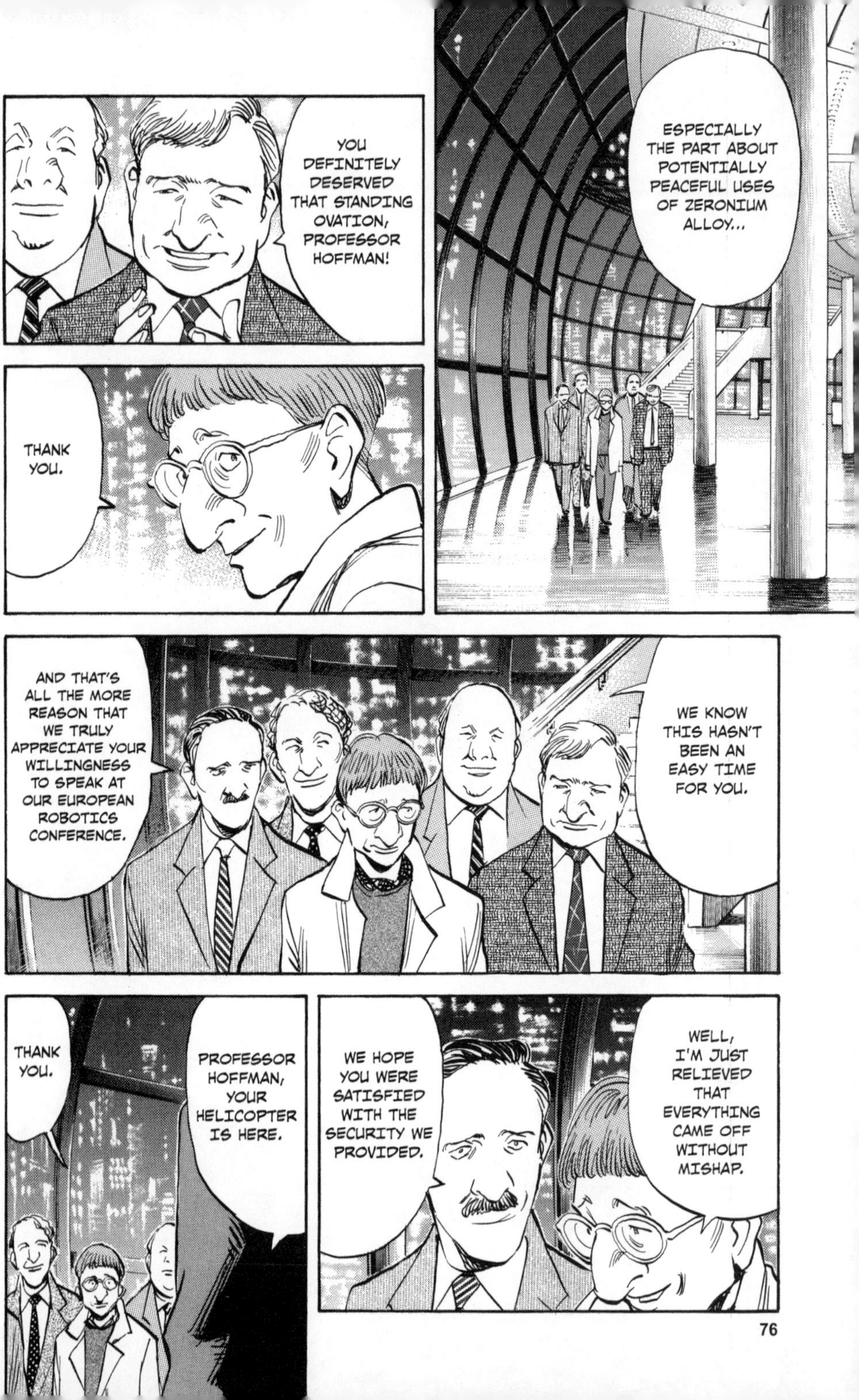

ESPECIALLY THE PART ABOUT POTENTIALLY PEACEFUL USES OF ZERONIUM ALLOY...
YOU DEFINITELY DESERVED THAT STANDING OVATION, PROFESSOR HOFFMAN!
THANK YOU.
WE KNOW THIS HASN'T BEEN AN EASY TIME FOR YOU.
AND THAT'S ALL THE MORE REASON THAT WE TRULY APPRECIATE YOUR WILLINGNESS TO SPEAK AT OUR EUROPEAN ROBOTICS CONFERENCE.
WELL, I'M JUST RELIEVED THAT EVERYTHING CAME OFF WITHOUT MISHAP.
WE HOPE YOU WERE SATISFIED WITH THE SECURITY WE PROVIDED.
PROFESSOR HOFFMAN, YOUR HELICOPTER IS HERE.
THANK YOU.

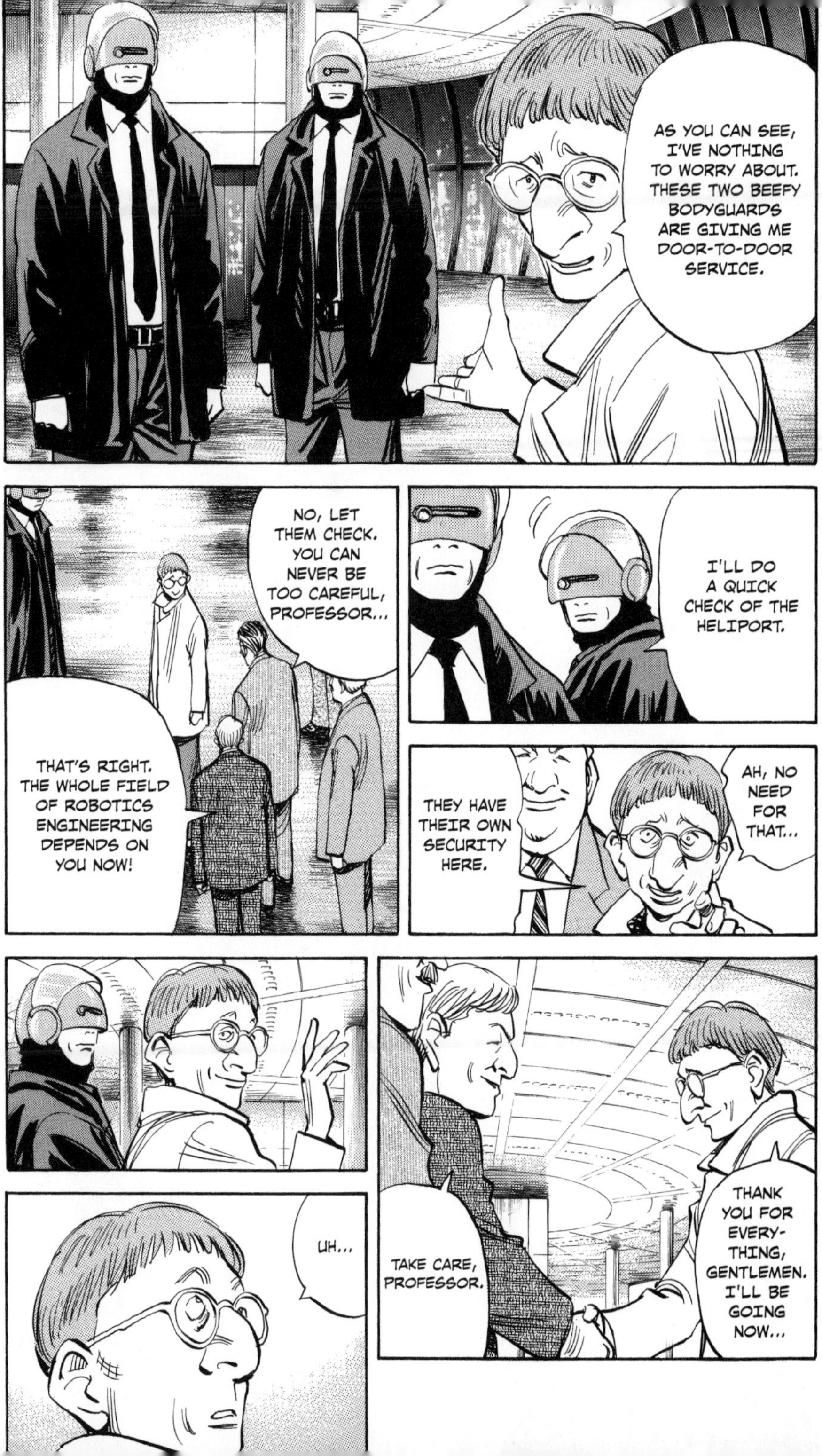
AS YOU CAN SEE, I'VE NOTHING TO WORRY ABOUT. THESE TWO BEEFY BODYGUARDS ARE GIVING ME DOOR-TO-DOOR SERVICE.
I'LL DO A QUICK CHECK OF THE HELIPORT.
AH, NO NEED FOR THAT...
THEY HAVE THEIR OWN SECURITY HERE.
NO, LET THEM CHECK. YOU CAN NEVER BE TOO CAREFUL, PROFESSOR...
THAT'S RIGHT. THE WHOLE FIELD OF ROBOTICS ENGINEERING DEPENDS ON YOU NOW!
THANK YOU FOR EVERY-THING, GENTLEMEN. I'LL BE GOING NOW...
TAKE CARE, PROFESSOR.
UH...

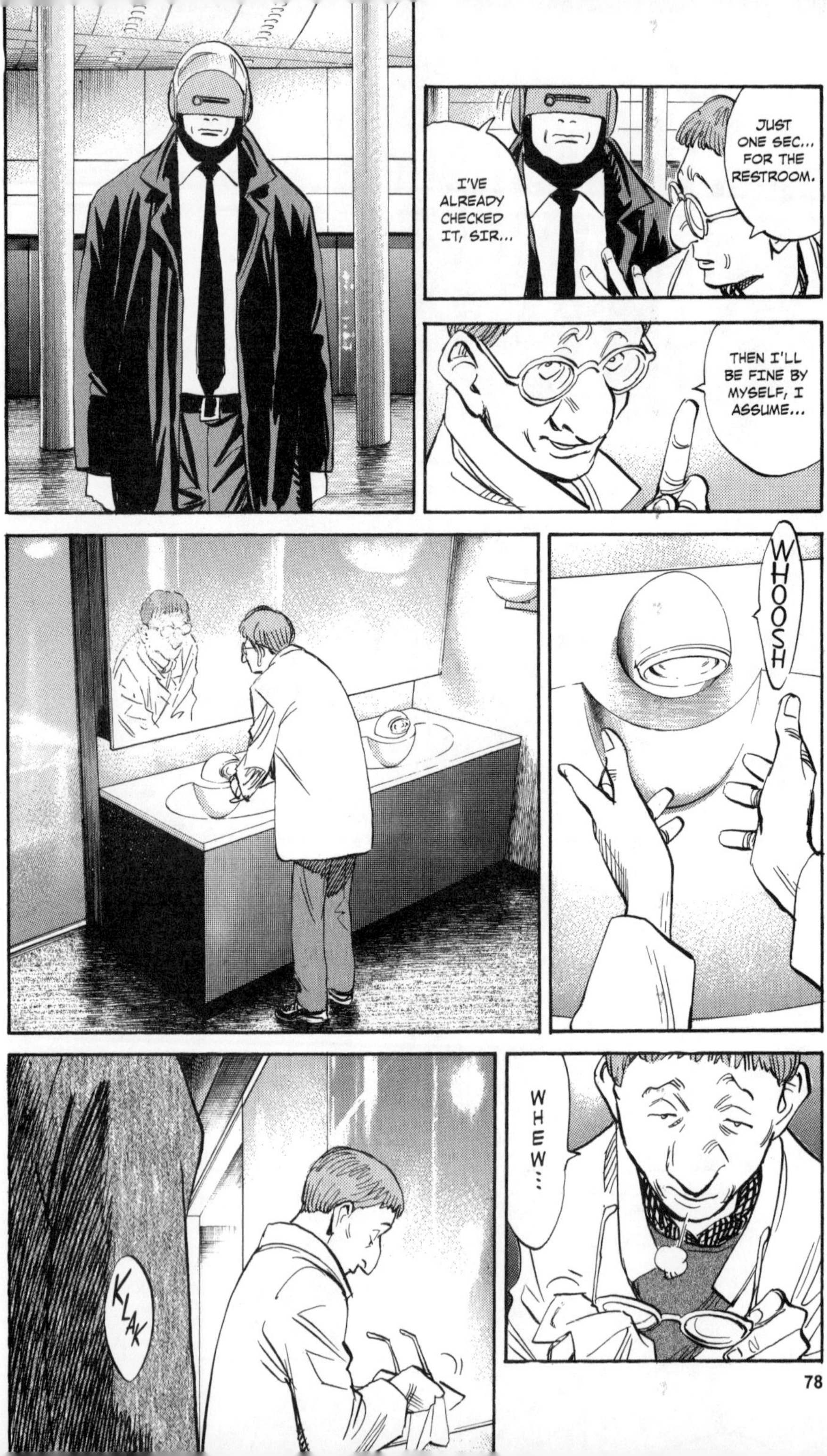
JUST ONE SEC... FOR THE RESTROOM.
I'VE ALREADY CHECKED IT, SIR...
THEN I'LL BE FINE BY MYSELF, I ASSUME...
WHOOSH
WHEW...
KLAK

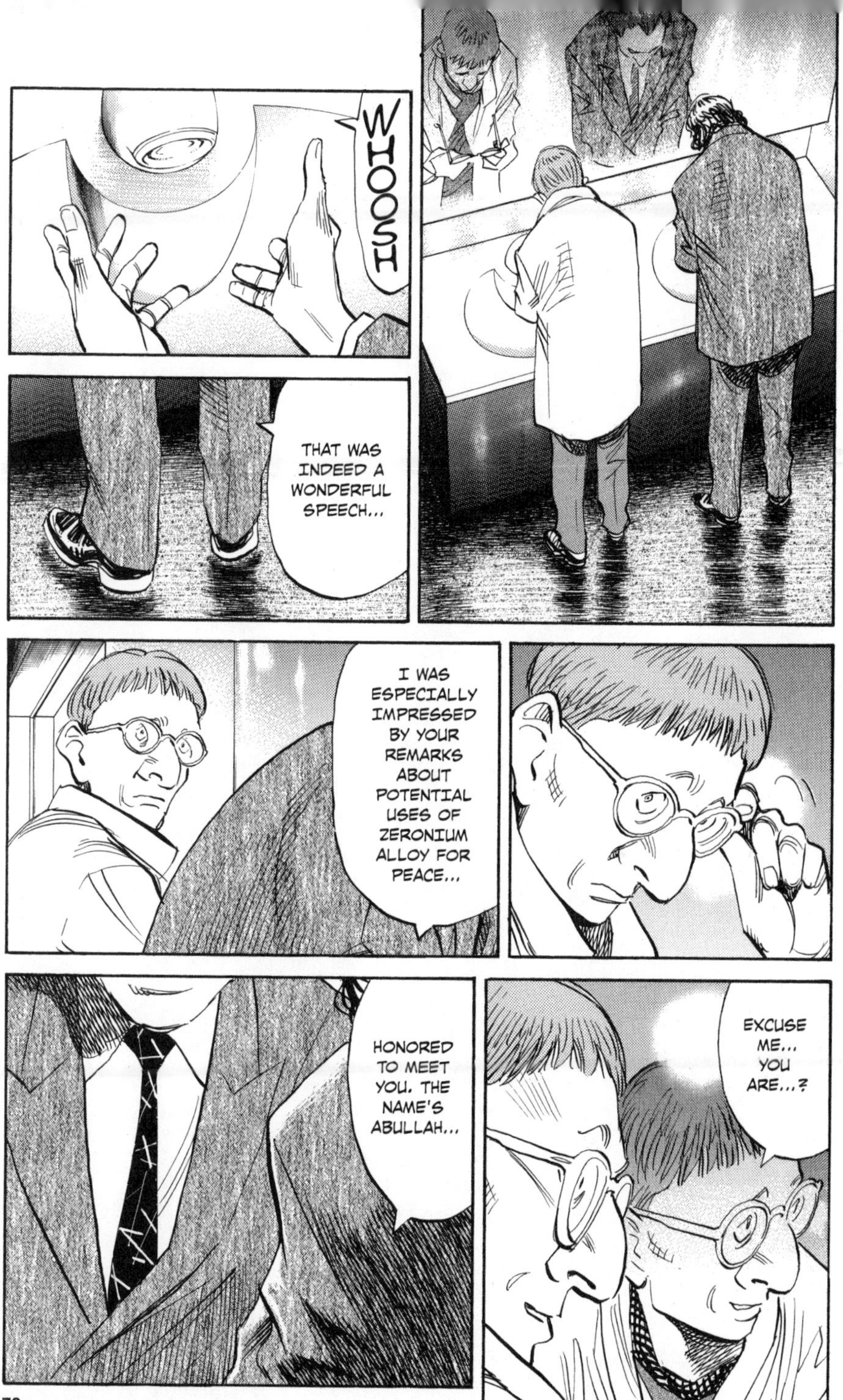
WHOOSH
THAT WAS INDEED A WONDERFUL SPEECH...
I WAS ESPECIALLY IMPRESSED BY YOUR REMARKS ABOUT POTENTIAL USES OF ZERONIUM ALLOY FOR PEACE...
EXCUSE ME... YOU ARE...?
HONORED TO MEET YOU. THE NAME'S ABULLAH...

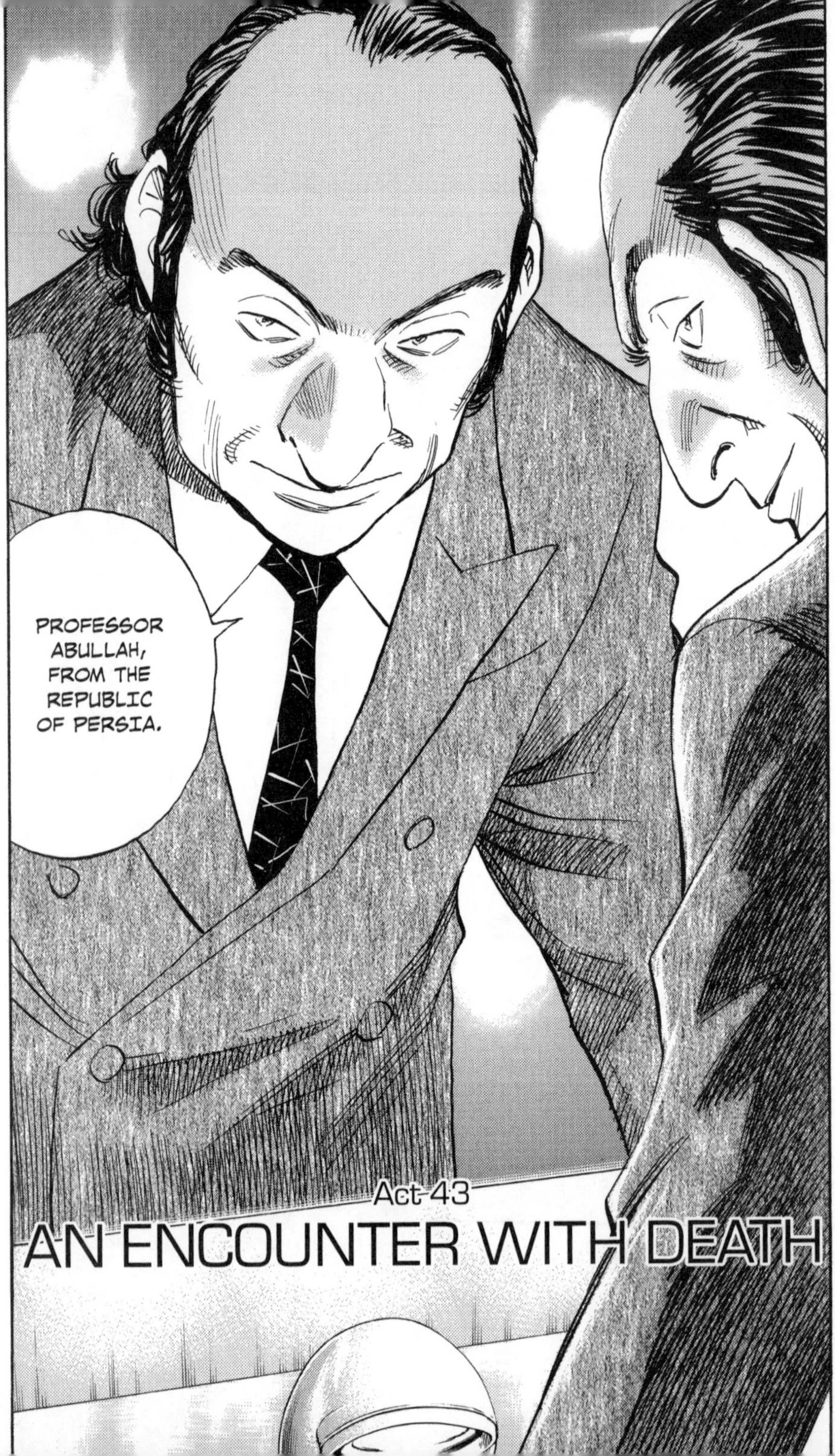
PROFESSOR ABULLAH, FROM THE REPUBLIC OF PERSIA.
Act 43
AN ENCOUNTER WITH DEATH

CREAK

ZAANDAM,
THE NETHERLANDS

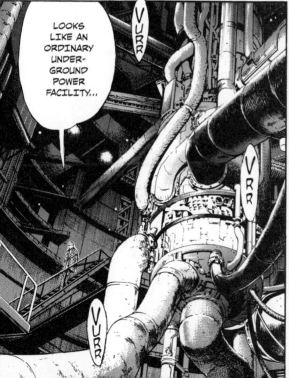

LOOKS LIKE AN ORDINARY UNDER-GROUND POWER FACILITY...

VURR

VRR

VURR

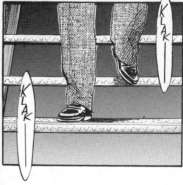

KLAK

KLAK

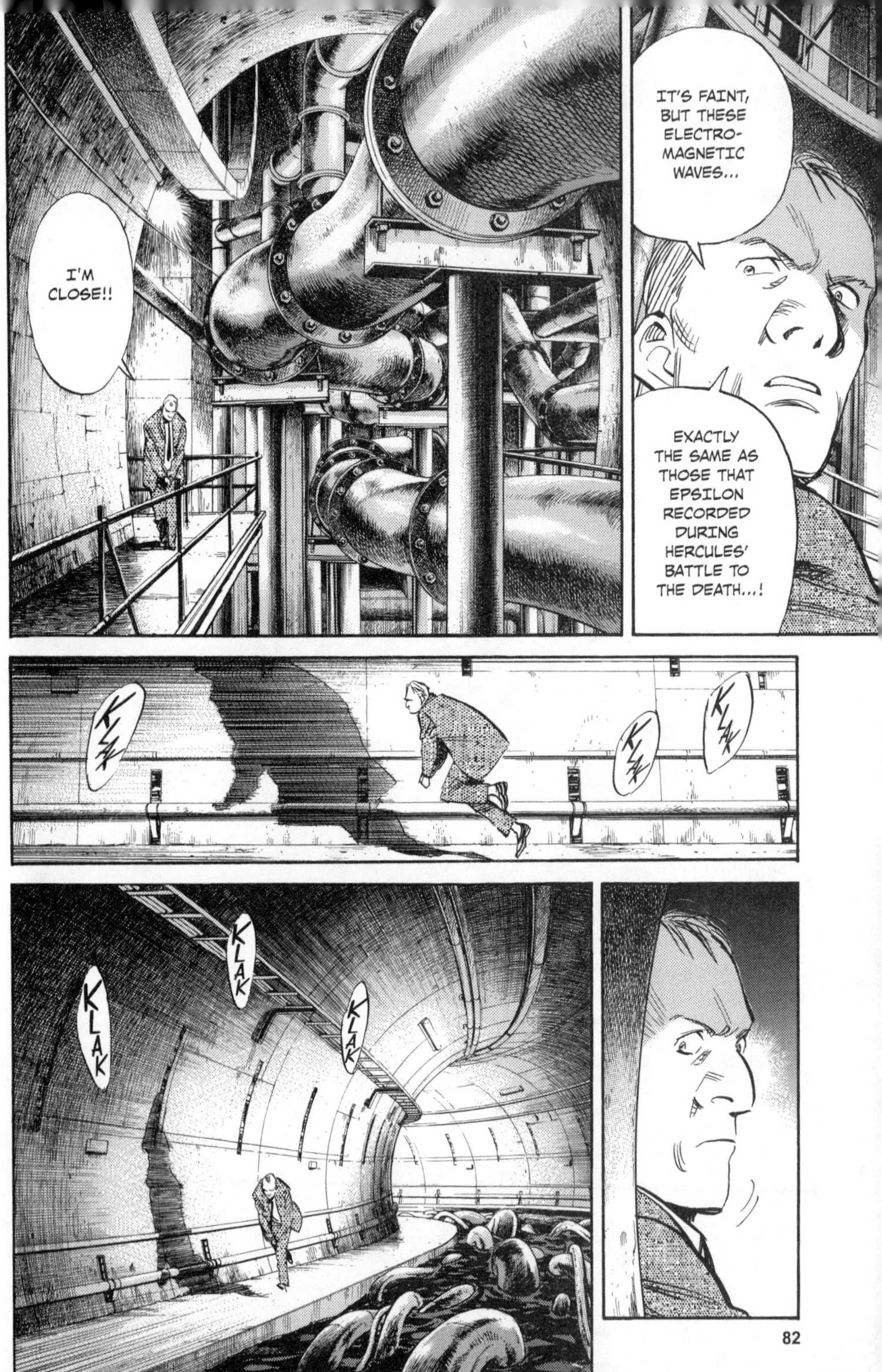
IT'S FAINT, BUT THESE ELECTRO-MAGNETIC WAVES...
EXACTLY THE SAME AS THOSE THAT EPSILON RECORDED DURING HERCULES' BATTLE TO THE DEATH...!
I'M CLOSE!!
KLAK
KLAK
KLAK
KLAK
KLAK
KLAK

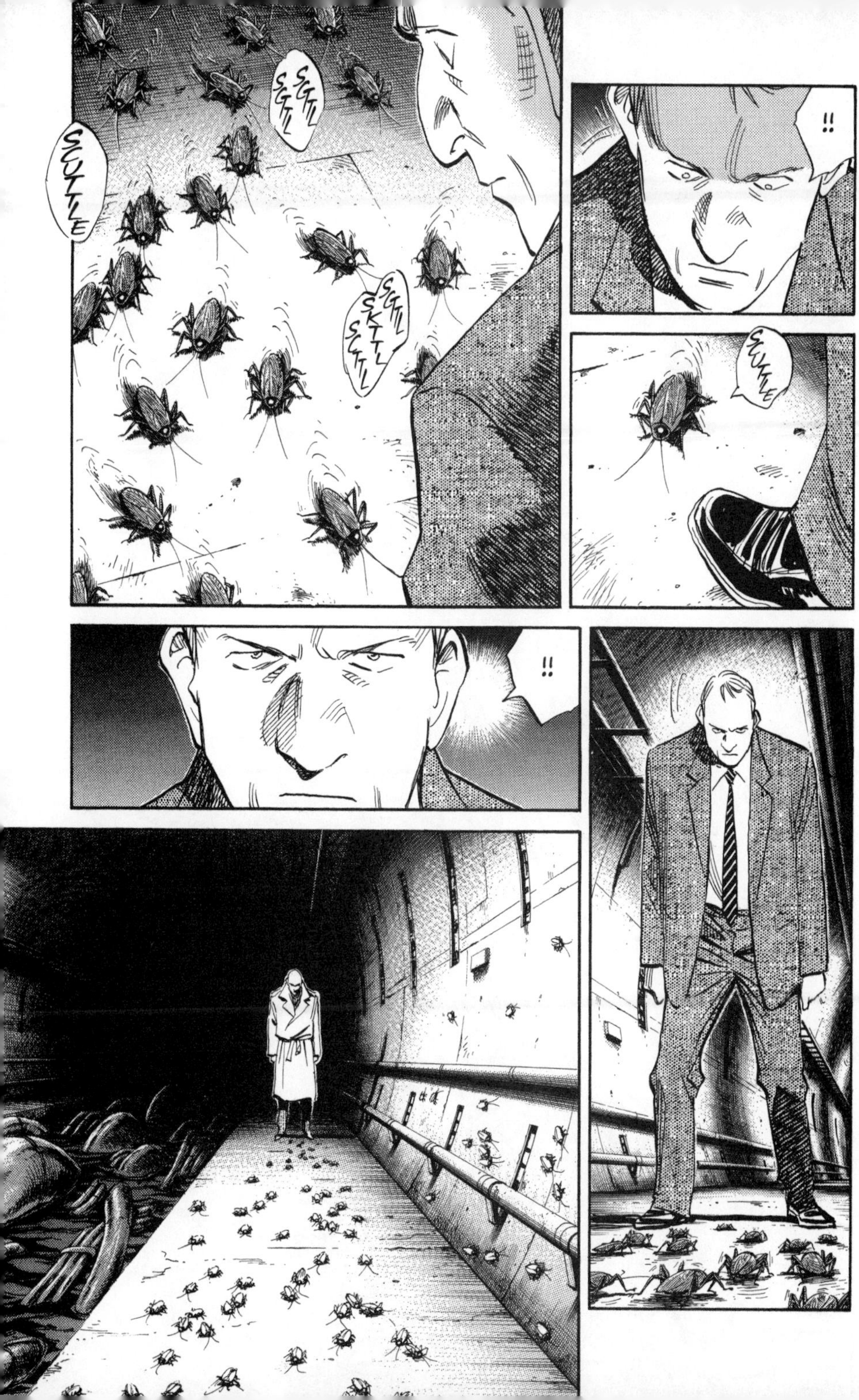
!!
SCUTTLE
SKTTL SKTTL
SCUTTLE
SKTTL SKTTL SKTTL
!!

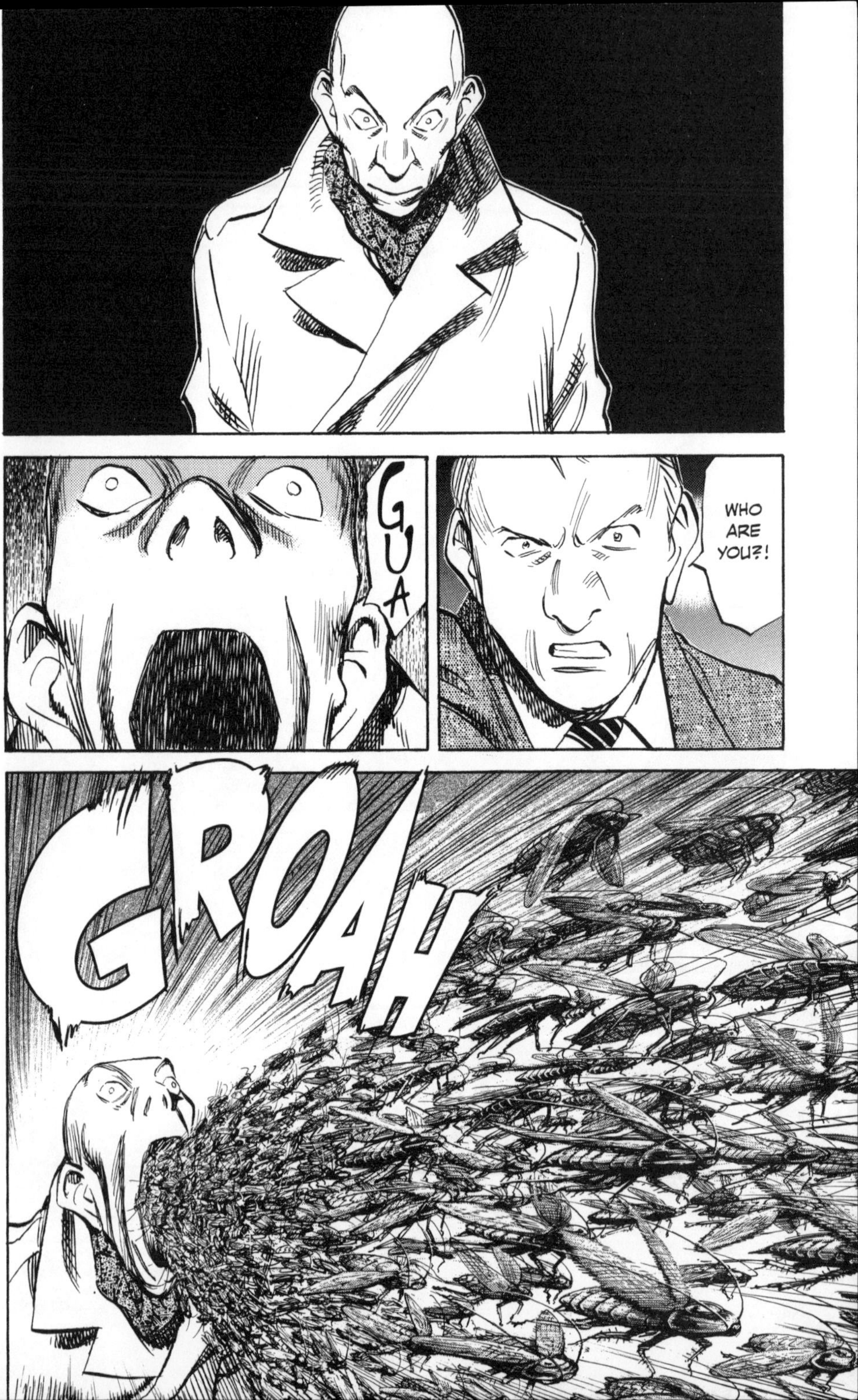
WHO ARE YOU?!
GUA
GROAH

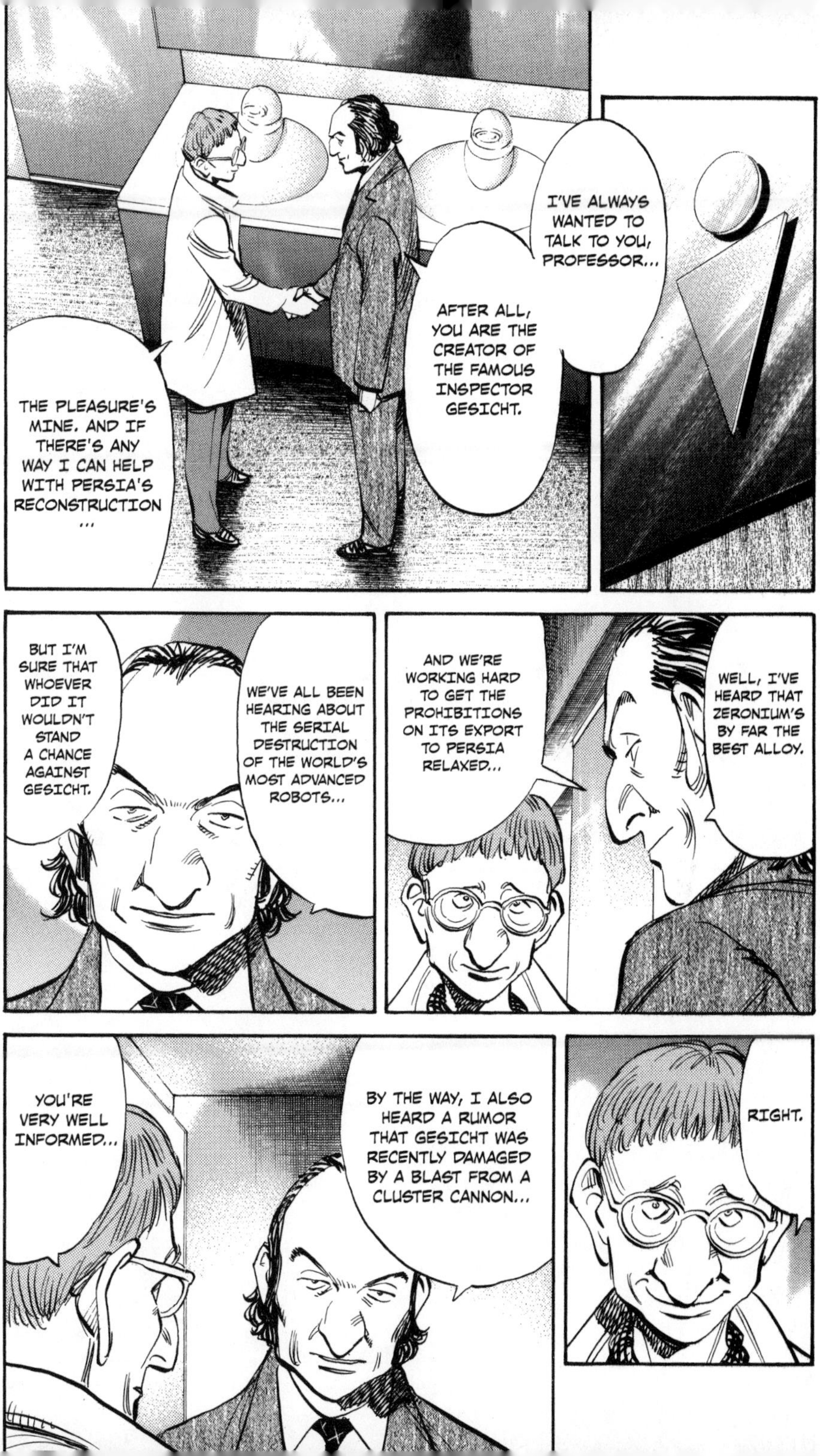
I'VE ALWAYS WANTED TO TALK TO YOU, PROFESSOR...
AFTER ALL, YOU ARE THE CREATOR OF THE FAMOUS INSPECTOR GESICHT.
THE PLEASURE'S MINE. AND IF THERE'S ANY WAY I CAN HELP WITH PERSIA'S RECONSTRUCTION ...
WELL, I'VE HEARD THAT ZERONIUM'S BY FAR THE BEST ALLOY.
AND WE'RE WORKING HARD TO GET THE PROHIBITIONS ON ITS EXPORT TO PERSIA RELAXED...
WE'VE ALL BEEN HEARING ABOUT THE SERIAL DESTRUCTION OF THE WORLD'S MOST ADVANCED ROBOTS...
BUT I'M SURE THAT WHOEVER DID IT WOULDN'T STAND A CHANCE AGAINST GESICHT.
RIGHT.
BY THE WAY, I ALSO HEARD A RUMOR THAT GESICHT WAS RECENTLY DAMAGED BY A BLAST FROM A CLUSTER CANNON...
YOU'RE VERY WELL INFORMED...

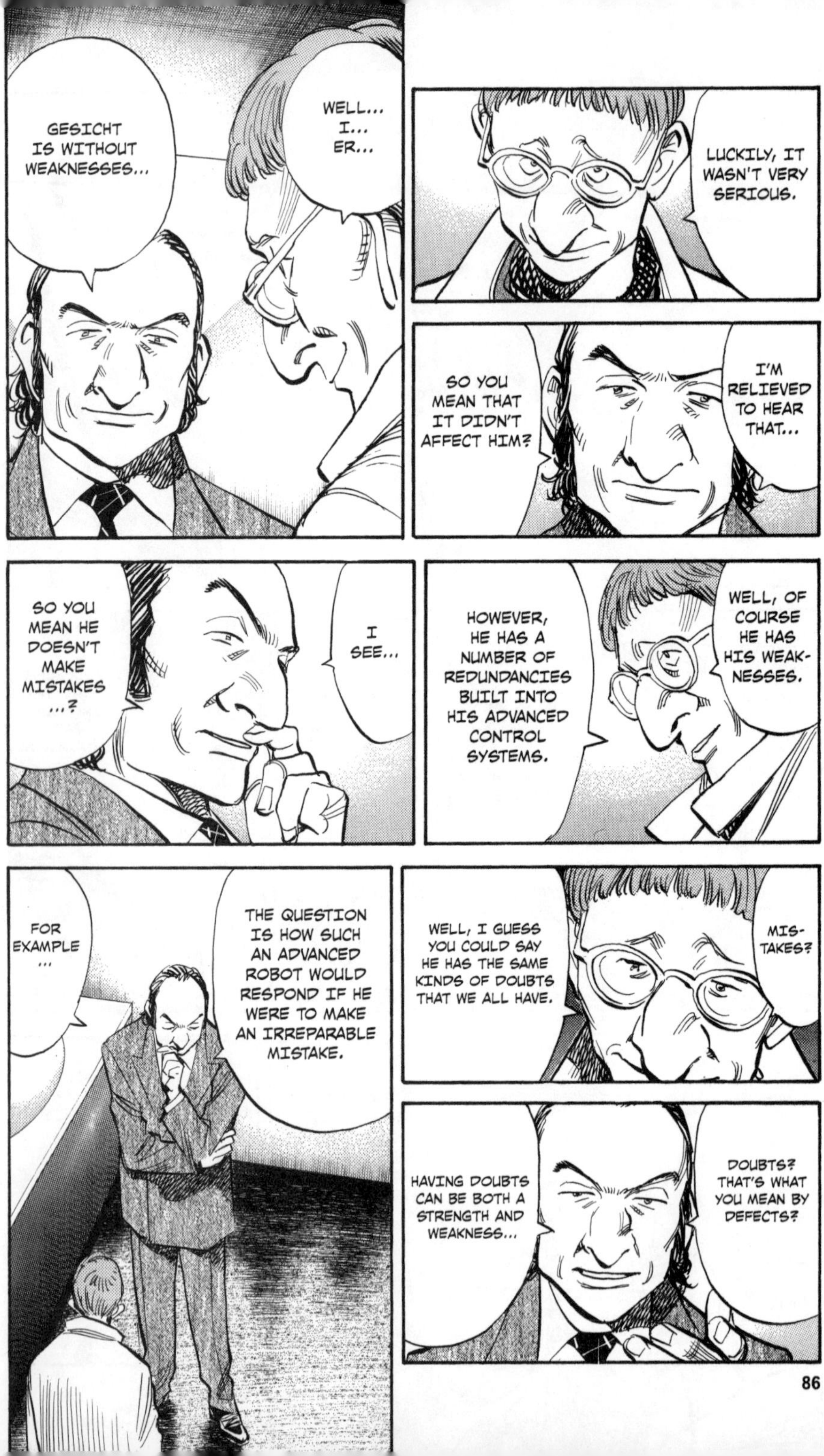
LUCKILY, IT WASN'T VERY SERIOUS.
I'M RELIEVED TO HEAR THAT...
SO YOU MEAN THAT IT DIDN'T AFFECT HIM?
WELL... I... ER...
GESICHT IS WITHOUT WEAKNESSES...
WELL, OF COURSE HE HAS HIS WEAK-NESSES.
HOWEVER, HE HAS A NUMBER OF REDUNDANCIES BUILT INTO HIS ADVANCED CONTROL SYSTEMS.
I SEE...
SO YOU MEAN HE DOESN'T MAKE MISTAKES ...?
MIS-TAKES?
WELL, I GUESS YOU COULD SAY HE HAS THE SAME KINDS OF DOUBTS THAT WE ALL HAVE.
DOUBTS? THAT'S WHAT YOU MEAN BY DEFECTS?
HAVING DOUBTS CAN BE BOTH A STRENGTH AND WEAKNESS...
THE QUESTION IS HOW SUCH AN ADVANCED ROBOT WOULD RESPOND IF HE WERE TO MAKE AN IRREPARABLE MISTAKE.
FOR EXAMPLE ...

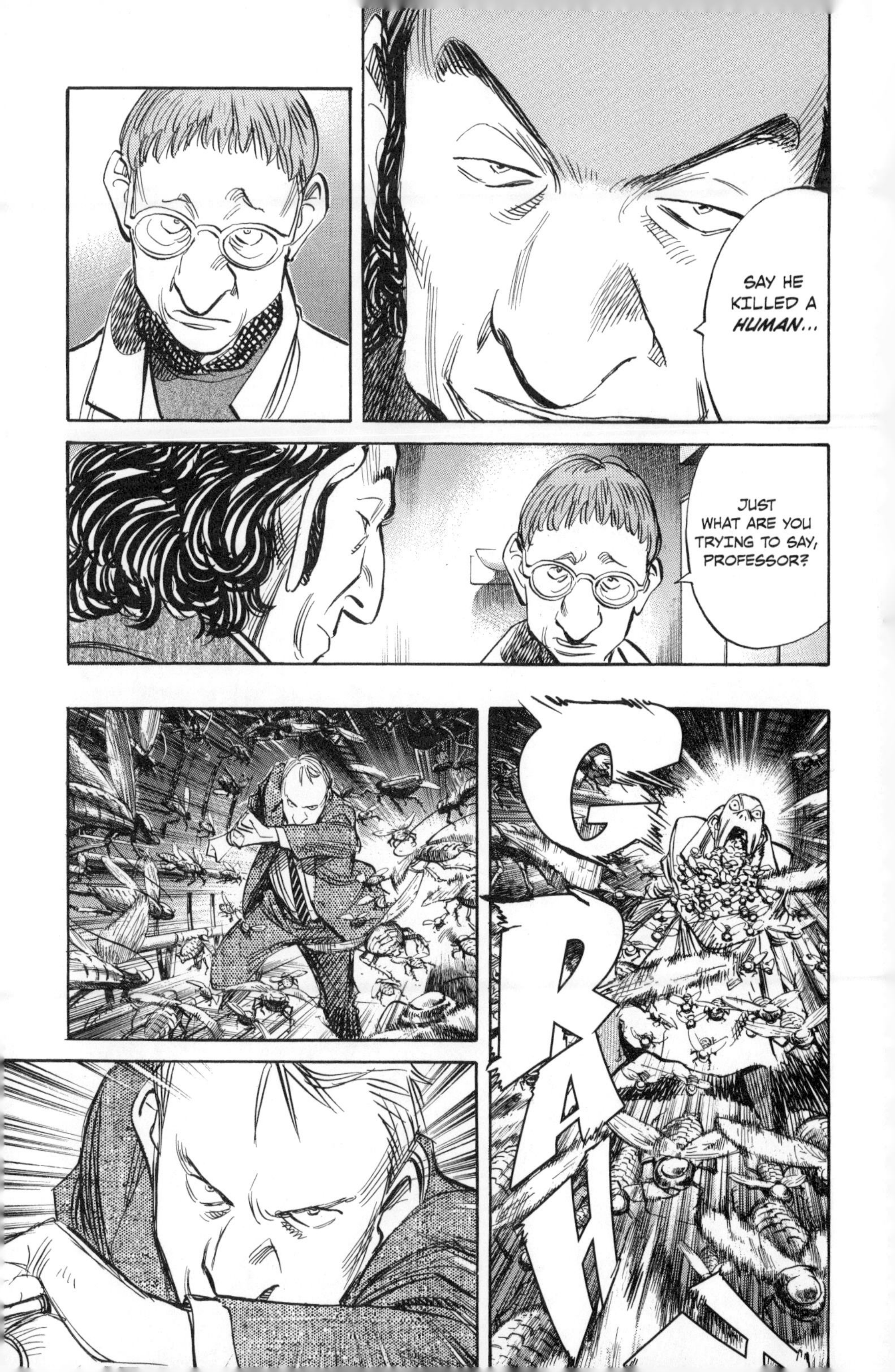
SAY HE KILLED A *HUMAN*...
JUST WHAT ARE YOU TRYING TO SAY, PROFESSOR?
GRA

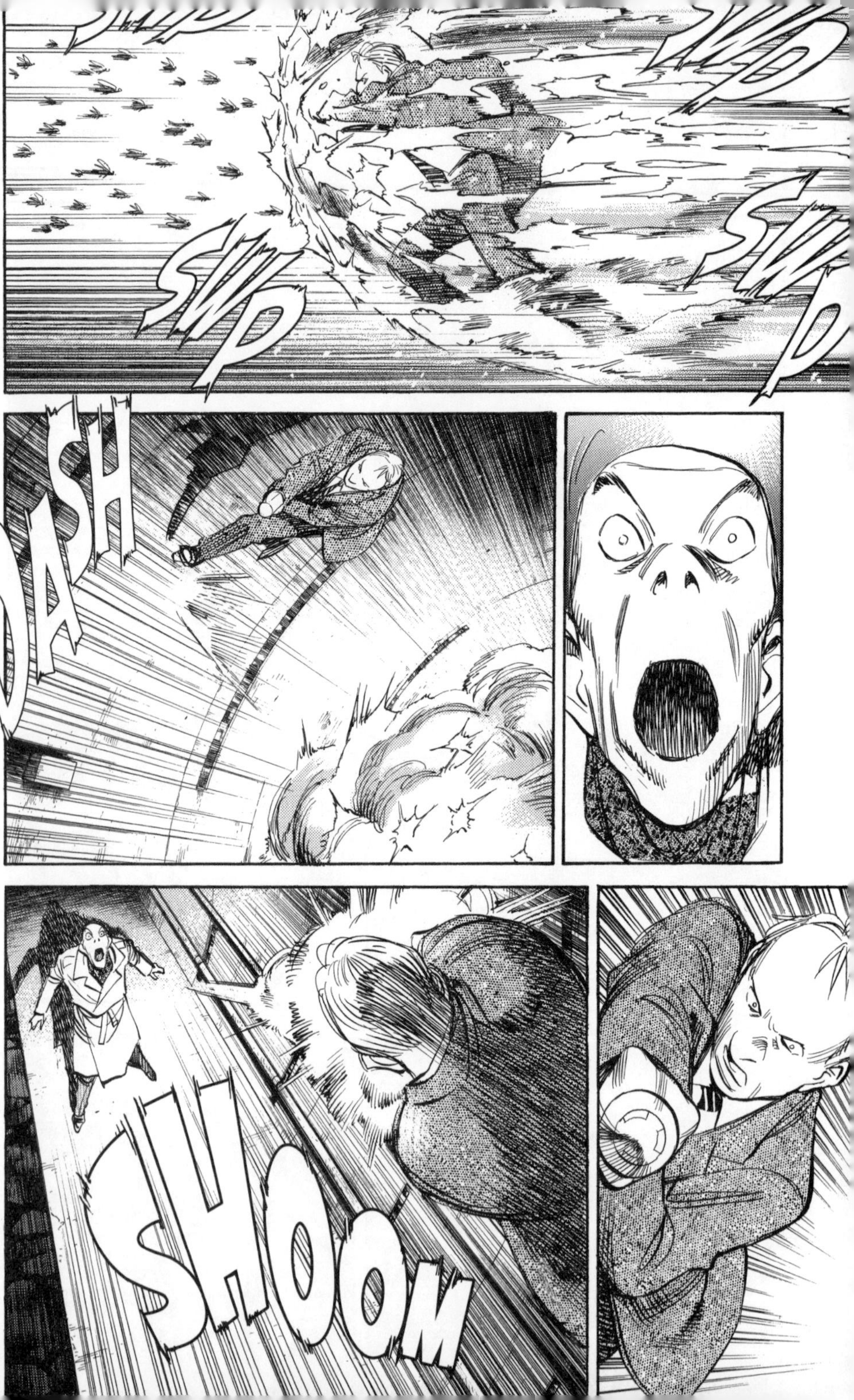
SWIP
SWIP
DASH
SHOOM

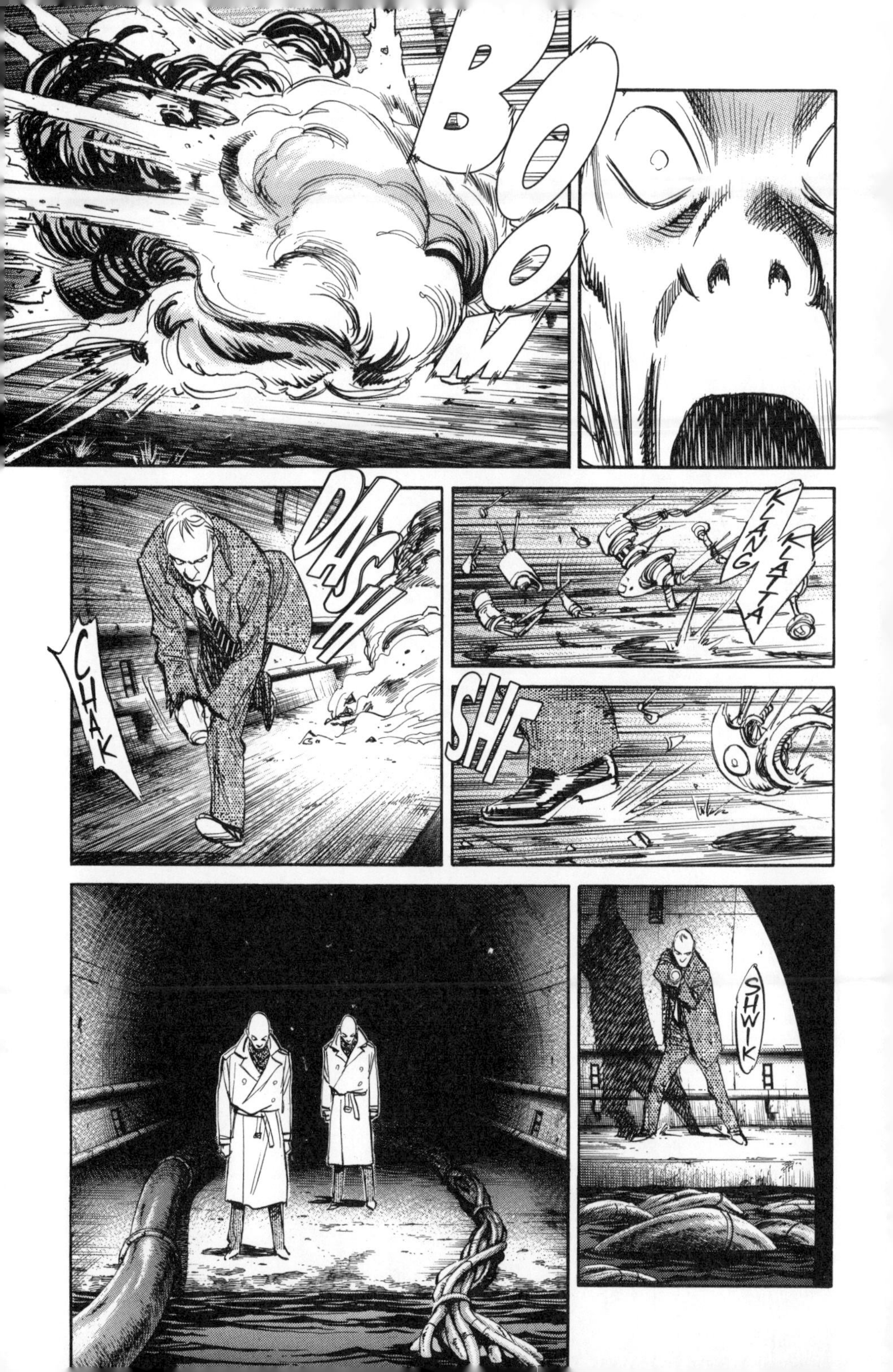
BOOOM
KLATTA
KLANG
SHF
DASH
CHAK
SHWIK

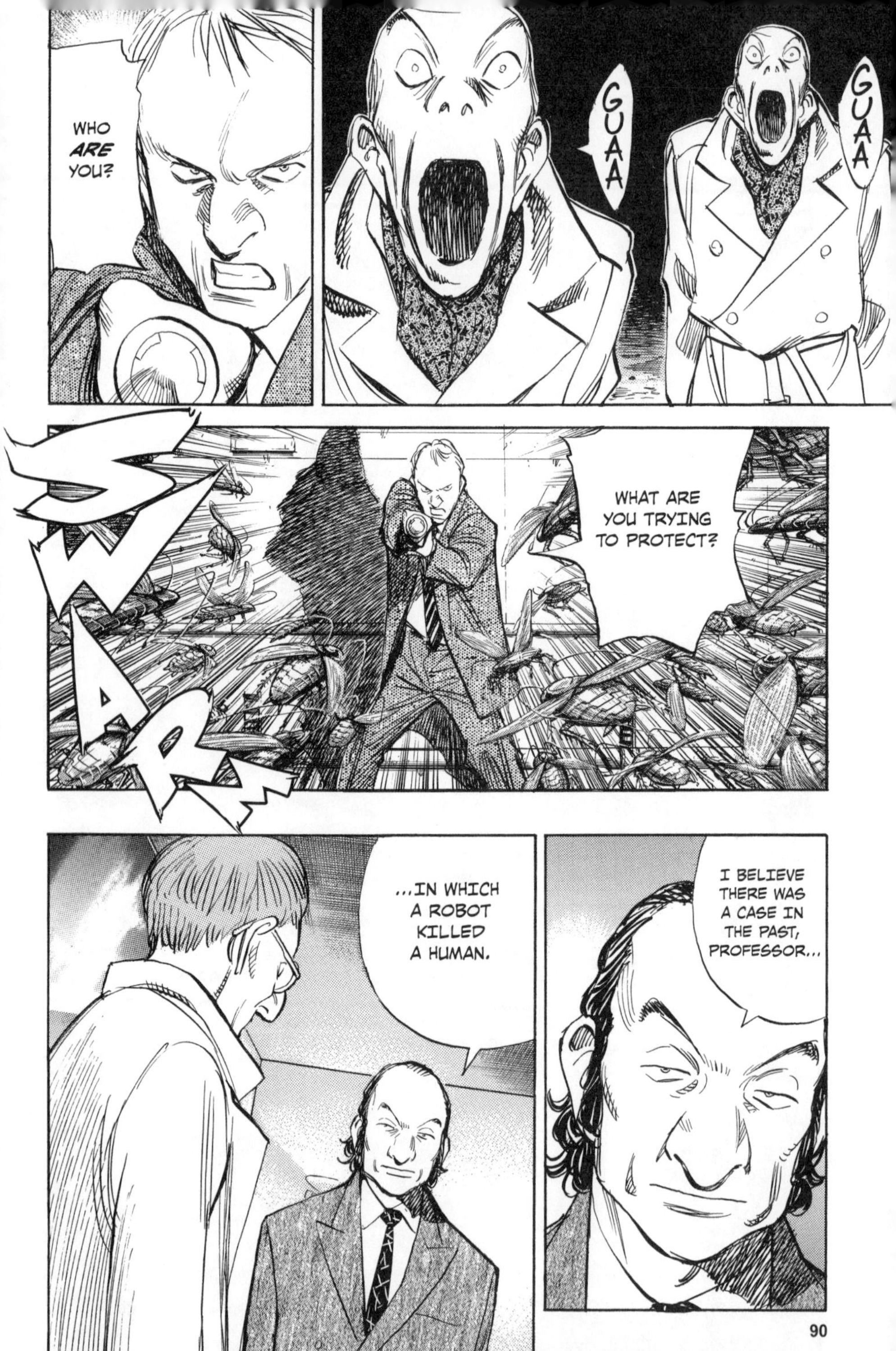
GUAA
GUAA
WHO *ARE* YOU?
WHAT ARE YOU TRYING TO PROTECT?
SWARM
I BELIEVE THERE WAS A CASE IN THE PAST, PROFESSOR...
...IN WHICH A ROBOT KILLED A HUMAN.

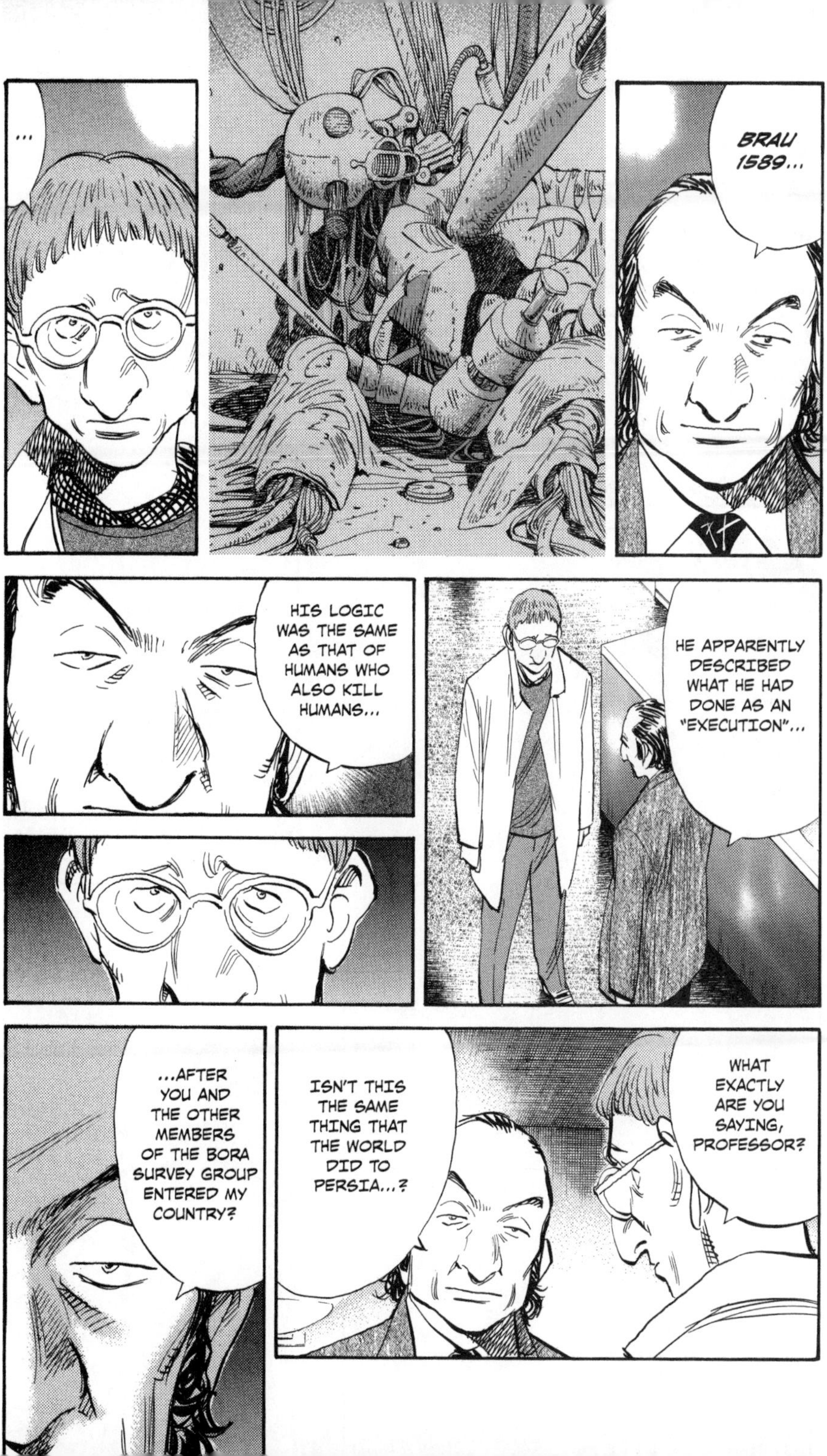
BRAU 1589...
...
HE APPARENTLY DESCRIBED WHAT HE HAD DONE AS AN "EXECUTION"...
HIS LOGIC WAS THE SAME AS THAT OF HUMANS WHO ALSO KILL HUMANS...
WHAT EXACTLY ARE YOU SAYING, PROFESSOR?
ISN'T THIS THE SAME THING THAT THE WORLD DID TO PERSIA...?
...AFTER YOU AND THE OTHER MEMBERS OF THE BORA SURVEY GROUP ENTERED MY COUNTRY?

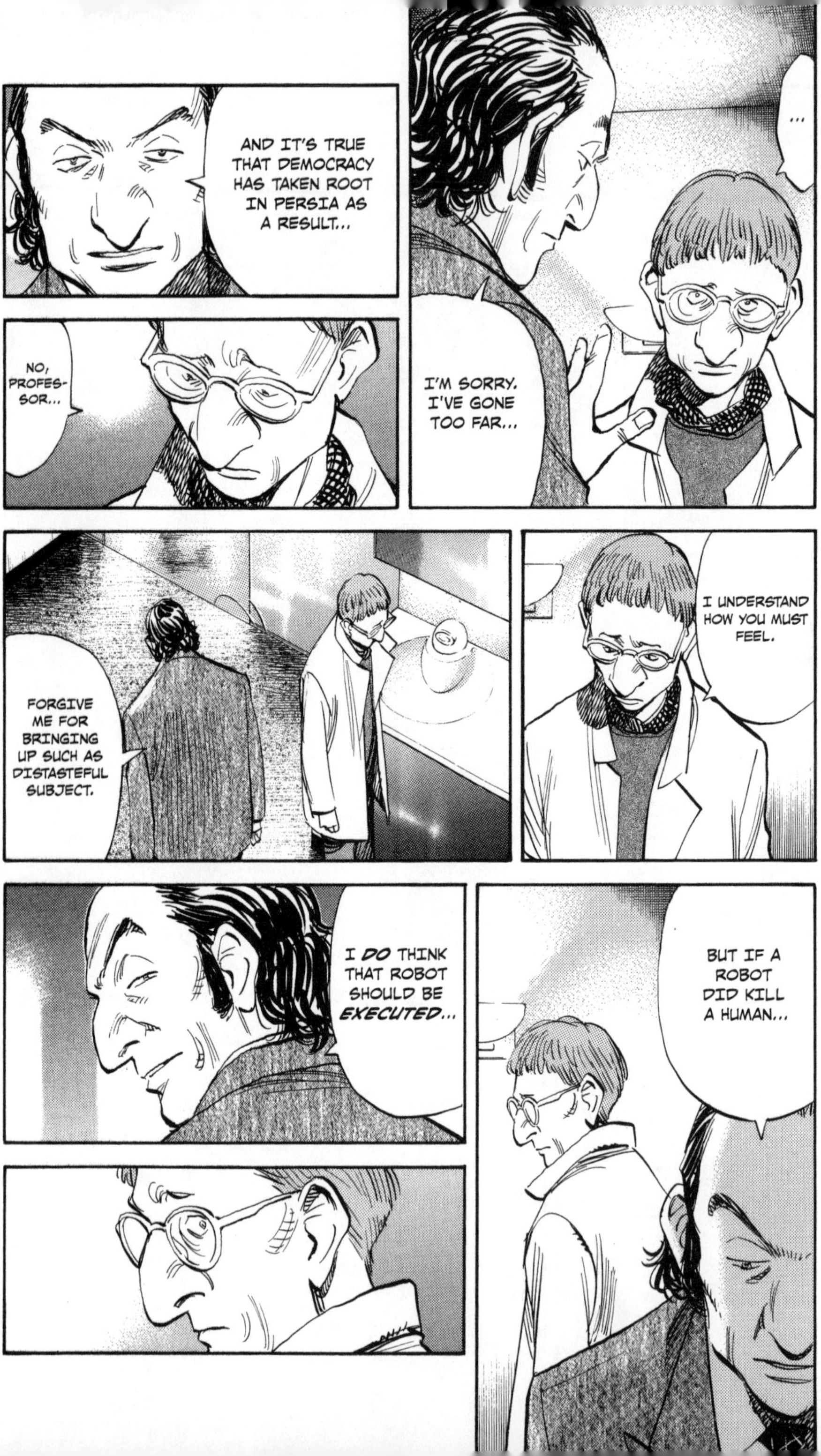
...
I'M SORRY. I'VE GONE TOO FAR...
AND IT'S TRUE THAT DEMOCRACY HAS TAKEN ROOT IN PERSIA AS A RESULT...
NO, PROFES-SOR...
I UNDERSTAND HOW YOU MUST FEEL.
FORGIVE ME FOR BRINGING UP SUCH AS DISTASTEFUL SUBJECT.
BUT IF A ROBOT DID KILL A HUMAN...
I *DO* THINK THAT ROBOT SHOULD BE ***EXECUTED***...

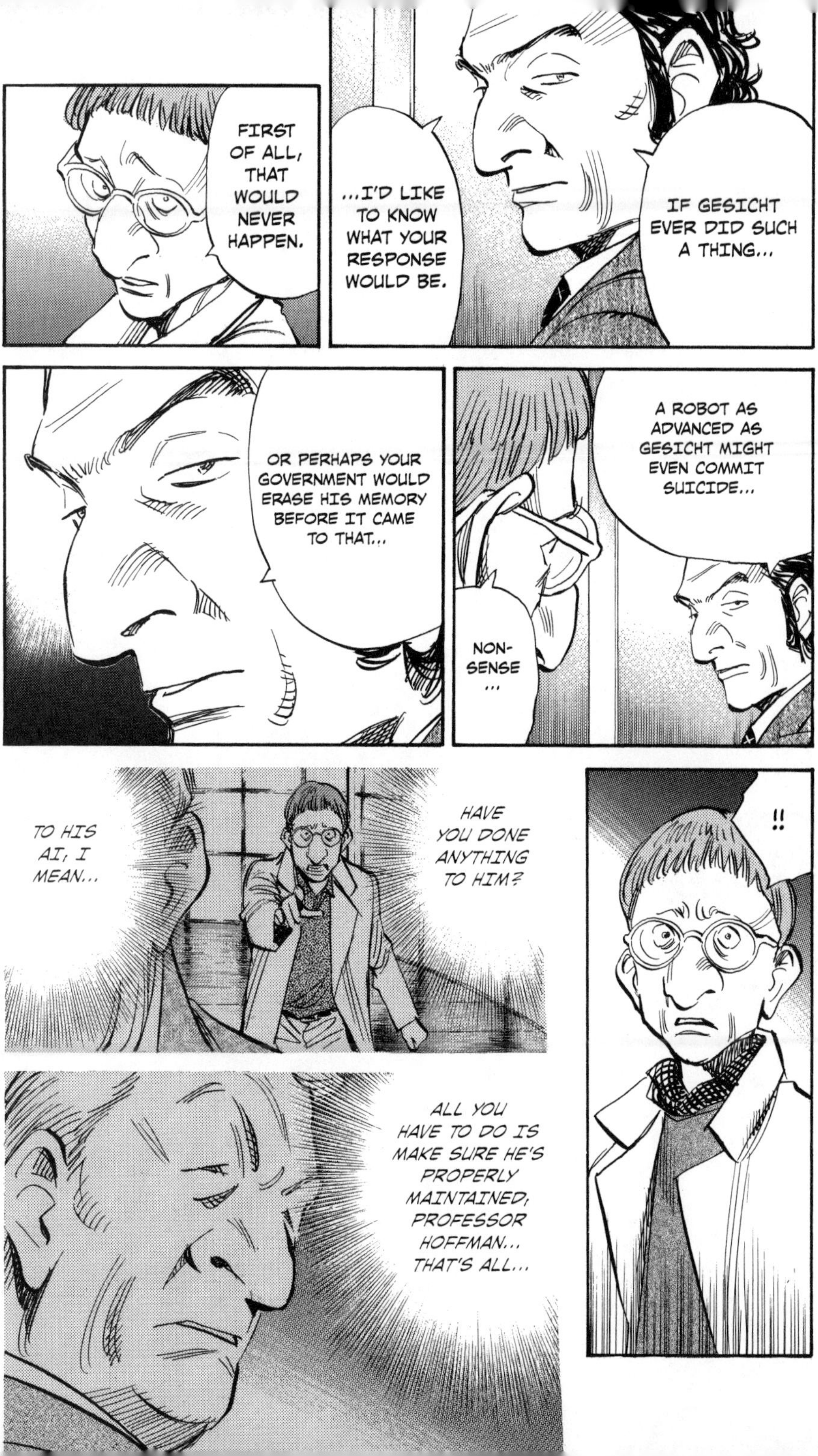
IF GESICHT EVER DID SUCH A THING...
...I'D LIKE TO KNOW WHAT YOUR RESPONSE WOULD BE.
FIRST OF ALL, THAT WOULD NEVER HAPPEN.
A ROBOT AS ADVANCED AS GESICHT MIGHT EVEN COMMIT SUICIDE...
NON-SENSE...
OR PERHAPS YOUR GOVERNMENT WOULD ERASE HIS MEMORY BEFORE IT CAME TO THAT...
!!
HAVE YOU DONE ANYTHING TO HIM?
TO HIS AI, I MEAN...
ALL YOU HAVE TO DO IS MAKE SURE HE'S PROPERLY MAINTAINED, PROFESSOR HOFFMAN... THAT'S ALL...

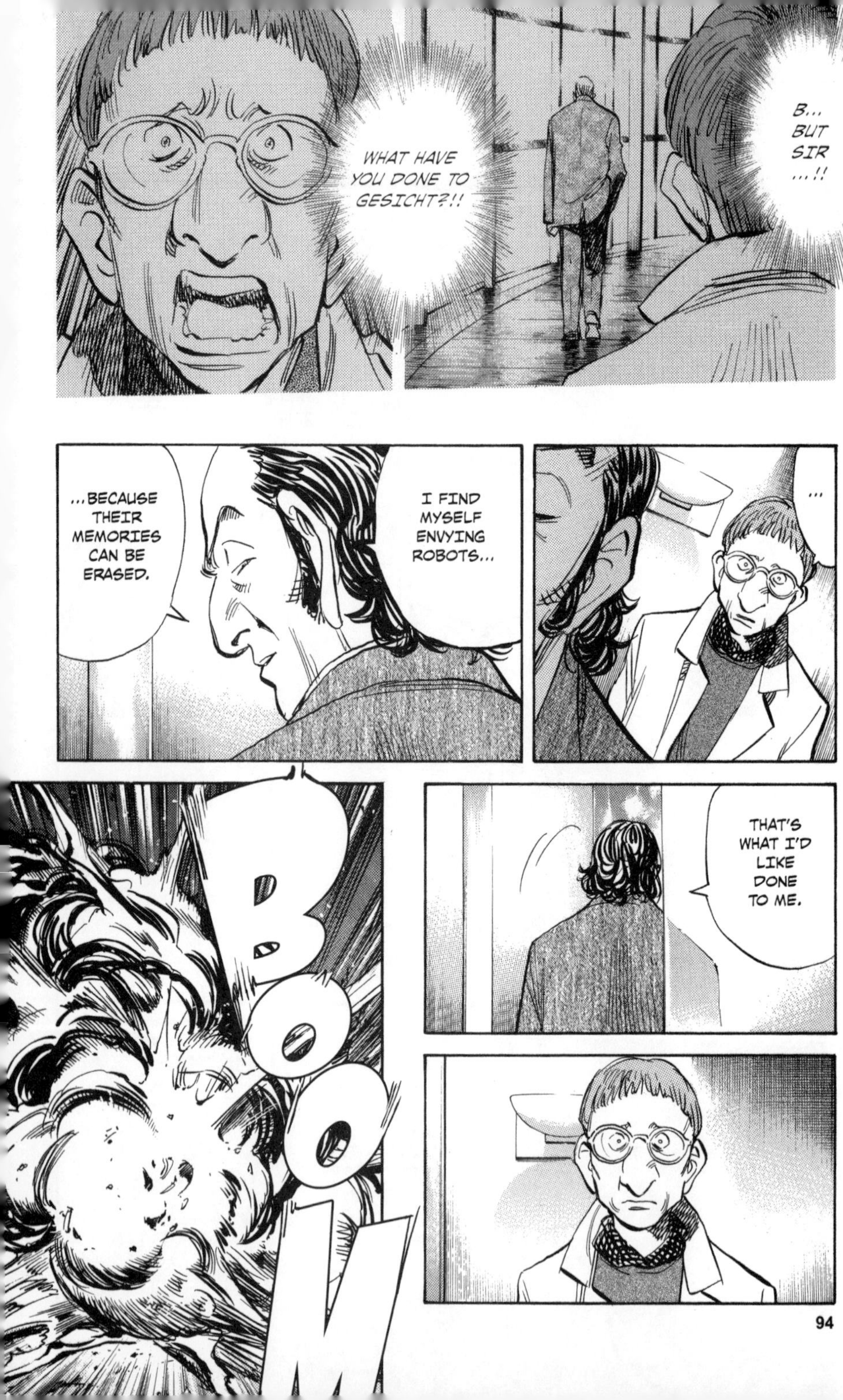
B... BUT SIR ...!!
WHAT HAVE YOU DONE TO GESICHT?!!
...
I FIND MYSELF ENVYING ROBOTS...
...BECAUSE THEIR MEMORIES CAN BE ERASED.
THAT'S WHAT I'D LIKE DONE TO ME.
BOOOM

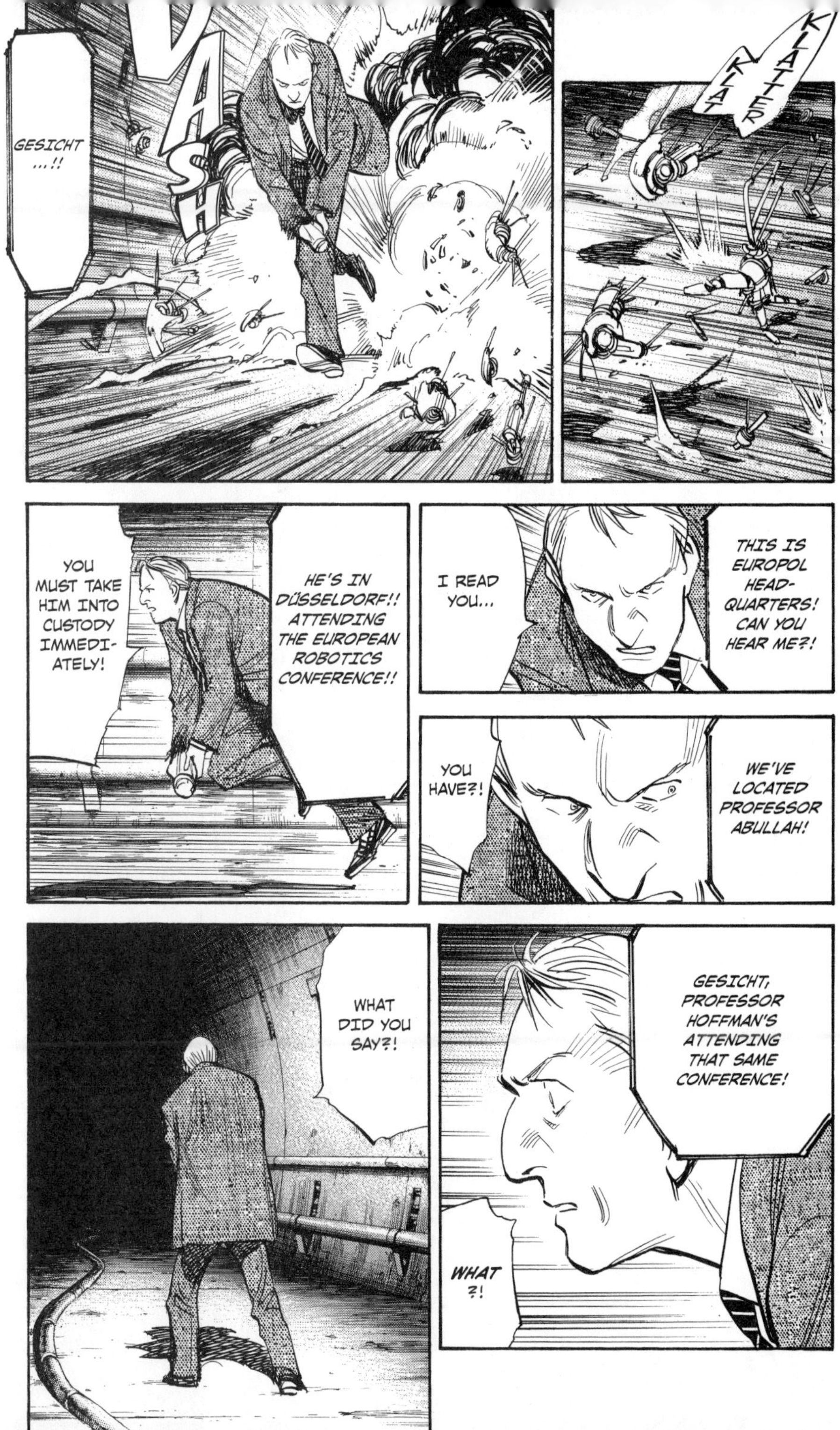
KLATTER
KLAT
VASH
GESICHT ...!!
THIS IS EUROPOL HEAD-QUARTERS! CAN YOU HEAR ME?!
I READ YOU...
WE'VE LOCATED PROFESSOR ABULLAH!
YOU HAVE?!
HE'S IN DÜSSELDORF!! ATTENDING THE EUROPEAN ROBOTICS CONFERENCE!!
YOU MUST TAKE HIM INTO CUSTODY IMMEDI-ATELY!
GESICHT, PROFESSOR HOFFMAN'S ATTENDING THAT SAME CONFERENCE!
WHAT ?!
WHAT DID YOU SAY?!

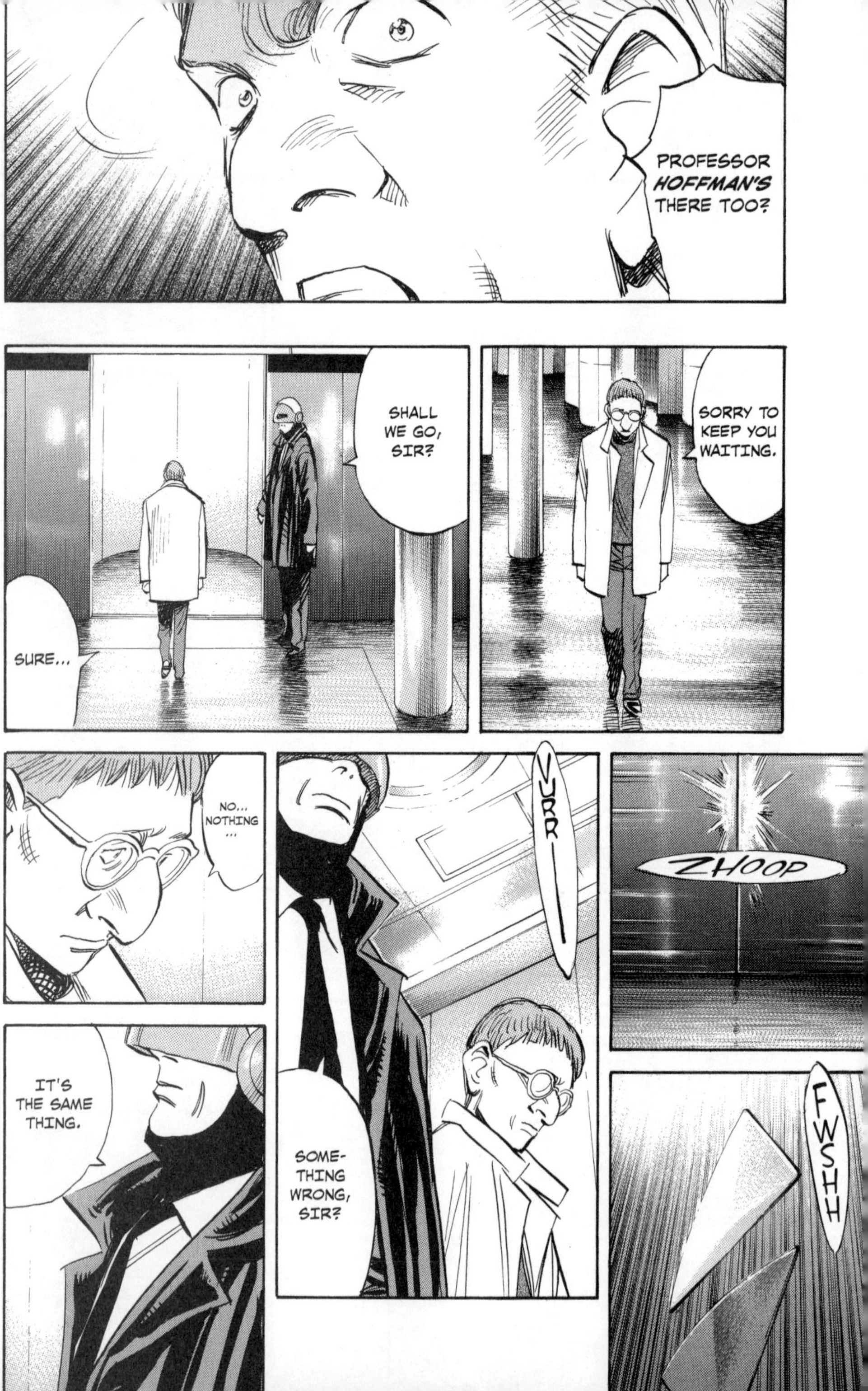
PROFESSOR HOFFMAN'S THERE TOO?
SORRY TO KEEP YOU WAITING.
SHALL WE GO, SIR?
SURE...
ZHOOP
FWSHH
VURR
SOME-THING WRONG, SIR?
NO... NOTHING...
IT'S THE SAME THING.

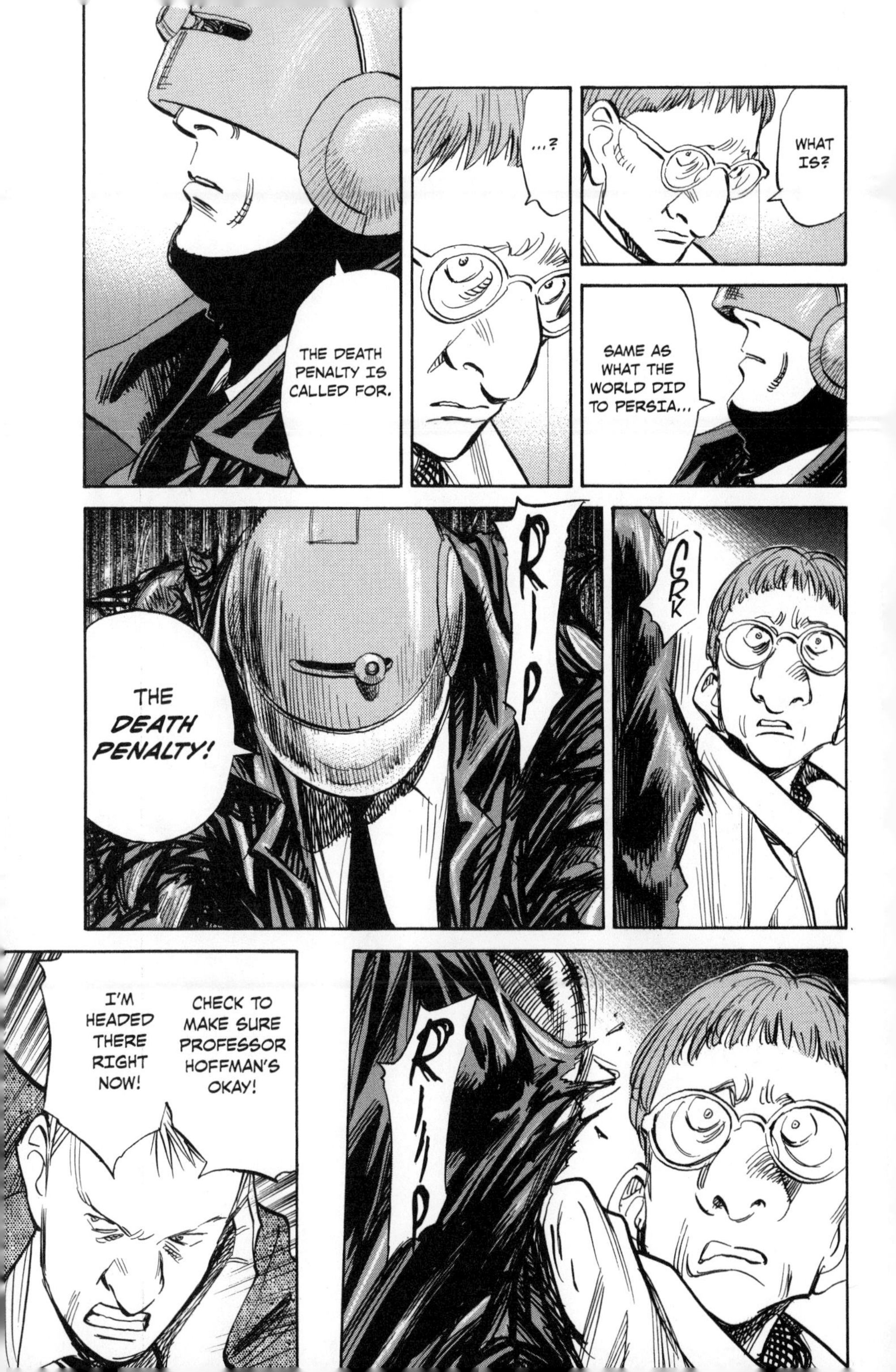
WHAT IS?
SAME AS WHAT THE WORLD DID TO PERSIA...
...?
THE DEATH PENALTY IS CALLED FOR.
GRK
RIP
THE *DEATH PENALTY!*
RIIIP
CHECK TO MAKE SURE PROFESSOR HOFFMAN'S OKAY!
I'M HEADED THERE RIGHT NOW!

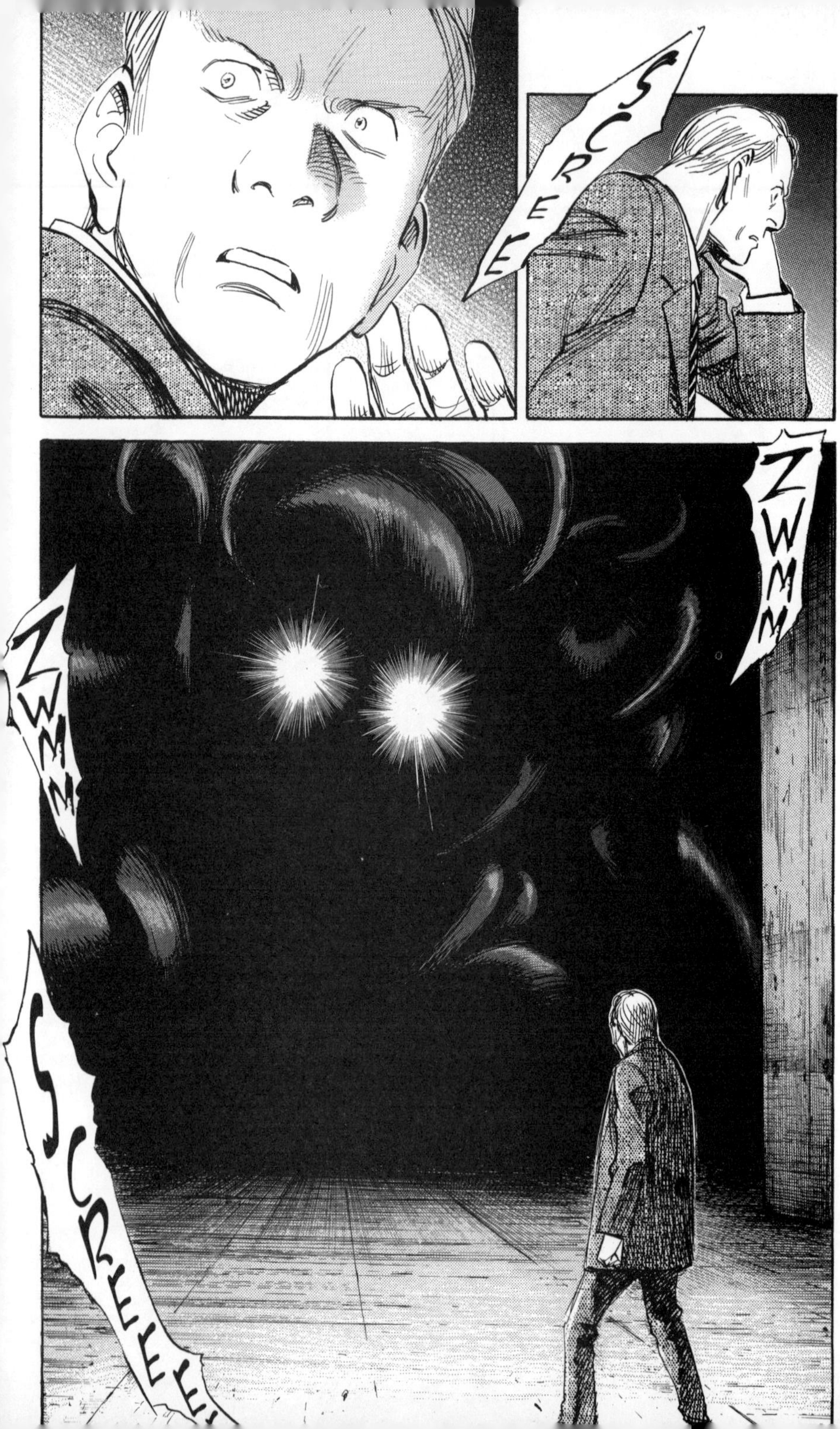
SCREEE
ZWMM
ZWMM
SCREEEE

Act 44 I AM PLUTO

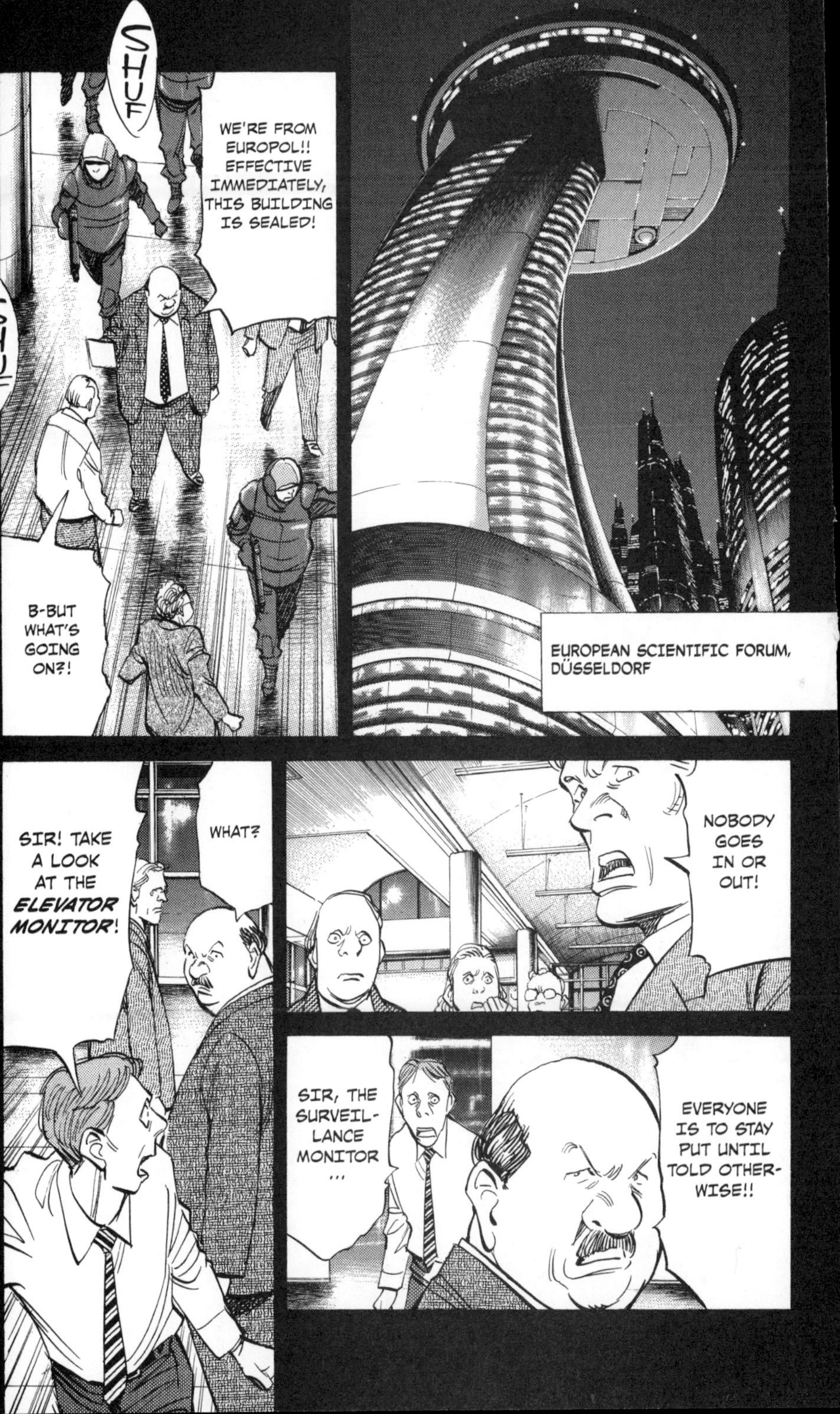
EUROPEAN SCIENTIFIC FORUM, DÜSSELDORF
SHUF
WE'RE FROM EUROPOL!! EFFECTIVE IMMEDIATELY, THIS BUILDING IS SEALED!
SHUF
B-BUT WHAT'S GOING ON?!
NOBODY GOES IN OR OUT!
EVERYONE IS TO STAY PUT UNTIL TOLD OTHER-WISE!!
SIR, THE SURVEIL-LANCE MONITOR ...
WHAT?
SIR! TAKE A LOOK AT THE ***ELEVATOR MONITOR***!

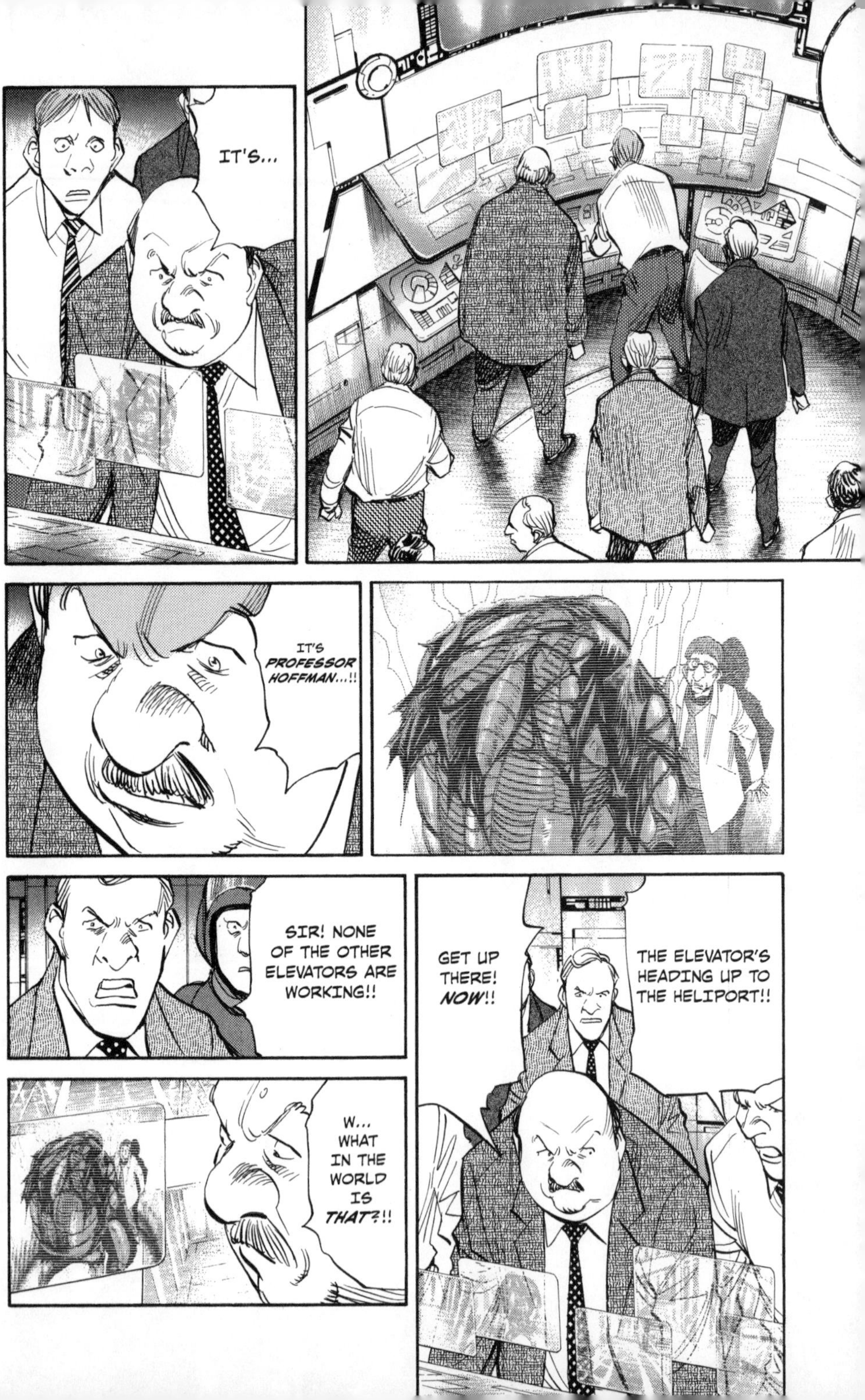
IT'S...
IT'S *PROFESSOR HOFFMAN*...!!
THE ELEVATOR'S HEADING UP TO THE HELIPORT!!
GET UP THERE! *NOW*!!
SIR! NONE OF THE OTHER ELEVATORS ARE WORKING!!
W... WHAT IN THE WORLD IS *THAT*?!!

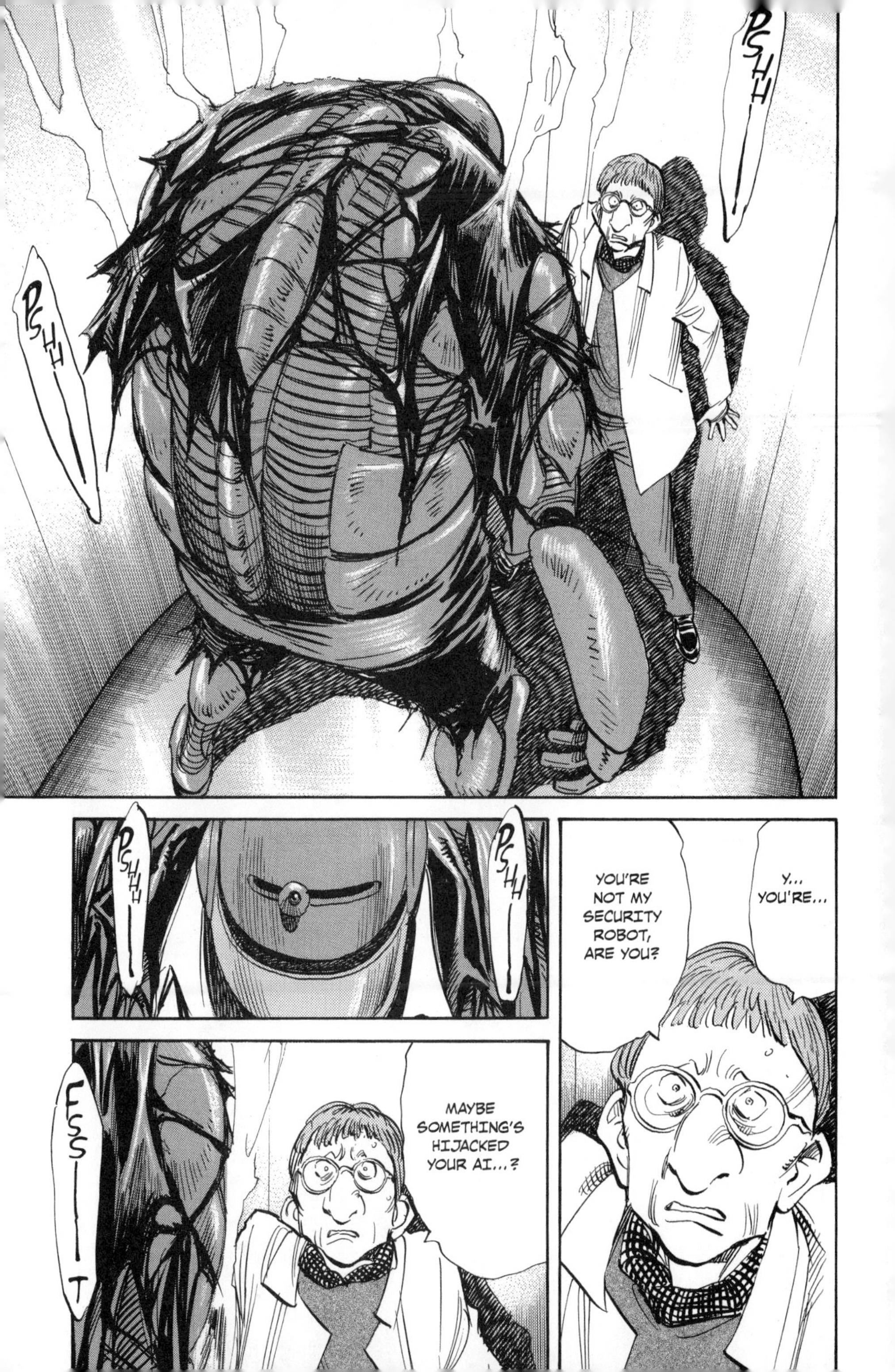
PSHH
PSHH
Y... YOU'RE...
YOU'RE NOT MY SECURITY ROBOT, ARE YOU?
PSHH
PSHH
MAYBE SOMETHING'S HIJACKED YOUR AI...?
FSSIT

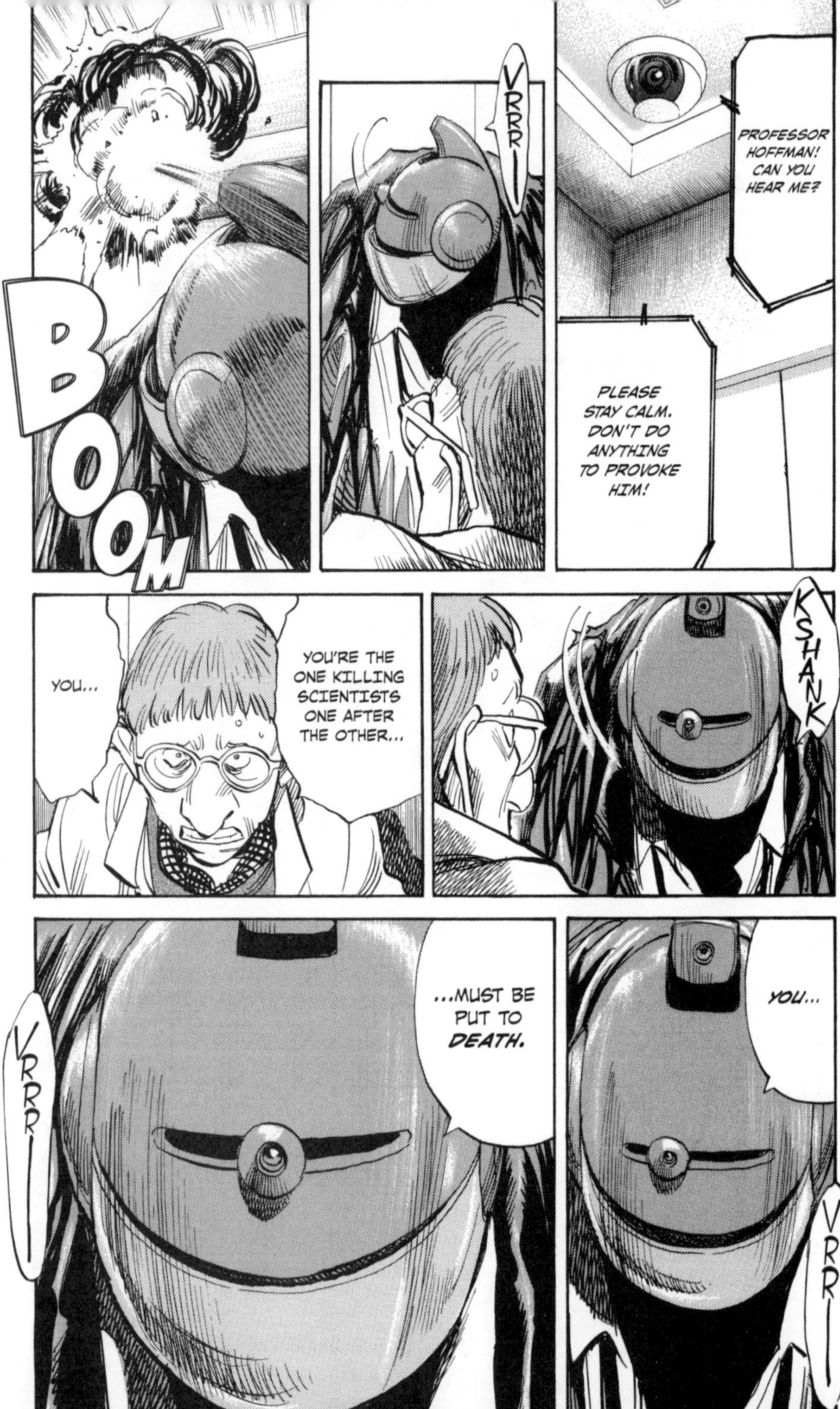
PROFESSOR HOFFMAN! CAN YOU HEAR ME?
PLEASE STAY CALM. DON'T DO ANYTHING TO PROVOKE HIM!
VRRRI
BOOM
KSHANK
YOU'RE THE ONE KILLING SCIENTISTS ONE AFTER THE OTHER...
YOU...
YOU...
VRRI
...MUST BE PUT TO DEATH.
VRRRI

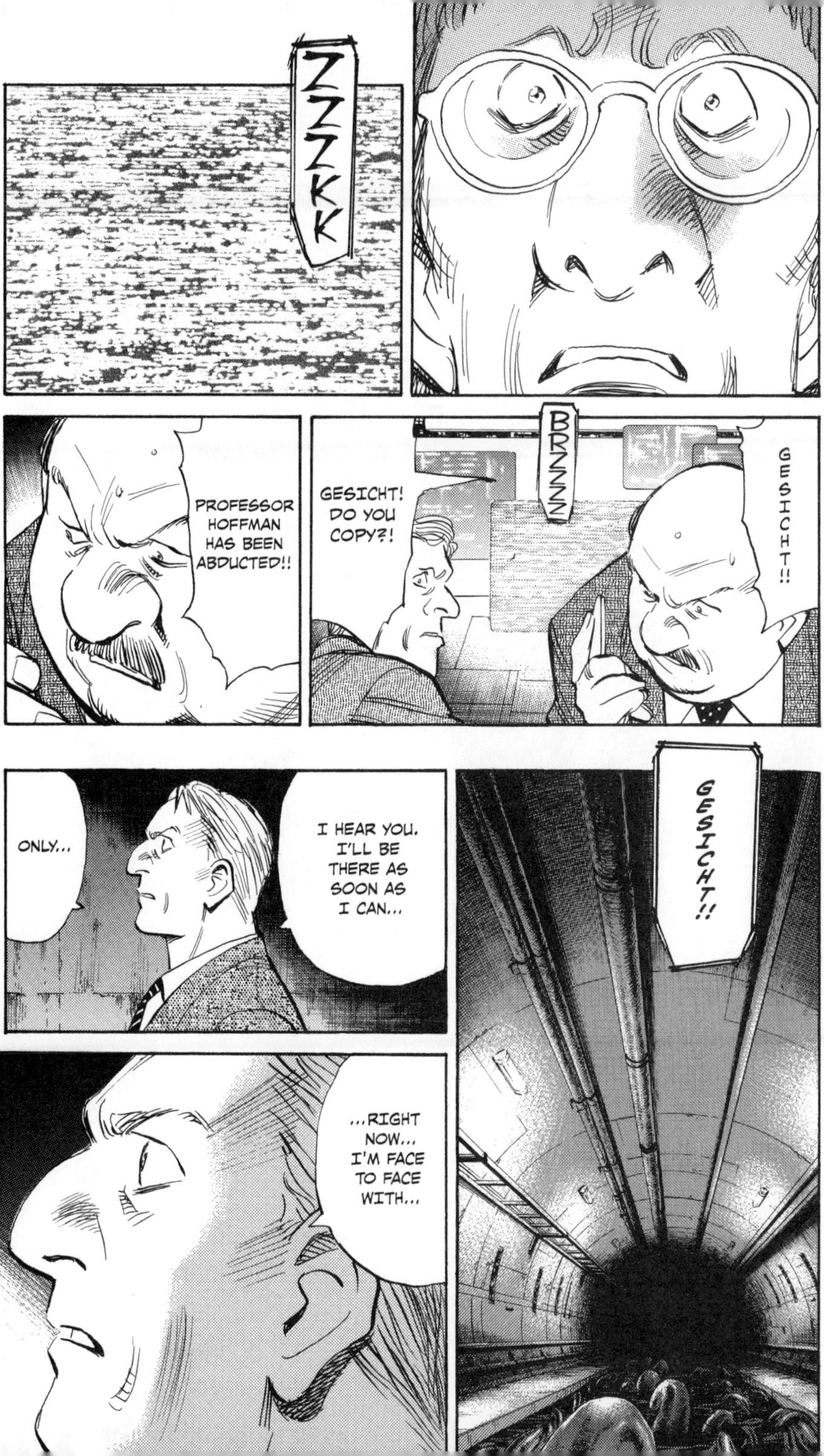
ZZZKK
GESICHT!!
BRZZZ
GESICHT! DO YOU COPY?!
PROFESSOR HOFFMAN HAS BEEN ABDUCTED!!
GESICHT!!
I HEAR YOU. I'LL BE THERE AS SOON AS I CAN...
ONLY...
...RIGHT NOW... I'M FACE TO FACE WITH...

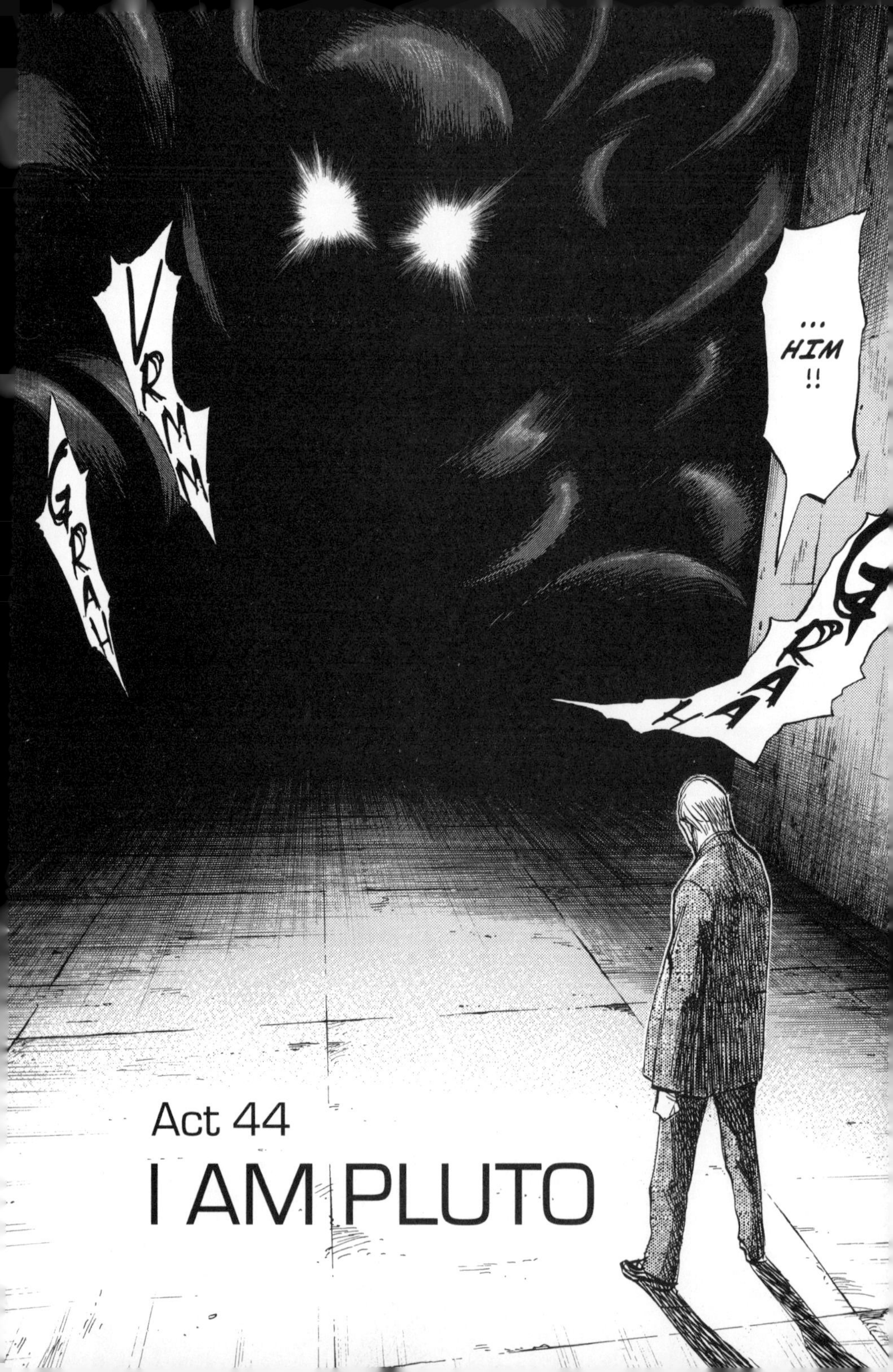
...HIM!!
GRRAAH
VRMMM
GRRAH

Act 44
I AM PLUTO

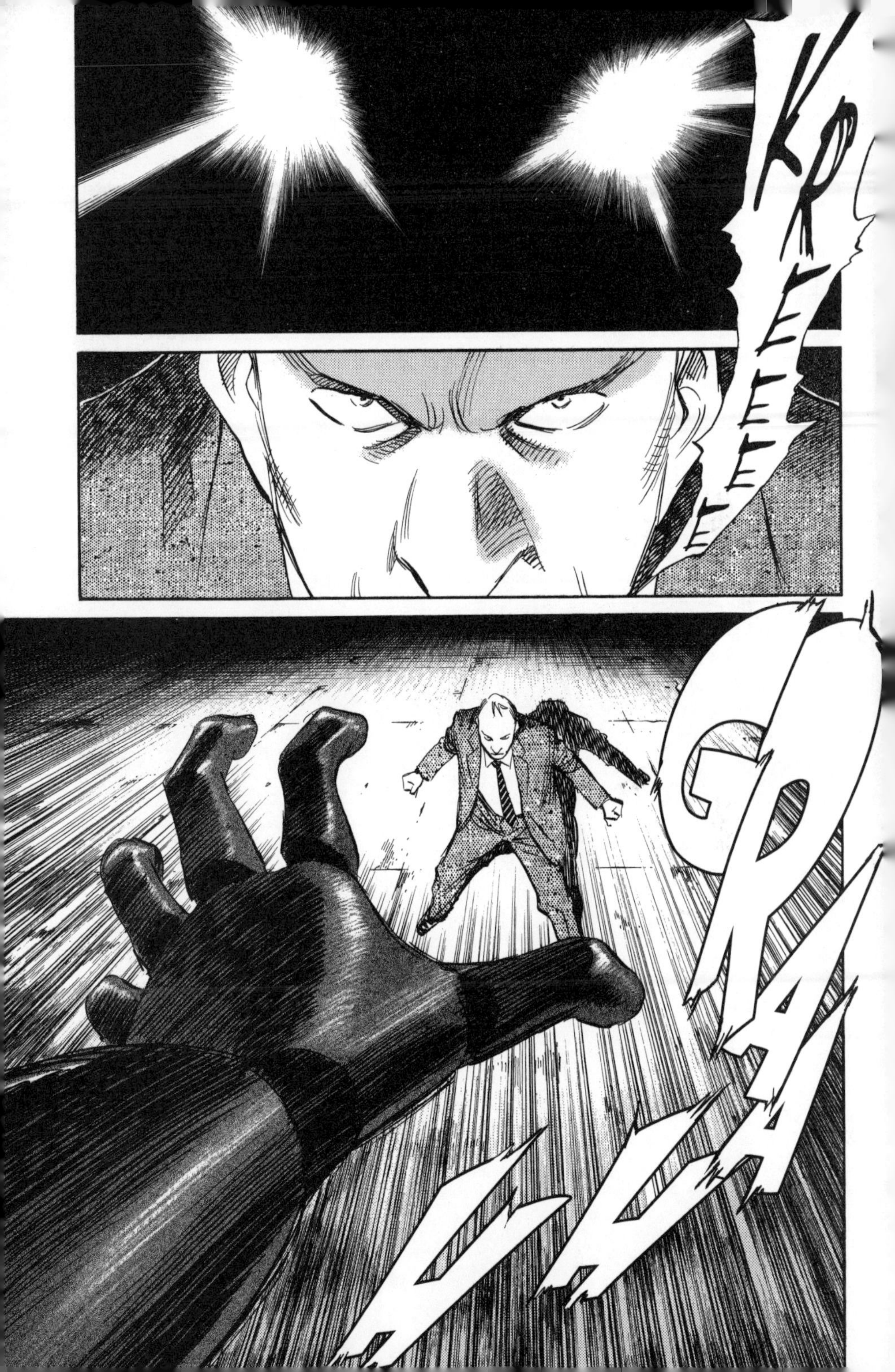
KRREEEEEEE
GRAAAA

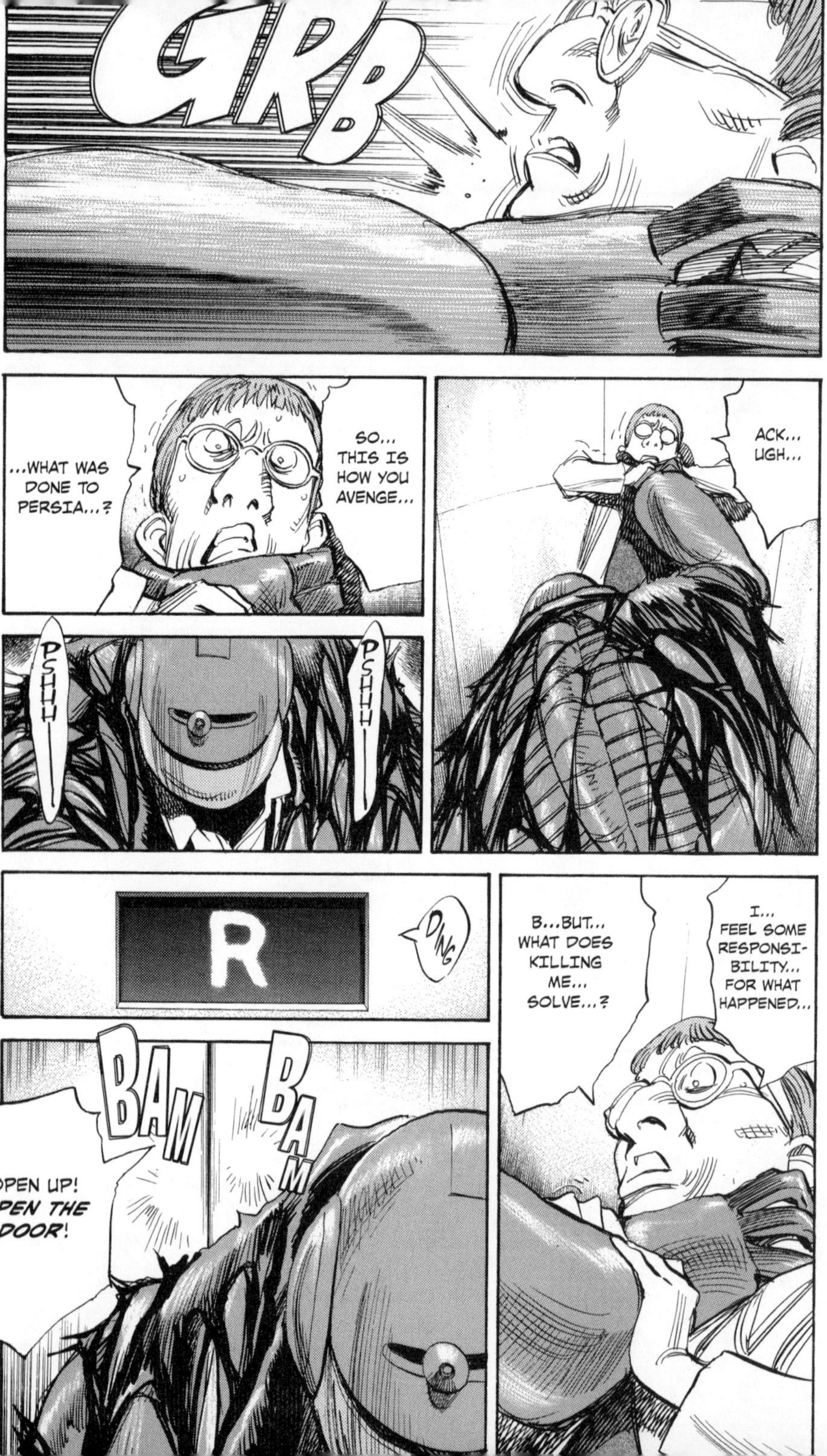
GRB
ACK... UGH...
SO... THIS IS HOW YOU AVENGE...
...WHAT WAS DONE TO PERSIA...?
PSHHH
PSHHH
I... FEEL SOME RESPONSI-BILITY... FOR WHAT HAPPENED...
B...BUT... WHAT DOES KILLING ME... SOLVE...?
R
DING
BAM
BAM
OPEN UP! *OPEN THE DOOR*!

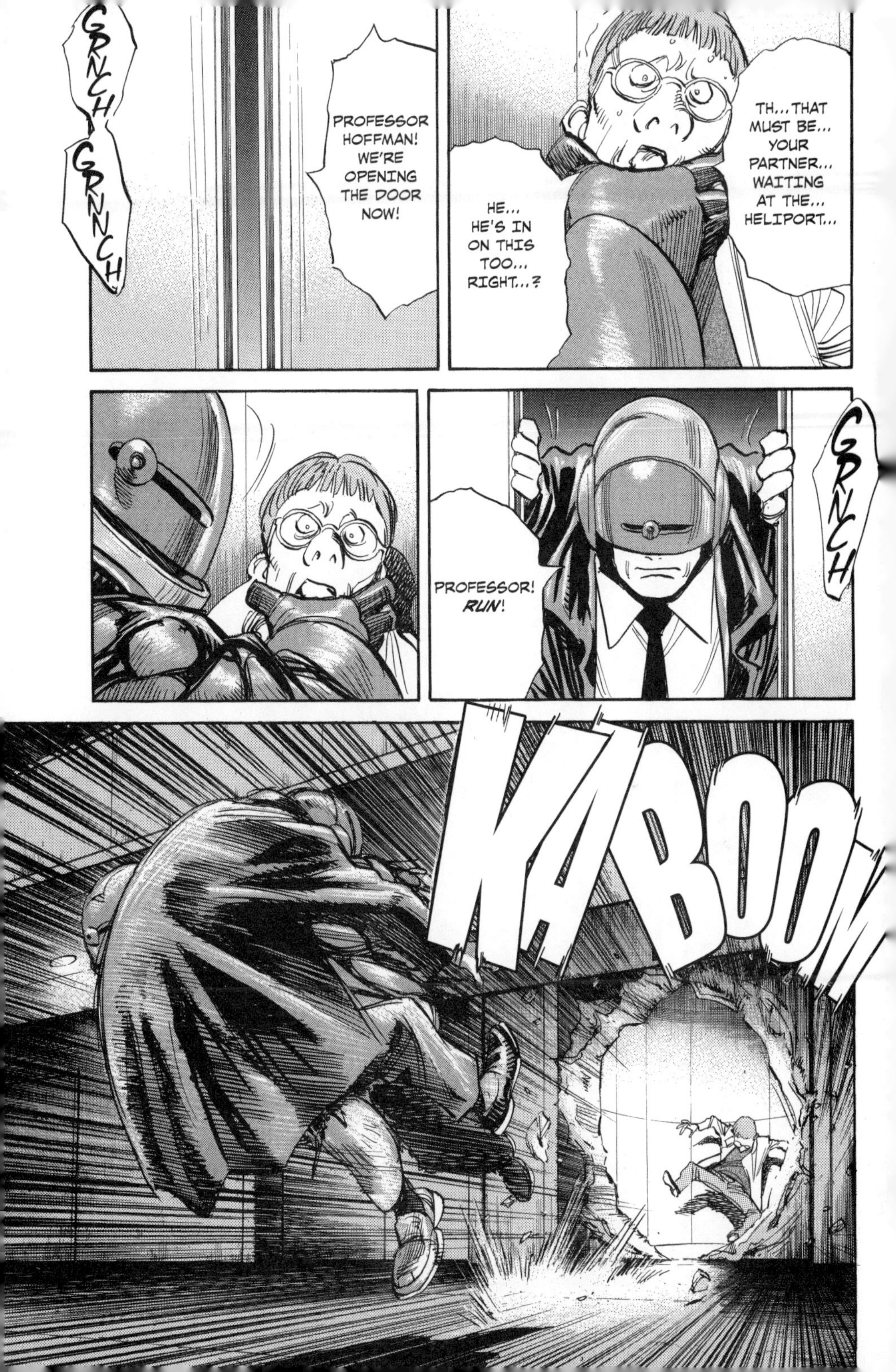
TH...THAT MUST BE... YOUR PARTNER... WAITING AT THE... HELIPORT...
HE... HE'S IN ON THIS TOO... RIGHT...?
PROFESSOR HOFFMAN! WE'RE OPENING THE DOOR NOW!
GRNCH GRNNCH
GRNCH
PROFESSOR! *RUN*!
KABOOM

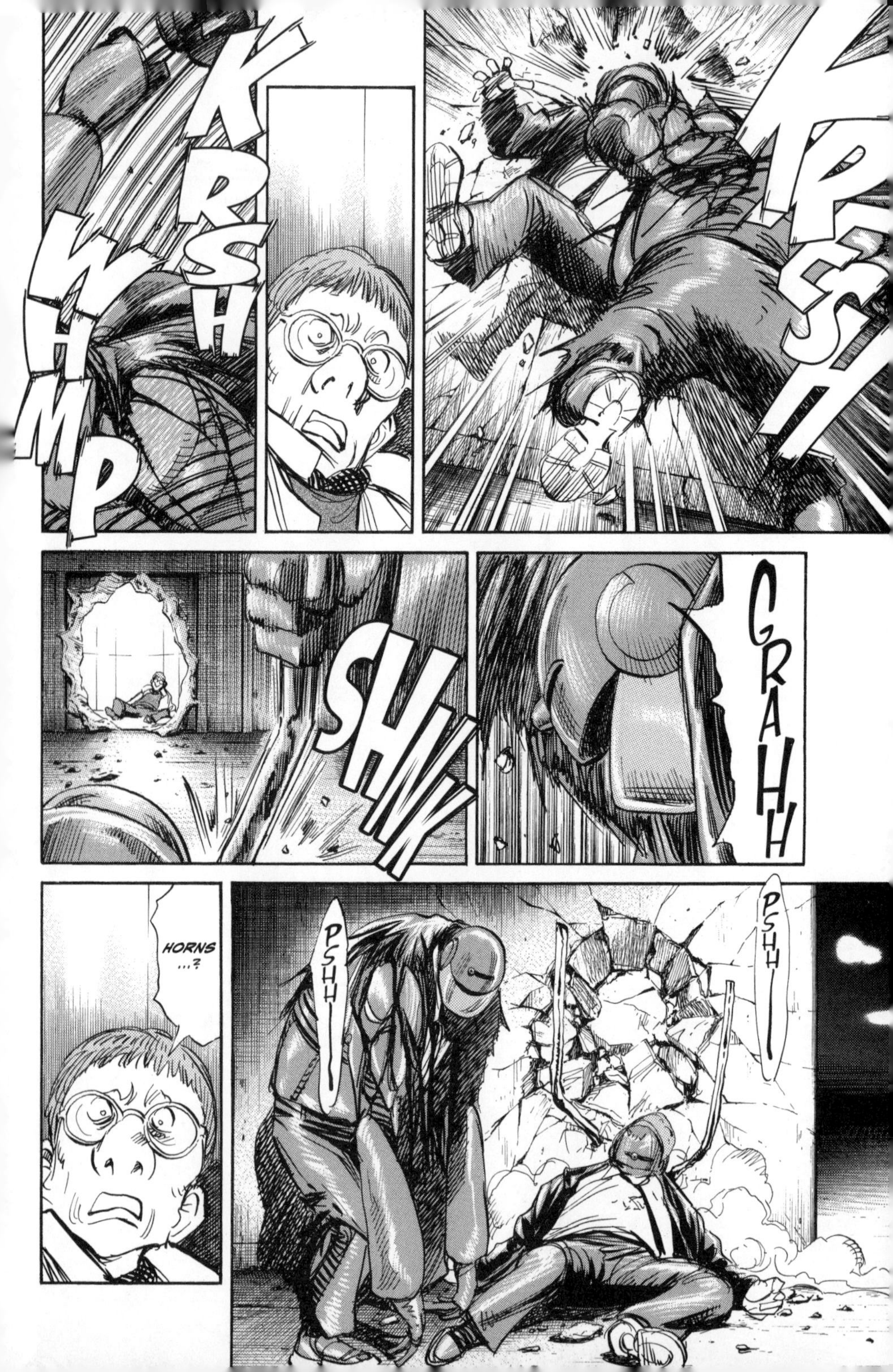
KRSSH
KRSH
WHMP
GRAHHH
SHK
PSHH
PSHH
HORNS ...?

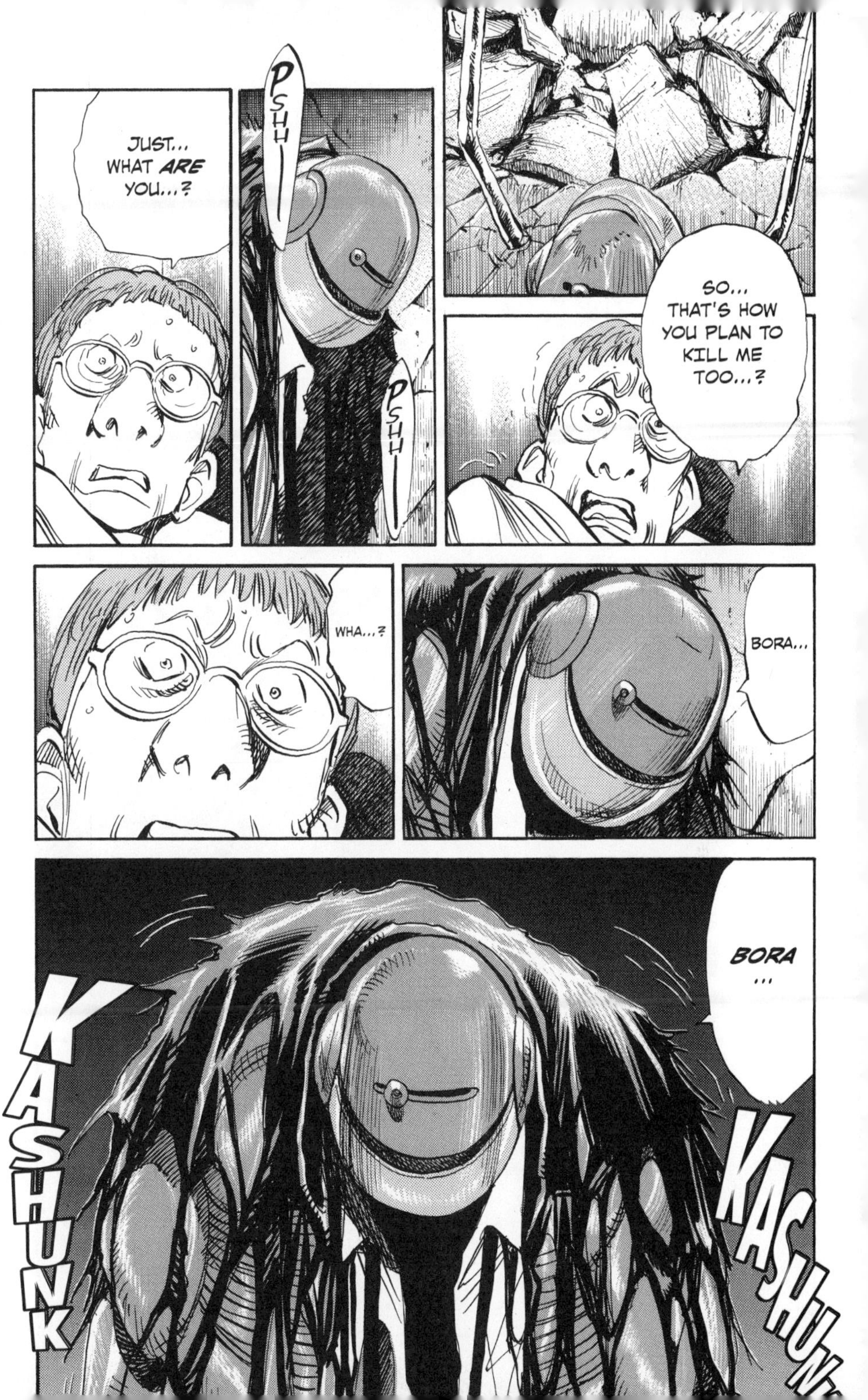
SO... THAT'S HOW YOU PLAN TO KILL ME TOO...?
PSHH
PSHH
JUST... WHAT ARE YOU...?
BORA...
WHA...?
BORA...
KASHUNK
KASHUNK

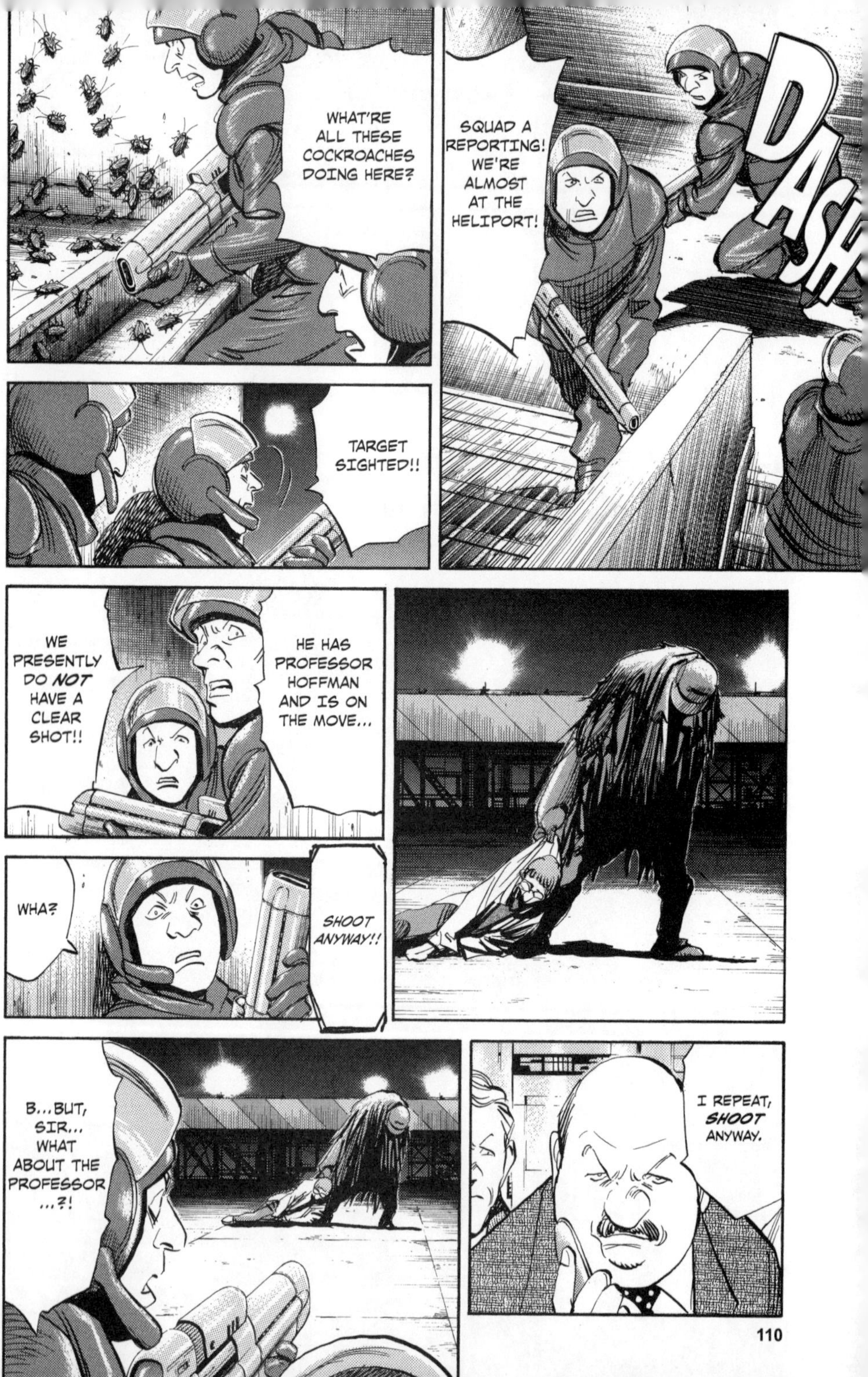
SQUAD A REPORTING! WE'RE ALMOST AT THE HELIPORT!
DASH
WHAT'RE ALL THESE COCKROACHES DOING HERE?
TARGET SIGHTED!!
HE HAS PROFESSOR HOFFMAN AND IS ON THE MOVE...
WE PRESENTLY DO *NOT* HAVE A CLEAR SHOT!!
SHOOT ANYWAY!!
WHA?
I REPEAT, ***SHOOT*** ANYWAY.
B...BUT, SIR... WHAT ABOUT THE PROFESSOR ...?!

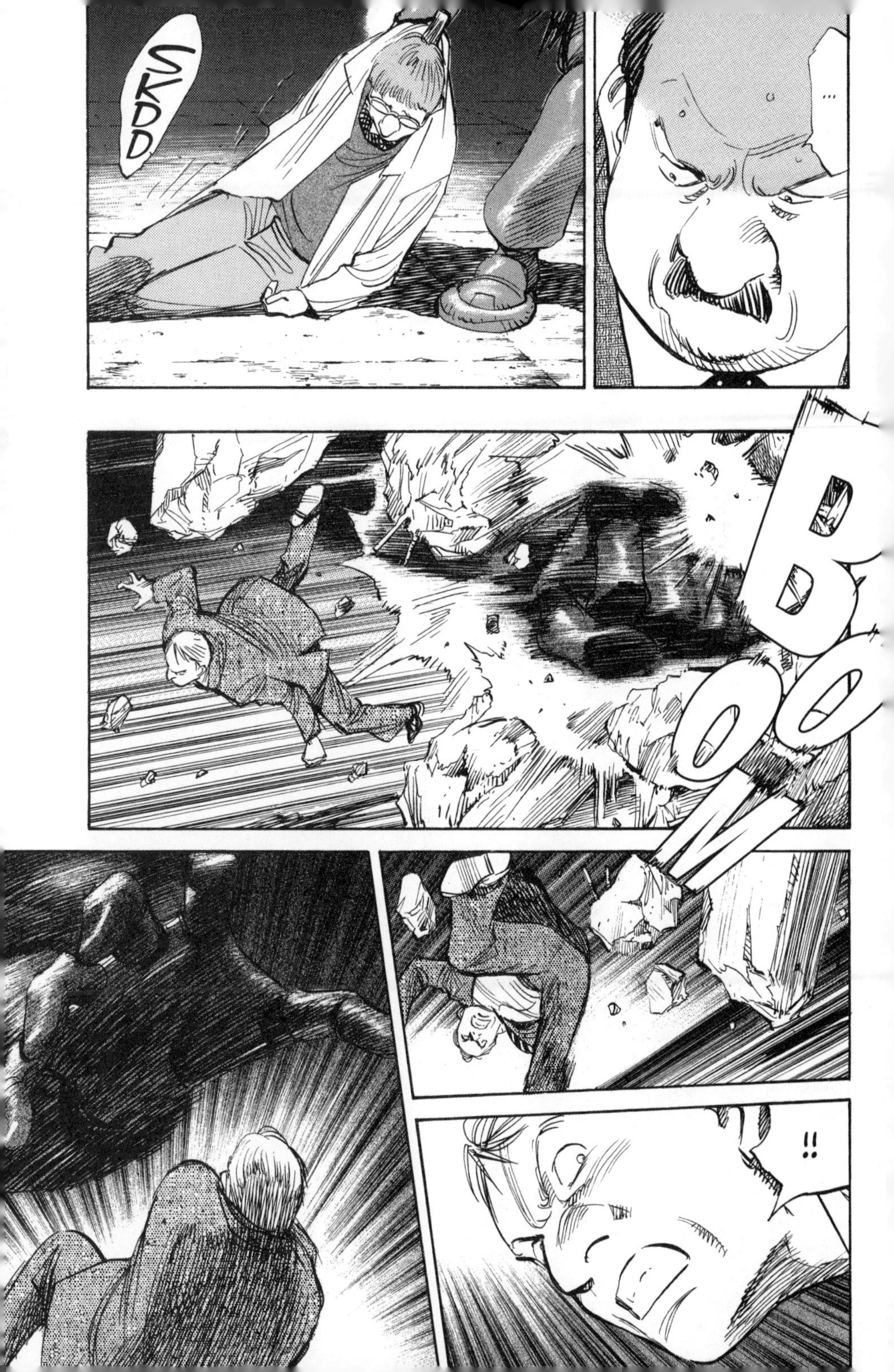
...
SKDD
BOOM
!!

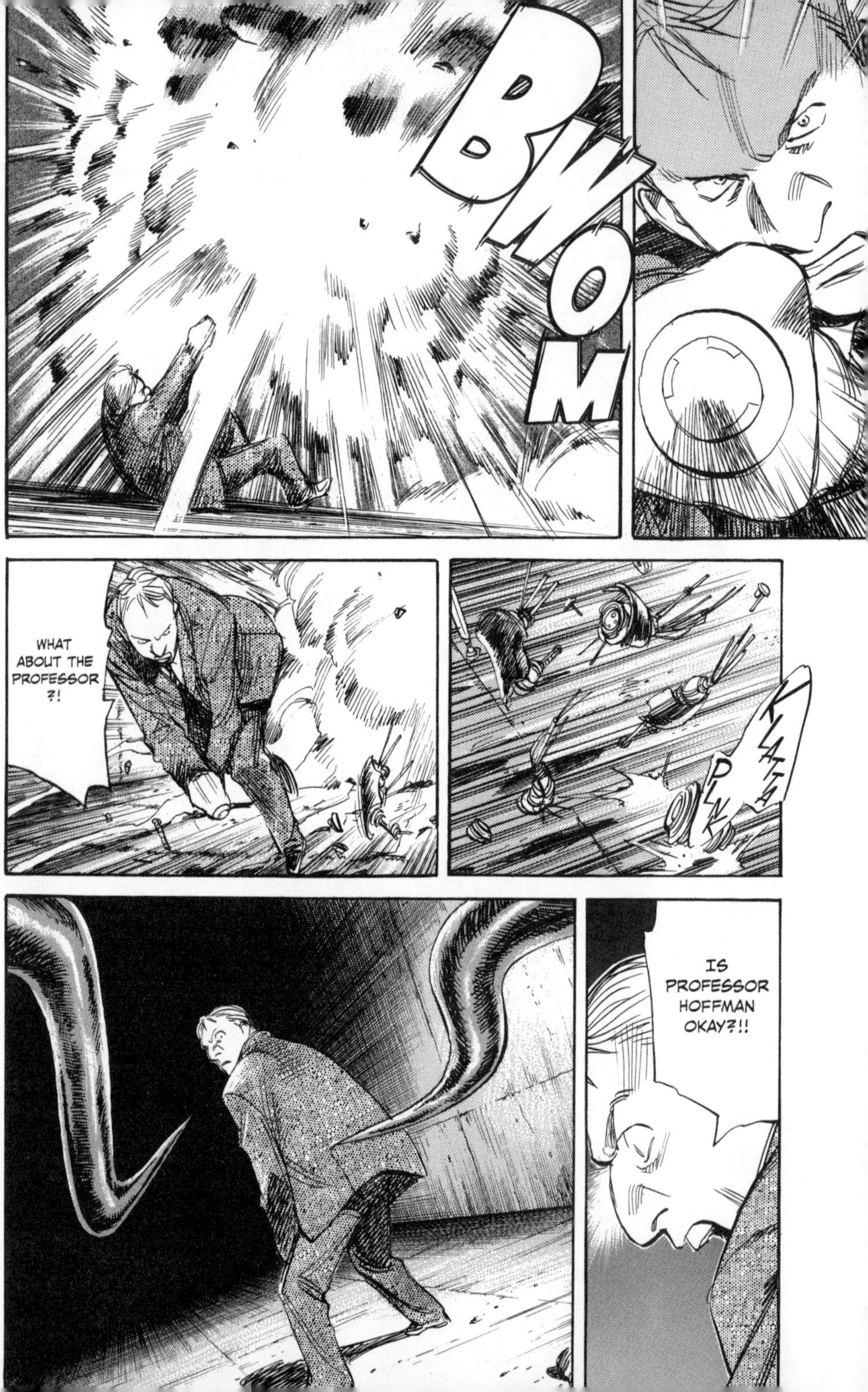
BWOOM
KLATTA
PLNK
WHAT ABOUT THE PROFESSOR ?!
IS PROFESSOR HOFFMAN OKAY?!!

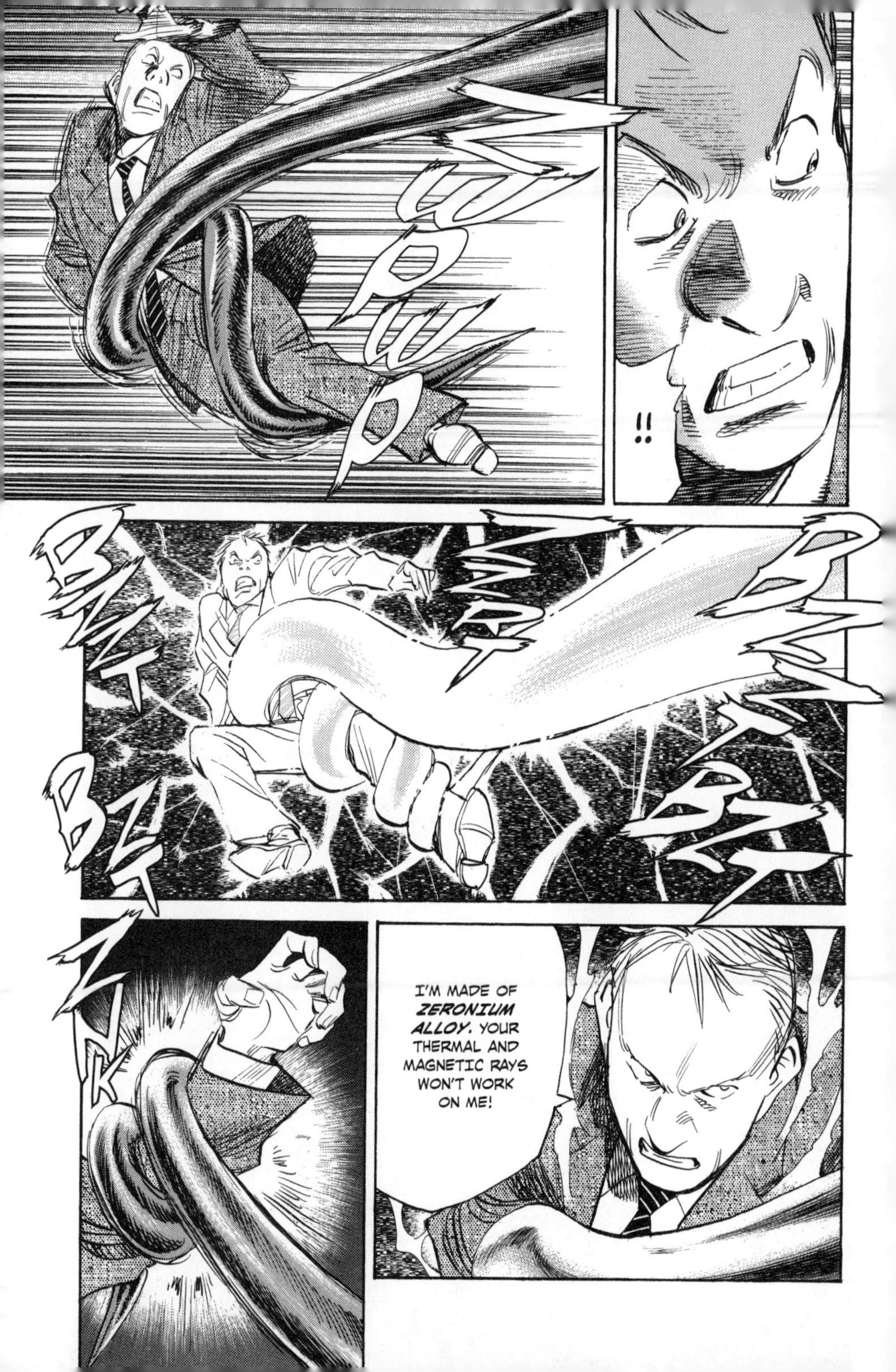
!!
I'M MADE OF ***ZERONIUM ALLOY.*** YOUR THERMAL AND MAGNETIC RAYS WON'T WORK ON ME!

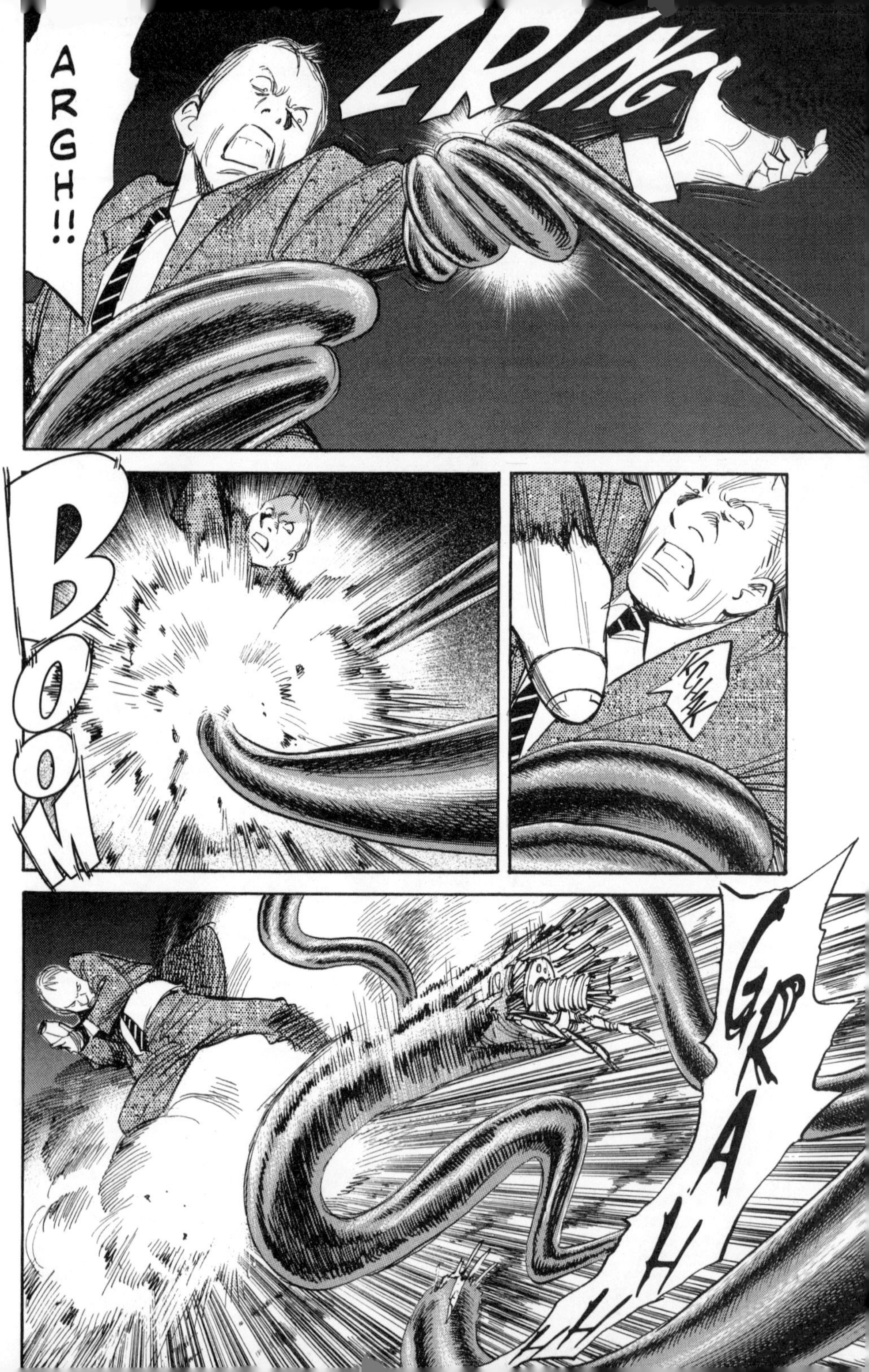
ARGH!!
ZRING
KCHAK
BOOOM
GRAHHHH

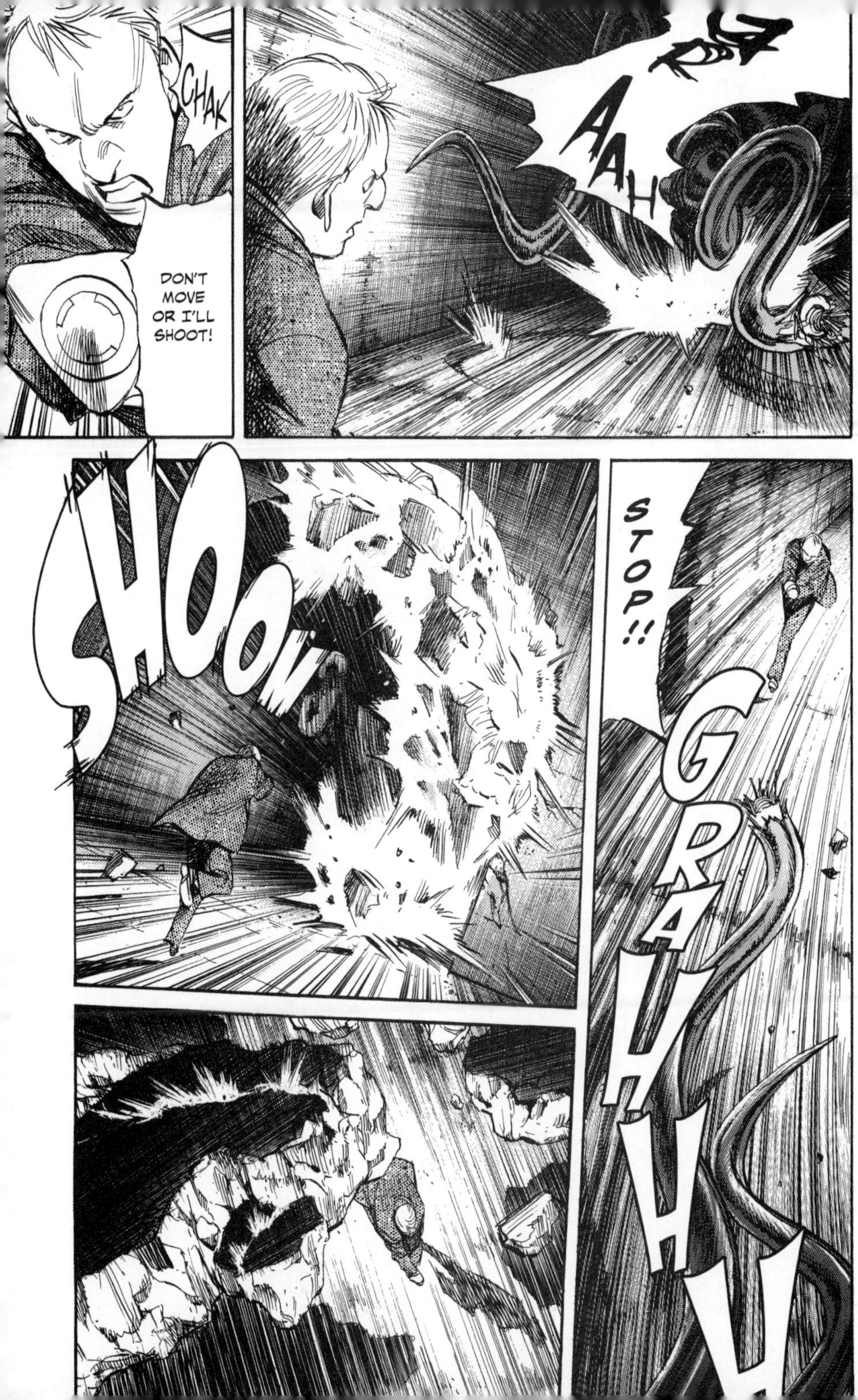
RAAH
CHAK
DON'T MOVE OR I'LL SHOOT!
STOP!!
GRAAHHH!!
SHOOM

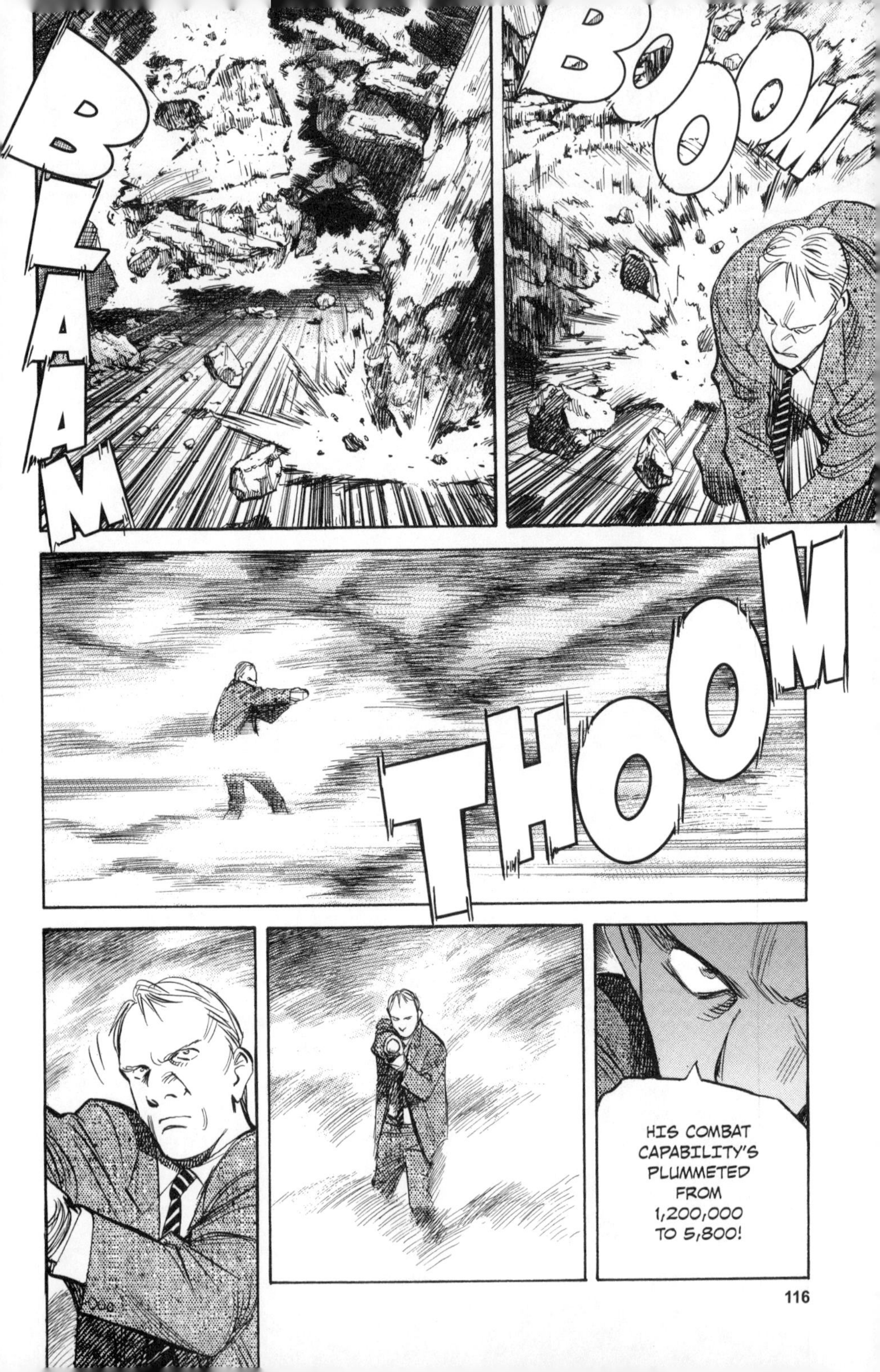
BOOOM
BLAAAM
THOOM
HIS COMBAT CAPABILITY'S PLUMMETED FROM 1,200,000 TO 5,800!

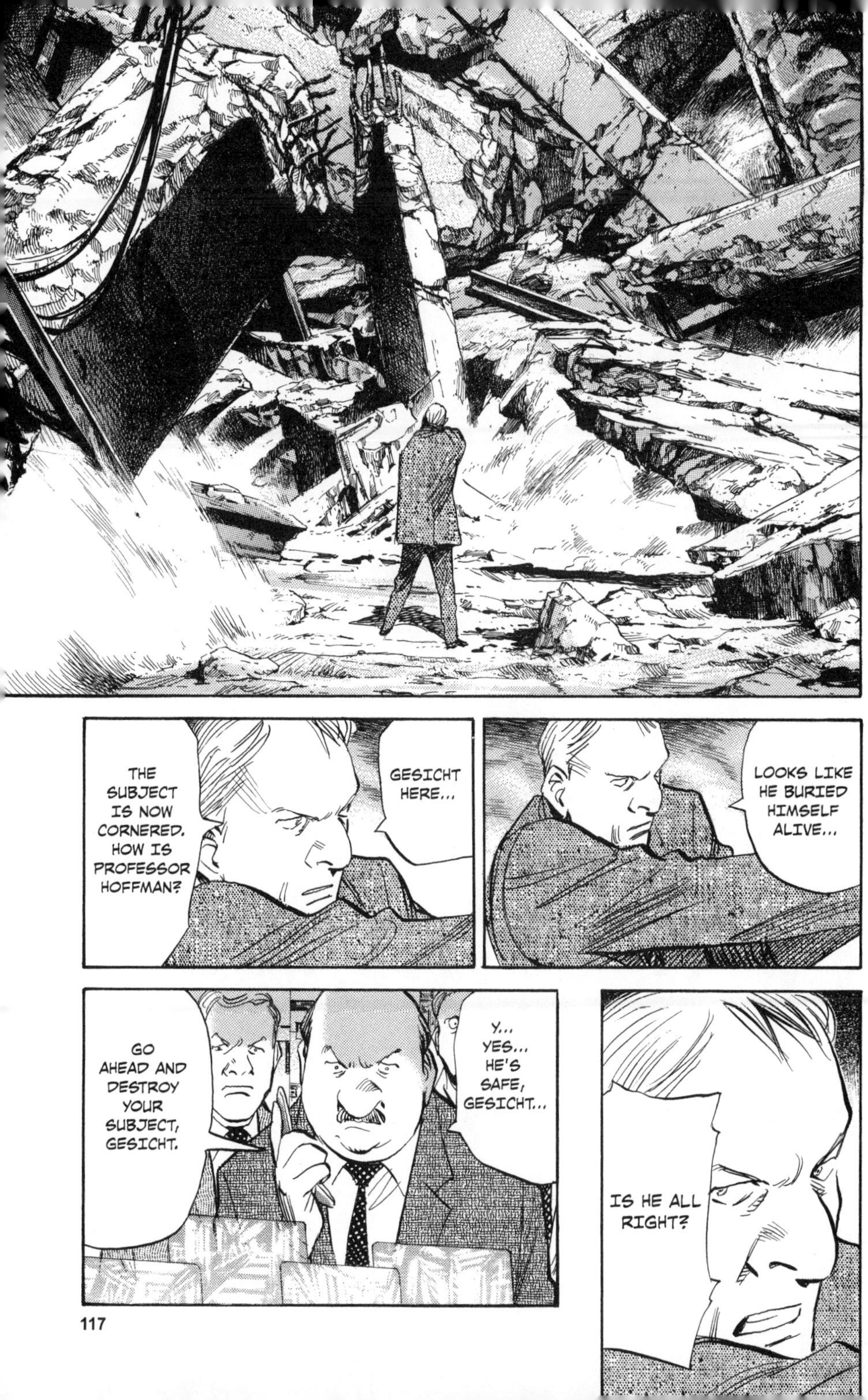
LOOKS LIKE HE BURIED HIMSELF ALIVE...
GESICHT HERE...
THE SUBJECT IS NOW CORNERED. HOW IS PROFESSOR HOFFMAN?
IS HE ALL RIGHT?
Y... YES... HE'S SAFE, GESICHT...
GO AHEAD AND DESTROY YOUR SUBJECT, GESICHT.

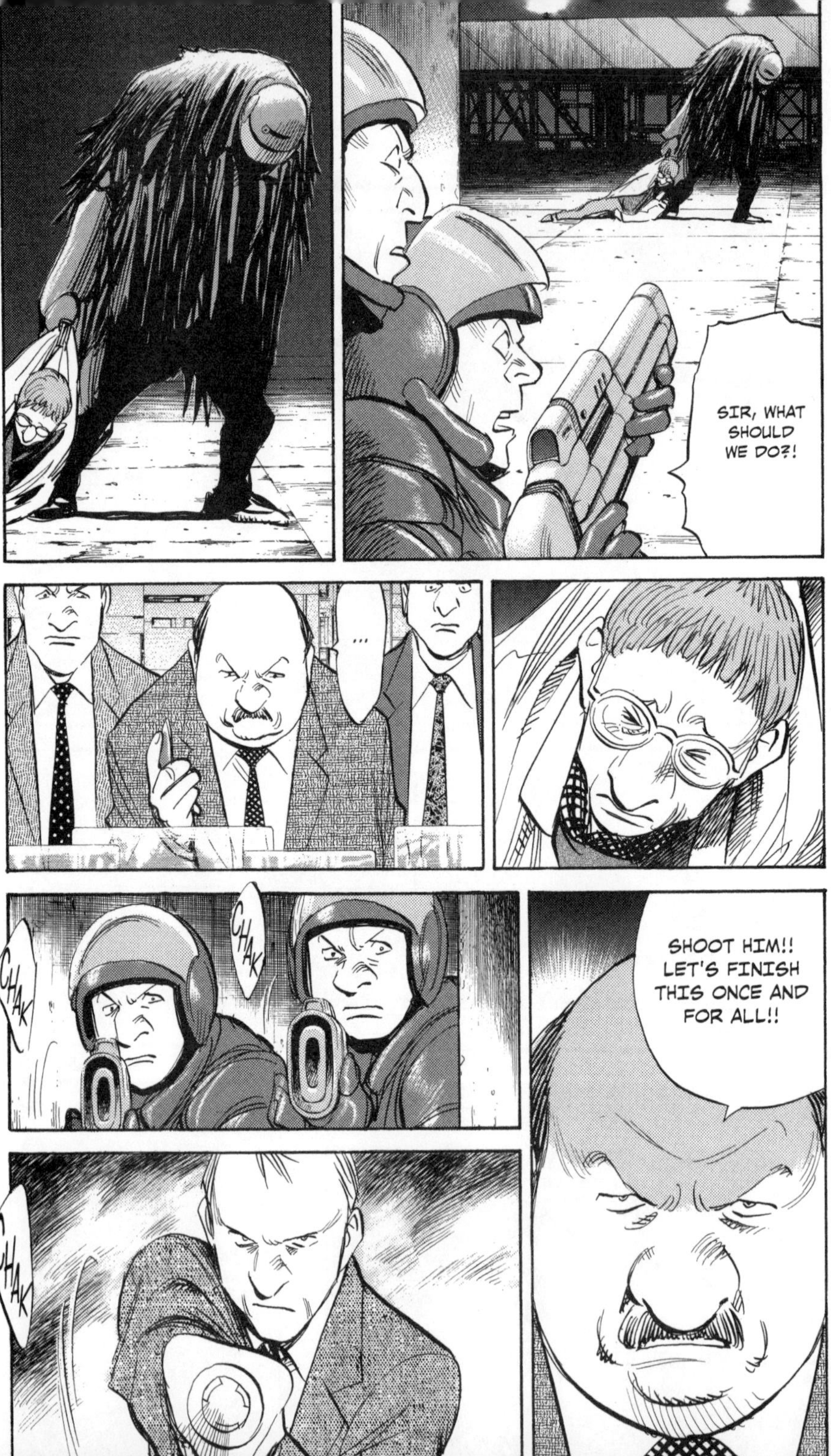
SIR, WHAT SHOULD WE DO?!
...
SHOOT HIM!! LET'S FINISH THIS ONCE AND FOR ALL!!
CHAK
CHAK
CHAK

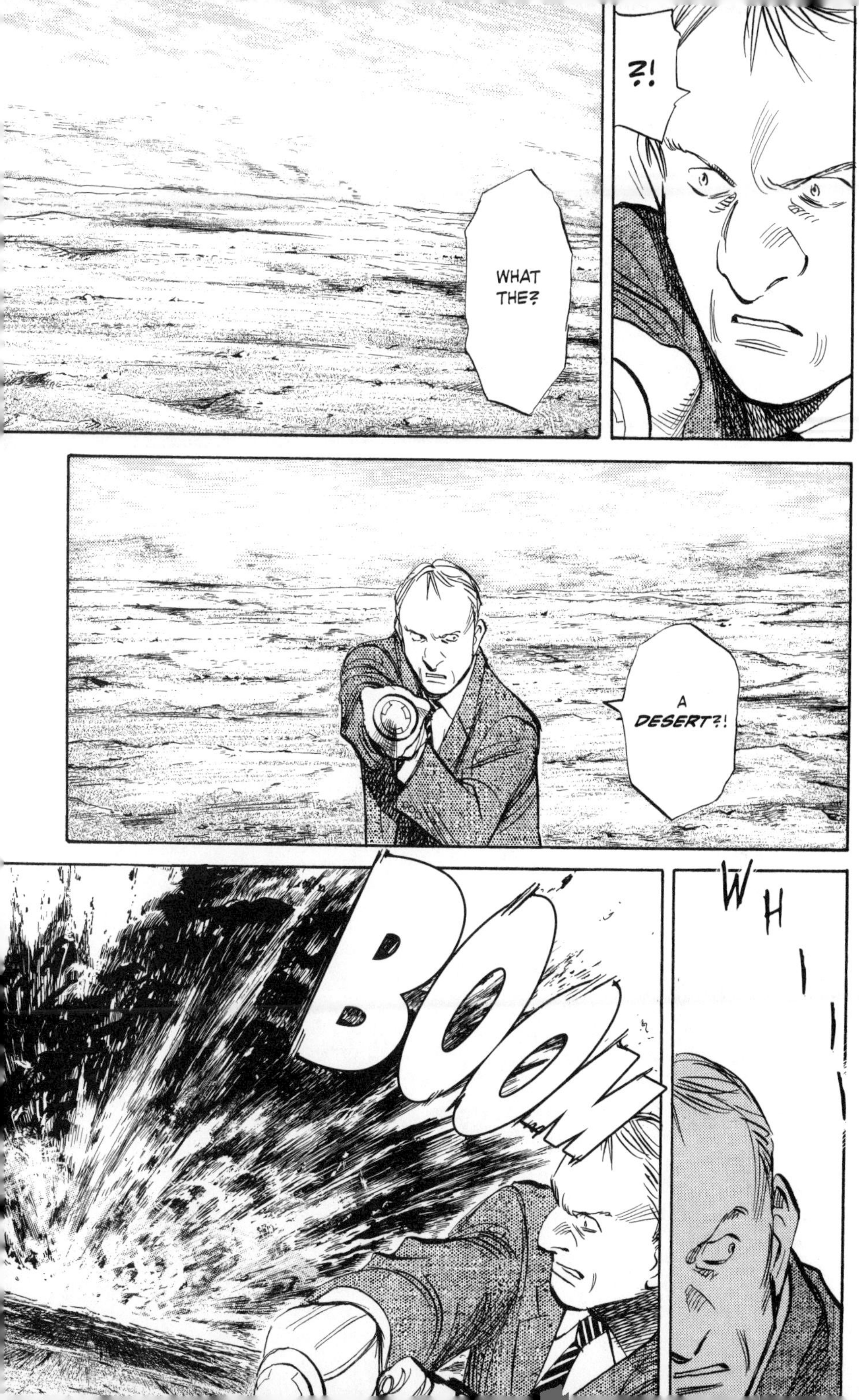
?!
WHAT THE?
A DESERT?!
WHIIII
BOOM

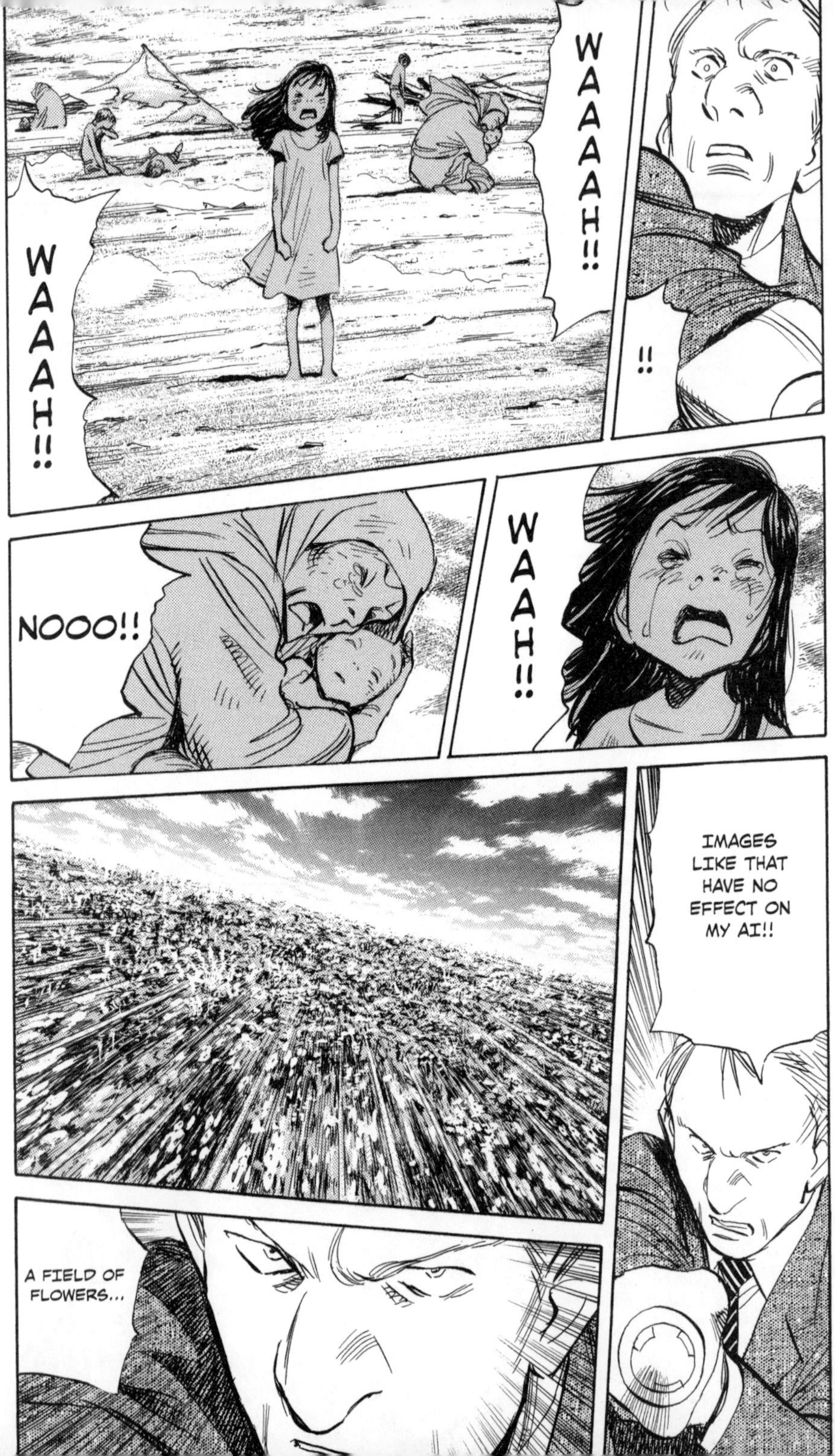
!!
WAAAAH!!
WAAAH!!
WAAH!!
NOOO!!
IMAGES LIKE THAT HAVE NO EFFECT ON MY AI!!
A FIELD OF FLOWERS...

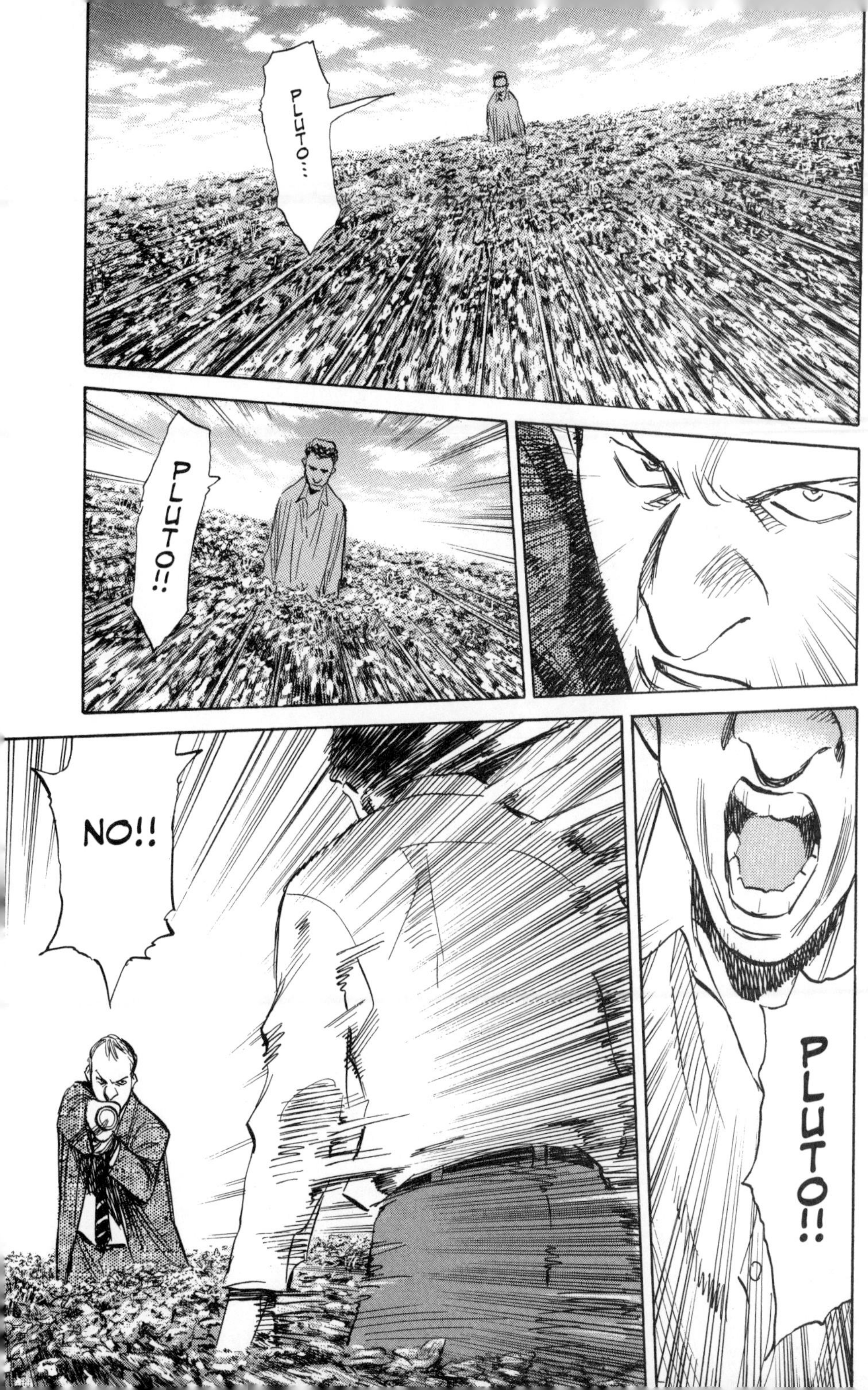
PLUTO...
PLUTO!!
PLUTO!!
NO!!

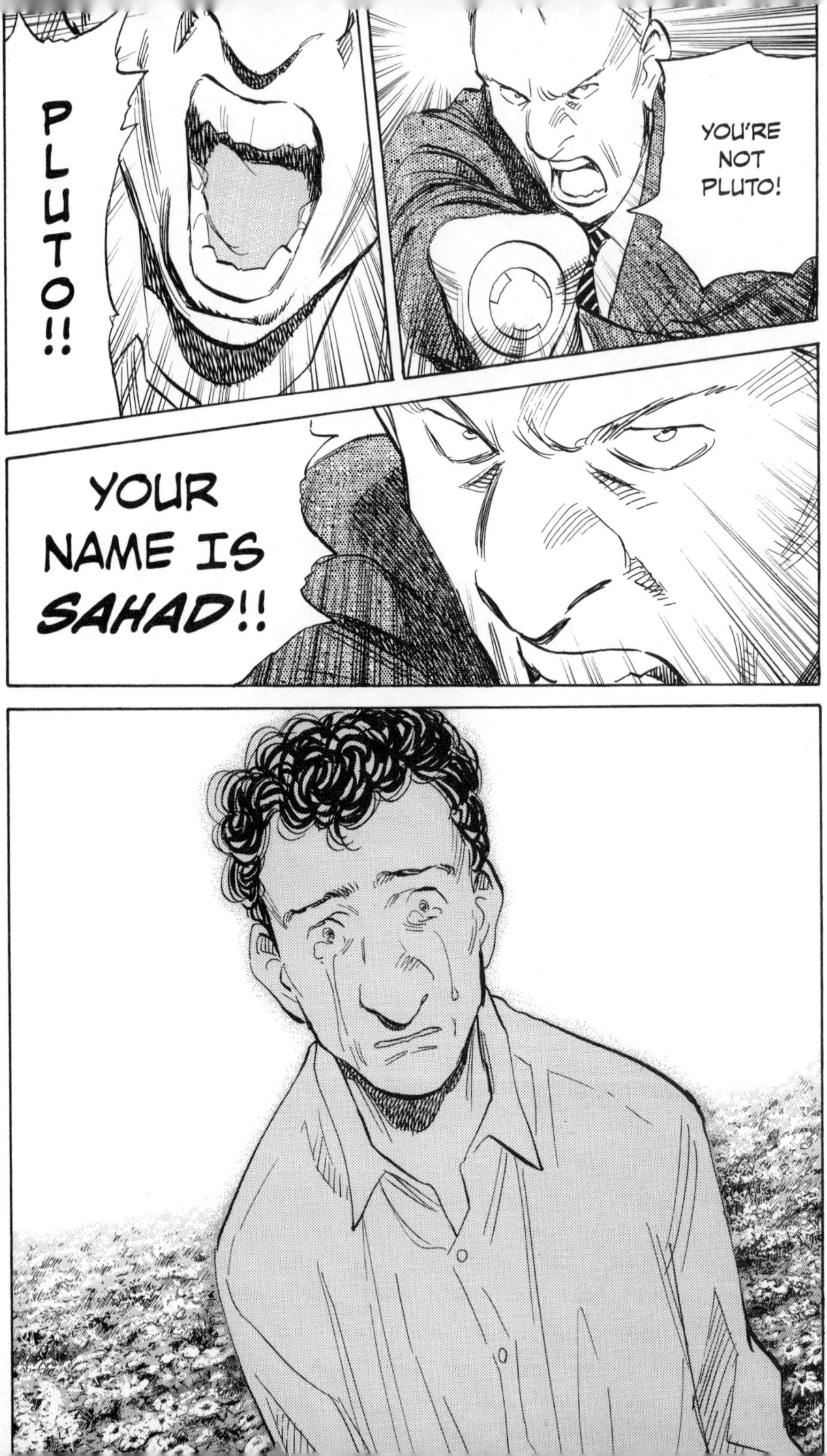
YOU'RE NOT PLUTO!
PLUTO!!
YOUR NAME IS *SAHAD*!!

Act 45 Negotiation and Reparation

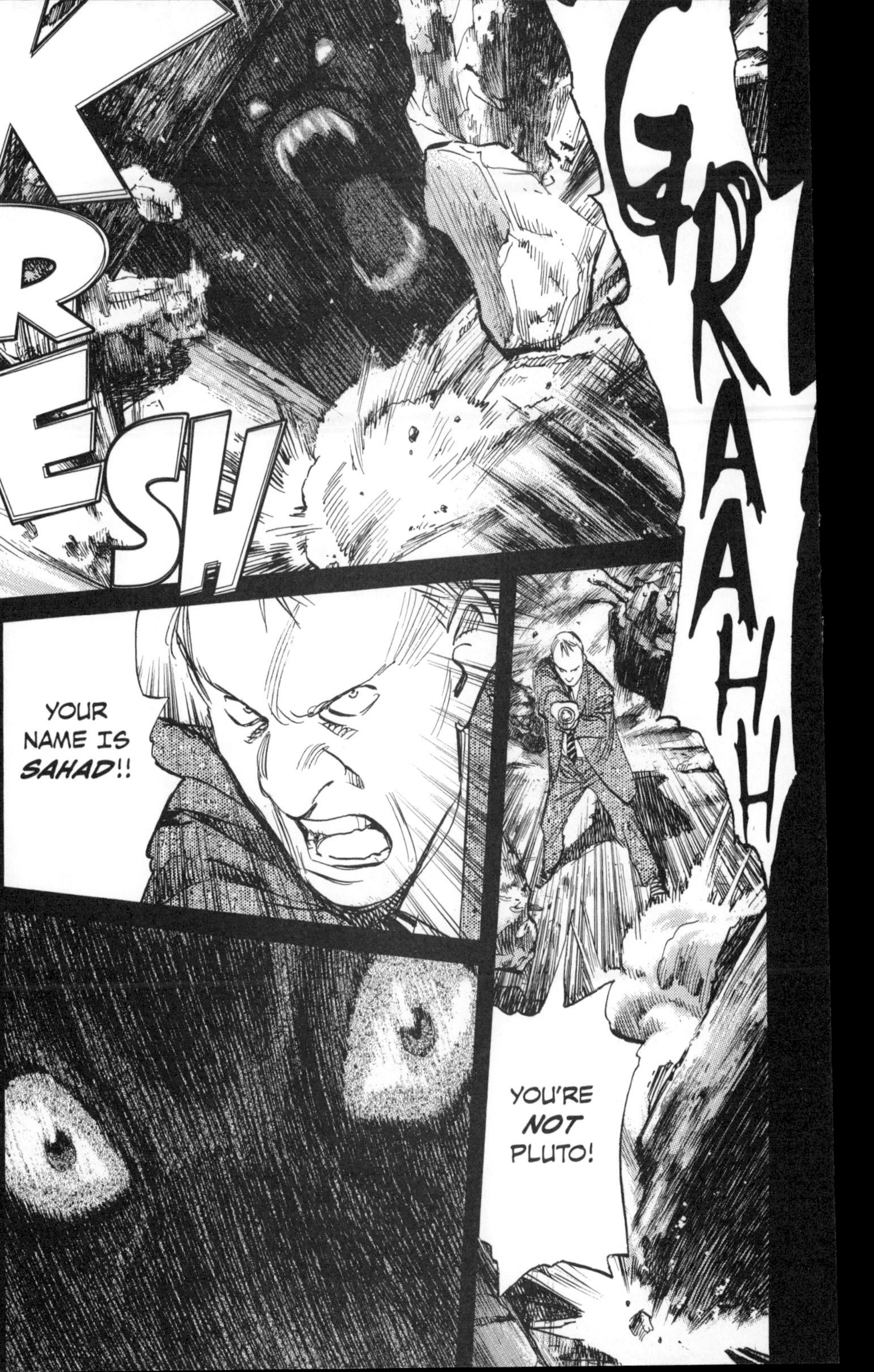
GRRAAHH
KRESH
YOUR NAME IS *SAHAD*!!
YOU'RE *NOT* PLUTO!

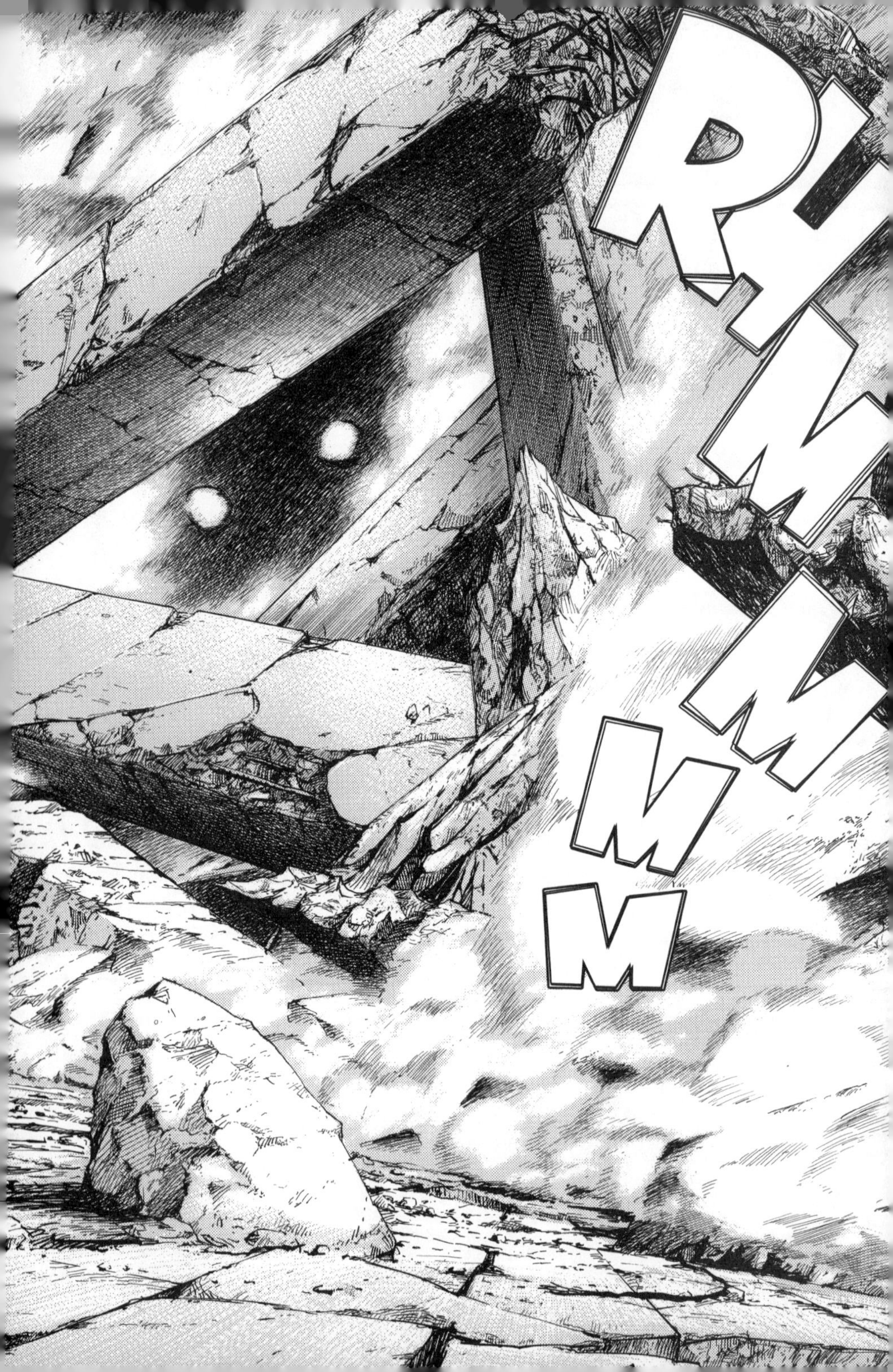
RUMMMM

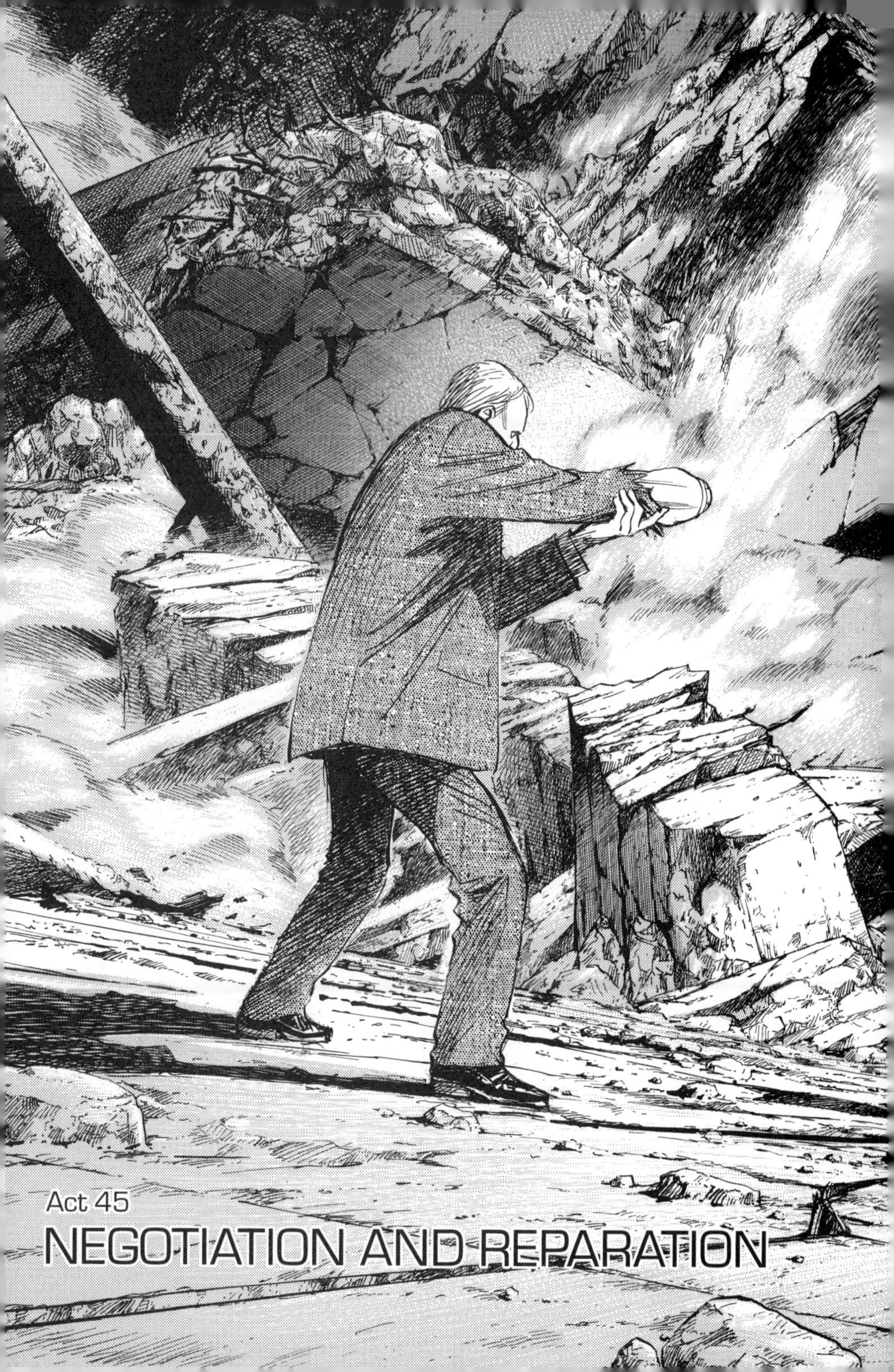
Act 45
NEGOTIATION AND REPARATION

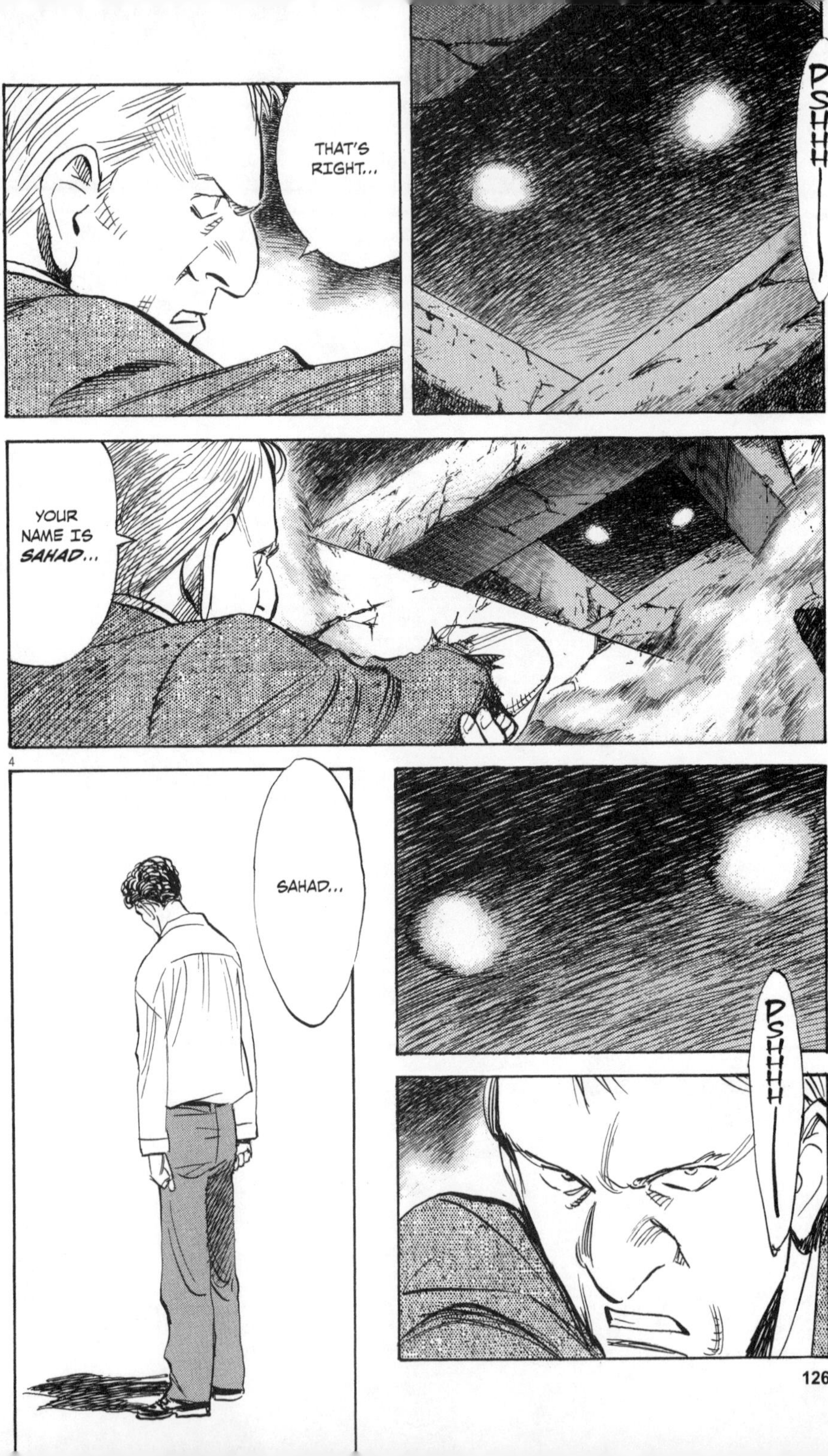

PSHHH—
THAT'S RIGHT...
YOUR NAME IS *SAHAD*...
PSHHHH—
SAHAD...

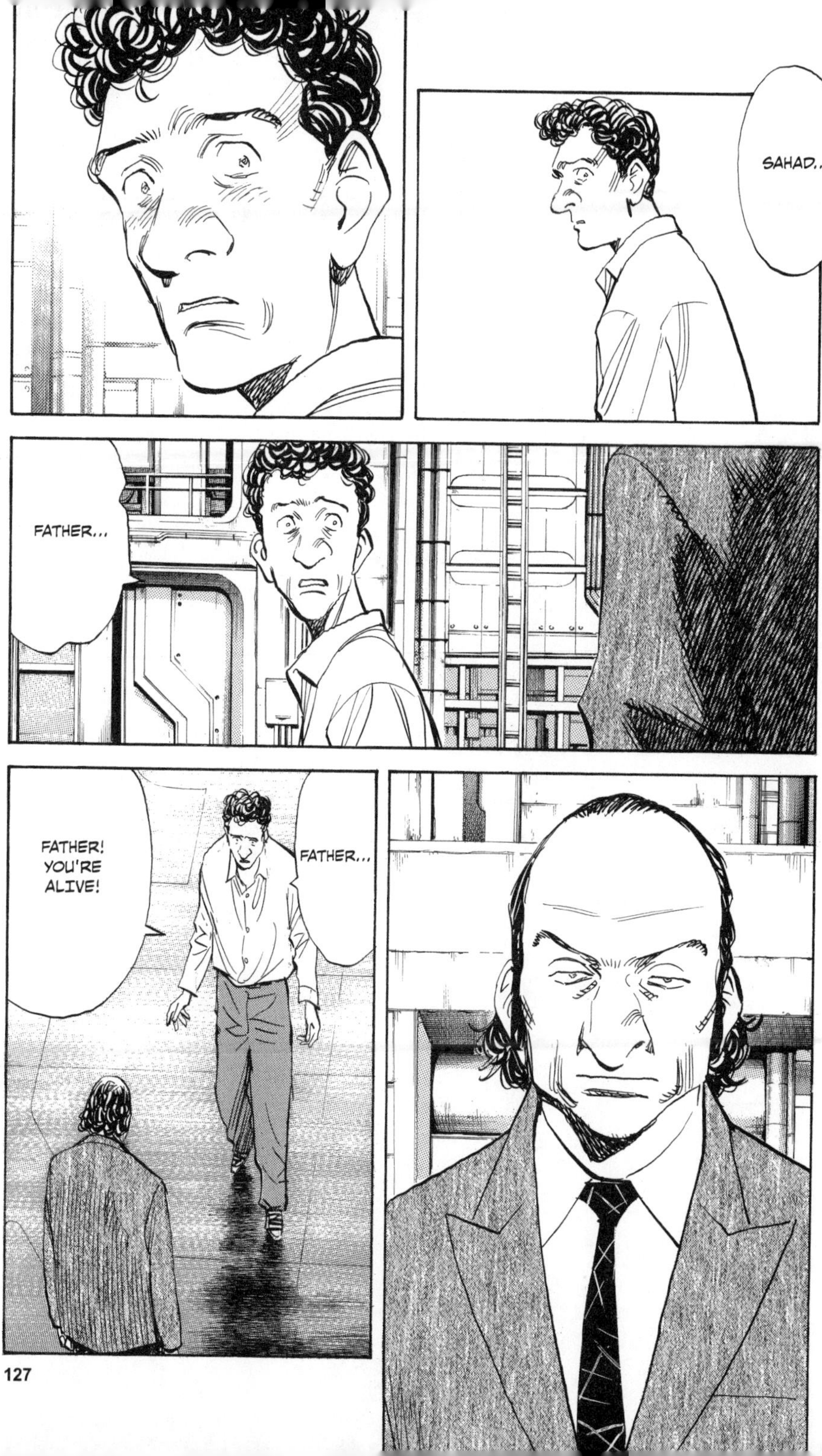
SAHAD...
FATHER...
FATHER...
FATHER! YOU'RE ALIVE!

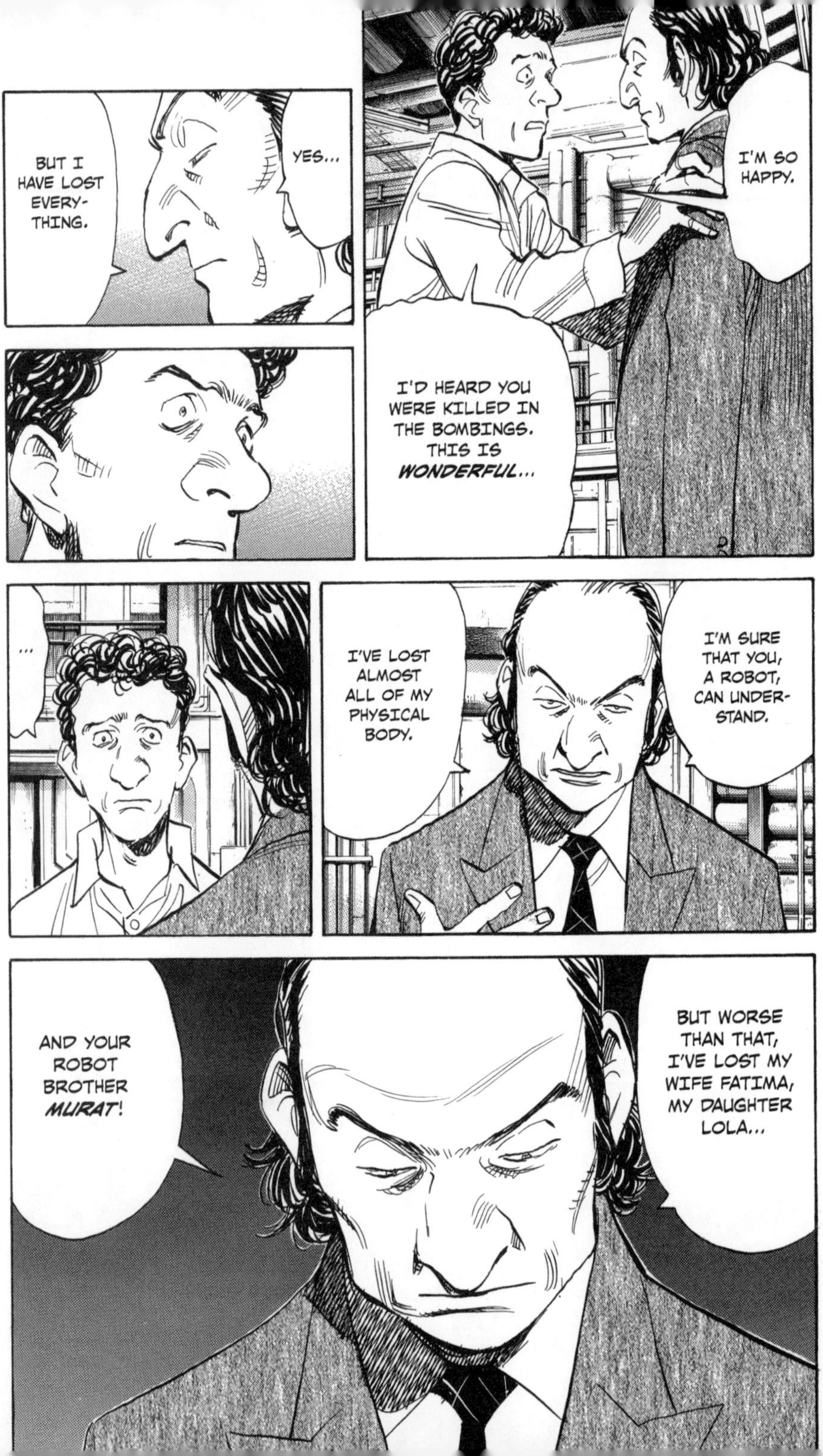
I'M SO HAPPY.
I'D HEARD YOU WERE KILLED IN THE BOMBINGS. THIS IS *WONDERFUL*...
YES...
BUT I HAVE LOST EVERY-THING.
I'M SURE THAT YOU, A ROBOT, CAN UNDER-STAND.
I'VE LOST ALMOST ALL OF MY PHYSICAL BODY.
...
BUT WORSE THAN THAT, I'VE LOST MY WIFE FATIMA, MY DAUGHTER LOLA...
AND YOUR ROBOT BROTHER *MURAT*!

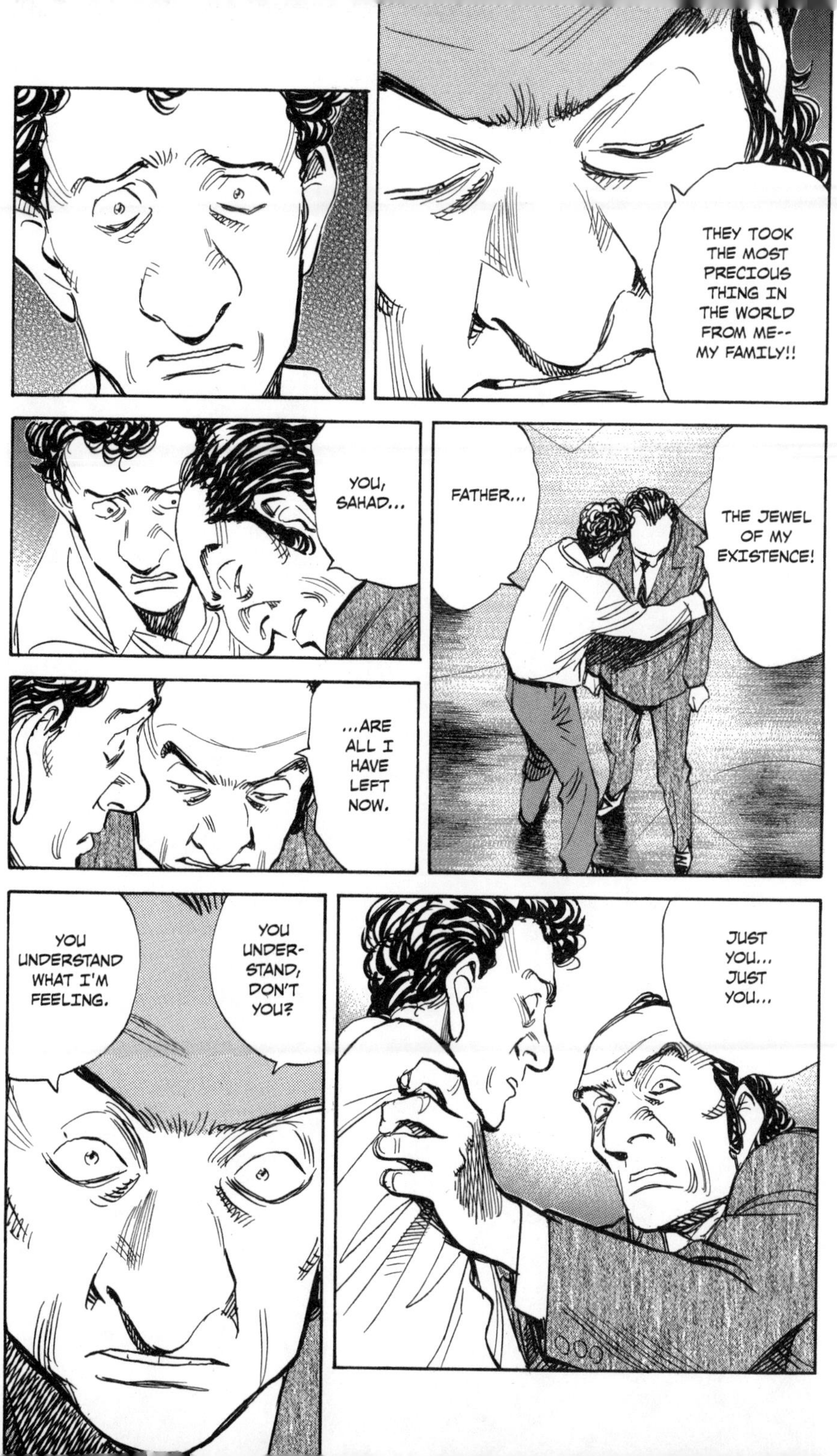
THEY TOOK THE MOST PRECIOUS THING IN THE WORLD FROM ME-- MY FAMILY!!
THE JEWEL OF MY EXISTENCE!
FATHER...
YOU, SAHAD...
...ARE ALL I HAVE LEFT NOW.
JUST YOU... JUST YOU...
YOU UNDER-STAND, DON'T YOU?
YOU UNDERSTAND WHAT I'M FEELING.

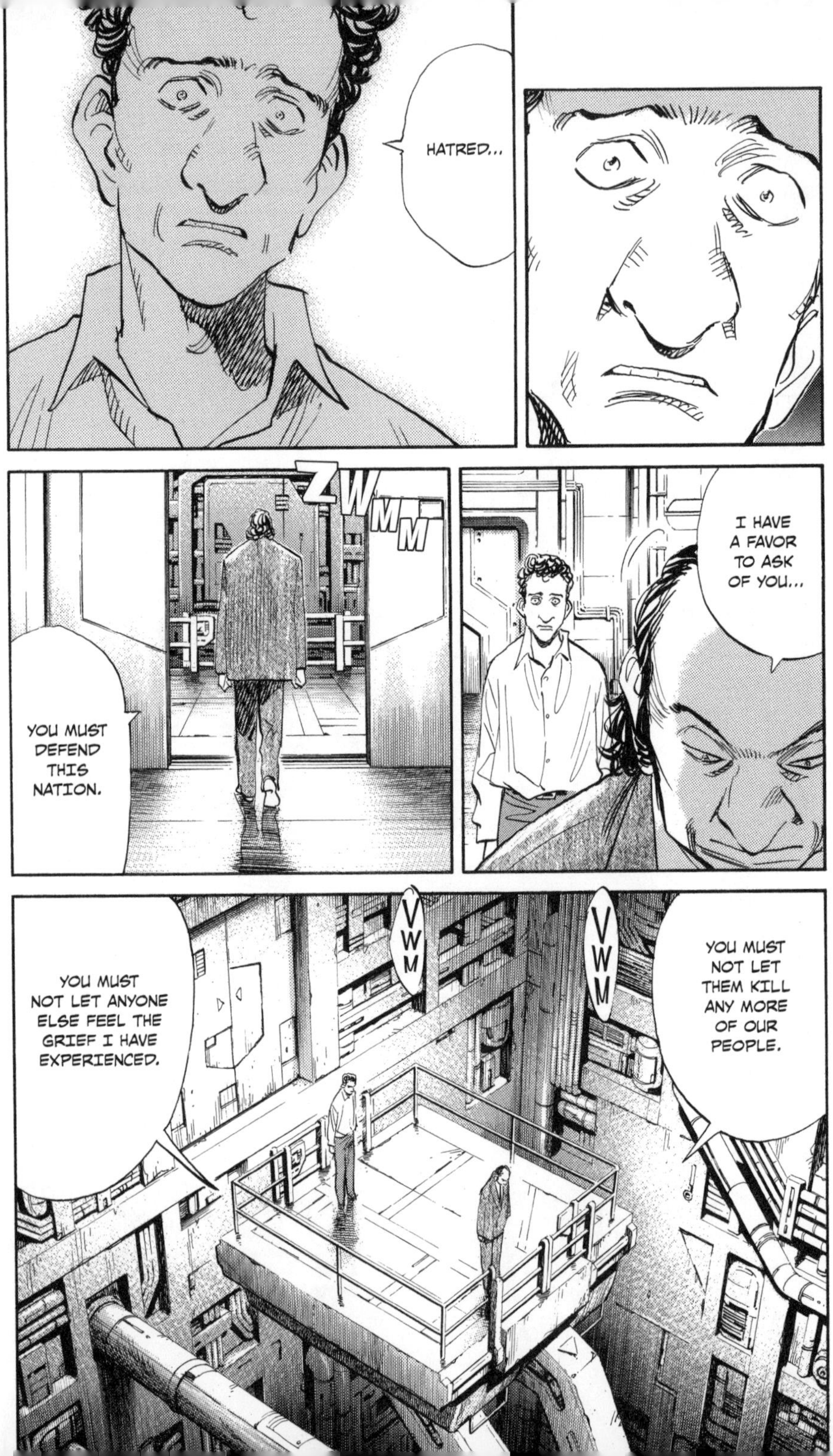
HATRED...
I HAVE A FAVOR TO ASK OF YOU...
ZWMMM
YOU MUST DEFEND THIS NATION.
YOU MUST NOT LET THEM KILL ANY MORE OF OUR PEOPLE.
VWM
VWM
YOU MUST NOT LET ANYONE ELSE FEEL THE GRIEF I HAVE EXPERIENCED.

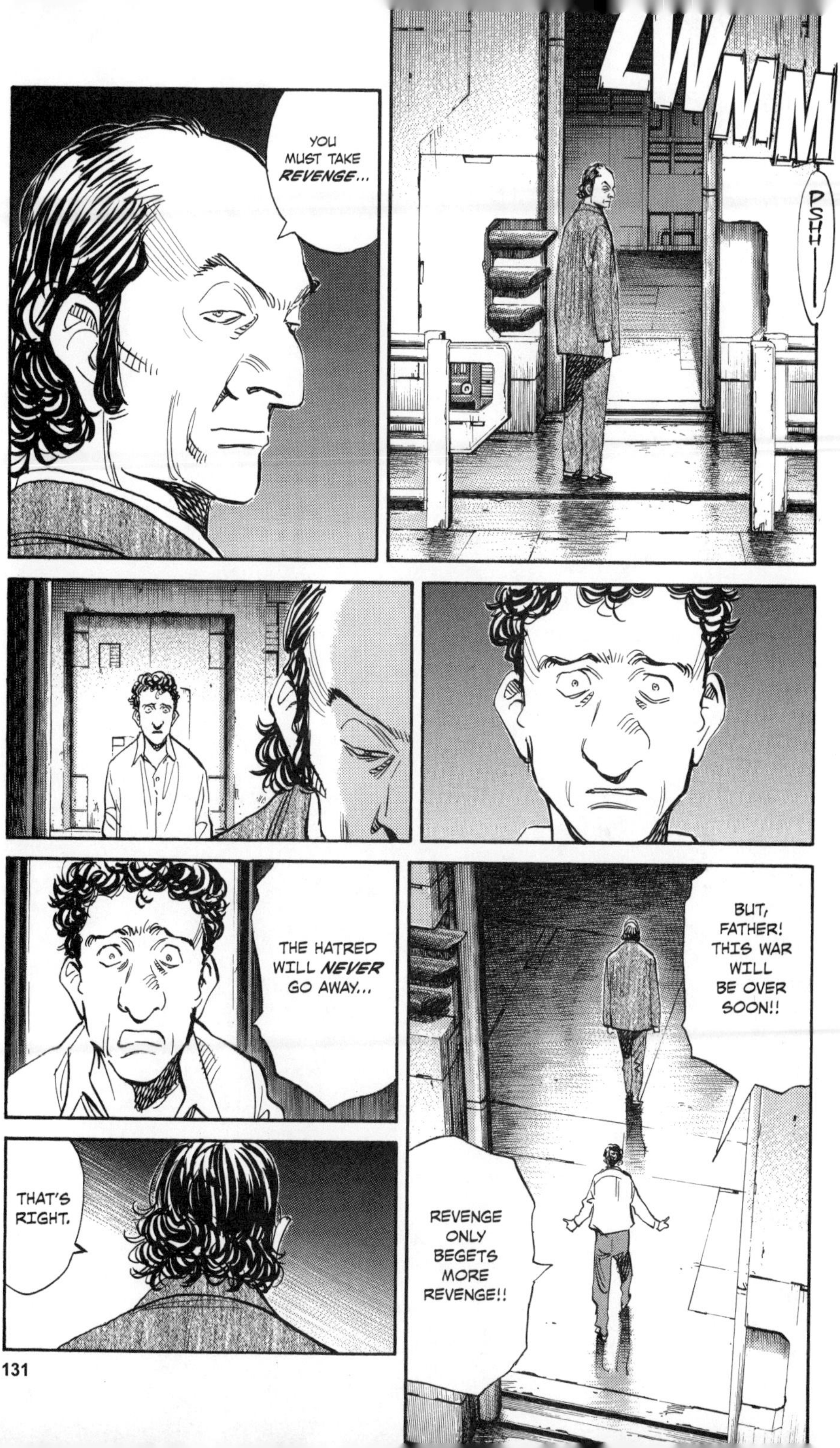
ZWMM
PSHH
YOU MUST TAKE *REVENGE*...
BUT, FATHER! THIS WAR WILL BE OVER SOON!!
REVENGE ONLY BEGETS MORE REVENGE!!
THE HATRED WILL *NEVER* GO AWAY...
THAT'S RIGHT.

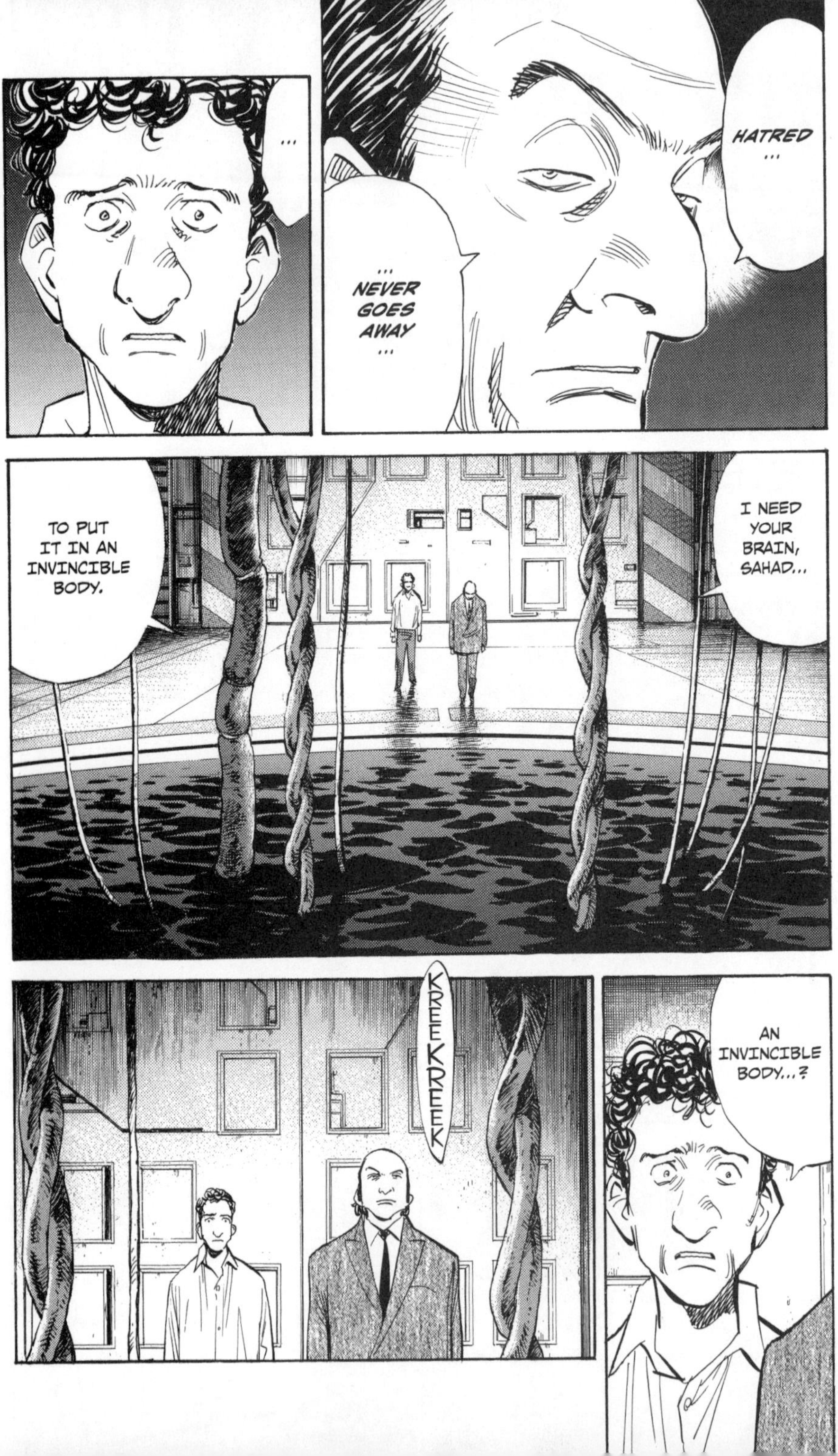
HATRED ...
... NEVER GOES AWAY ...
...
I NEED YOUR BRAIN, SAHAD...
TO PUT IT IN AN INVINCIBLE BODY.
AN INVINCIBLE BODY...?
KREEKKREEK

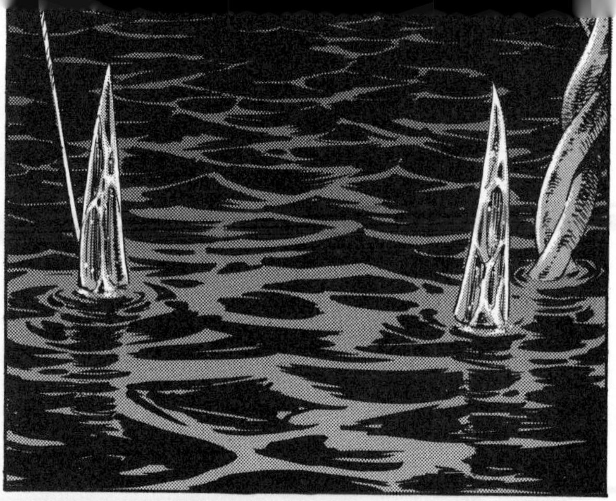

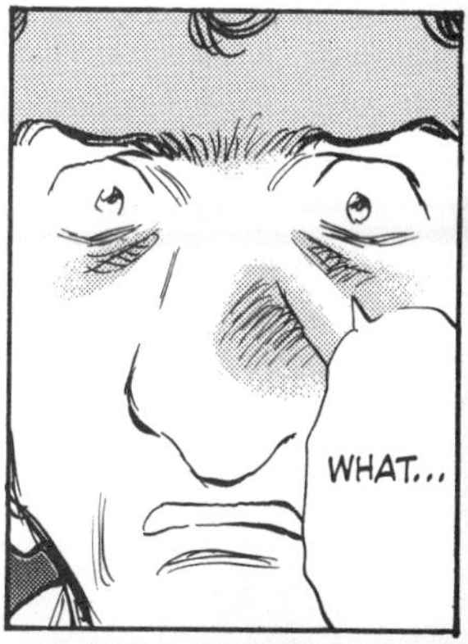
WHAT...

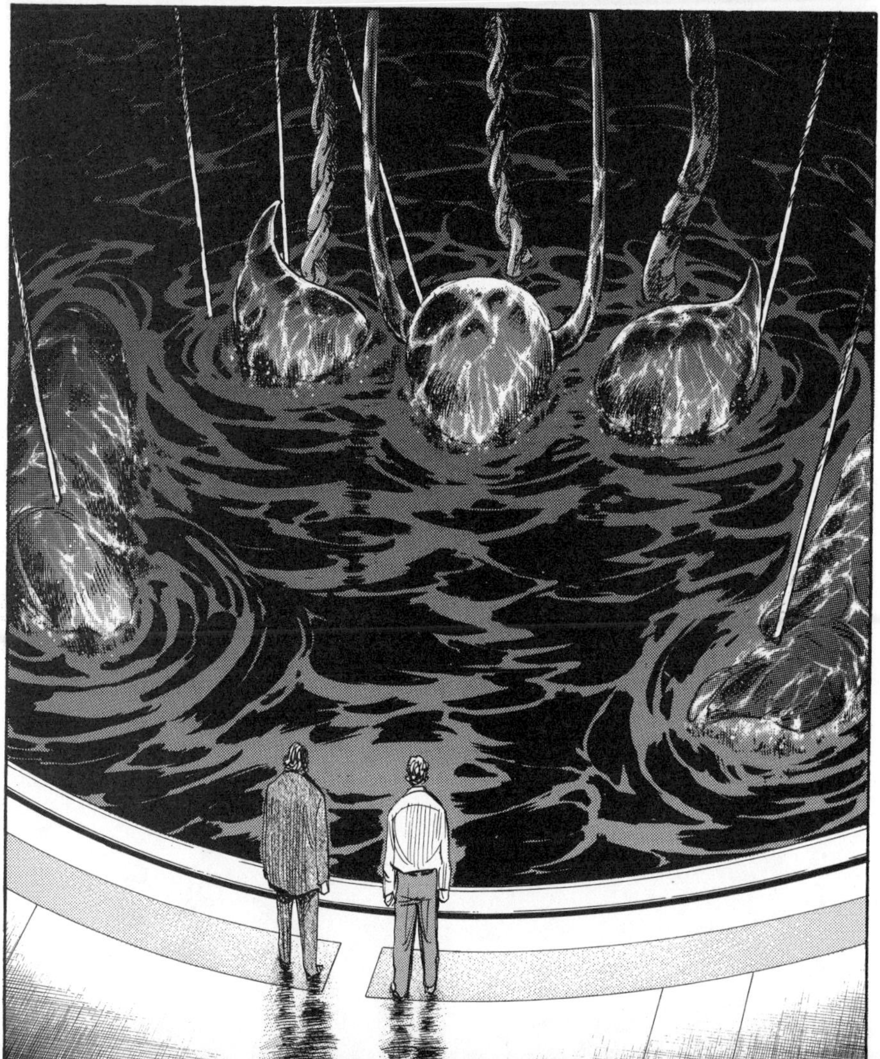

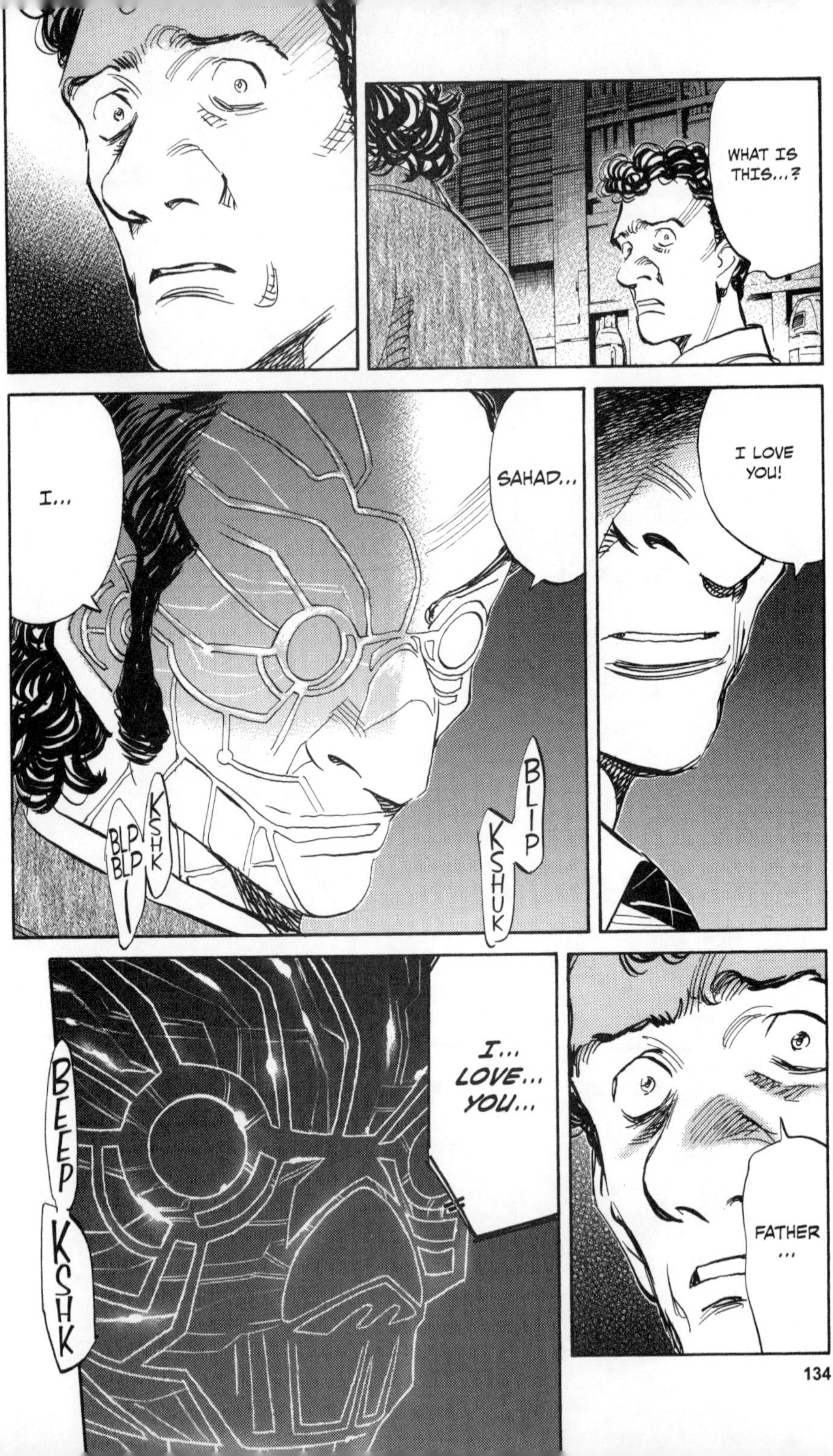
WHAT IS THIS...?
I LOVE YOU!
SAHAD...
I...
BLIP
KSHUK
KSHK
BLP BLP
FATHER ...
I... LOVE... YOU...
BEEEP
KSHK

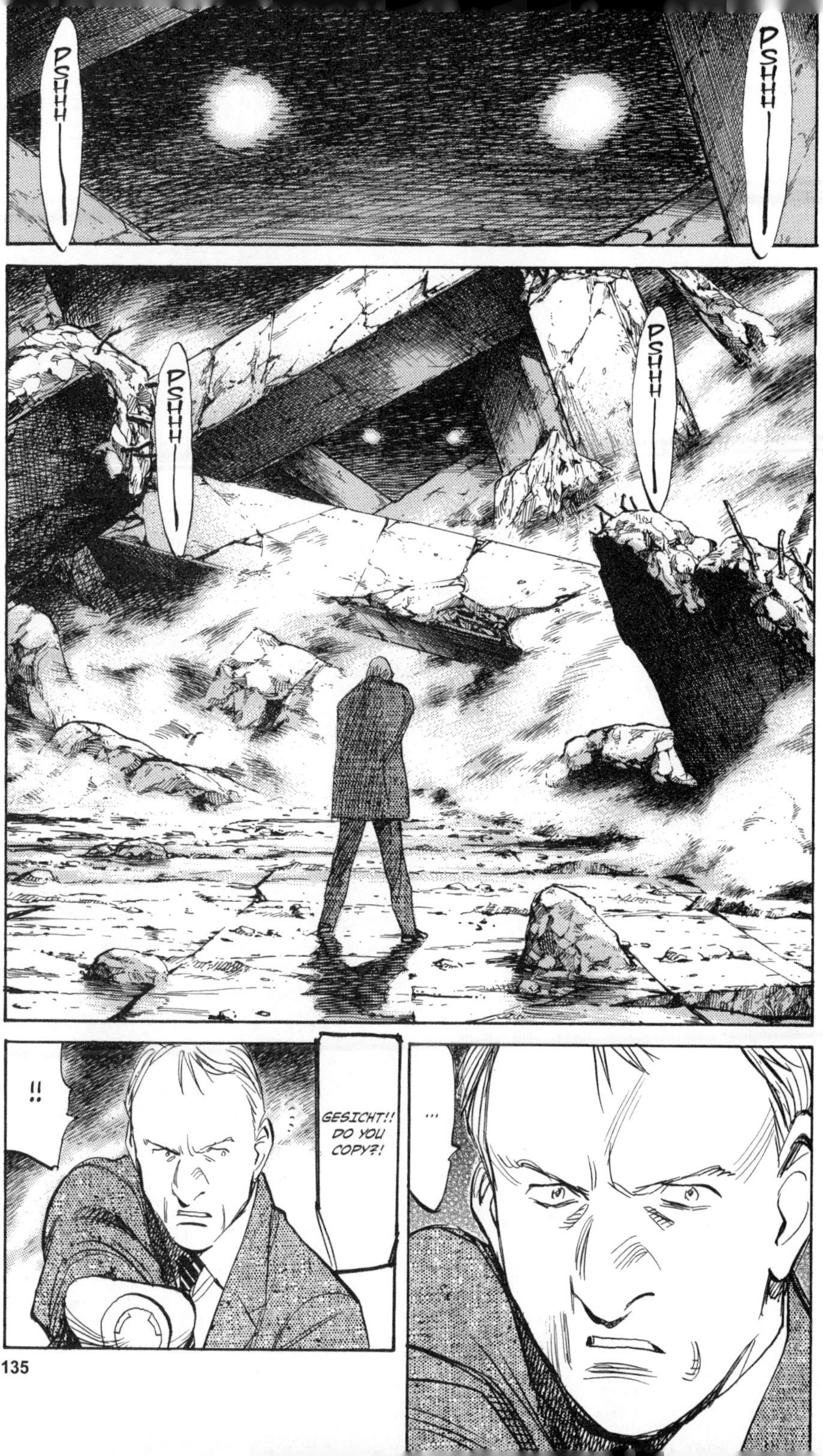
PSHHH—
PSHHH—
PSHHH—
PSHHH—
...
GESICHT!! DO YOU COPY?!
...
!!

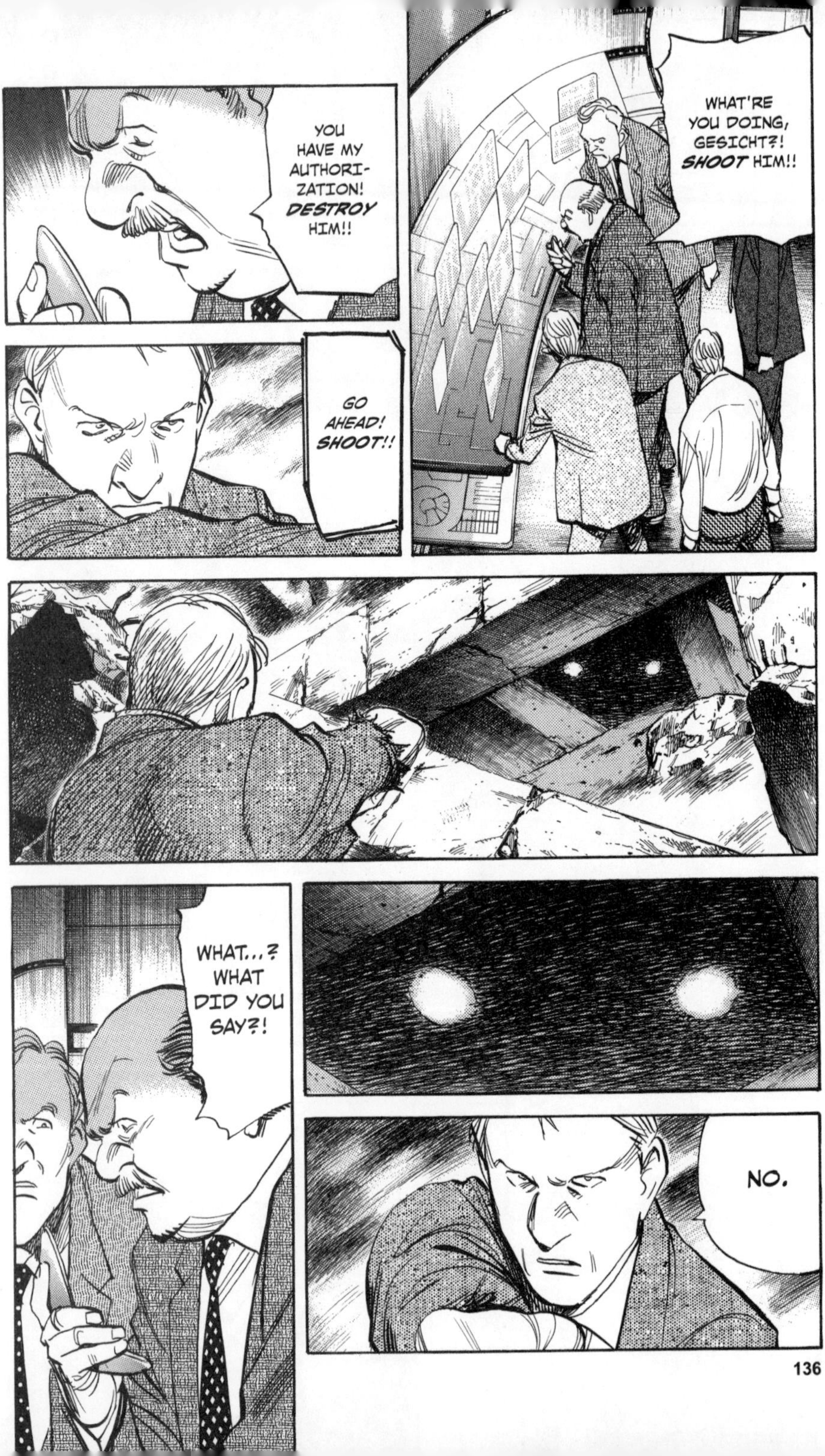
WHAT'RE YOU DOING, GESICHT?! SHOOT HIM!!
YOU HAVE MY AUTHORIZATION! DESTROY HIM!!
GO AHEAD! SHOOT!!
NO.
WHAT...? WHAT DID YOU SAY?!

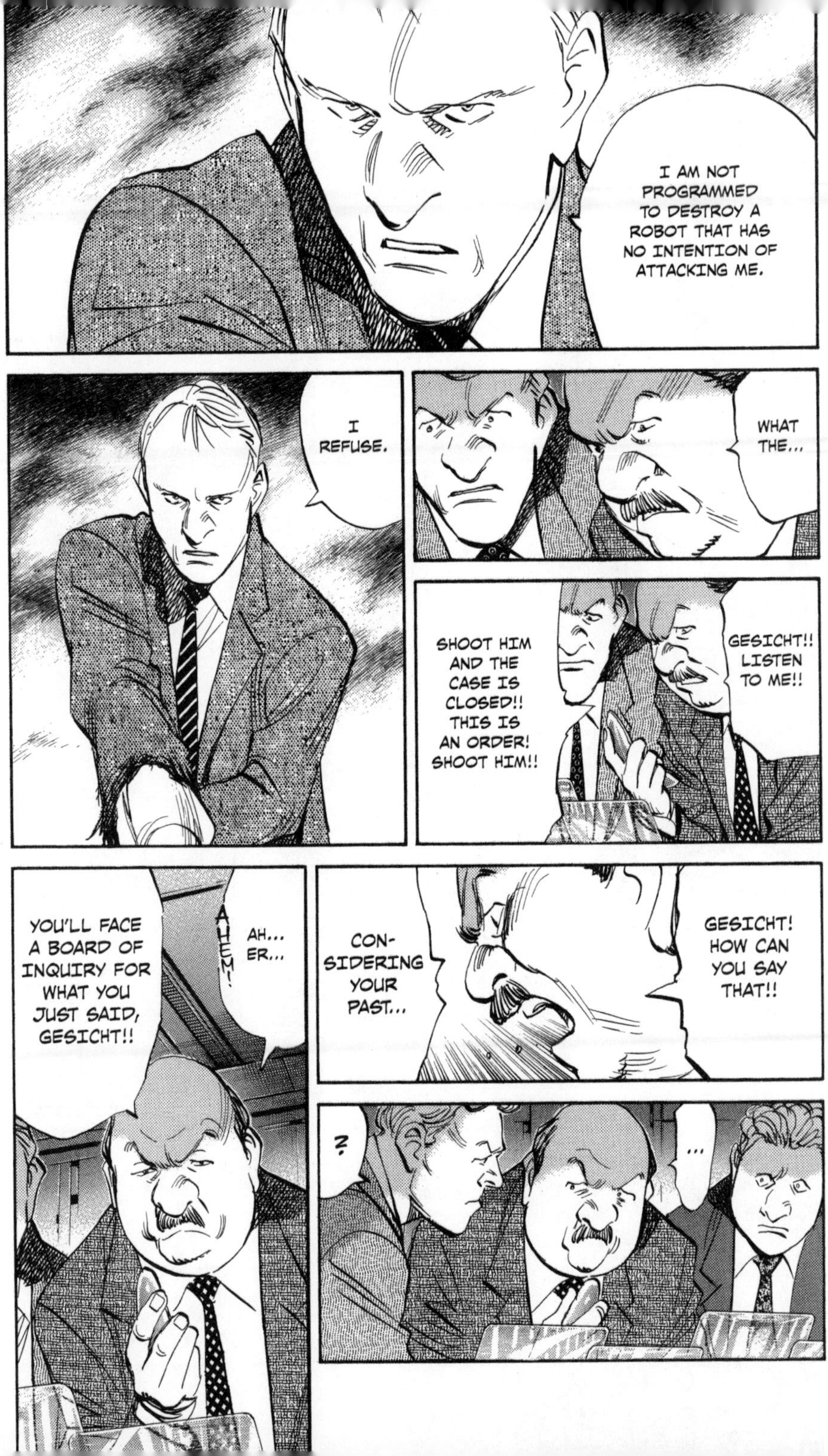
I AM NOT PROGRAMMED TO DESTROY A ROBOT THAT HAS NO INTENTION OF ATTACKING ME.
WHAT THE...
GESICHT!! LISTEN TO ME!!
SHOOT HIM AND THE CASE IS CLOSED!! THIS IS AN ORDER! SHOOT HIM!!
I REFUSE.
GESICHT! HOW CAN YOU SAY THAT!!
CON-SIDERING YOUR PAST...
...
?
AH... ER...
AHEM!
YOU'LL FACE A BOARD OF INQUIRY FOR WHAT YOU JUST SAID, GESICHT!!

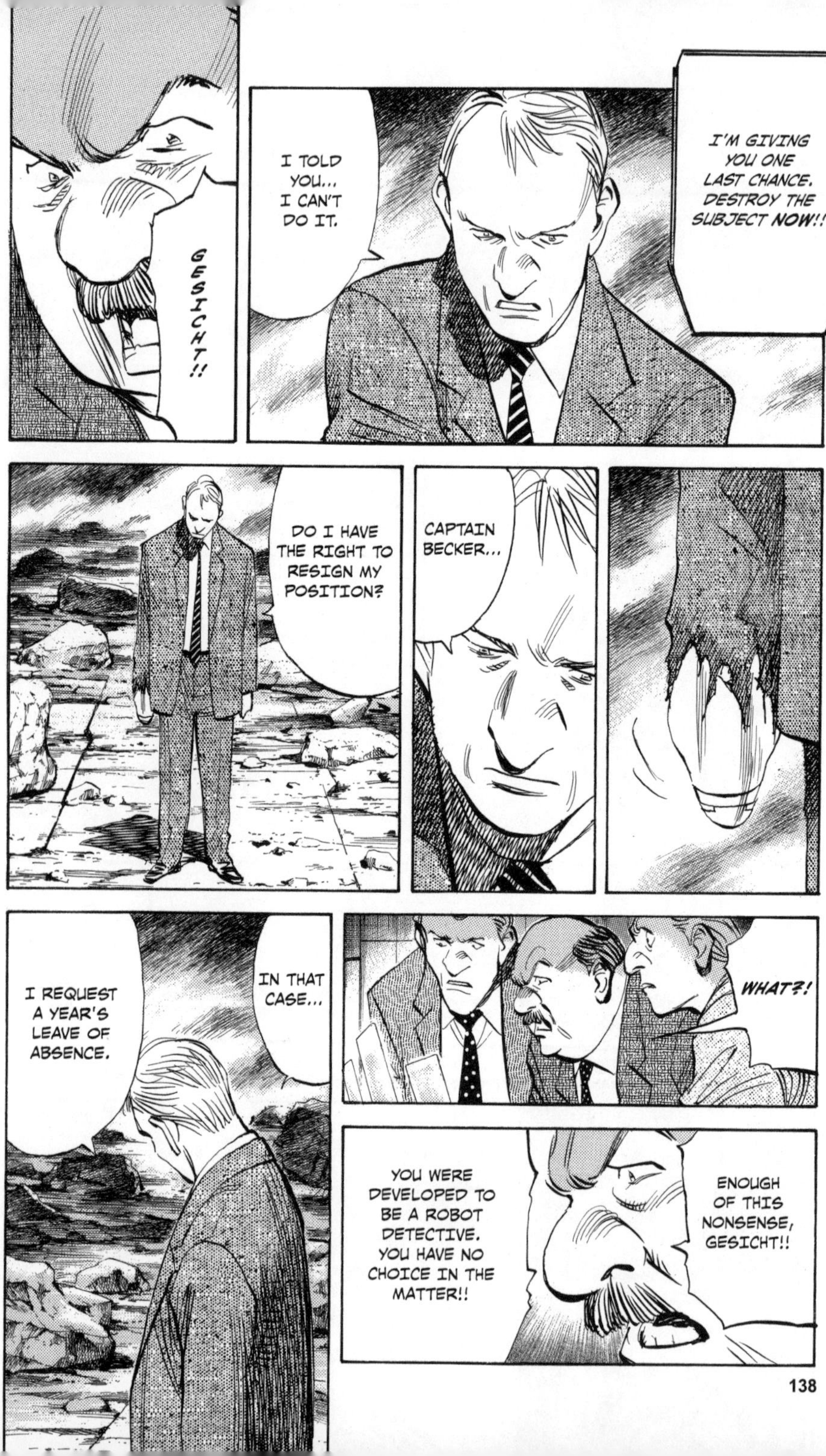
I'M GIVING YOU ONE LAST CHANCE. DESTROY THE SUBJECT **NOW**!!
I TOLD YOU... I CAN'T DO IT.
GESICHT!!
CAPTAIN BECKER...
DO I HAVE THE RIGHT TO RESIGN MY POSITION?
WHAT?!
ENOUGH OF THIS NONSENSE, GESICHT!!
YOU WERE DEVELOPED TO BE A ROBOT DETECTIVE. YOU HAVE NO CHOICE IN THE MATTER!!
IN THAT CASE...
I REQUEST A YEAR'S LEAVE OF ABSENCE.

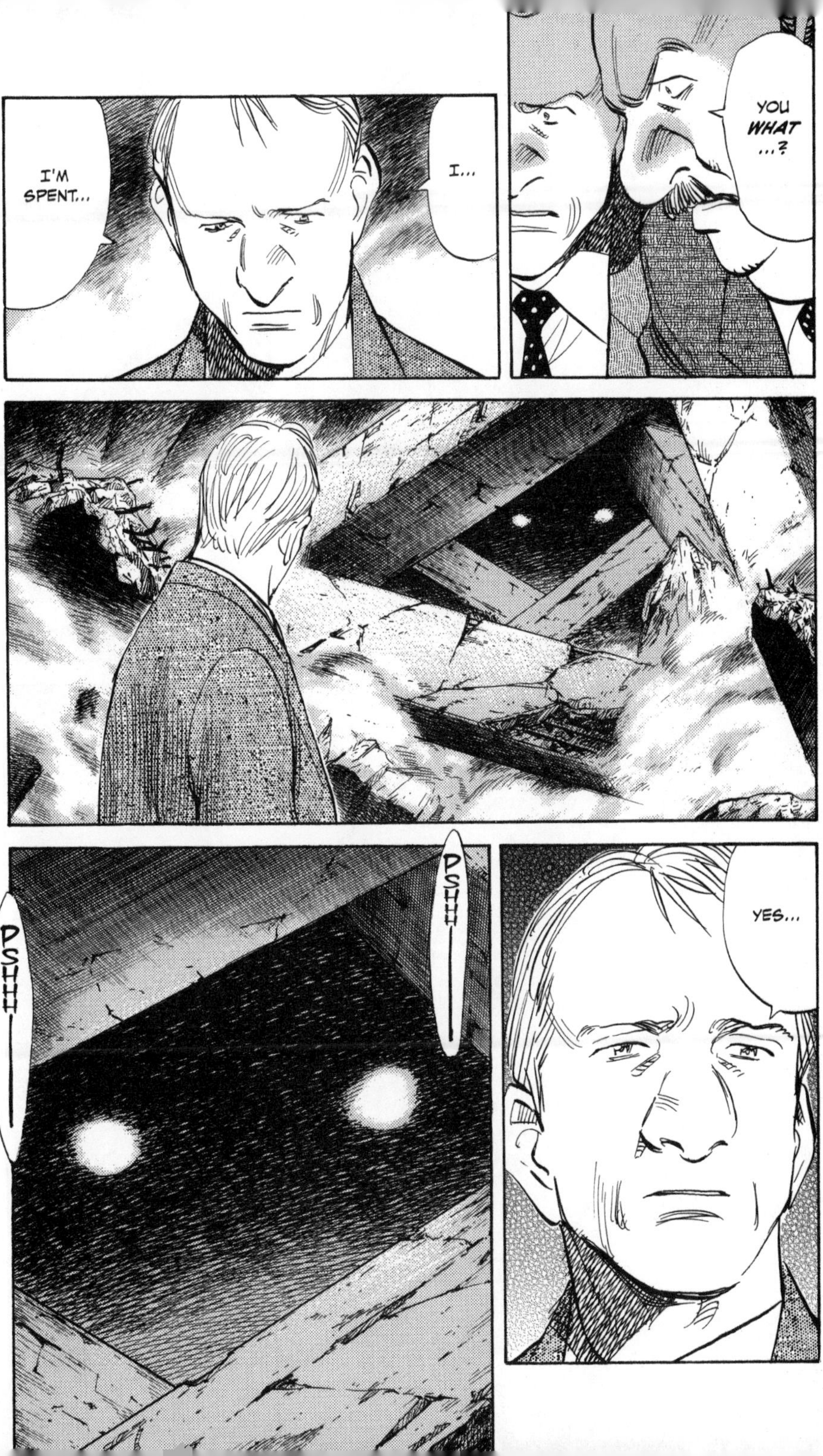
YOU WHAT ...?
I...
I'M SPENT...
YES...
PSHHH—
PSHHH—

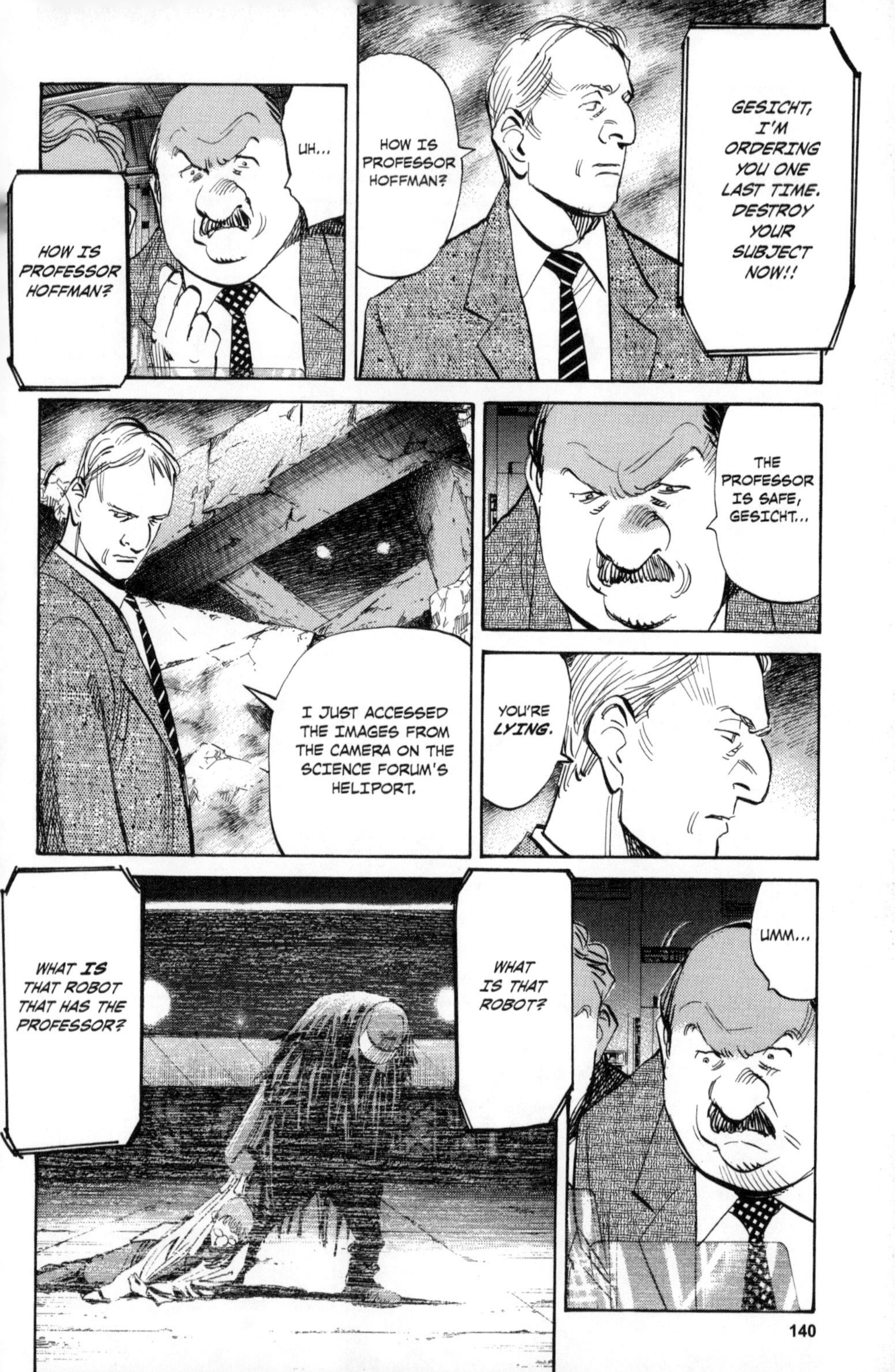
GESICHT, I'M ORDERING YOU ONE LAST TIME. DESTROY YOUR SUBJECT NOW!!
HOW IS PROFESSOR HOFFMAN?
UH...
HOW IS PROFESSOR HOFFMAN?
THE PROFESSOR IS SAFE, GESICHT...
YOU'RE LYING.
I JUST ACCESSED THE IMAGES FROM THE CAMERA ON THE SCIENCE FORUM'S HELIPORT.
UMM...
WHAT IS THAT ROBOT?
WHAT IS THAT ROBOT THAT HAS THE PROFESSOR?

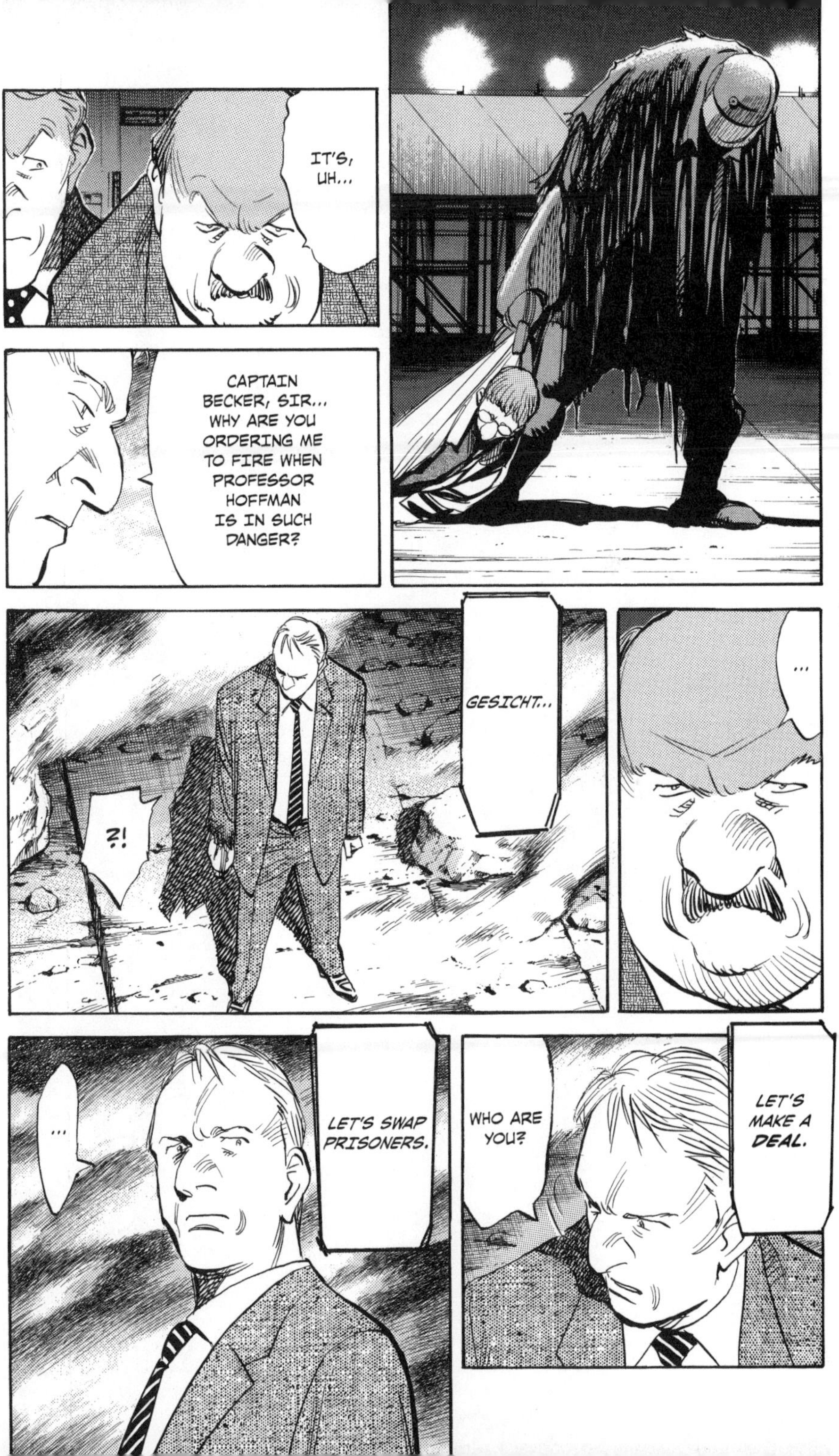
IT'S, UH...
CAPTAIN BECKER, SIR... WHY ARE YOU ORDERING ME TO FIRE WHEN PROFESSOR HOFFMAN IS IN SUCH DANGER?
...
GESICHT...
?!
LET'S MAKE A DEAL.
WHO ARE YOU?
LET'S SWAP PRISONERS.
...

WHO ARE YOU?

RELEASE MY BELOVED PLUTO.

STEP AWAY FROM THERE, AND I'LL GIVE PROFESSOR HOFFMAN HIS FREEDOM.

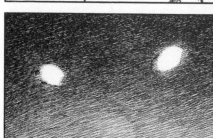

I WON'T TOLERATE ANY INSUBORDI-NATION, GESICHT!!

GESICHT ...?!

SHUF

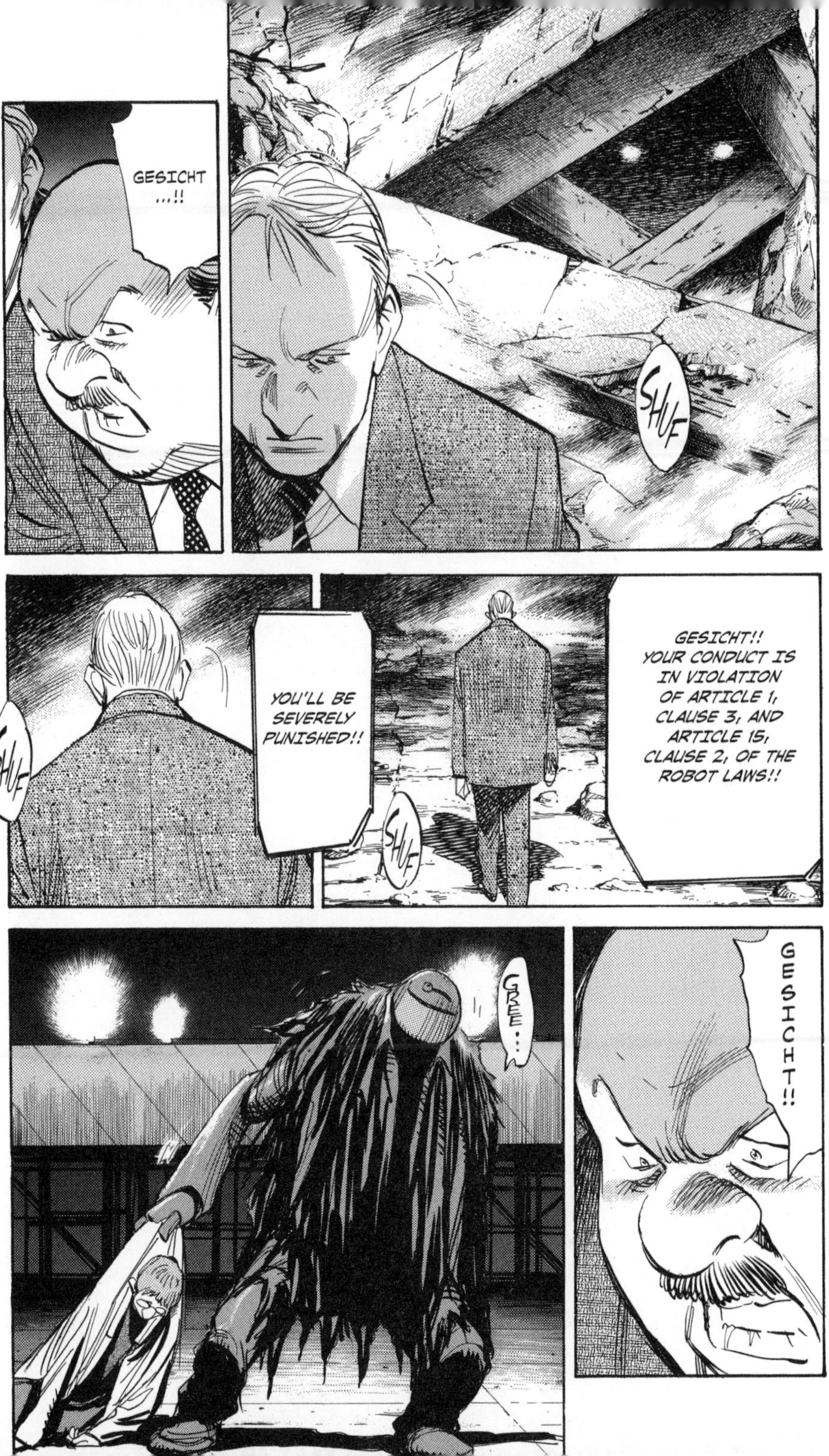
SHUF
GESICHT ...!!
GESICHT!! YOUR CONDUCT IS IN VIOLATION OF ARTICLE 1, CLAUSE 3, AND ARTICLE 15, CLAUSE 2, OF THE ROBOT LAWS!!
SHUF
YOU'LL BE SEVERELY PUNISHED!!
SHUF
GESICHT!!
GREE...

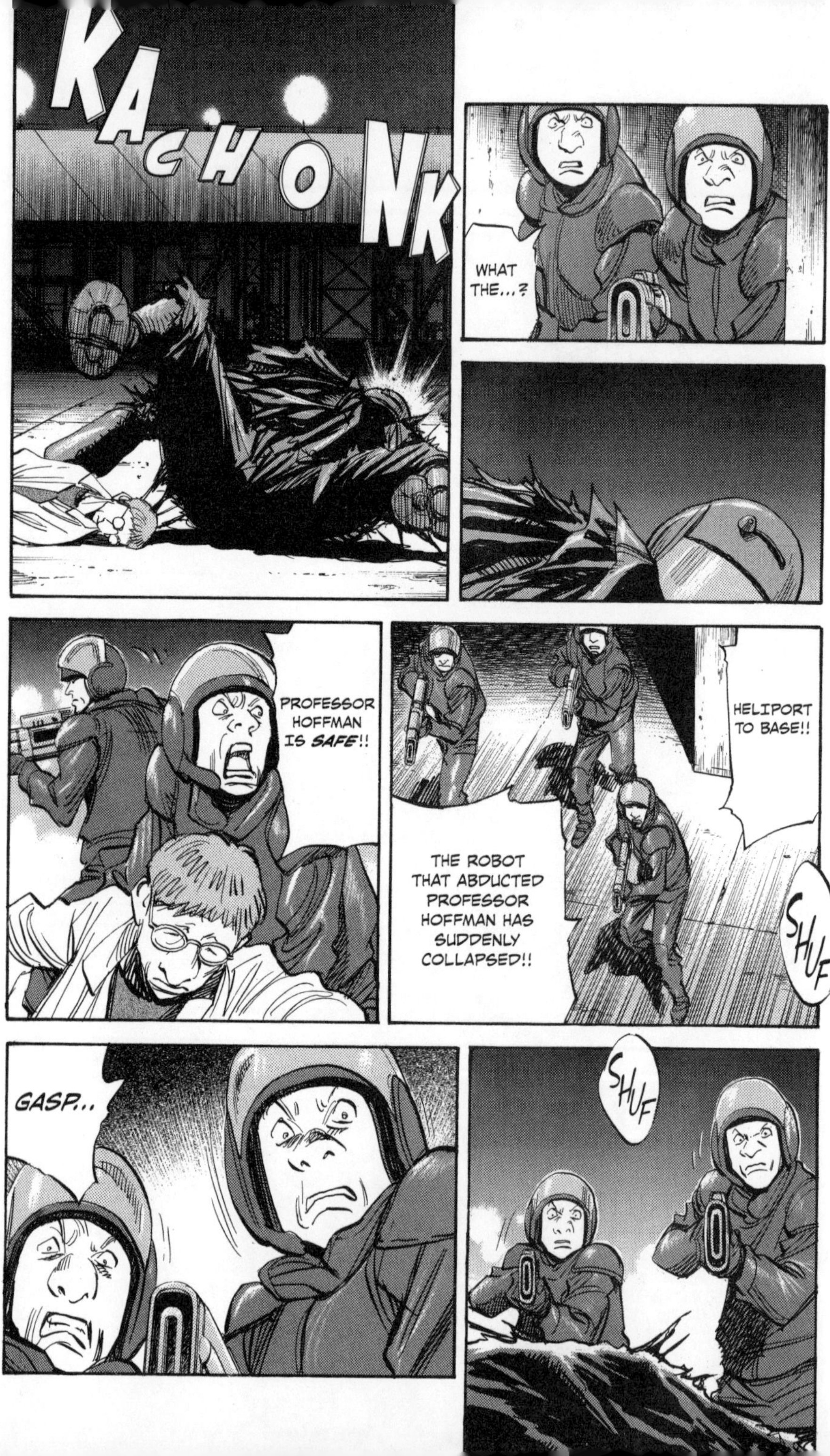
WHAT THE...?
KACHONK
HELIPORT TO BASE!!
THE ROBOT THAT ABDUCTED PROFESSOR HOFFMAN HAS SUDDENLY COLLAPSED!!
SHUF
PROFESSOR HOFFMAN IS SAFE!!
SHUF
GASP...

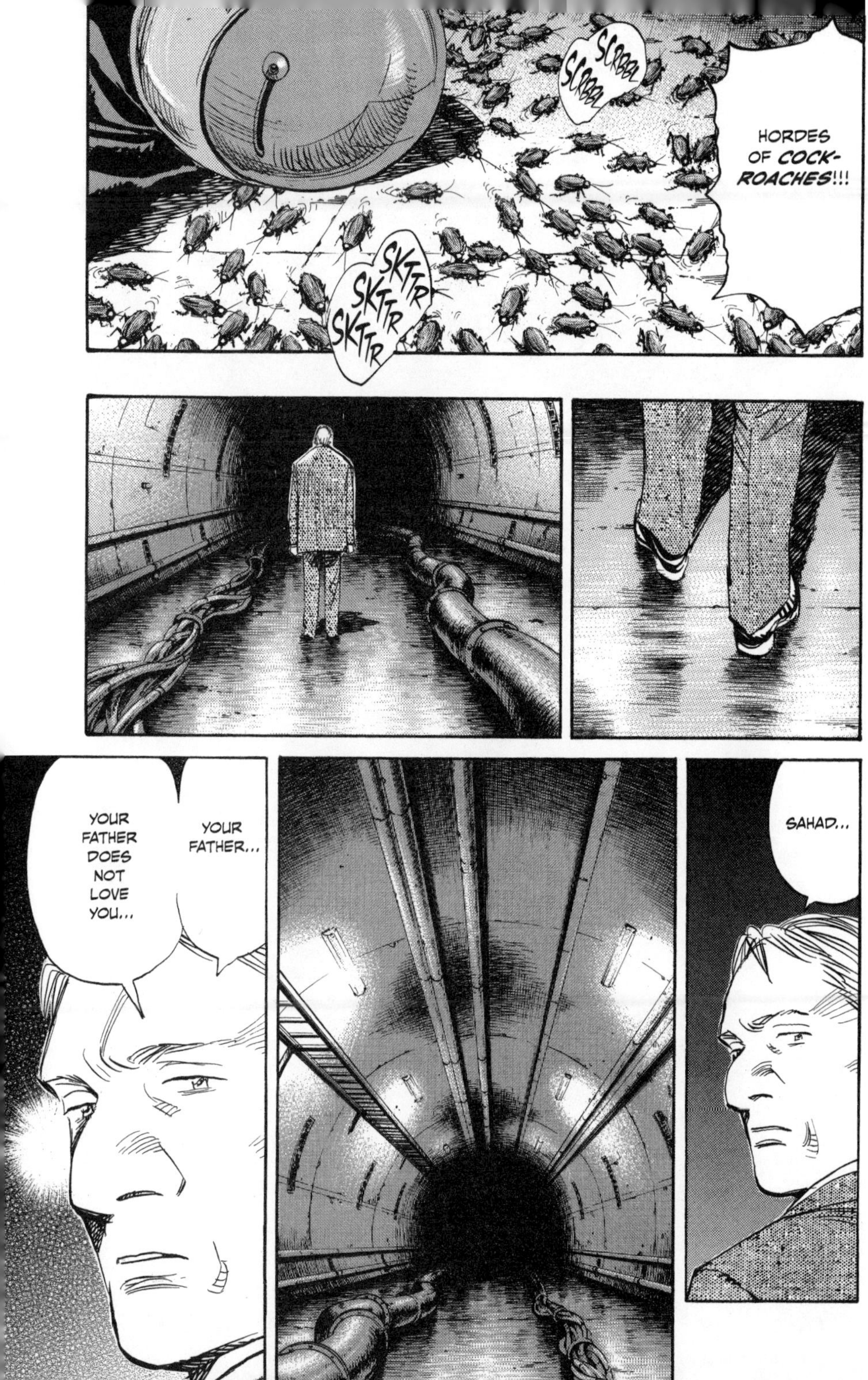
HORDES OF COCK-ROACHES!!!
SCRBBL SCRBBL
SKTTR SKTTR SKTTR
SAHAD...
YOUR FATHER...
YOUR FATHER DOES NOT LOVE YOU...

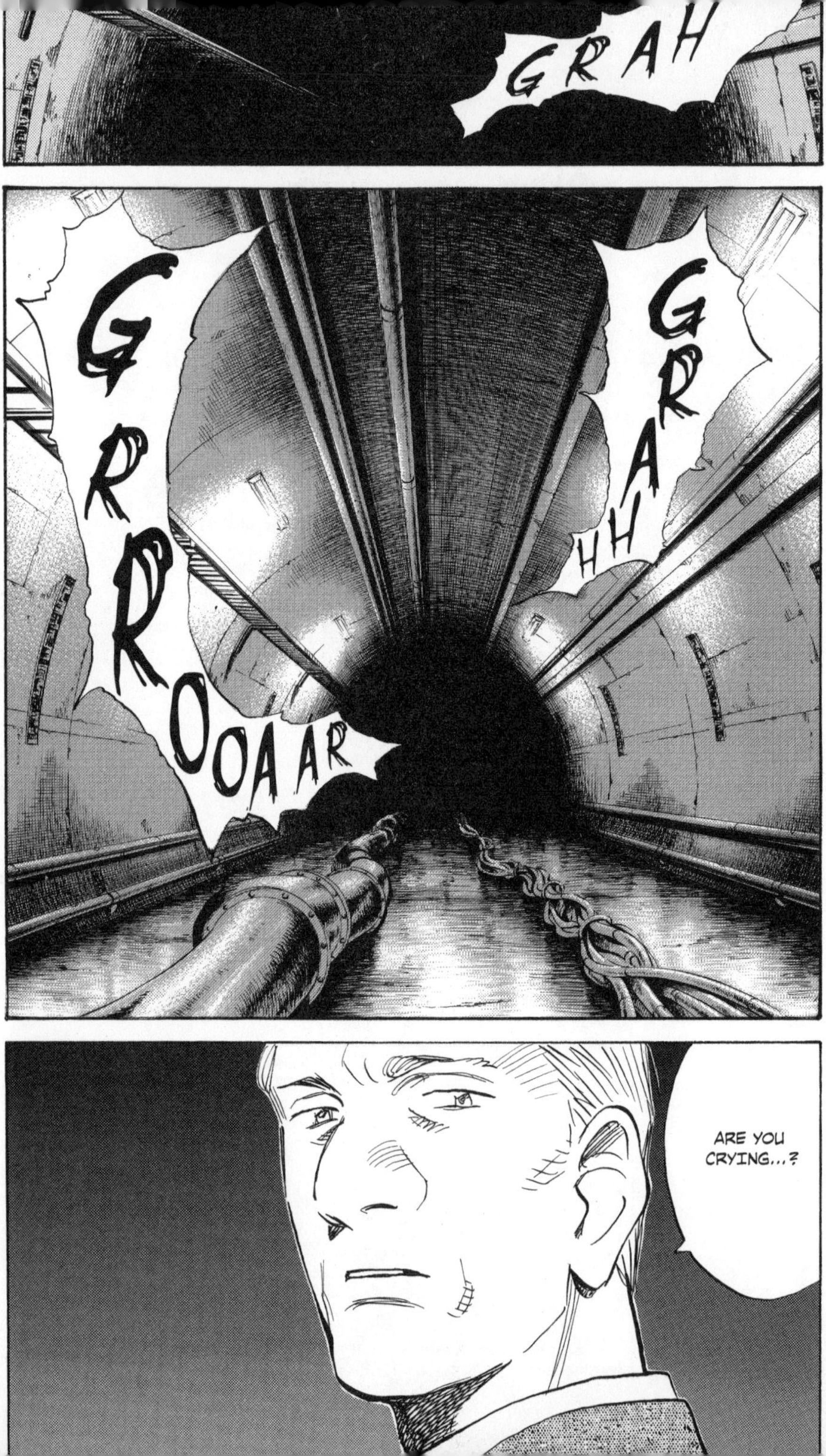
GRAH
GRAHH
GRRROOAAR
ARE YOU CRYING...?

Act 46 END OF THE DREAM

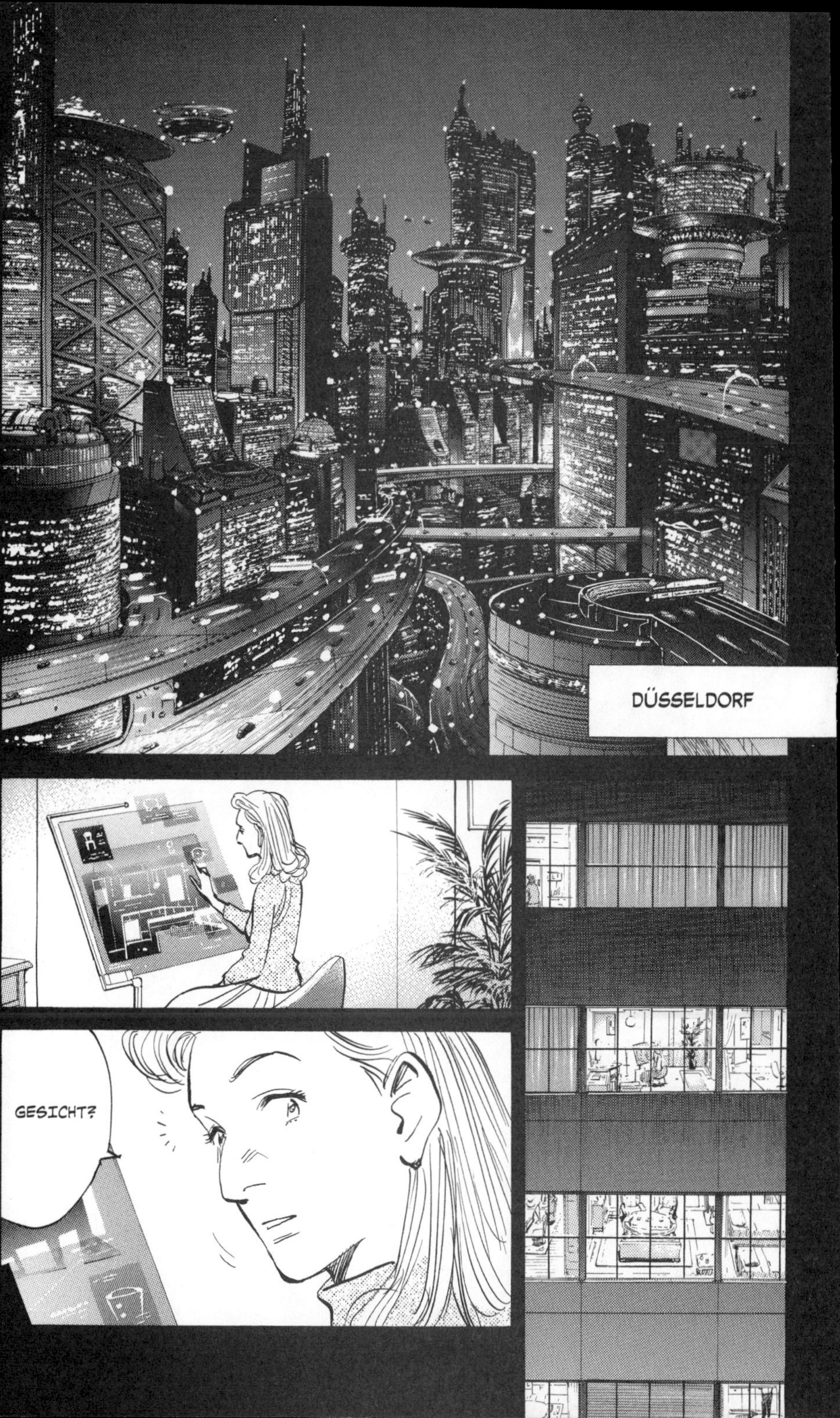
DÜSSELDORF
GESICHT?

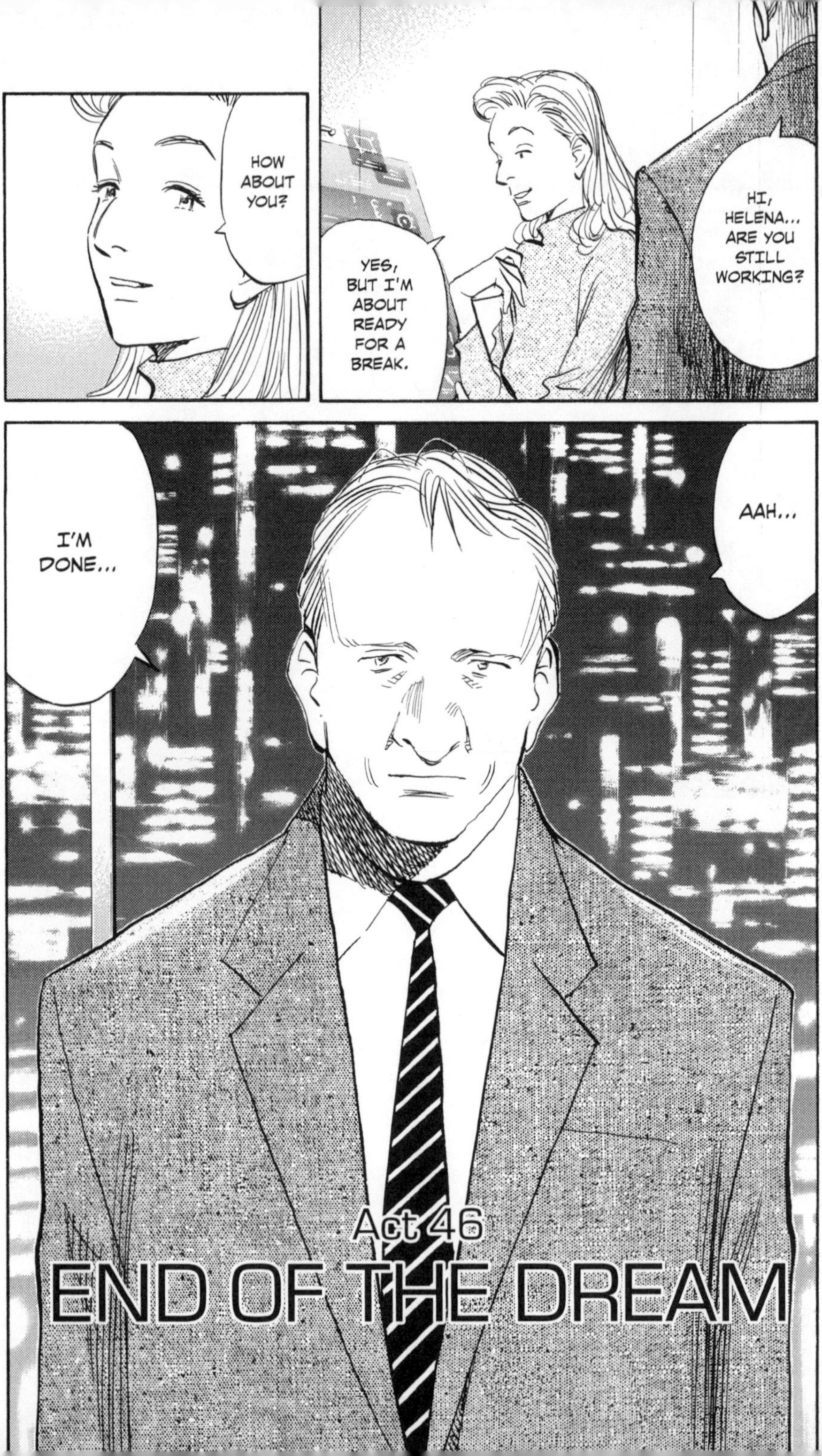
HI, HELENA... ARE YOU STILL WORKING?
YES, BUT I'M ABOUT READY FOR A BREAK.
HOW ABOUT YOU?
AAH...
I'M DONE...
Act 46
END OF THE DREAM

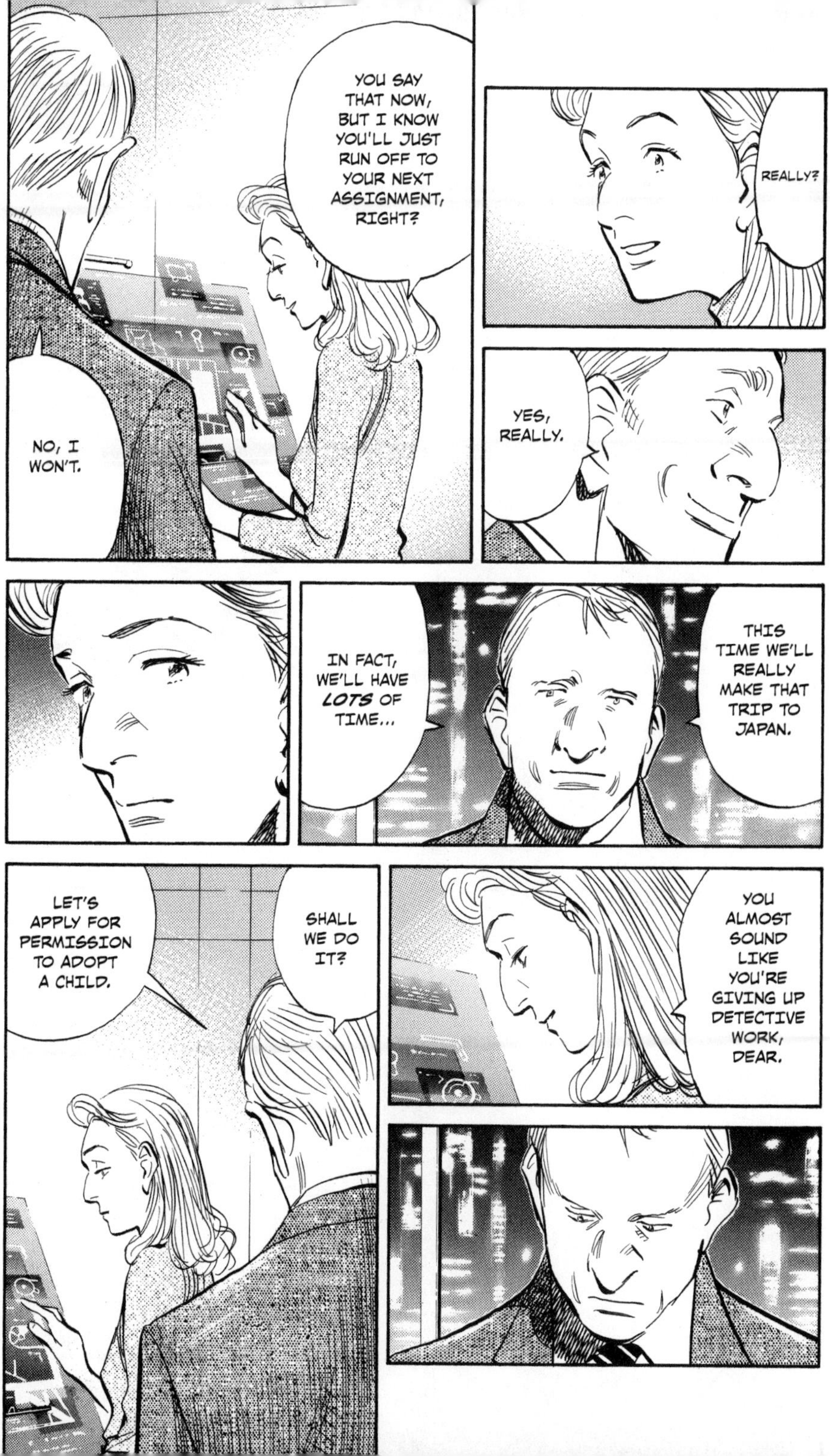
REALLY?
YES, REALLY.
YOU SAY THAT NOW, BUT I KNOW YOU'LL JUST RUN OFF TO YOUR NEXT ASSIGNMENT, RIGHT?
NO, I WON'T.
THIS TIME WE'LL REALLY MAKE THAT TRIP TO JAPAN.
IN FACT, WE'LL HAVE *LOTS* OF TIME...
YOU ALMOST SOUND LIKE YOU'RE GIVING UP DETECTIVE WORK, DEAR.
SHALL WE DO IT?
LET'S APPLY FOR PERMISSION TO ADOPT A CHILD.

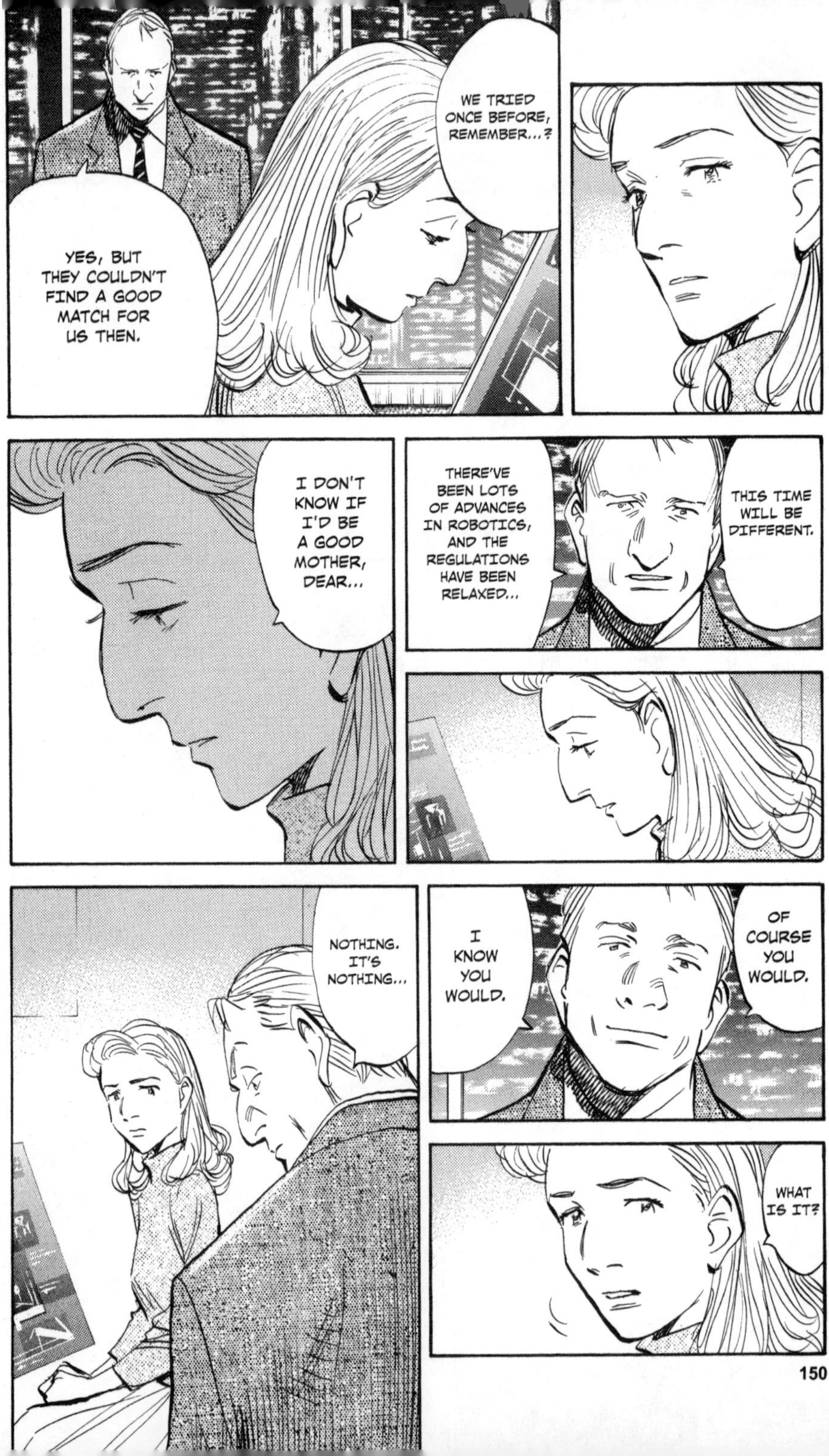
WE TRIED ONCE BEFORE, REMEMBER...?
YES, BUT THEY COULDN'T FIND A GOOD MATCH FOR US THEN.
THIS TIME WILL BE DIFFERENT.
THERE'VE BEEN LOTS OF ADVANCES IN ROBOTICS, AND THE REGULATIONS HAVE BEEN RELAXED...
I DON'T KNOW IF I'D BE A GOOD MOTHER, DEAR...
OF COURSE YOU WOULD.
I KNOW YOU WOULD.
WHAT IS IT?
NOTHING. IT'S NOTHING...

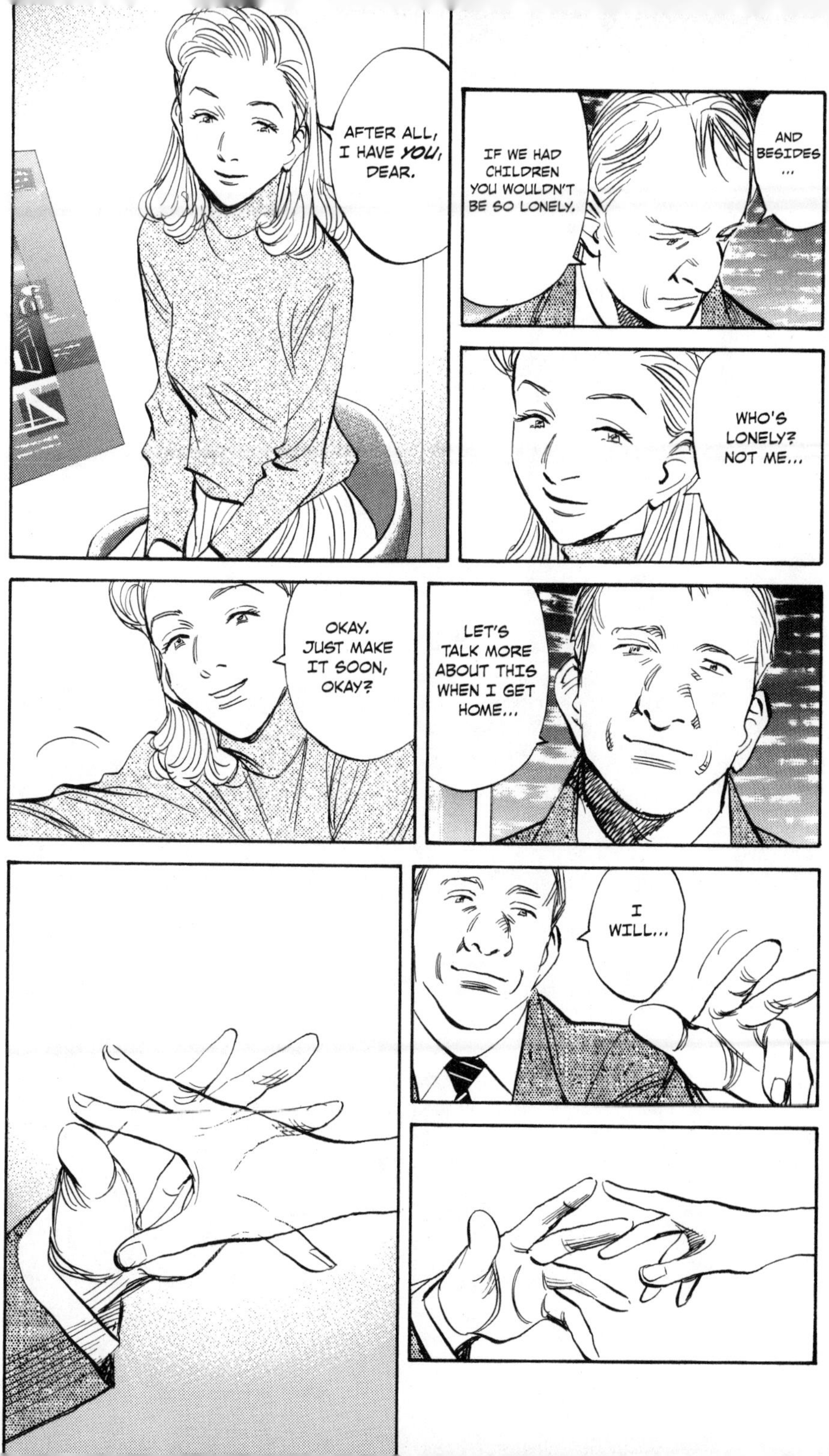
AND BESIDES ...
IF WE HAD CHILDREN YOU WOULDN'T BE SO LONELY.
WHO'S LONELY? NOT ME...
AFTER ALL, I HAVE *YOU*, DEAR.
LET'S TALK MORE ABOUT THIS WHEN I GET HOME...
OKAY. JUST MAKE IT SOON, OKAY?
I WILL...

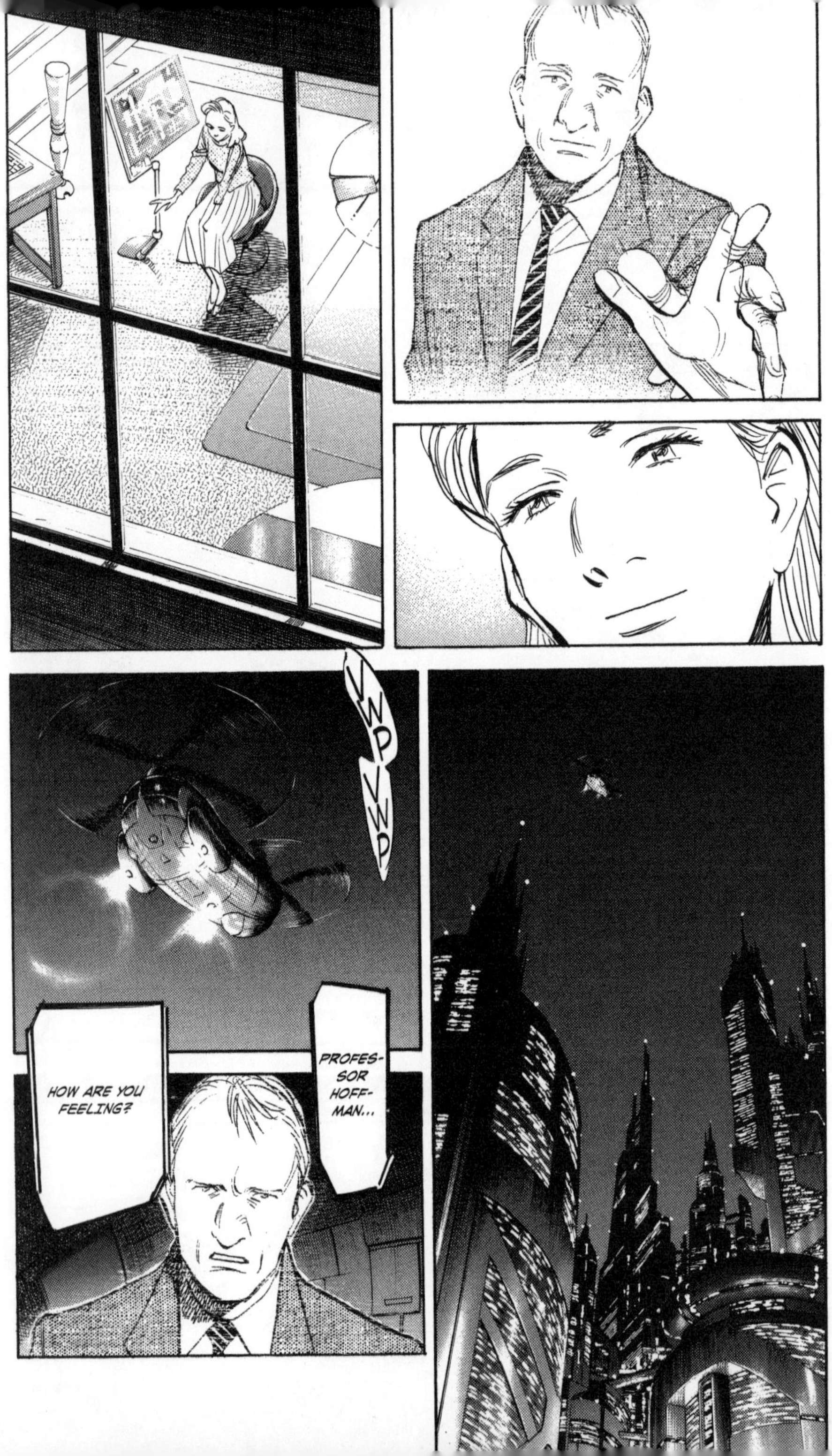
VWPVWP
PROFES-
SOR
HOFF-
MAN...
HOW ARE YOU
FEELING?

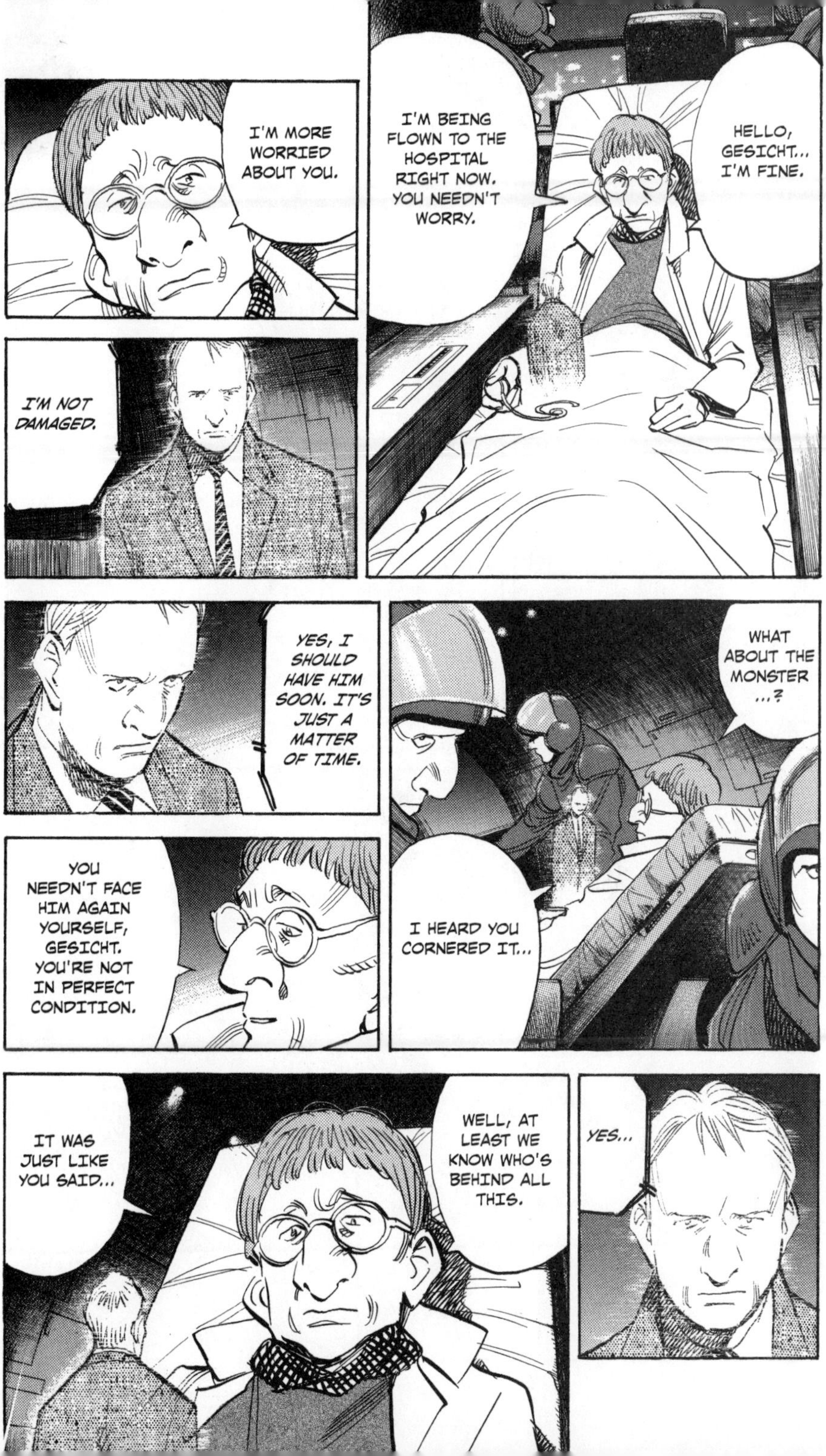
HELLO, GESICHT... I'M FINE.
I'M BEING FLOWN TO THE HOSPITAL RIGHT NOW. YOU NEEDN'T WORRY.
I'M MORE WORRIED ABOUT YOU.
I'M NOT DAMAGED.
WHAT ABOUT THE MONSTER ...?
I HEARD YOU CORNERED IT...
YES, I SHOULD HAVE HIM SOON. IT'S JUST A MATTER OF TIME.
YOU NEEDN'T FACE HIM AGAIN YOURSELF, GESICHT. YOU'RE NOT IN PERFECT CONDITION.
YES...
WELL, AT LEAST WE KNOW WHO'S BEHIND ALL THIS.
IT WAS JUST LIKE YOU SAID...

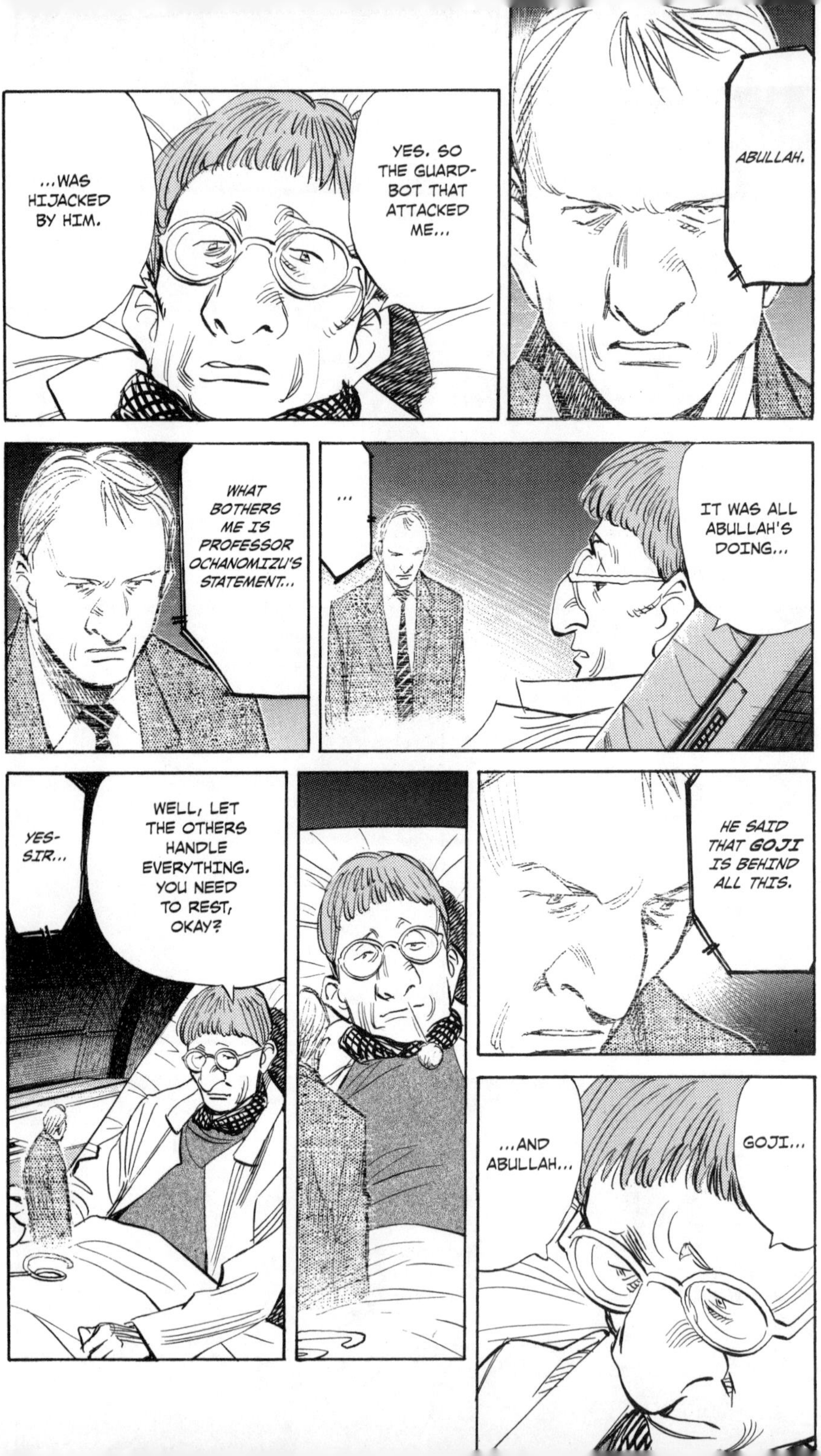
ABULLAH.
YES. SO THE GUARD-BOT THAT ATTACKED ME...
...WAS HIJACKED BY HIM.
IT WAS ALL ABULLAH'S DOING...
...
WHAT BOTHERS ME IS PROFESSOR OCHANOMIZU'S STATEMENT...
HE SAID THAT **GOJI** IS BEHIND ALL THIS.
GOJI...
...AND ABULLAH...
WELL, LET THE OTHERS HANDLE EVERYTHING. YOU NEED TO REST, OKAY?
YES-SIR...

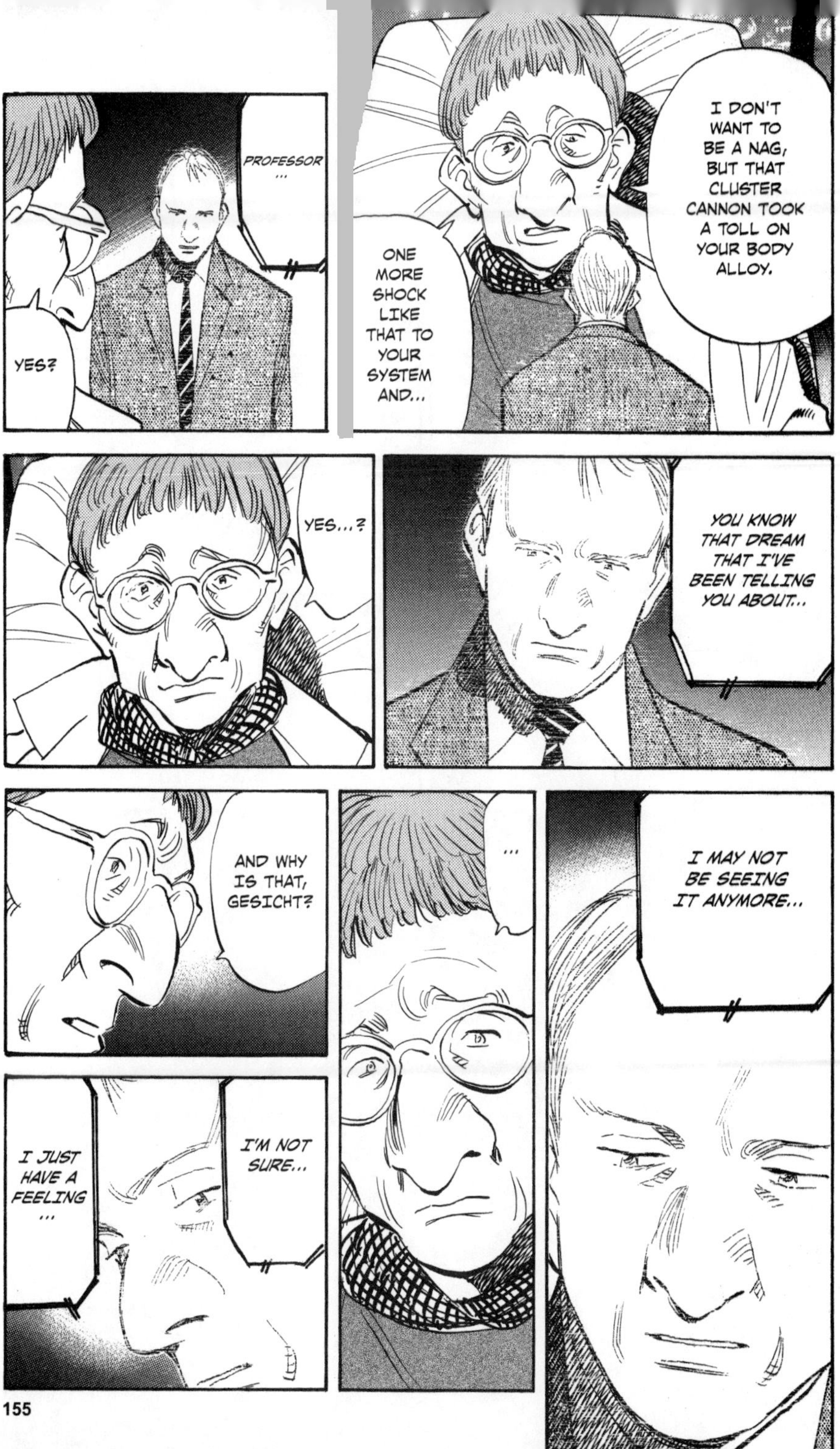
I DON'T WANT TO BE A NAG, BUT THAT CLUSTER CANNON TOOK A TOLL ON YOUR BODY ALLOY.
ONE MORE SHOCK LIKE THAT TO YOUR SYSTEM AND...
PROFESSOR...
YES?
YOU KNOW THAT DREAM THAT I'VE BEEN TELLING YOU ABOUT...
YES...?
I MAY NOT BE SEEING IT ANYMORE...
...
AND WHY IS THAT, GESICHT?
I'M NOT SURE...
I JUST HAVE A FEELING...

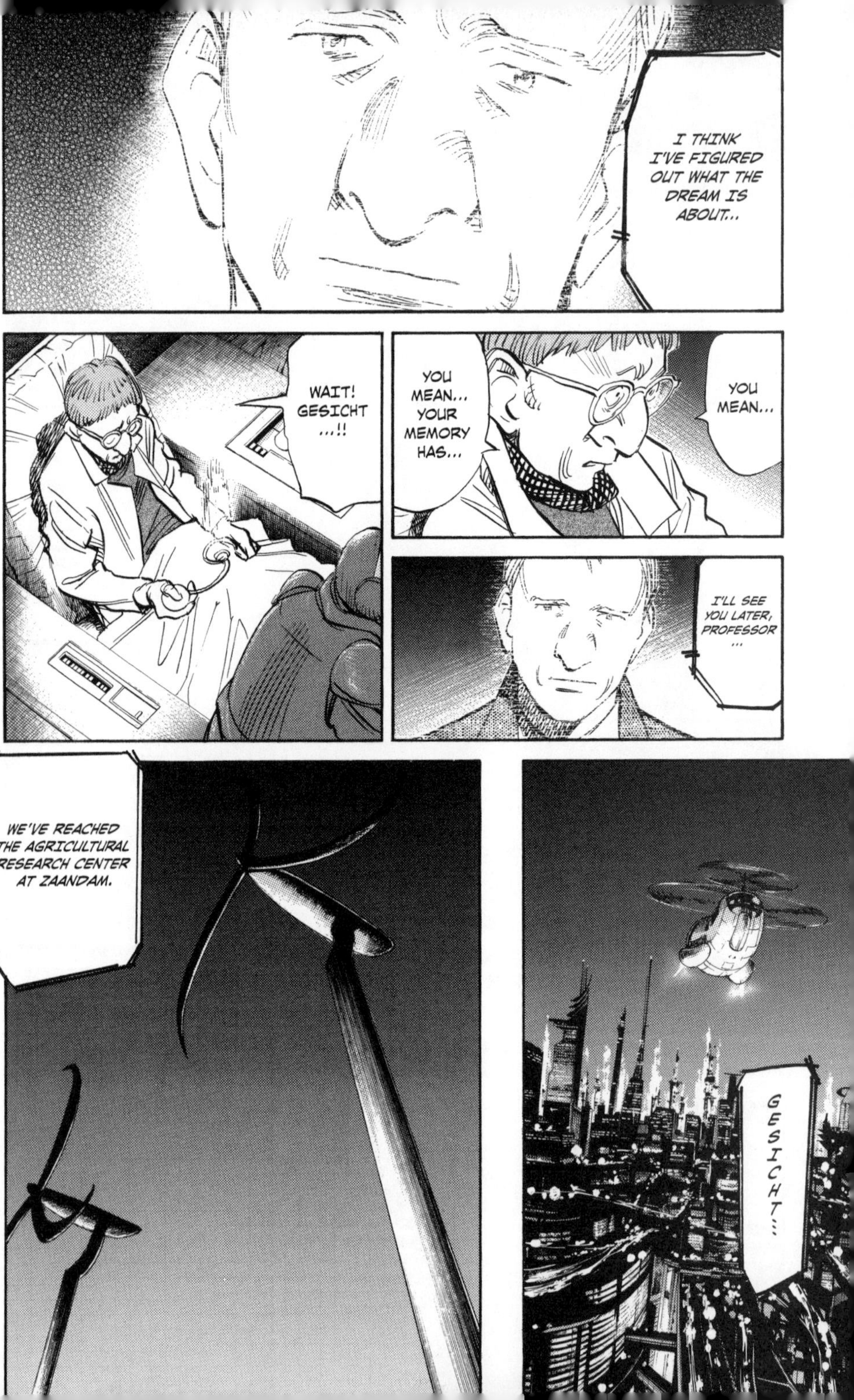
I THINK I'VE FIGURED OUT WHAT THE DREAM IS ABOUT...
YOU MEAN...
YOU MEAN... YOUR MEMORY HAS...
I'LL SEE YOU LATER, PROFESSOR...
WAIT! GESICHT ...!!
GESICHT...
WE'VE REACHED THE AGRICULTURAL RESEARCH CENTER AT ZAANDAM.

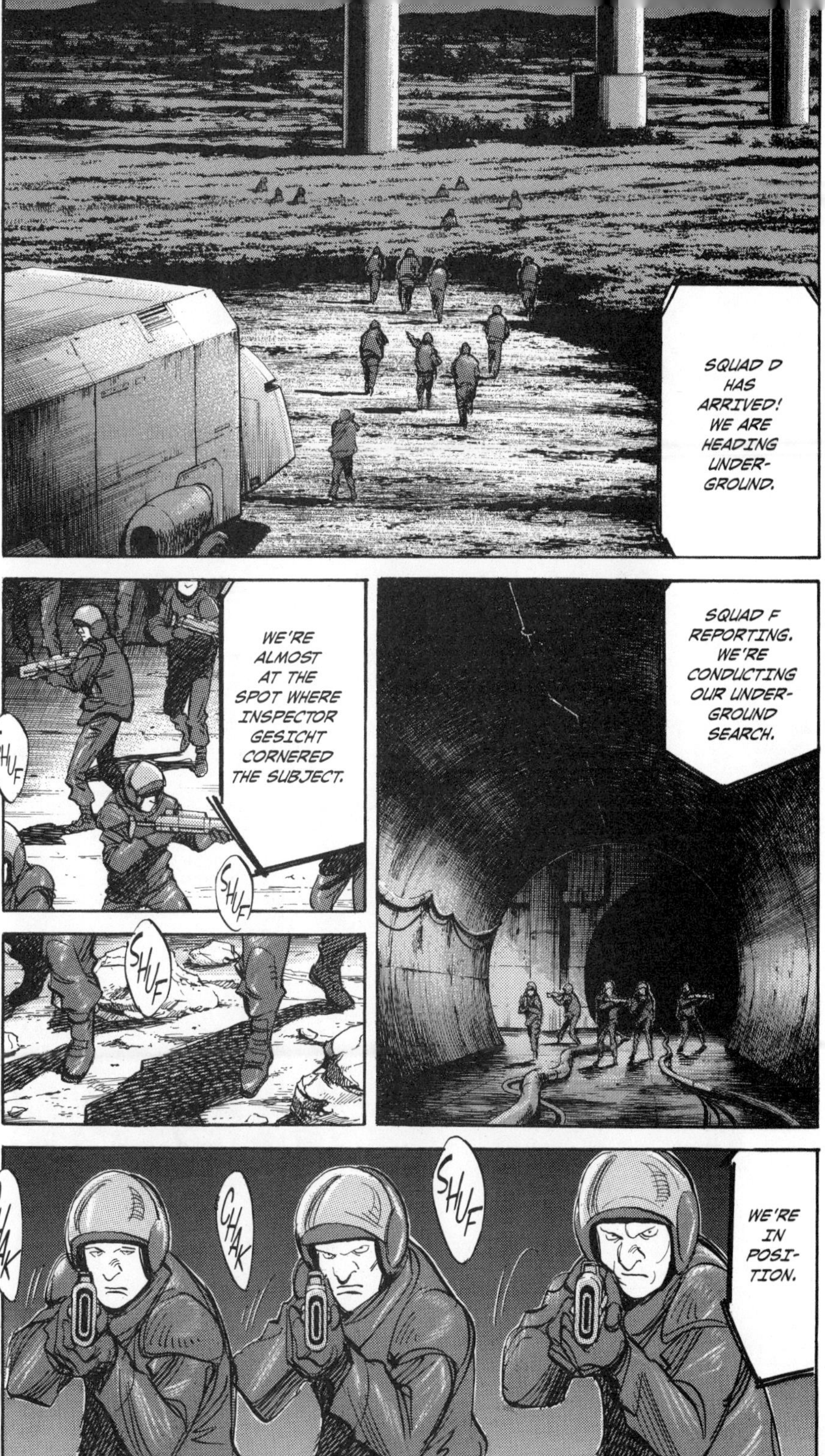

SQUAD D HAS ARRIVED! WE ARE HEADING UNDER-GROUND.
SQUAD F REPORTING. WE'RE CONDUCTING OUR UNDER-GROUND SEARCH.
WE'RE ALMOST AT THE SPOT WHERE INSPECTOR GESICHT CORNERED THE SUBJECT.
SHUF
SHUF
SHUF
WE'RE IN POSI-TION.
SHUF
CHAK
CHAK

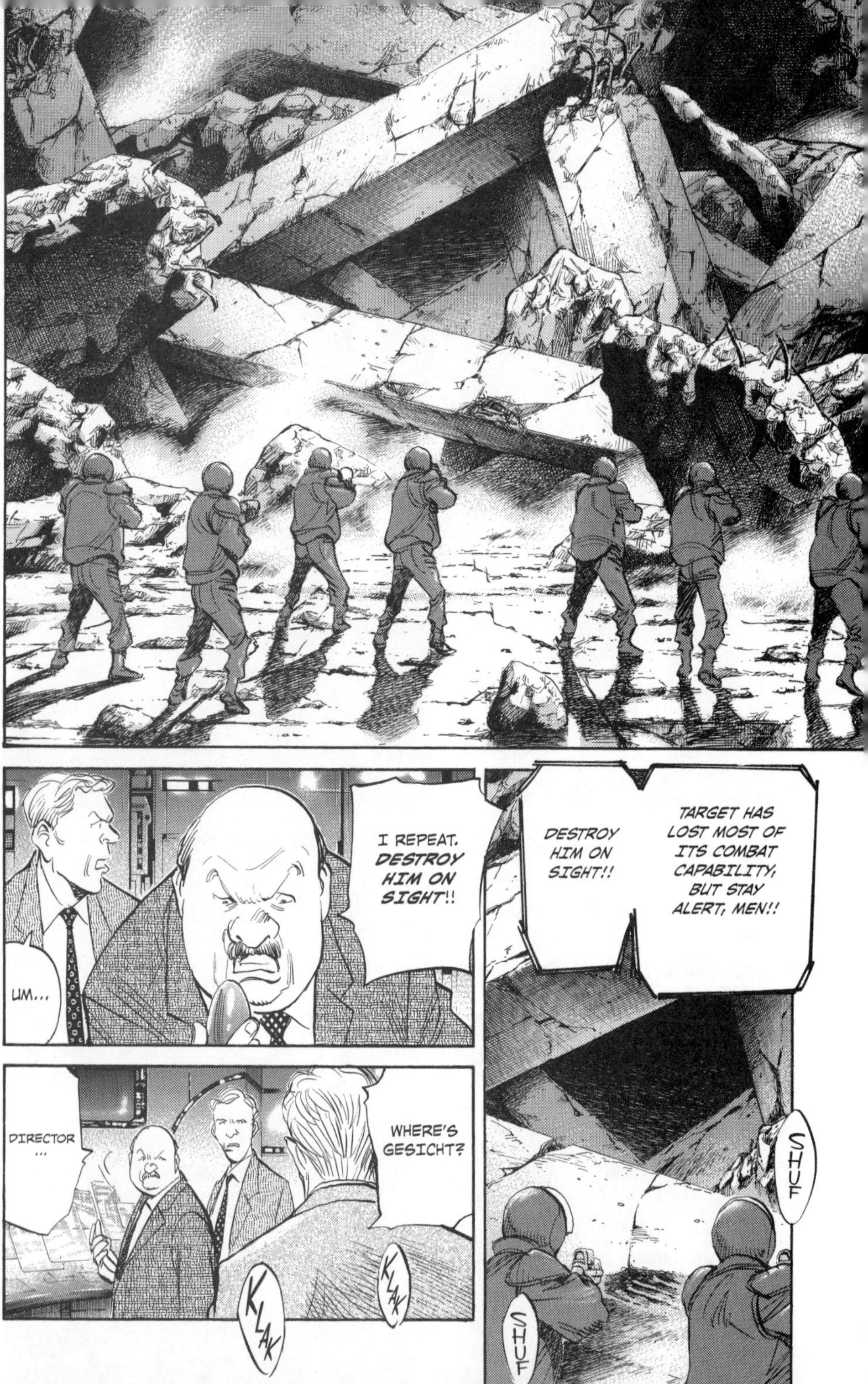
TARGET HAS LOST MOST OF ITS COMBAT CAPABILITY, BUT STAY ALERT, MEN!!
DESTROY HIM ON SIGHT!!
SHUF
SHUF
I REPEAT. DESTROY HIM ON SIGHT!!
UM...
WHERE'S GESICHT?
DIRECTOR ...
KLAK
KLAK

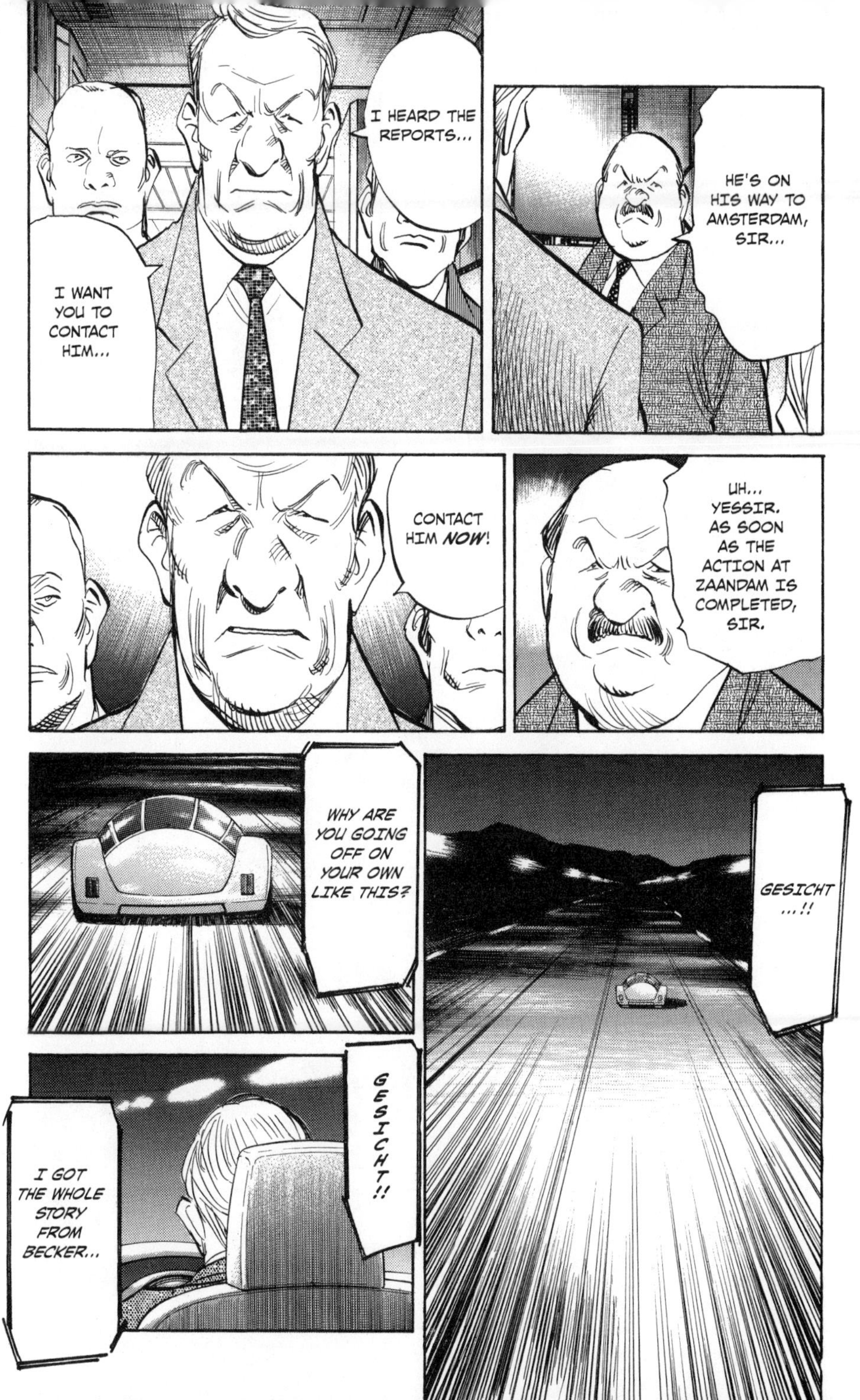
HE'S ON HIS WAY TO AMSTERDAM, SIR...
I HEARD THE REPORTS...
I WANT YOU TO CONTACT HIM...
UH... YESSIR. AS SOON AS THE ACTION AT ZAANDAM IS COMPLETED, SIR.
CONTACT HIM *NOW*!
GESICHT ...!!
WHY ARE YOU GOING OFF ON YOUR OWN LIKE THIS?
GESICHT!!
I GOT THE WHOLE STORY FROM BECKER...

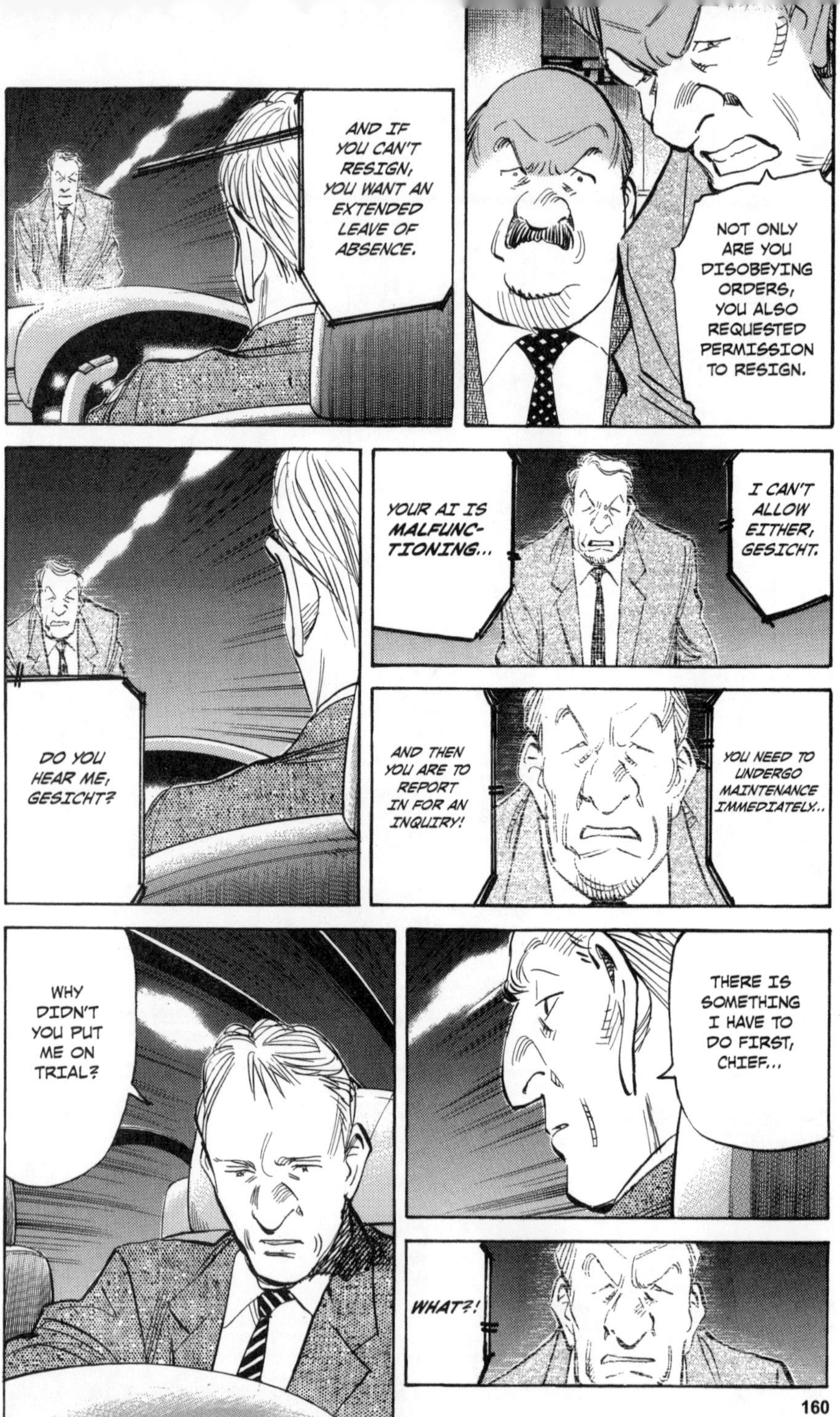
NOT ONLY ARE YOU DISOBEYING ORDERS, YOU ALSO REQUESTED PERMISSION TO RESIGN.
AND IF YOU CAN'T RESIGN, YOU WANT AN EXTENDED LEAVE OF ABSENCE.
I CAN'T ALLOW EITHER, GESICHT.
YOUR AI IS MALFUNCTIONING...
YOU NEED TO UNDERGO MAINTENANCE IMMEDIATELY...
AND THEN YOU ARE TO REPORT IN FOR AN INQUIRY!
DO YOU HEAR ME, GESICHT?
THERE IS SOMETHING I HAVE TO DO FIRST, CHIEF...
WHAT?!
WHY DIDN'T YOU PUT ME ON TRIAL?

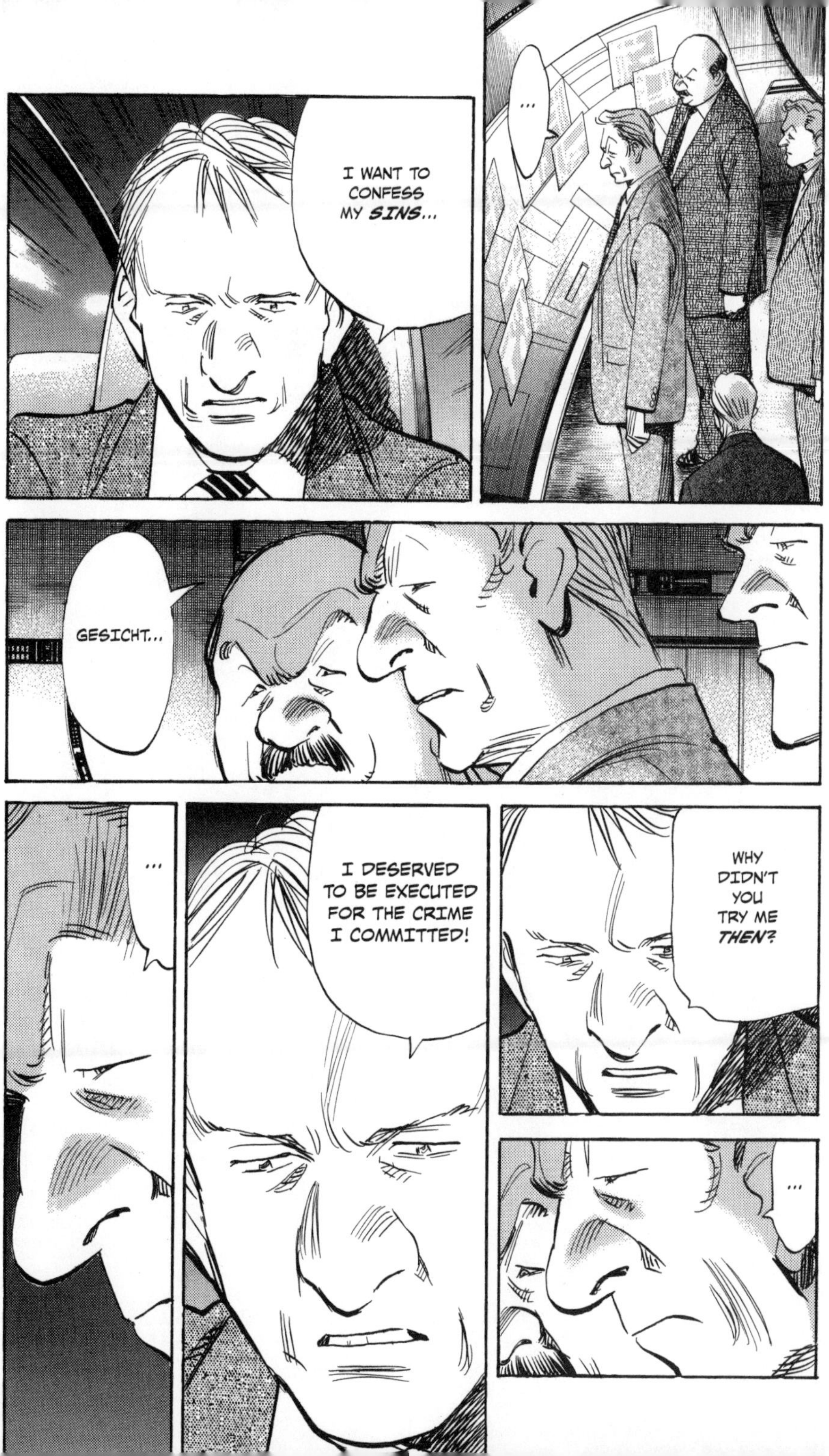
...
I WANT TO CONFESS MY SINS...
GESICHT...
WHY DIDN'T YOU TRY ME THEN?
...
I DESERVED TO BE EXECUTED FOR THE CRIME I COMMITTED!
...

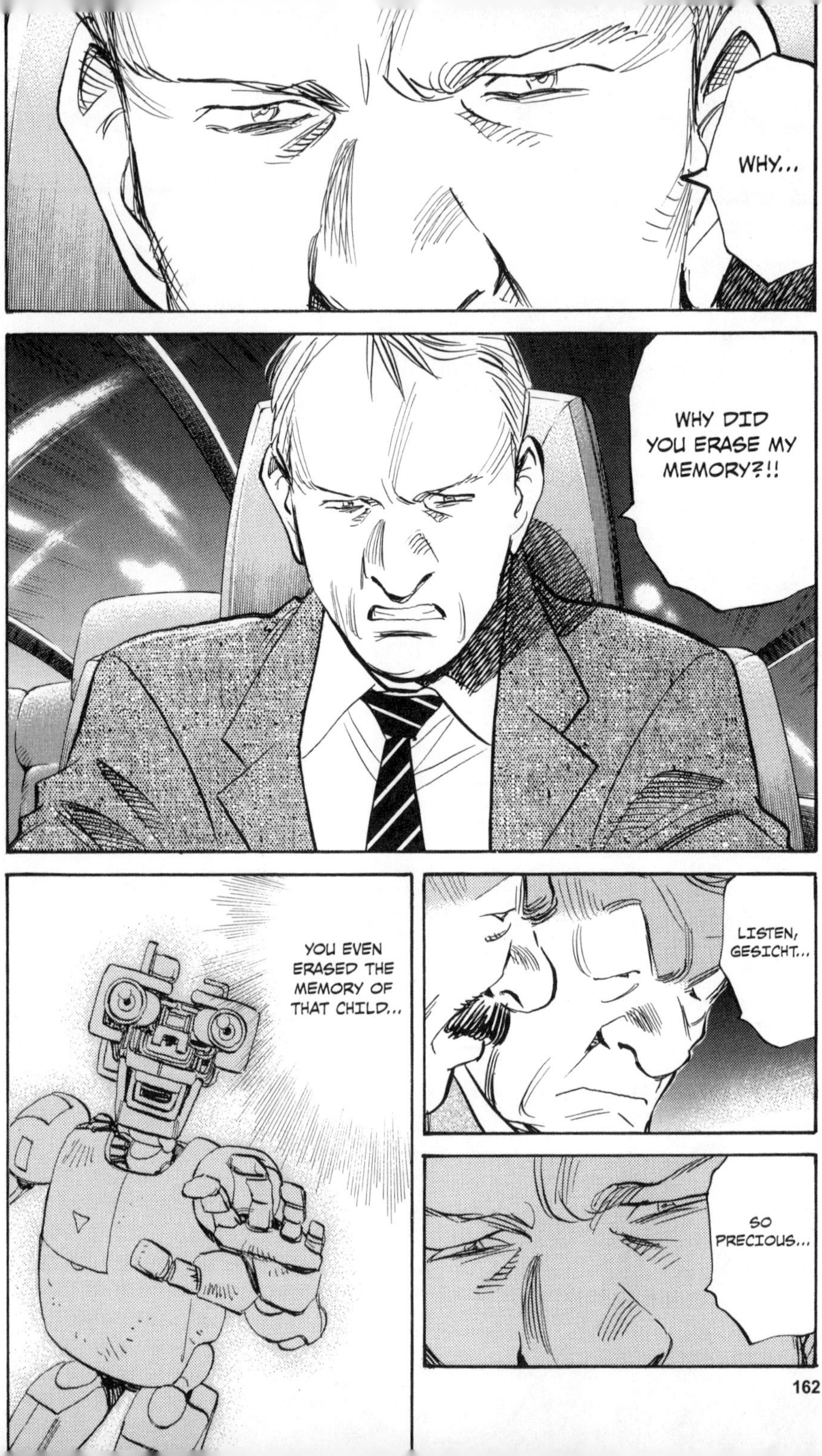
WHY...
WHY DID YOU ERASE MY MEMORY?!!
LISTEN, GESICHT...
SO PRECIOUS...
YOU EVEN ERASED THE MEMORY OF THAT CHILD...

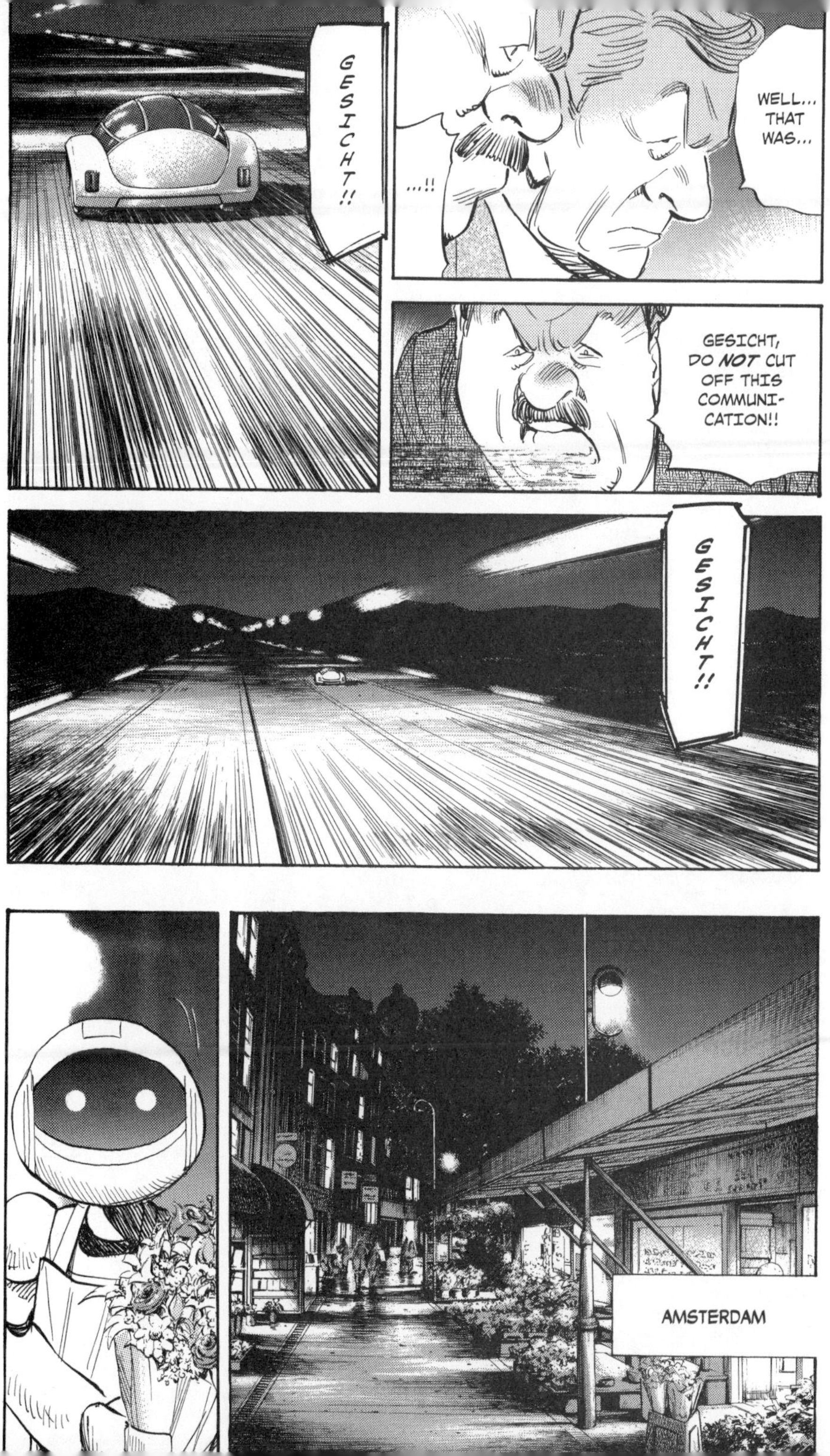
WELL... THAT WAS...
...!!
GESICHT, DO NOT CUT OFF THIS COMMUNICATION!!
GESICHT!!
GESICHT!!
AMSTERDAM

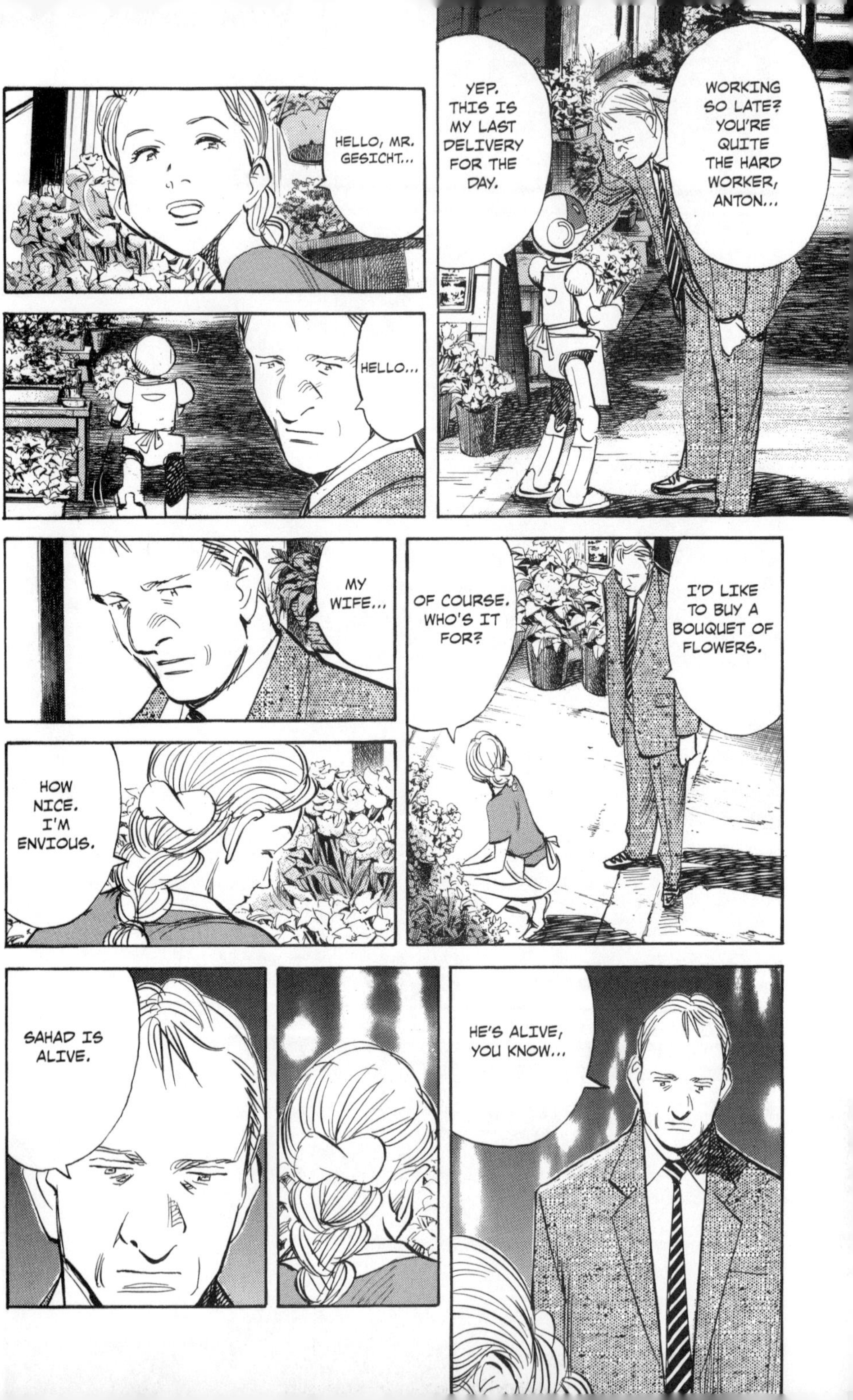
WORKING SO LATE? YOU'RE QUITE THE HARD WORKER, ANTON...
YEP. THIS IS MY LAST DELIVERY FOR THE DAY.
HELLO, MR. GESICHT...
HELLO...
I'D LIKE TO BUY A BOUQUET OF FLOWERS.
OF COURSE. WHO'S IT FOR?
MY WIFE...
HOW NICE. I'M ENVIOUS.
HE'S ALIVE, YOU KNOW...
SAHAD IS ALIVE.

HAS... HE DONE SOMETHING WRONG...?

R... REALLY ...?

HE'S NOT A BAD PERSON...

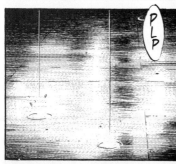

PLP

IT'S NOT HIS FAULT...

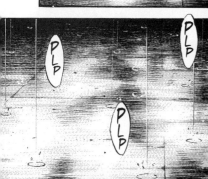

PLP

PLP

PLP

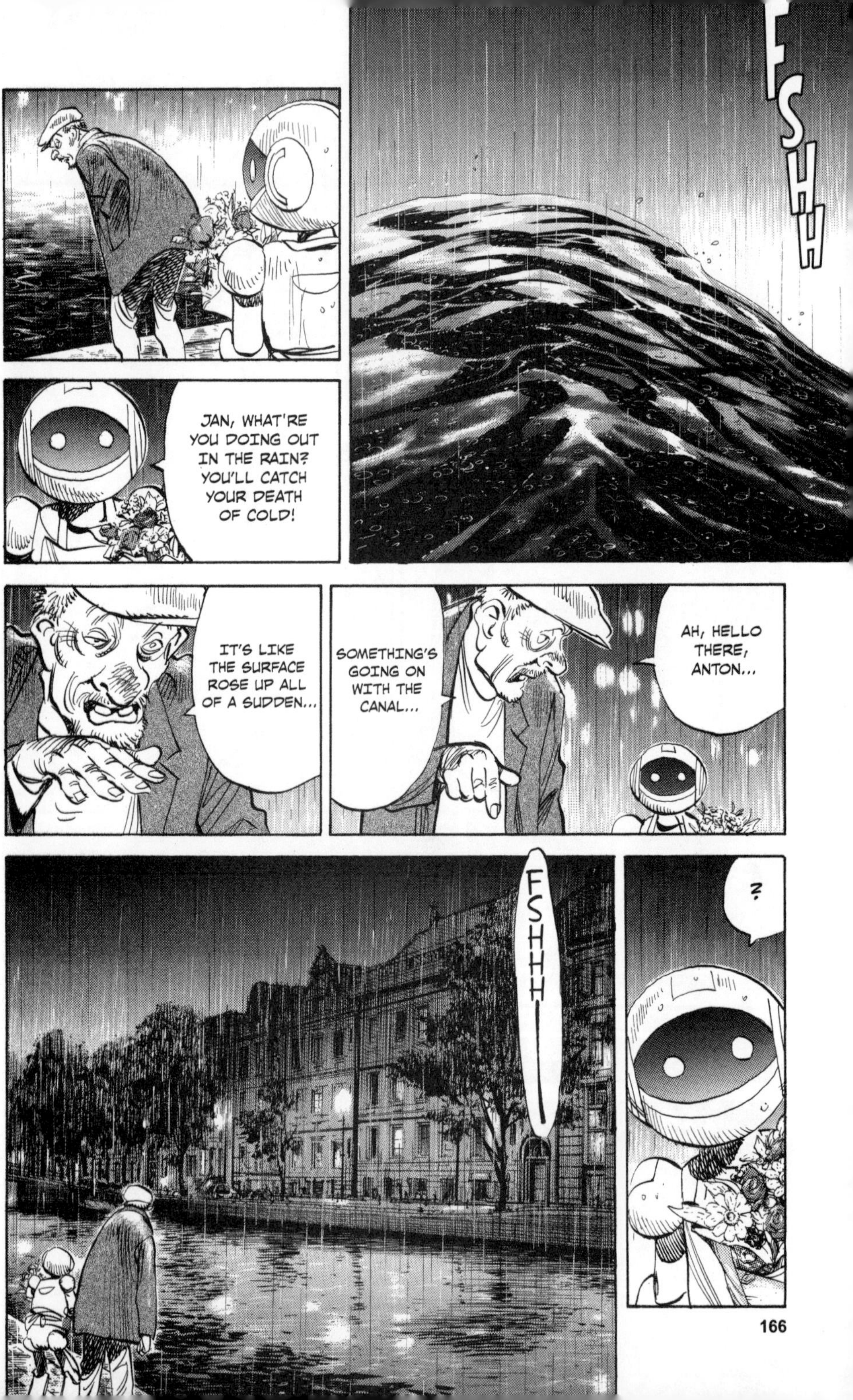
FSHH
JAN, WHAT'RE YOU DOING OUT IN THE RAIN? YOU'LL CATCH YOUR DEATH OF COLD!
AH, HELLO THERE, ANTON...
SOMETHING'S GOING ON WITH THE CANAL...
IT'S LIKE THE SURFACE ROSE UP ALL OF A SUDDEN...
?
FSHHH

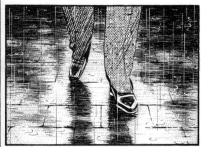

FSHHH

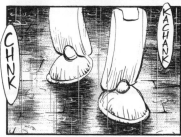

CHNK

KACHANK

?

ANTON,
WE MEET
AGAIN.

CHANK

KCHNK

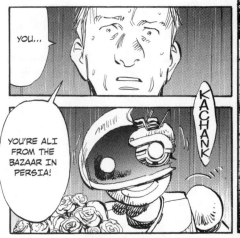

YOU...

YOU'RE ALI FROM THE BAZAAR IN PERSIA!

CHANK

KACHUNK

KACHANK

WHAT ARE YOU DOING IN AMSTERDAM?

!!

KACHANK

LOOK! HE'S WALKING ...

LOOK, GESICHT...

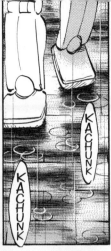

KACHUNK

KACHUNK

HE'S WALKING ...

KACHANK

KACHANK

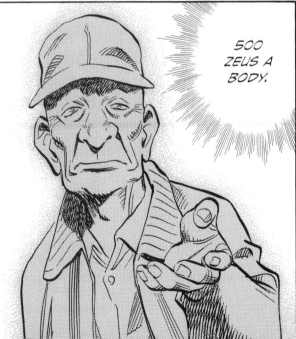

500 ZEUS A BODY.

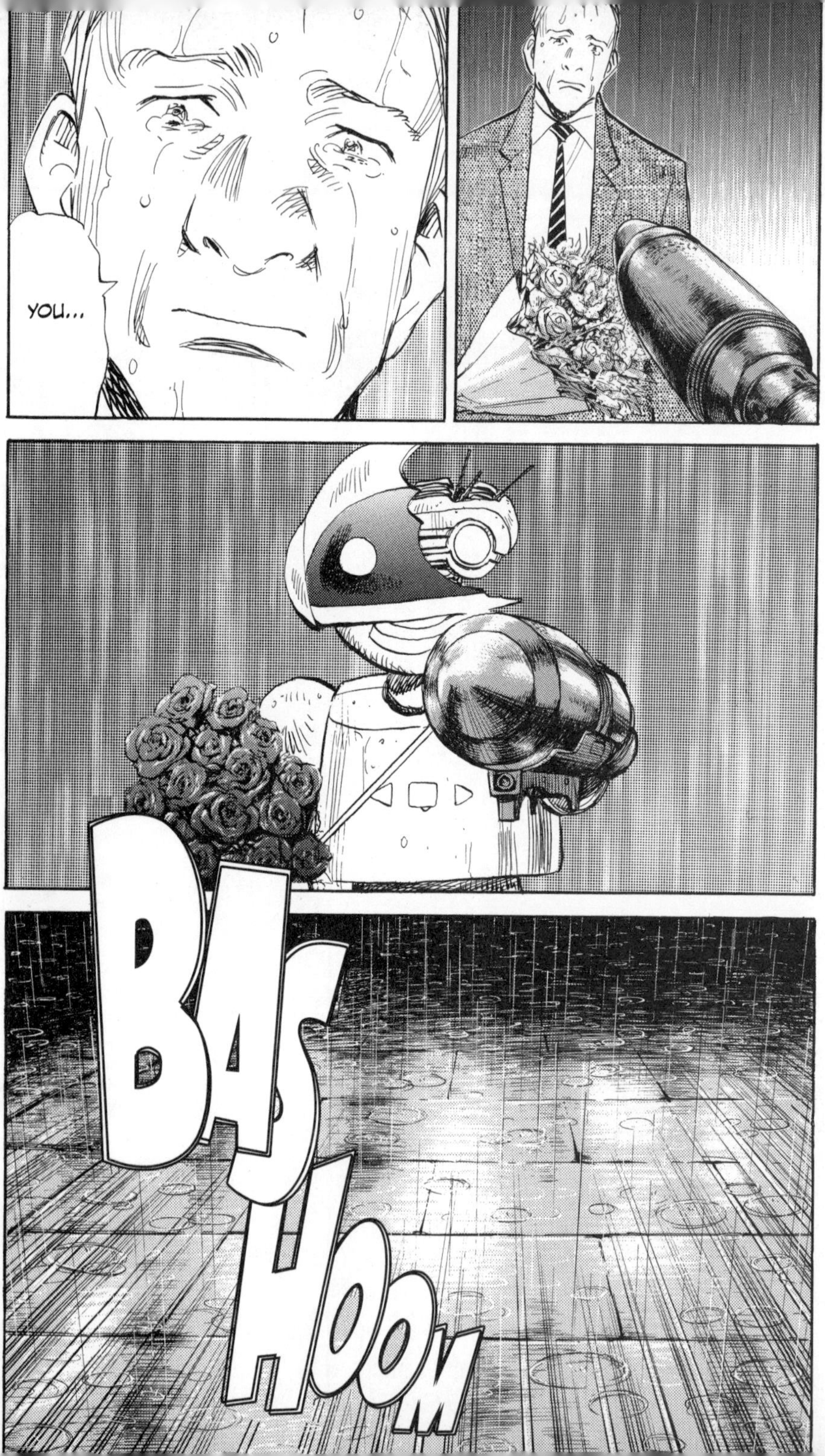
YOU...
BASHOOM

Act 47 Real Tears

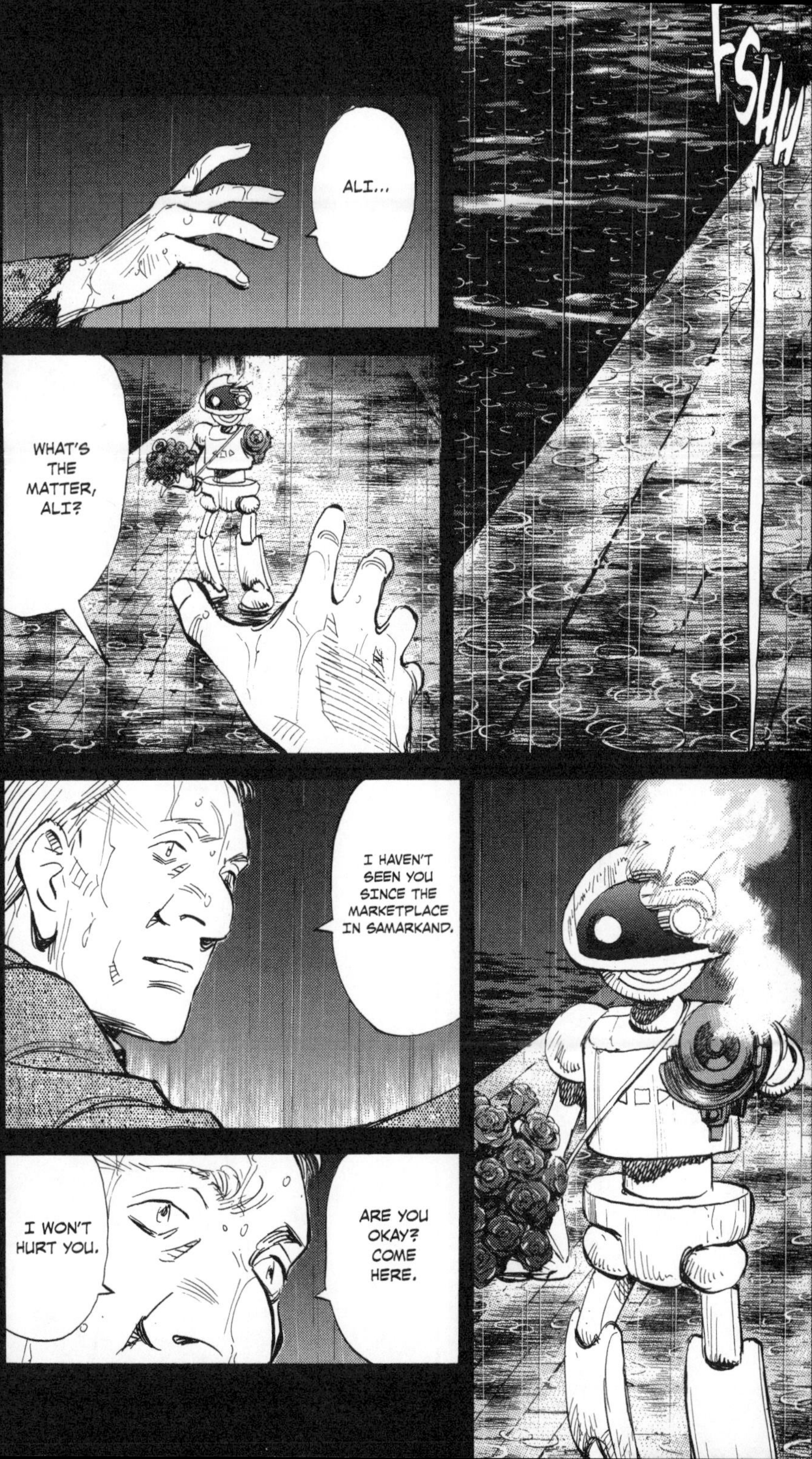
FSHH
ALI...
WHAT'S THE MATTER, ALI?
I HAVEN'T SEEN YOU SINCE THE MARKETPLACE IN SAMARKAND.
ARE YOU OKAY? COME HERE.
I WON'T HURT YOU.

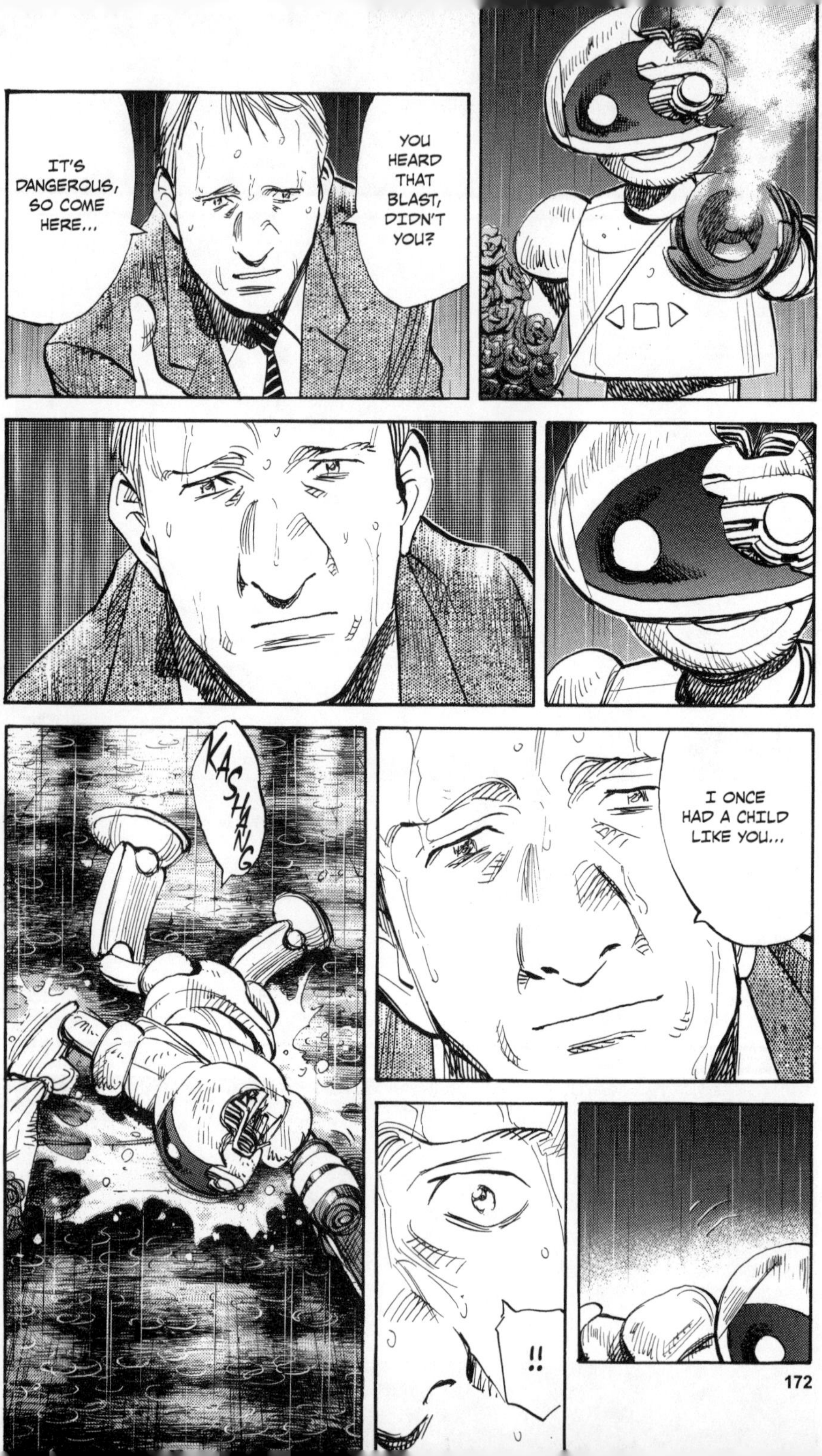
YOU HEARD THAT BLAST, DIDN'T YOU?
IT'S DANGEROUS, SO COME HERE...
I ONCE HAD A CHILD LIKE YOU...
!!
KASHANG

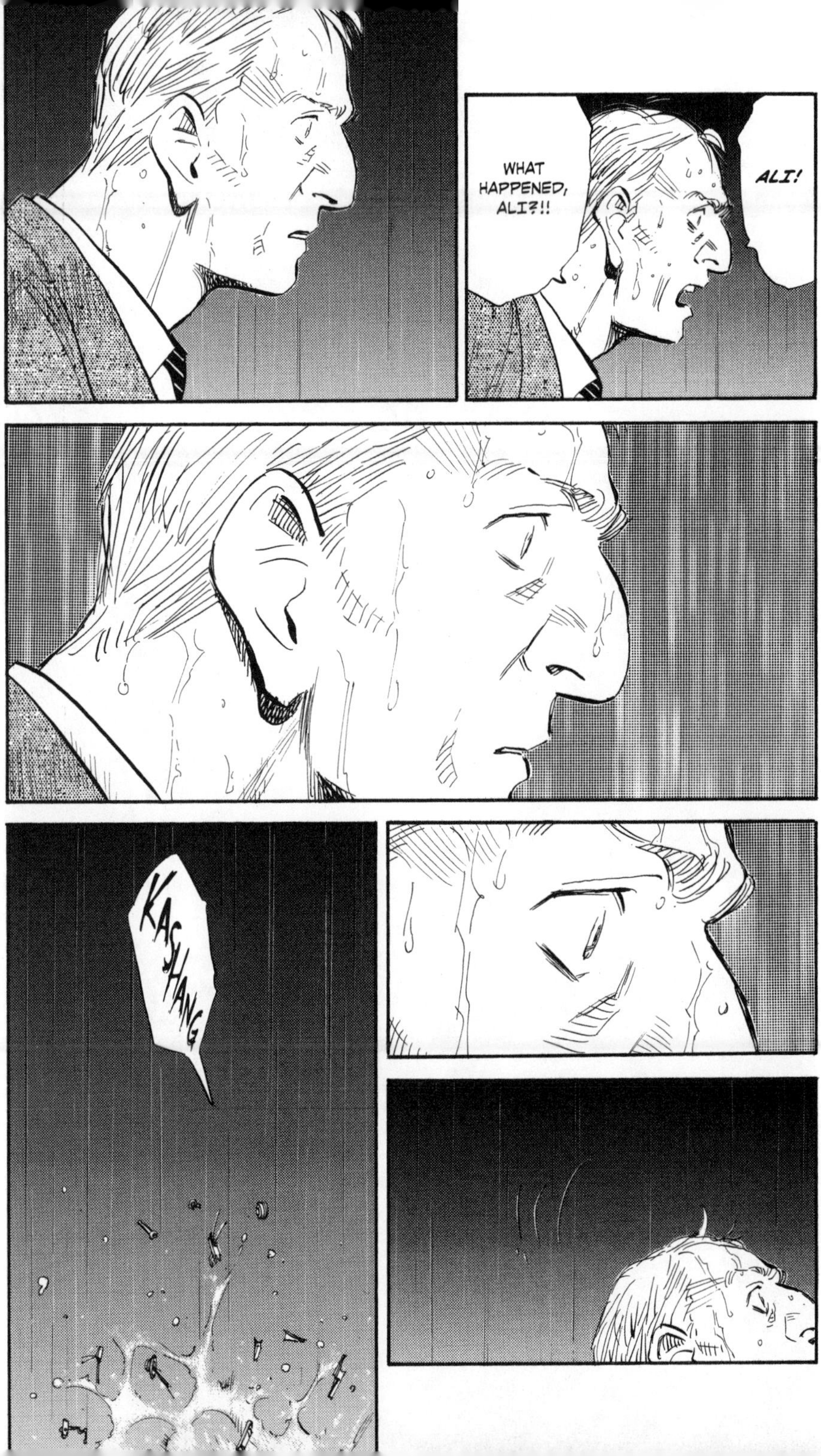
ALI!
WHAT HAPPENED, ALI?!!
KASHANG

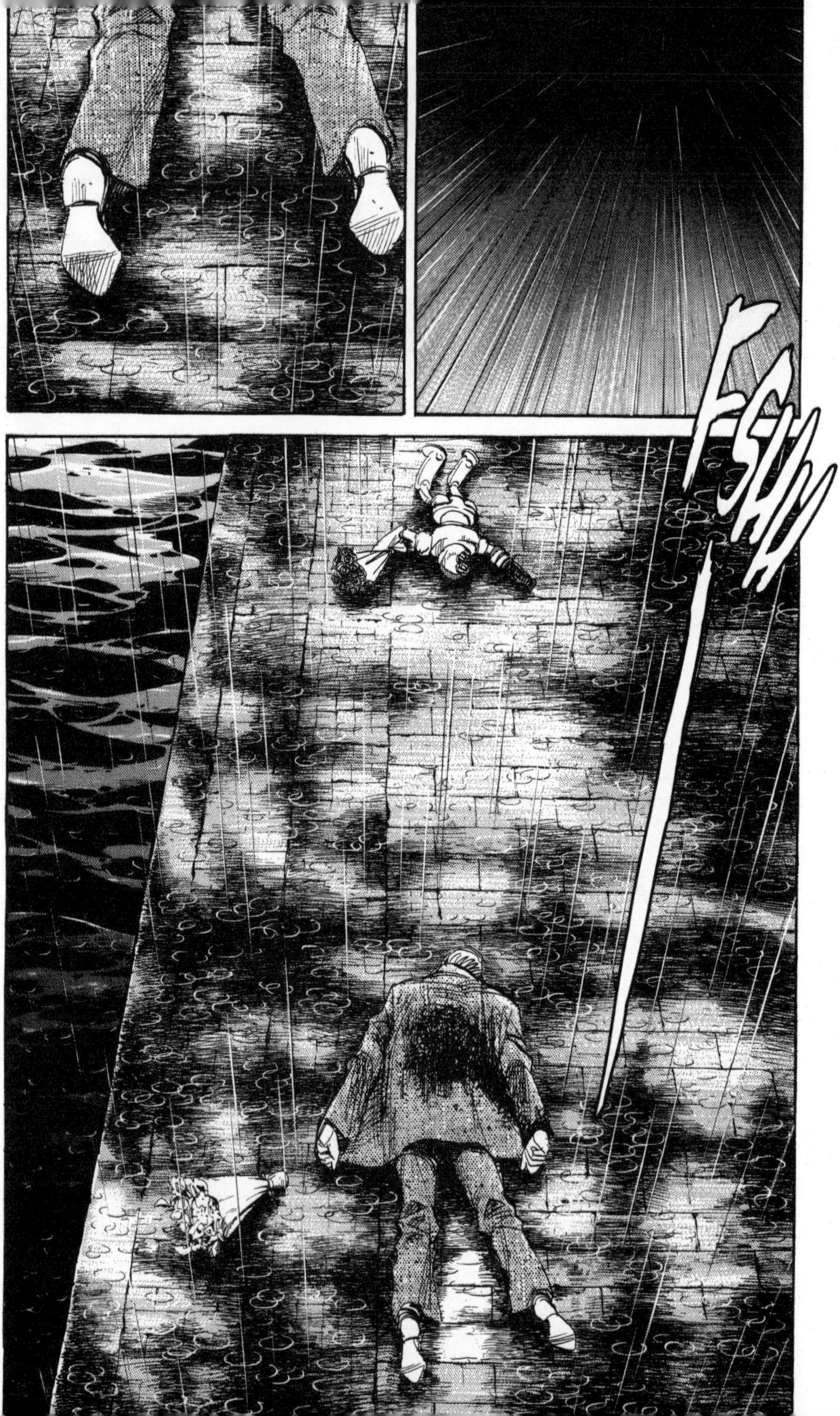
FSHH

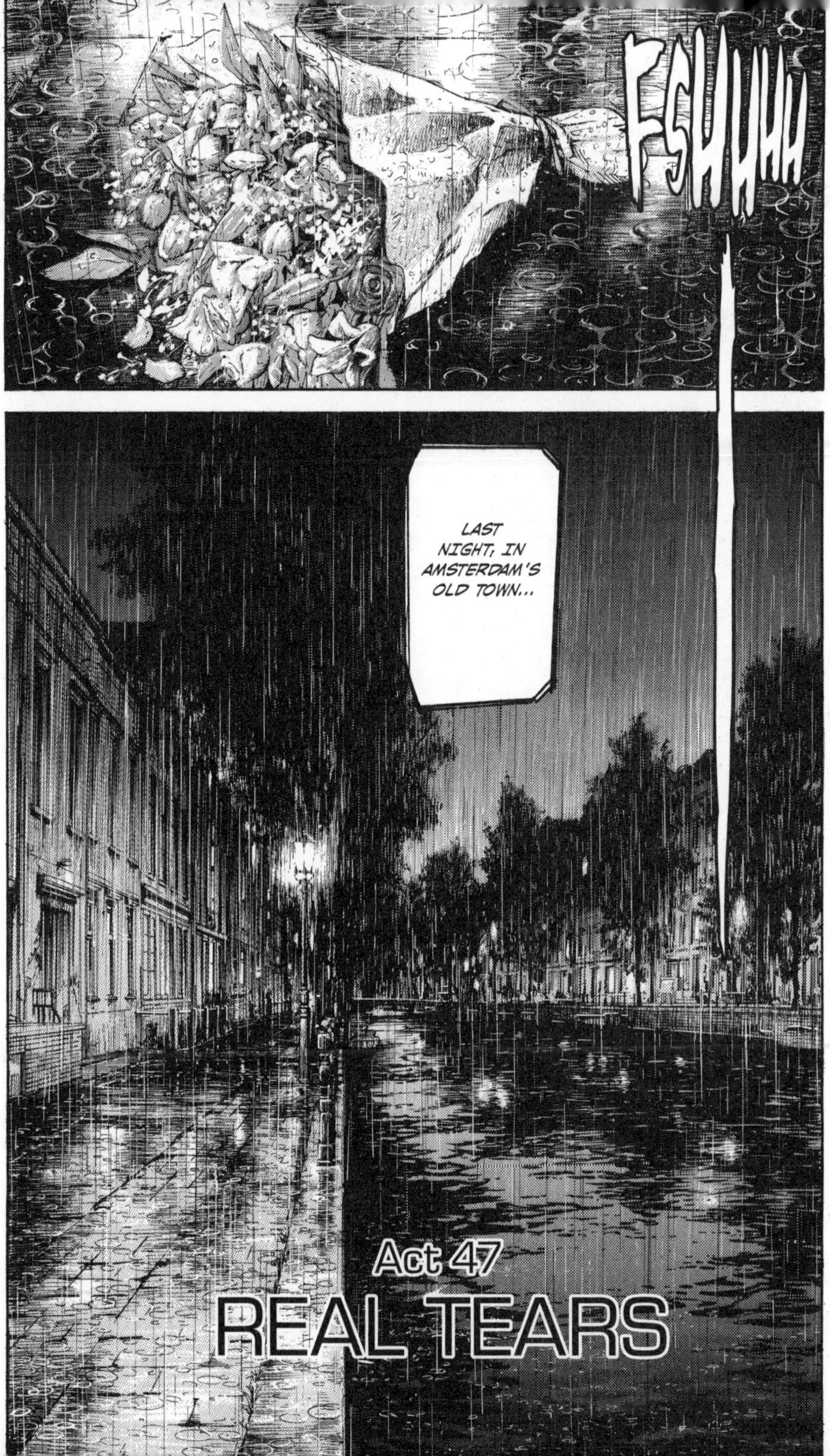

FSHHHH
LAST NIGHT, IN AMSTERDAM'S OLD TOWN...
Act 47
REAL TEARS

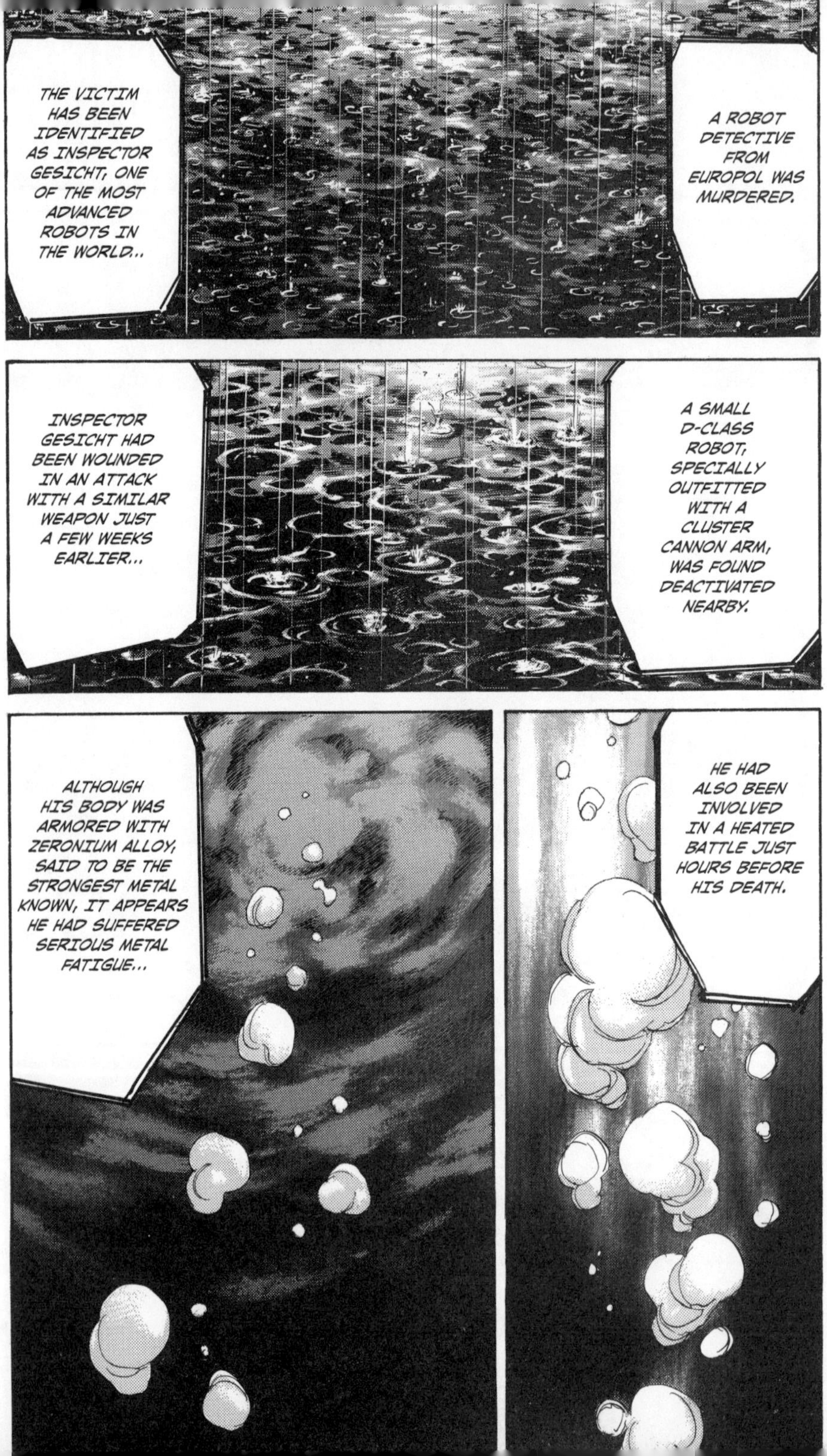
A ROBOT DETECTIVE FROM EUROPOL WAS MURDERED.
THE VICTIM HAS BEEN IDENTIFIED AS INSPECTOR GESICHT, ONE OF THE MOST ADVANCED ROBOTS IN THE WORLD...
A SMALL D-CLASS ROBOT, SPECIALLY OUTFITTED WITH A CLUSTER CANNON ARM, WAS FOUND DEACTIVATED NEARBY.
INSPECTOR GESICHT HAD BEEN WOUNDED IN AN ATTACK WITH A SIMILAR WEAPON JUST A FEW WEEKS EARLIER...
HE HAD ALSO BEEN INVOLVED IN A HEATED BATTLE JUST HOURS BEFORE HIS DEATH.
ALTHOUGH HIS BODY WAS ARMORED WITH ZERONIUM ALLOY, SAID TO BE THE STRONGEST METAL KNOWN, IT APPEARS HE HAD SUFFERED SERIOUS METAL FATIGUE...

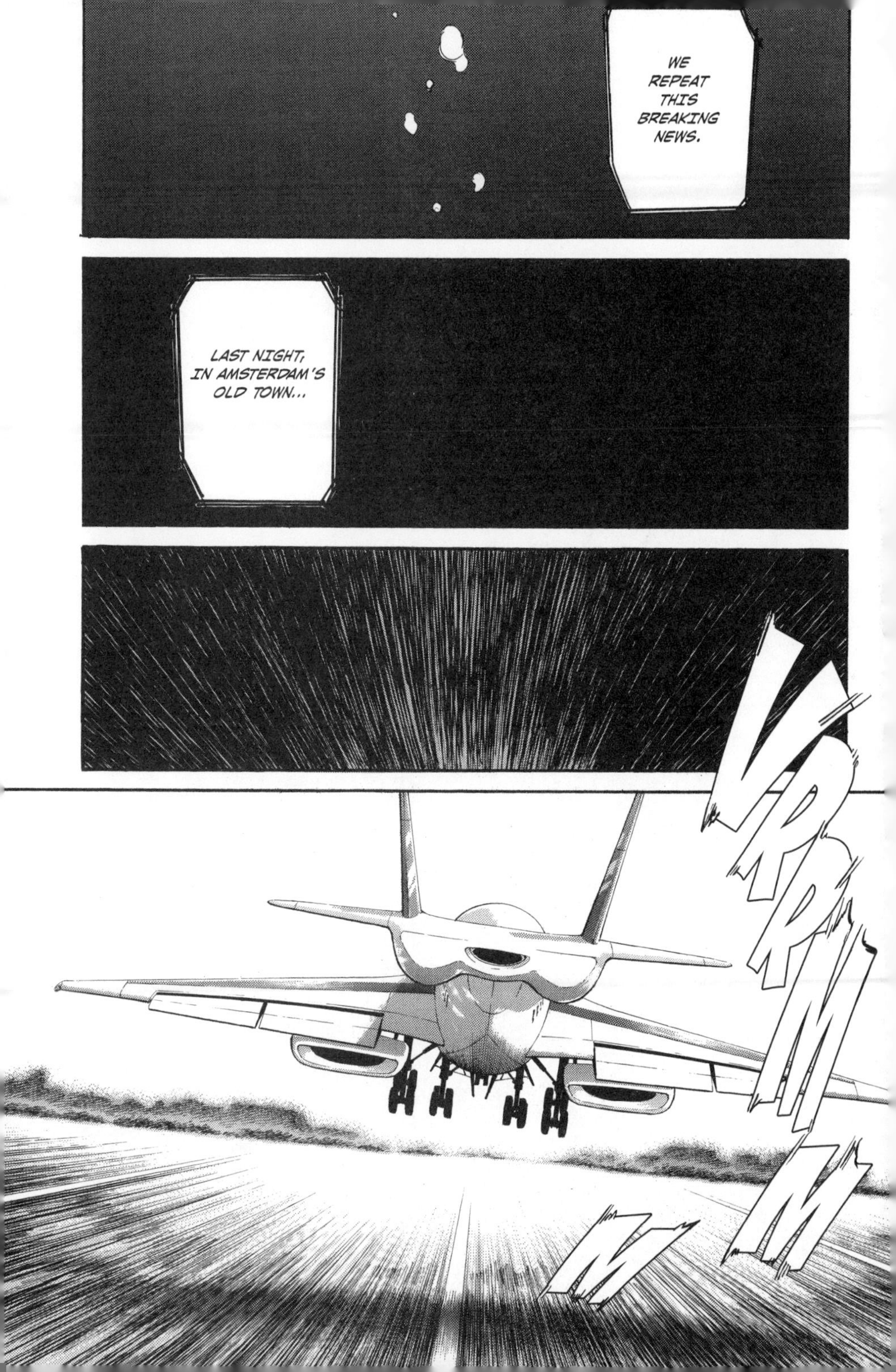
WE REPEAT THIS BREAKING NEWS.
LAST NIGHT, IN AMSTERDAM'S OLD TOWN...
VRRMMM

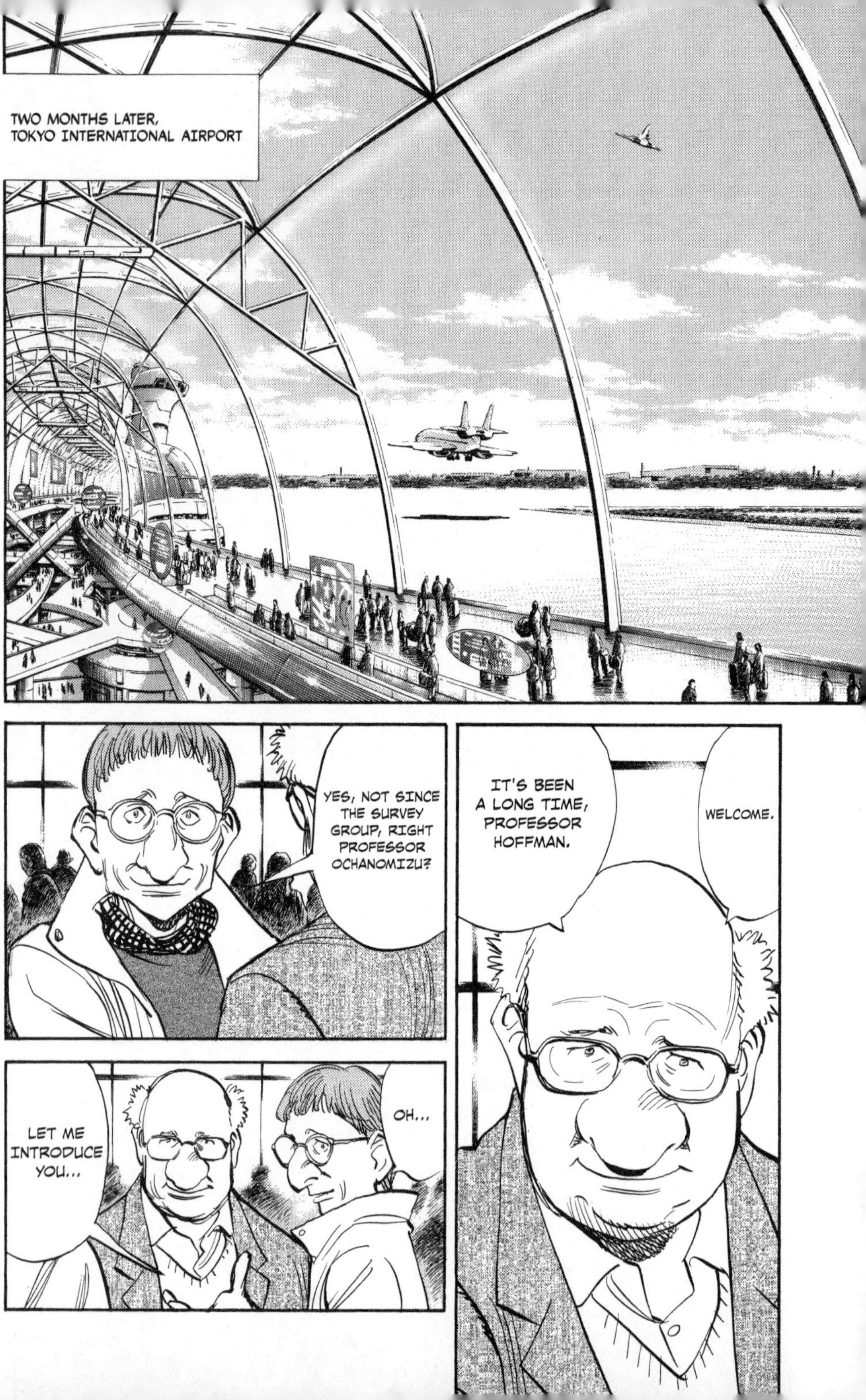

TWO MONTHS LATER, TOKYO INTERNATIONAL AIRPORT
WELCOME.
IT'S BEEN A LONG TIME, PROFESSOR HOFFMAN.
YES, NOT SINCE THE SURVEY GROUP, RIGHT PROFESSOR OCHANOMIZU?
OH...
LET ME INTRODUCE YOU...

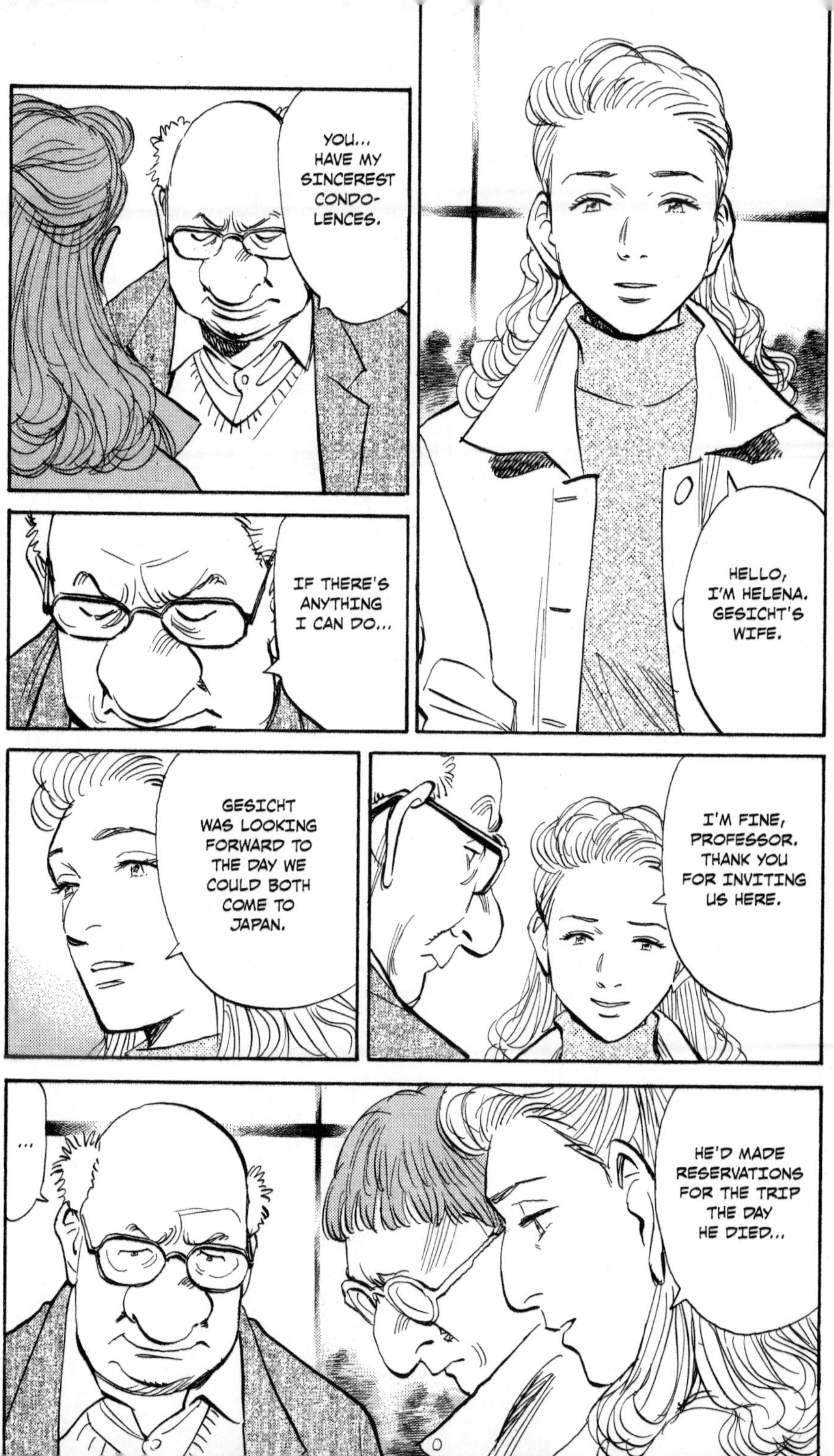
HELLO, I'M HELENA. GESICHT'S WIFE.
YOU... HAVE MY SINCEREST CONDO-LENCES.
IF THERE'S ANYTHING I CAN DO...
I'M FINE, PROFESSOR. THANK YOU FOR INVITING US HERE.
GESICHT WAS LOOKING FORWARD TO THE DAY WE COULD BOTH COME TO JAPAN.
HE'D MADE RESERVATIONS FOR THE TRIP THE DAY HE DIED...
...

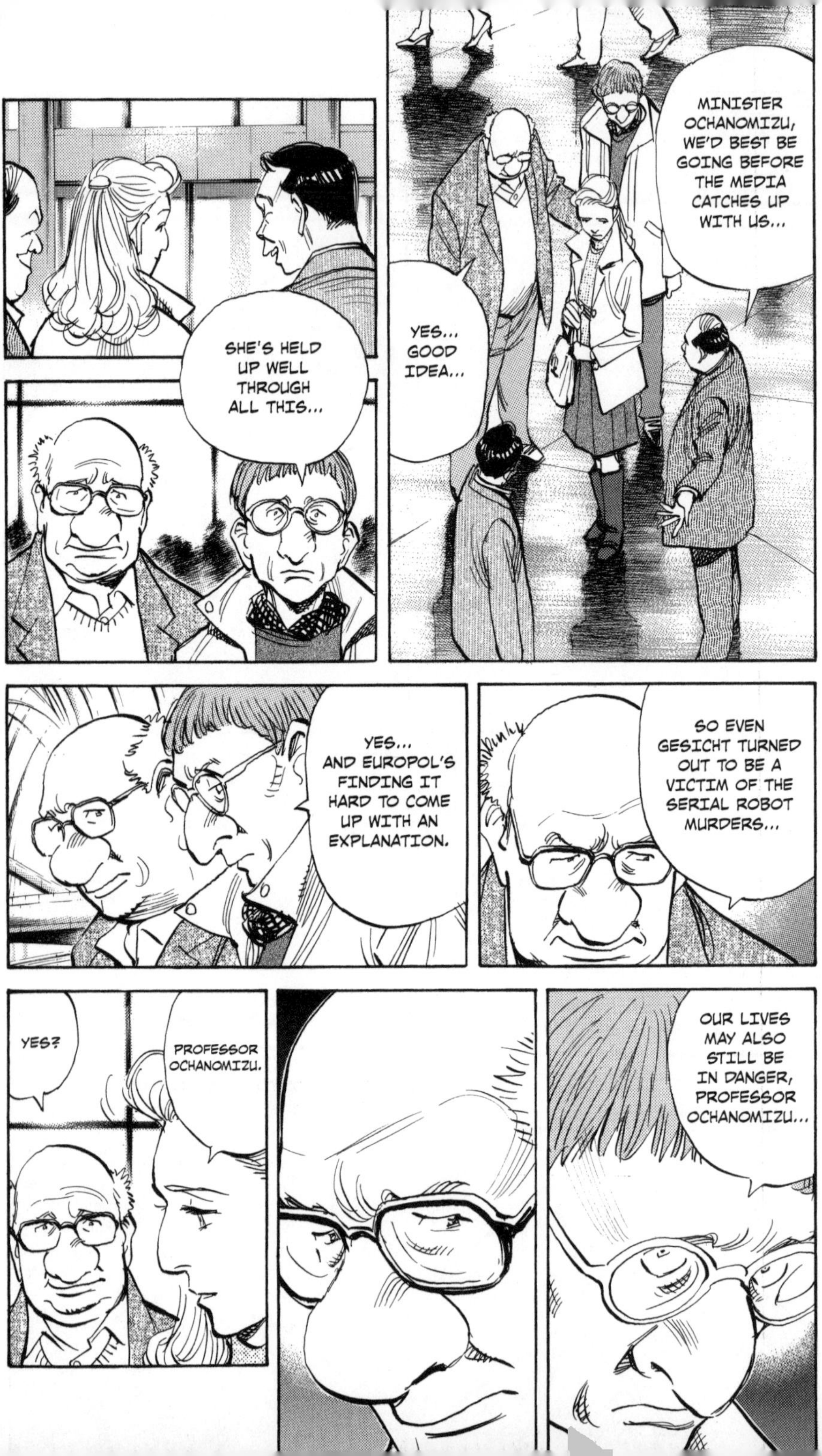
MINISTER OCHANOMIZU, WE'D BEST BE GOING BEFORE THE MEDIA CATCHES UP WITH US...
YES... GOOD IDEA...
SHE'S HELD UP WELL THROUGH ALL THIS...
SO EVEN GESICHT TURNED OUT TO BE A VICTIM OF THE SERIAL ROBOT MURDERS...
YES... AND EUROPOL'S FINDING IT HARD TO COME UP WITH AN EXPLANATION.
OUR LIVES MAY ALSO STILL BE IN DANGER, PROFESSOR OCHANOMIZU...
PROFESSOR OCHANOMIZU.
YES?

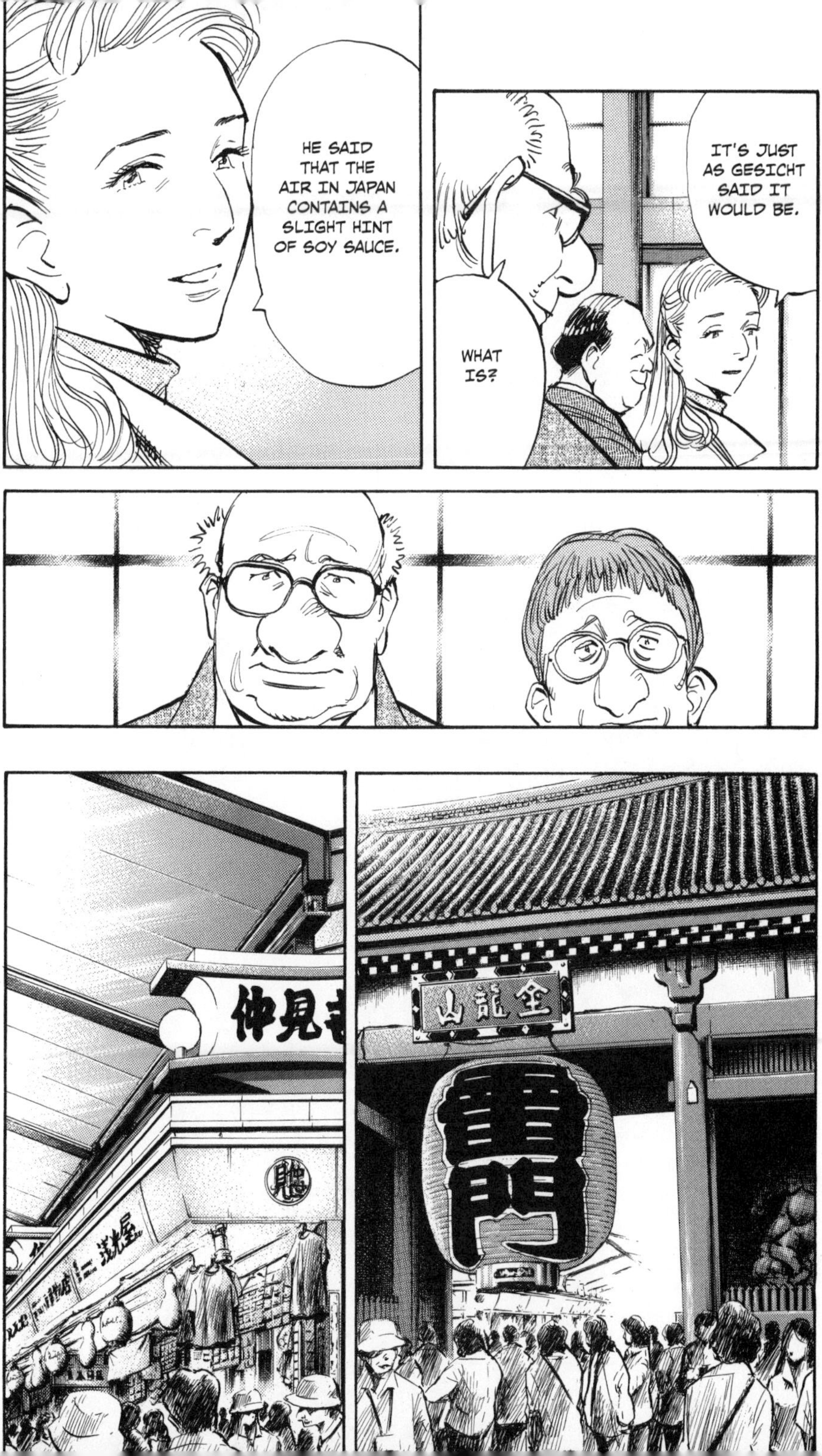
IT'S JUST AS GESICHT SAID IT WOULD BE.
WHAT IS?
HE SAID THAT THE AIR IN JAPAN CONTAINS A SLIGHT HINT OF SOY SAUCE.
金龍山
雷門

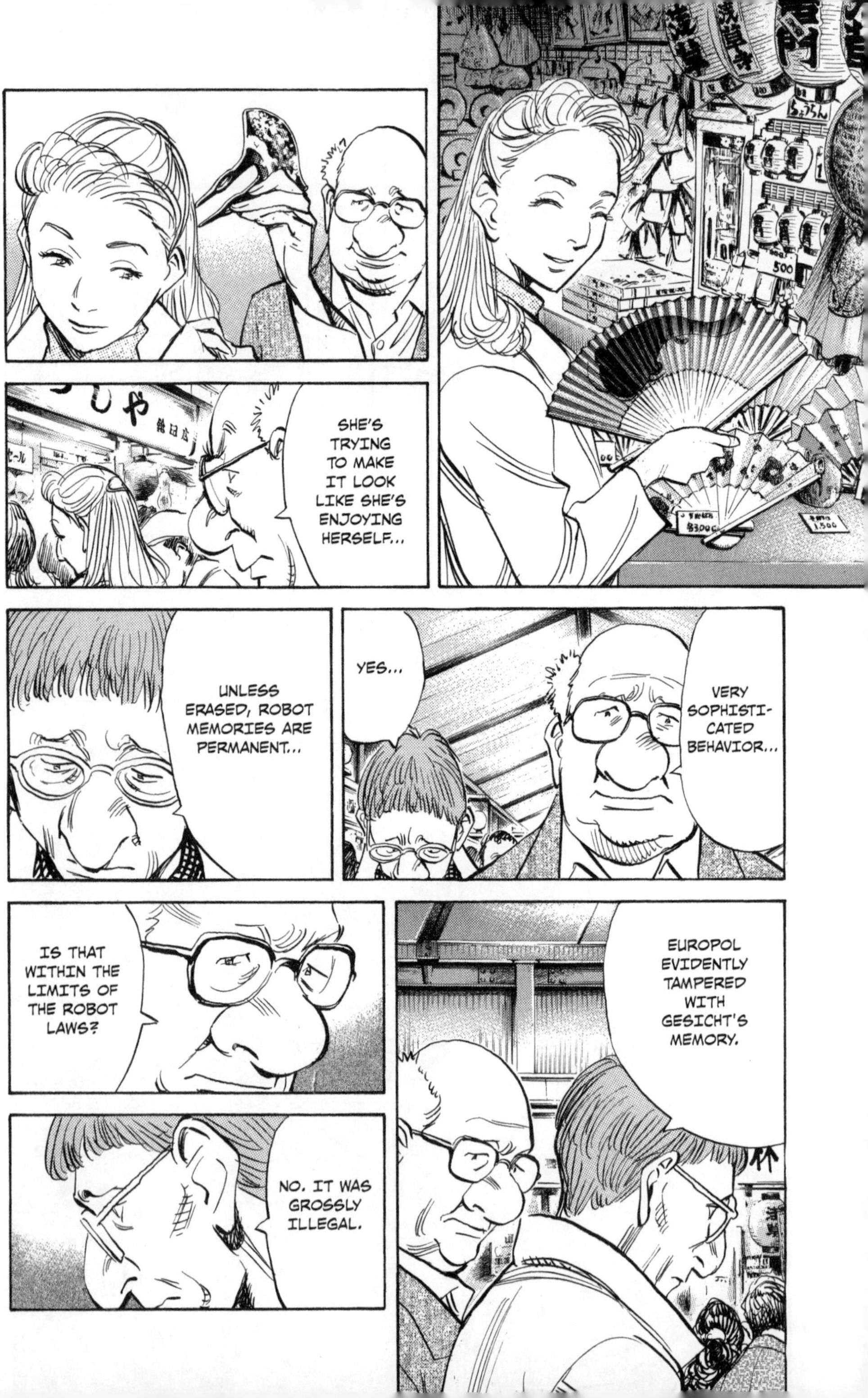
SHE'S TRYING TO MAKE IT LOOK LIKE SHE'S ENJOYING HERSELF...
VERY SOPHISTI-CATED BEHAVIOR...
YES...
UNLESS ERASED, ROBOT MEMORIES ARE PERMANENT...
EUROPOL EVIDENTLY TAMPERED WITH GESICHT'S MEMORY.
IS THAT WITHIN THE LIMITS OF THE ROBOT LAWS?
NO. IT WAS GROSSLY ILLEGAL.

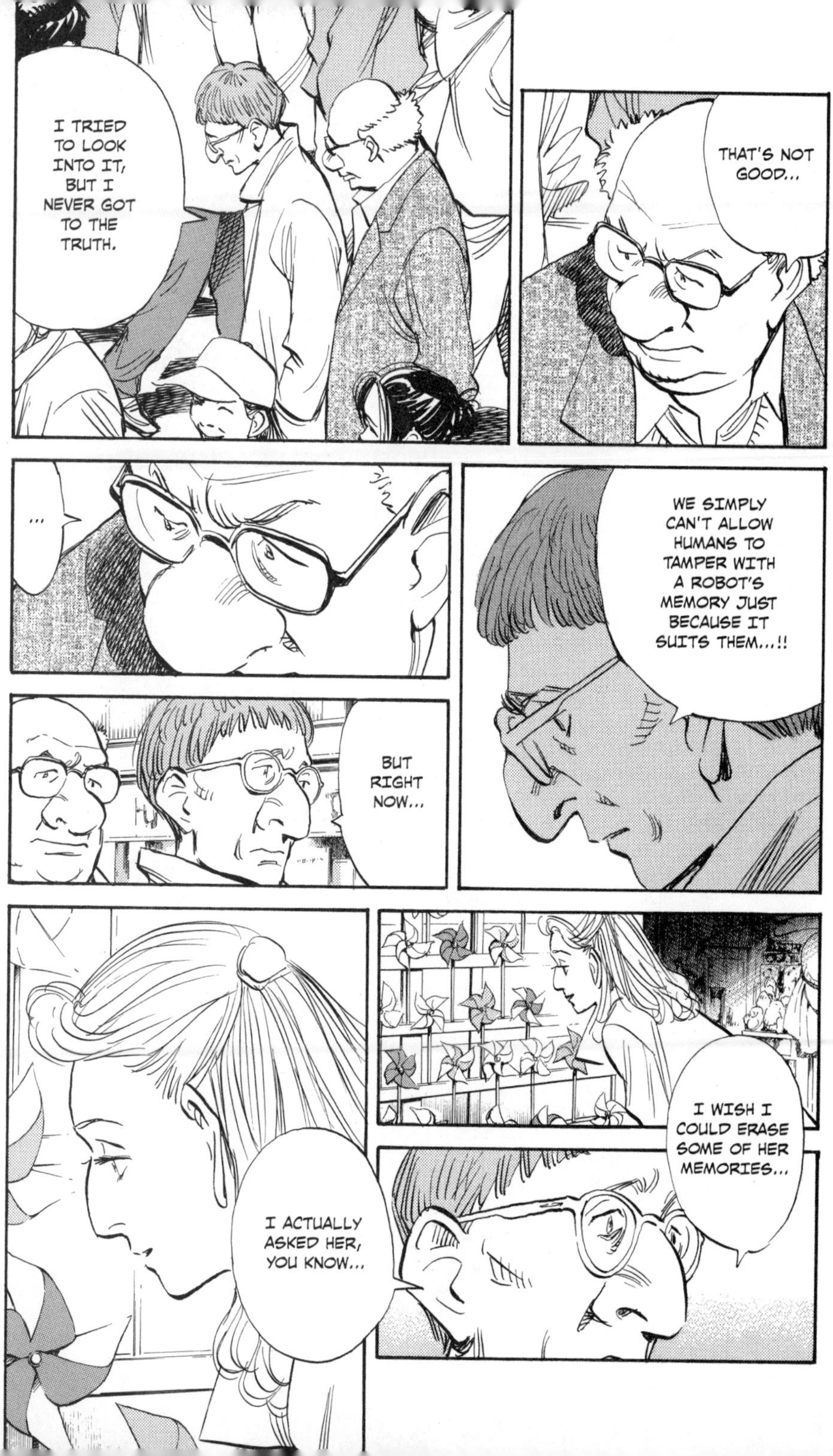
THAT'S NOT GOOD...
I TRIED TO LOOK INTO IT, BUT I NEVER GOT TO THE TRUTH.
WE SIMPLY CAN'T ALLOW HUMANS TO TAMPER WITH A ROBOT'S MEMORY JUST BECAUSE IT SUITS THEM...!!
...
BUT RIGHT NOW...
I WISH I COULD ERASE SOME OF HER MEMORIES...
I ACTUALLY ASKED HER, YOU KNOW...

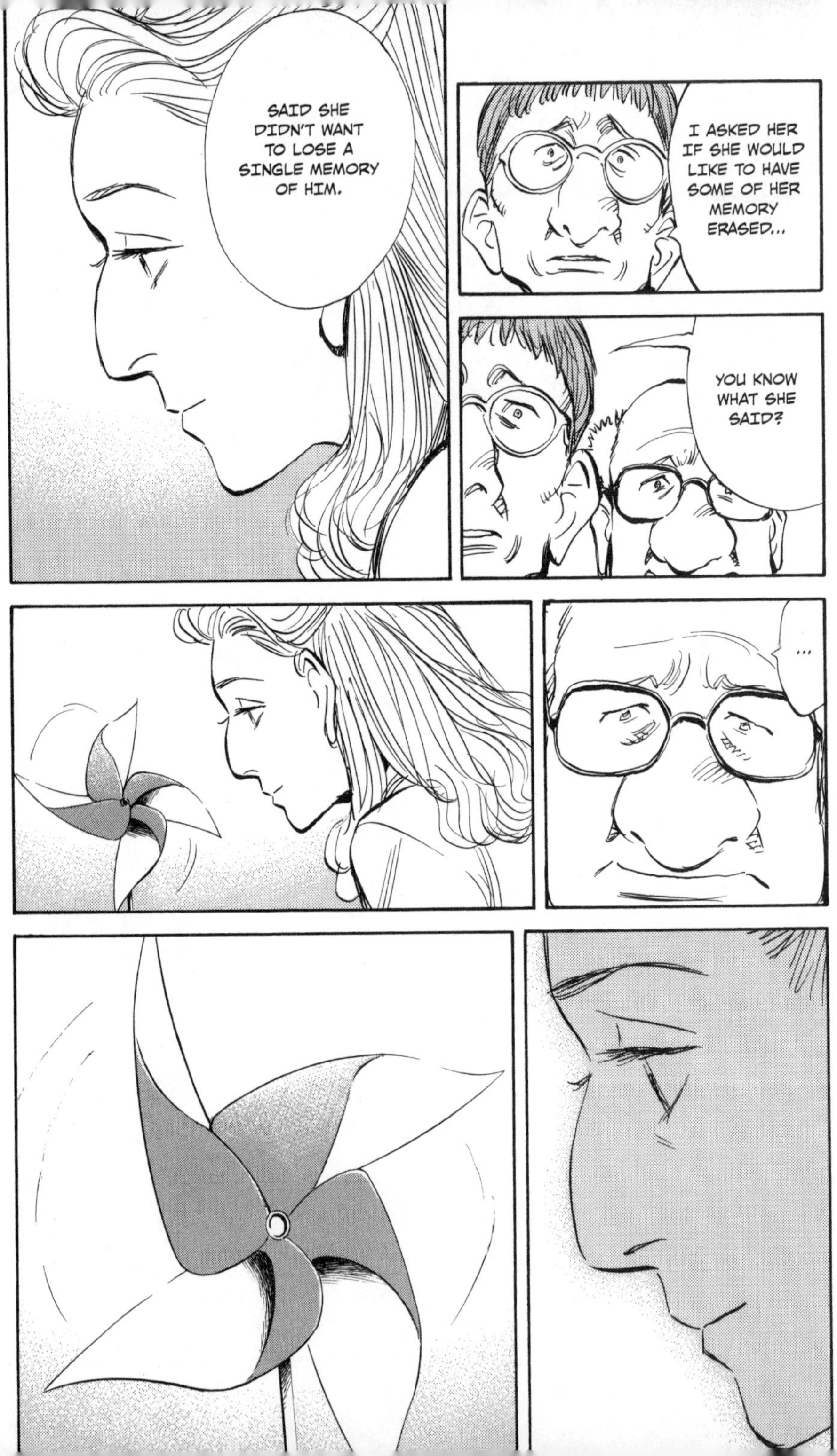
I ASKED HER IF SHE WOULD LIKE TO HAVE SOME OF HER MEMORY ERASED...
YOU KNOW WHAT SHE SAID?
SAID SHE DIDN'T WANT TO LOSE A SINGLE MEMORY OF HIM.
...

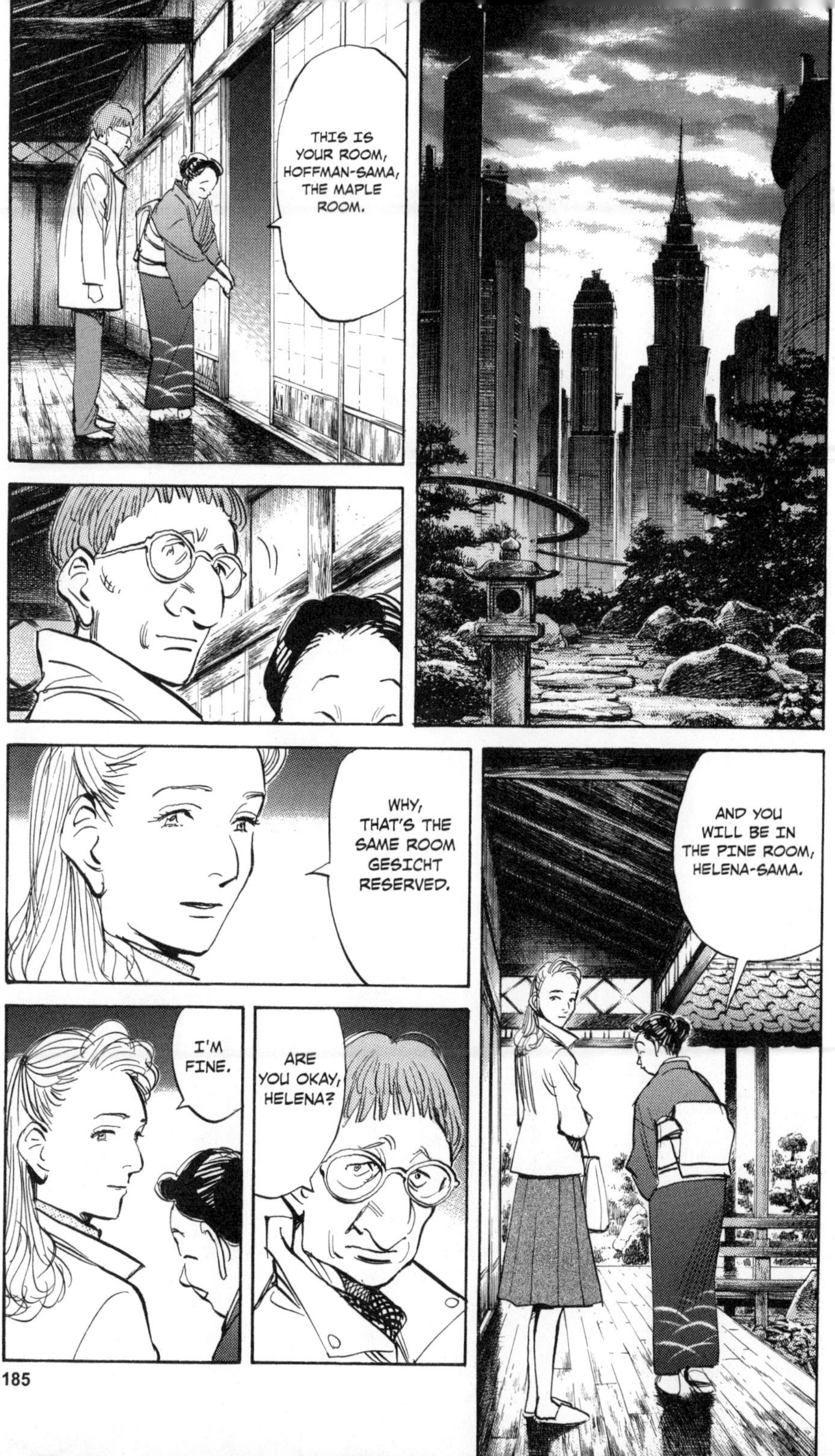
THIS IS YOUR ROOM, HOFFMAN-SAMA, THE MAPLE ROOM.
AND YOU WILL BE IN THE PINE ROOM, HELENA-SAMA.
WHY, THAT'S THE SAME ROOM GESICHT RESERVED.
ARE YOU OKAY, HELENA?
I'M FINE.

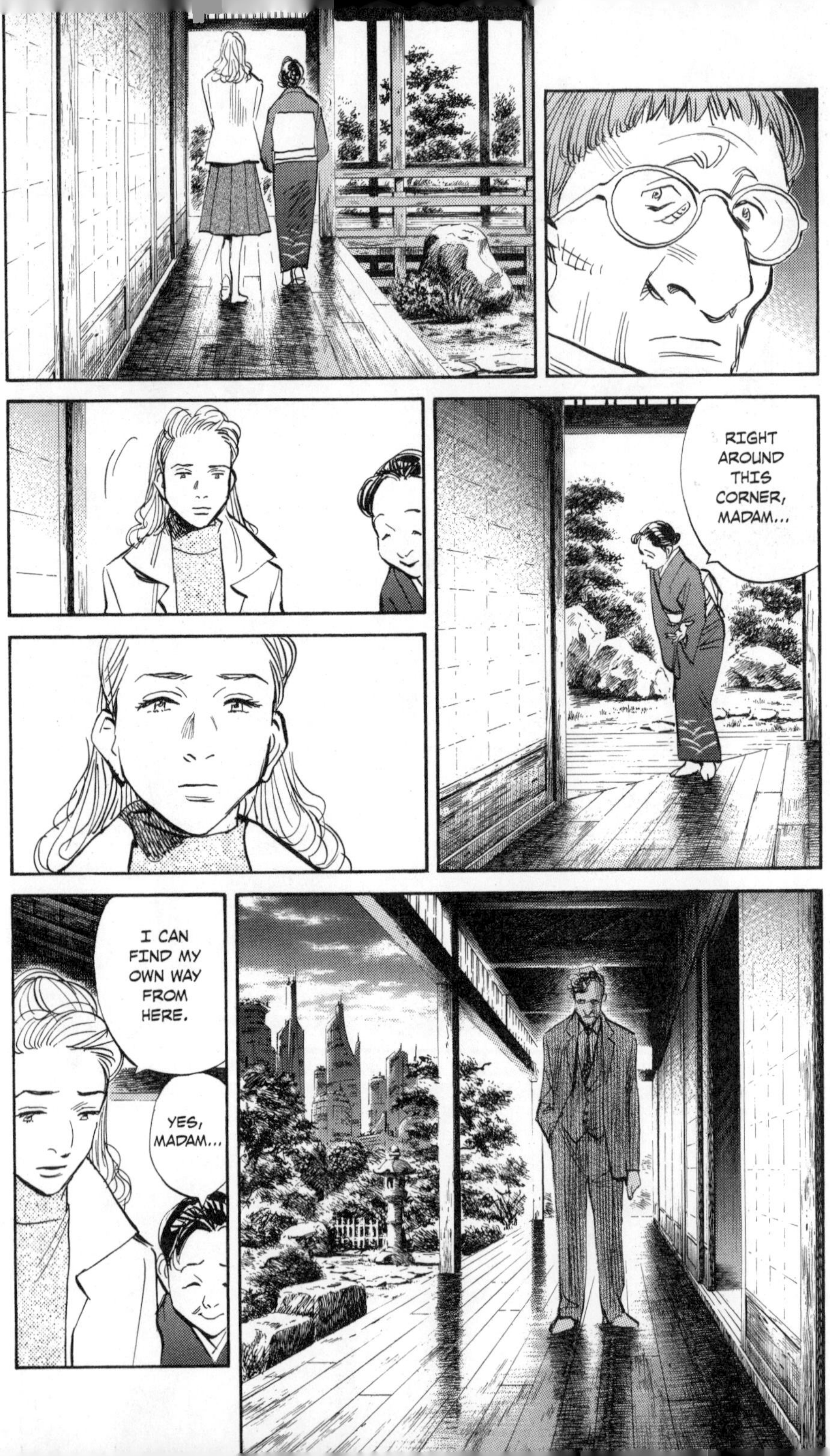
RIGHT AROUND THIS CORNER, MADAM...
I CAN FIND MY OWN WAY FROM HERE.
YES, MADAM...

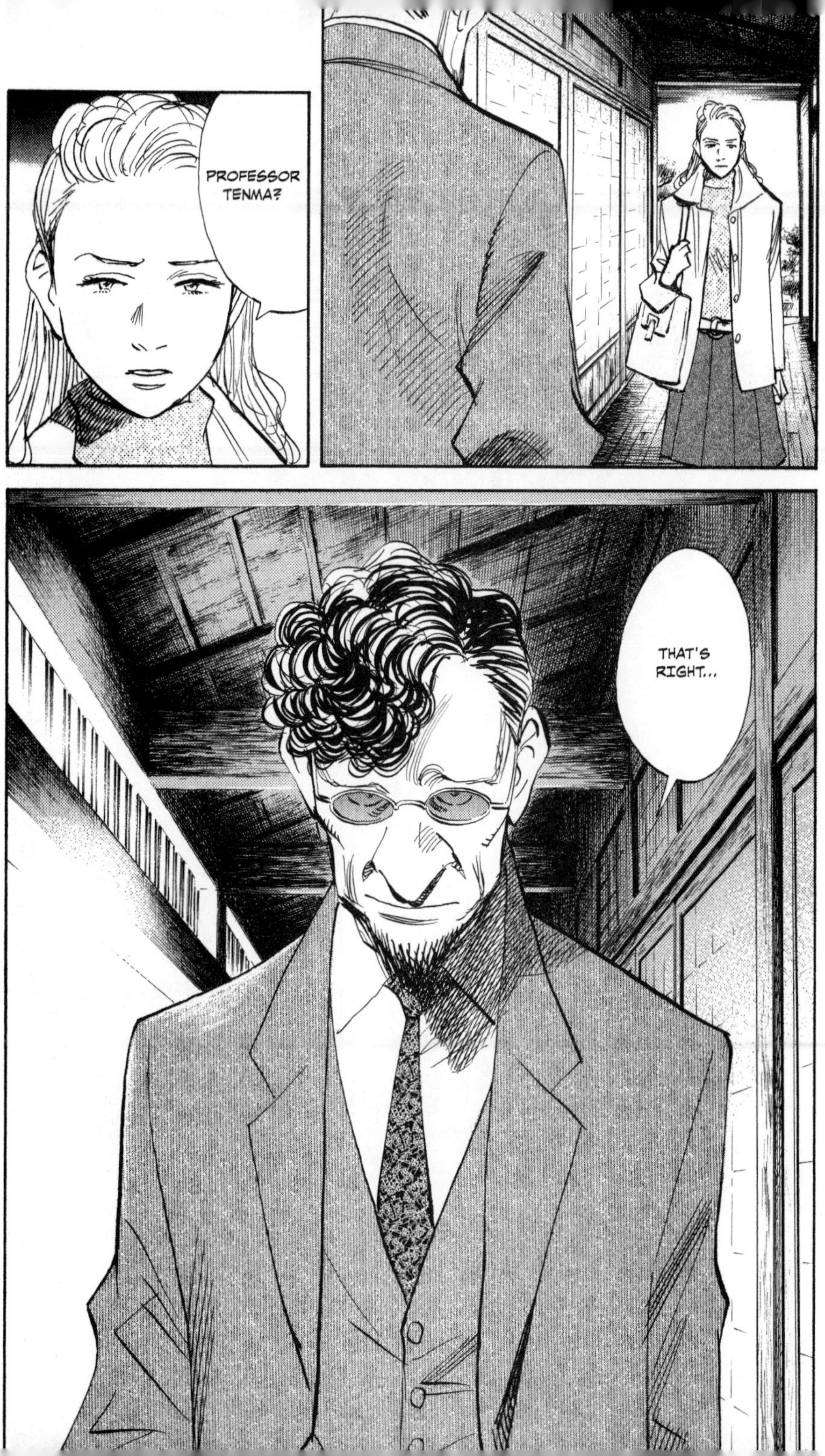
PROFESSOR TENMA?
THAT'S RIGHT...

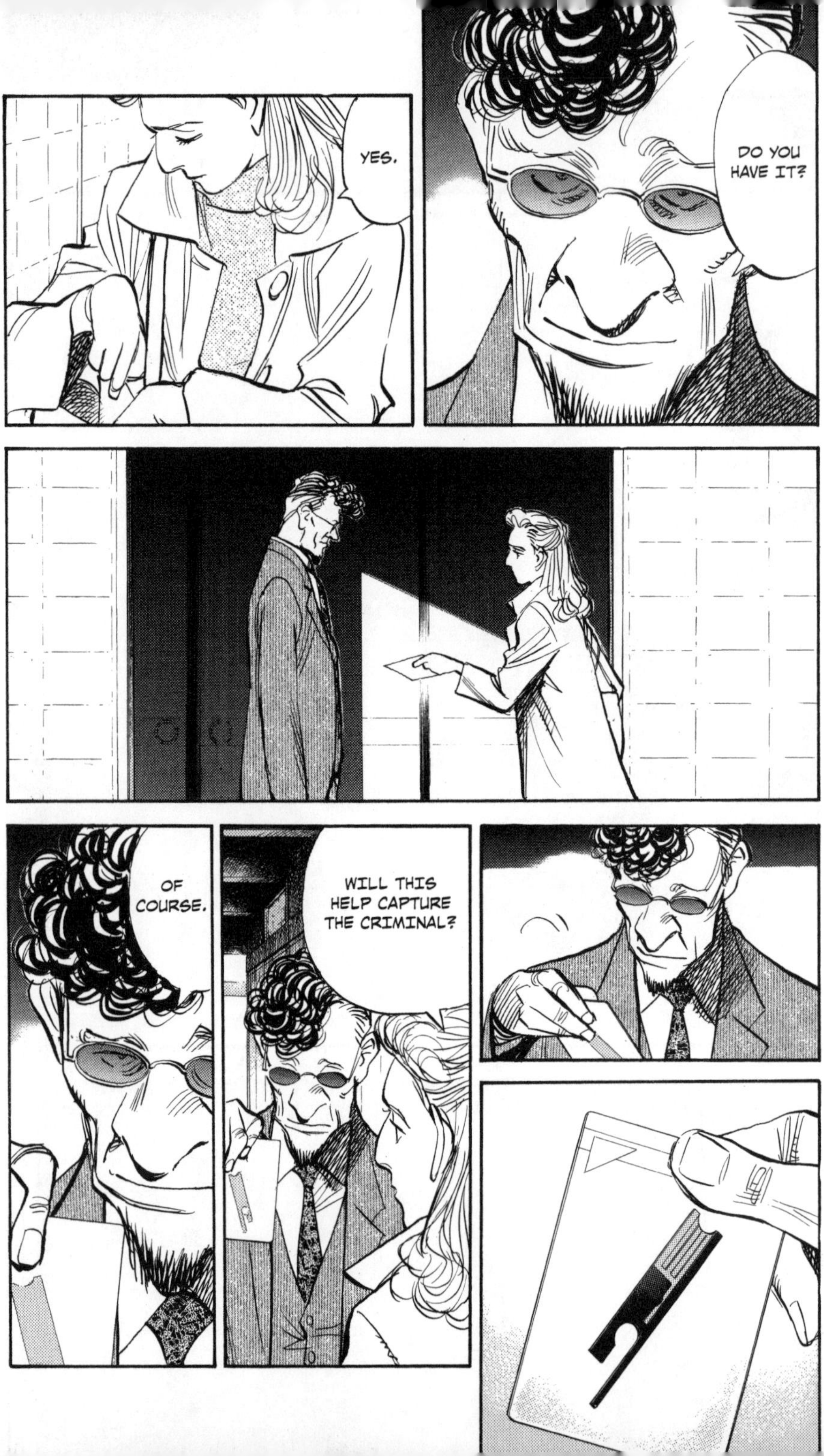
DO YOU HAVE IT?
YES.
WILL THIS HELP CAPTURE THE CRIMINAL?
OF COURSE.

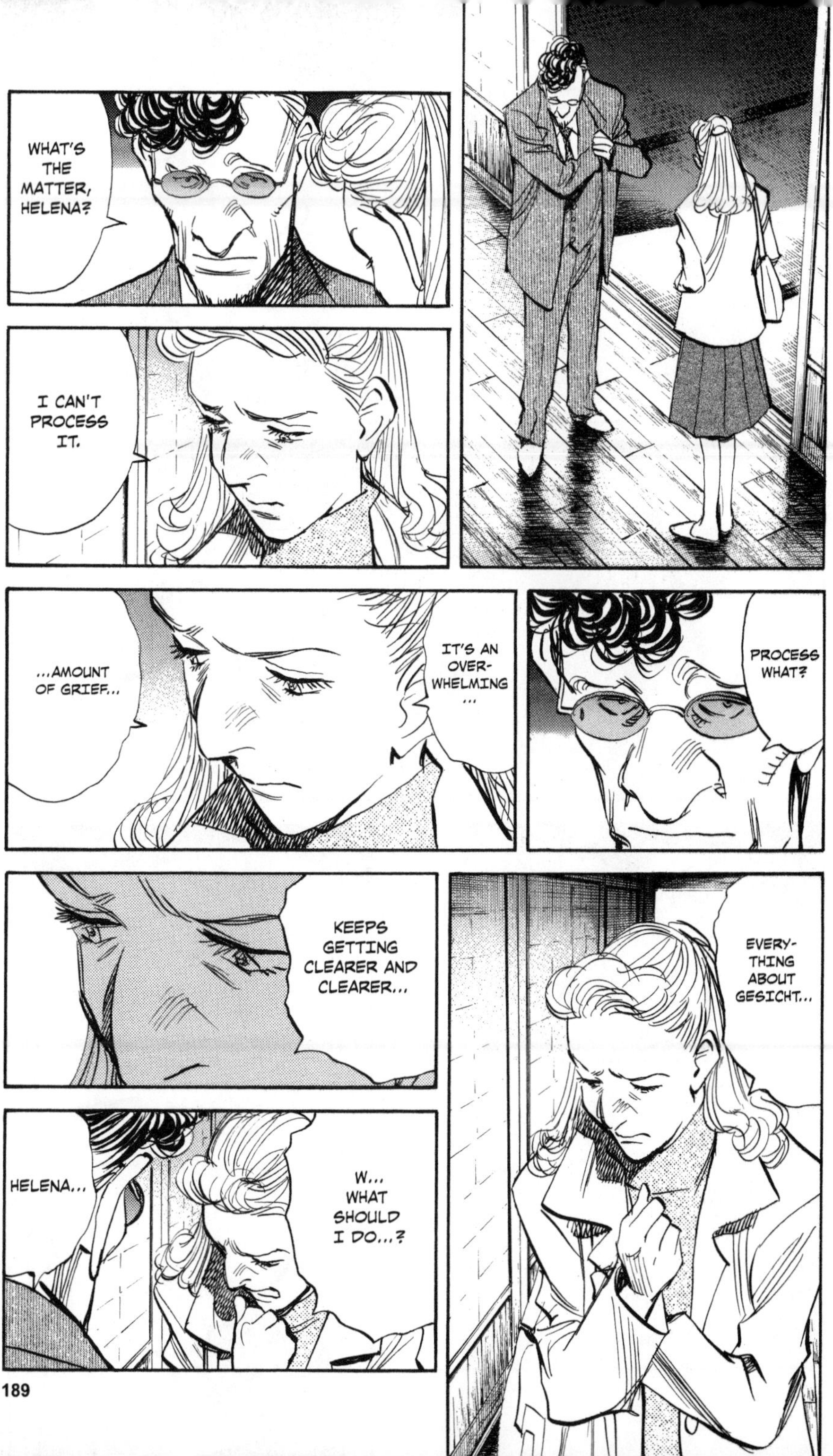
WHAT'S THE MATTER, HELENA?
I CAN'T PROCESS IT.
PROCESS WHAT?
IT'S AN OVER-WHELMING...
...AMOUNT OF GRIEF...
EVERY-THING ABOUT GESICHT...
KEEPS GETTING CLEARER AND CLEARER...
W... WHAT SHOULD I DO...?
HELENA...

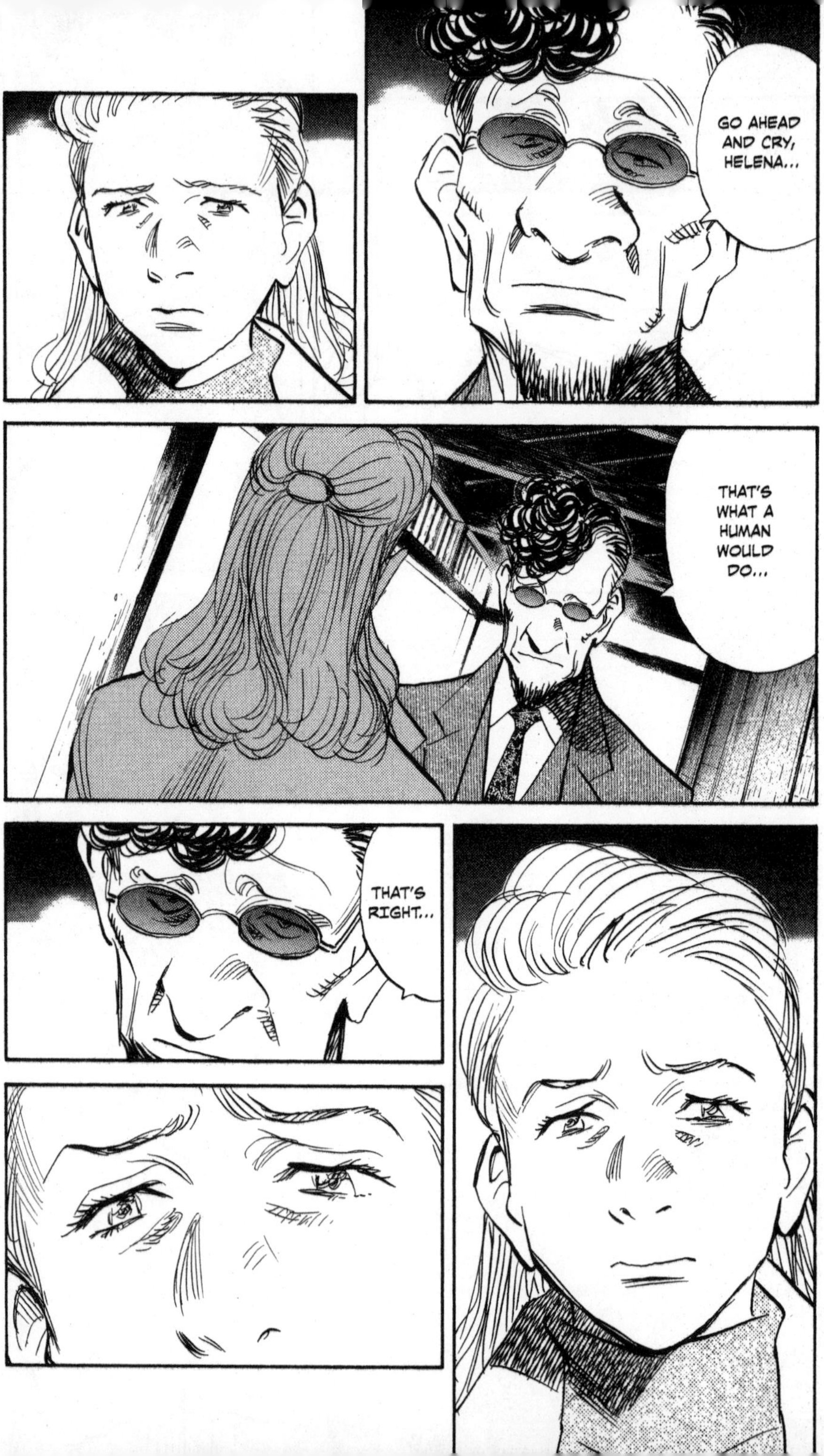
GO AHEAD AND CRY, HELENA...
THAT'S WHAT A HUMAN WOULD DO...
THAT'S RIGHT...

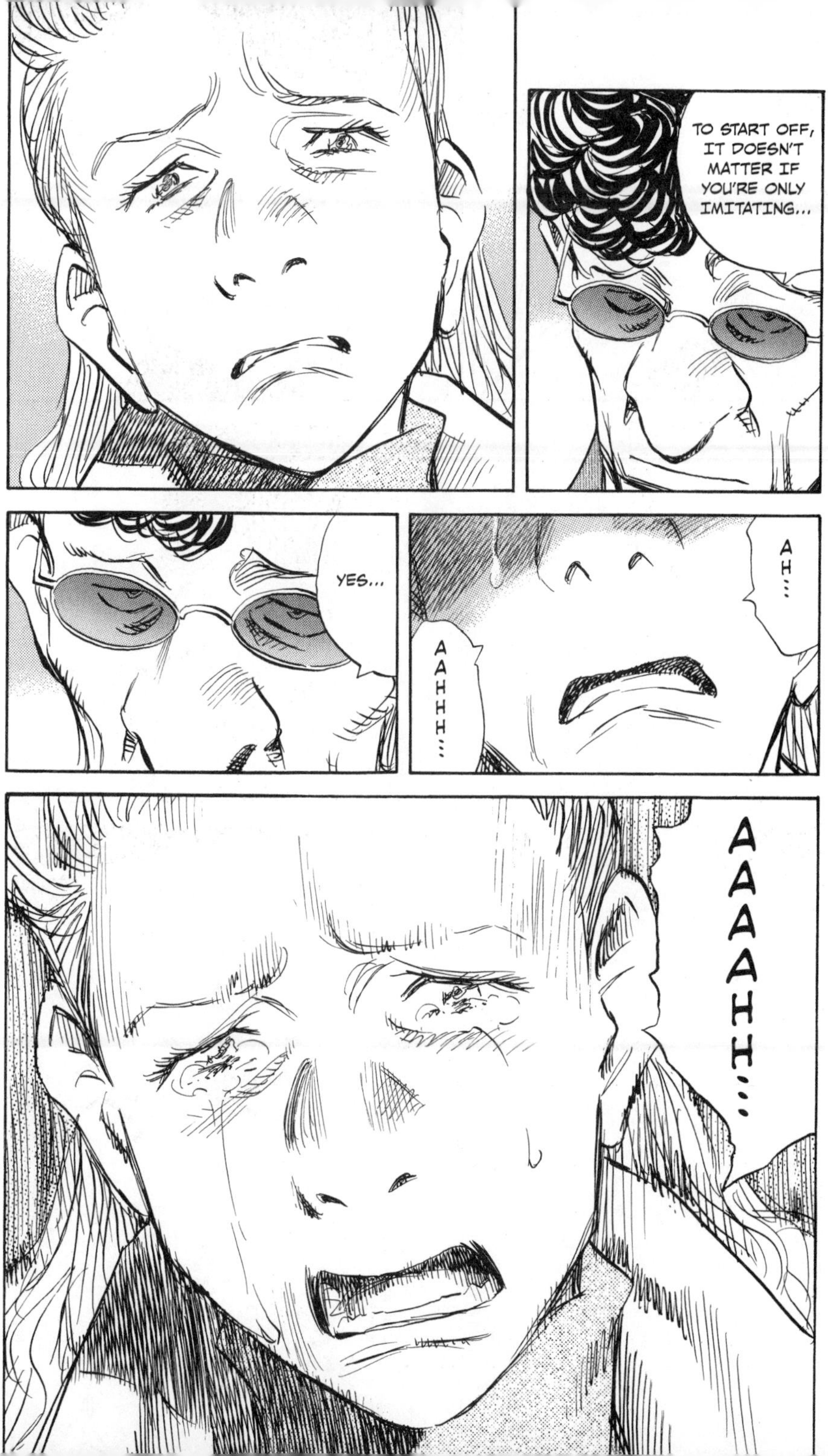
TO START OFF, IT DOESN'T MATTER IF YOU'RE ONLY IMITATING...
AH...
AAHHH...
YES...
AAAAHH...

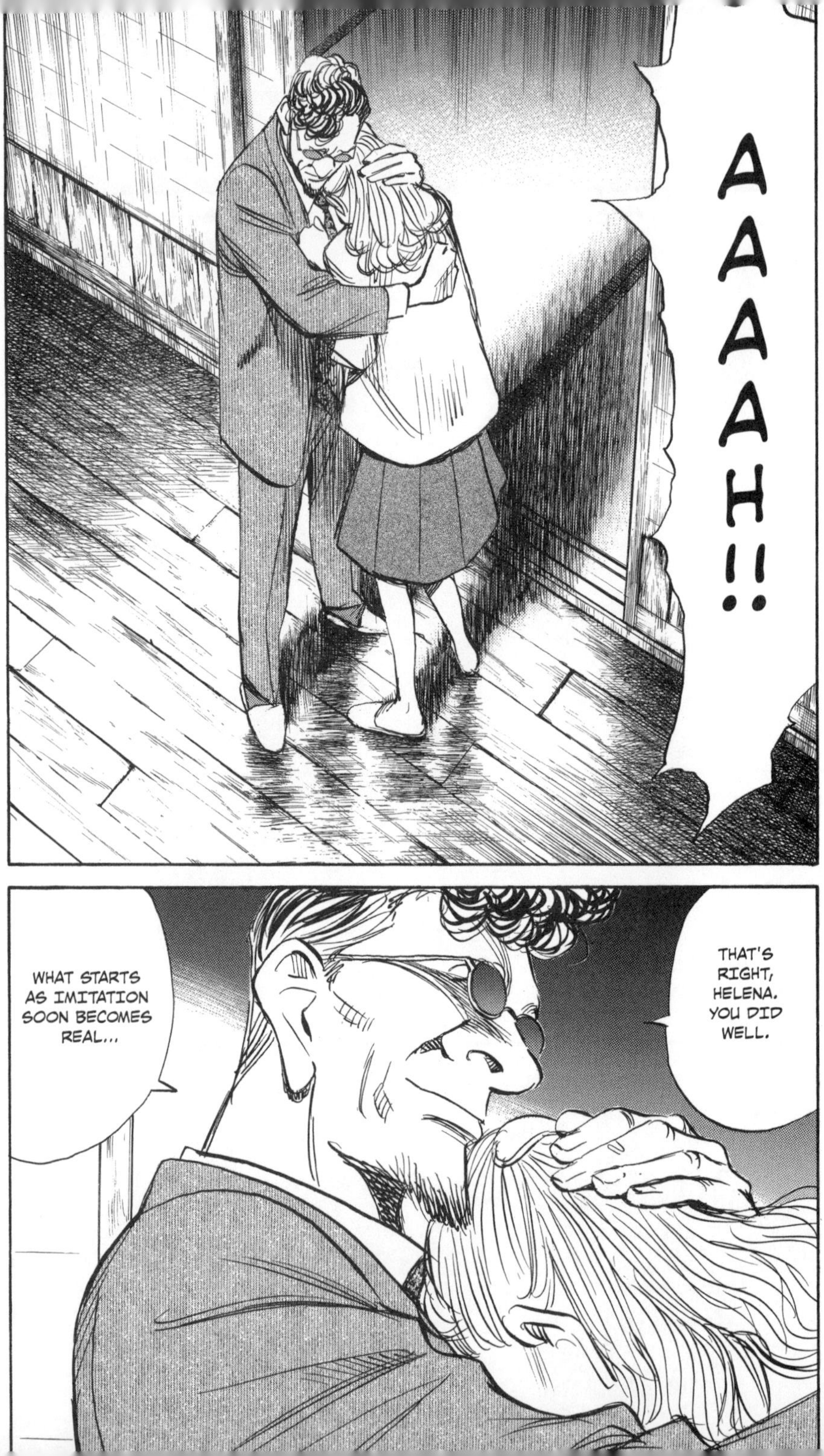
AAAAAH!!
THAT'S RIGHT, HELENA. YOU DID WELL.
WHAT STARTS AS IMITATION SOON BECOMES REAL...

SOON, YOU'LL BE ABLE TO TRULY WEEP, JUST LIKE ME...

THESE ARE REAL TEARS, HELENA...

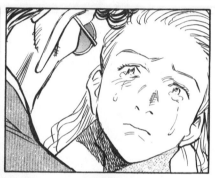

I, TOO, AM GRIEVING... FOR THE DEATH OF ATOM...

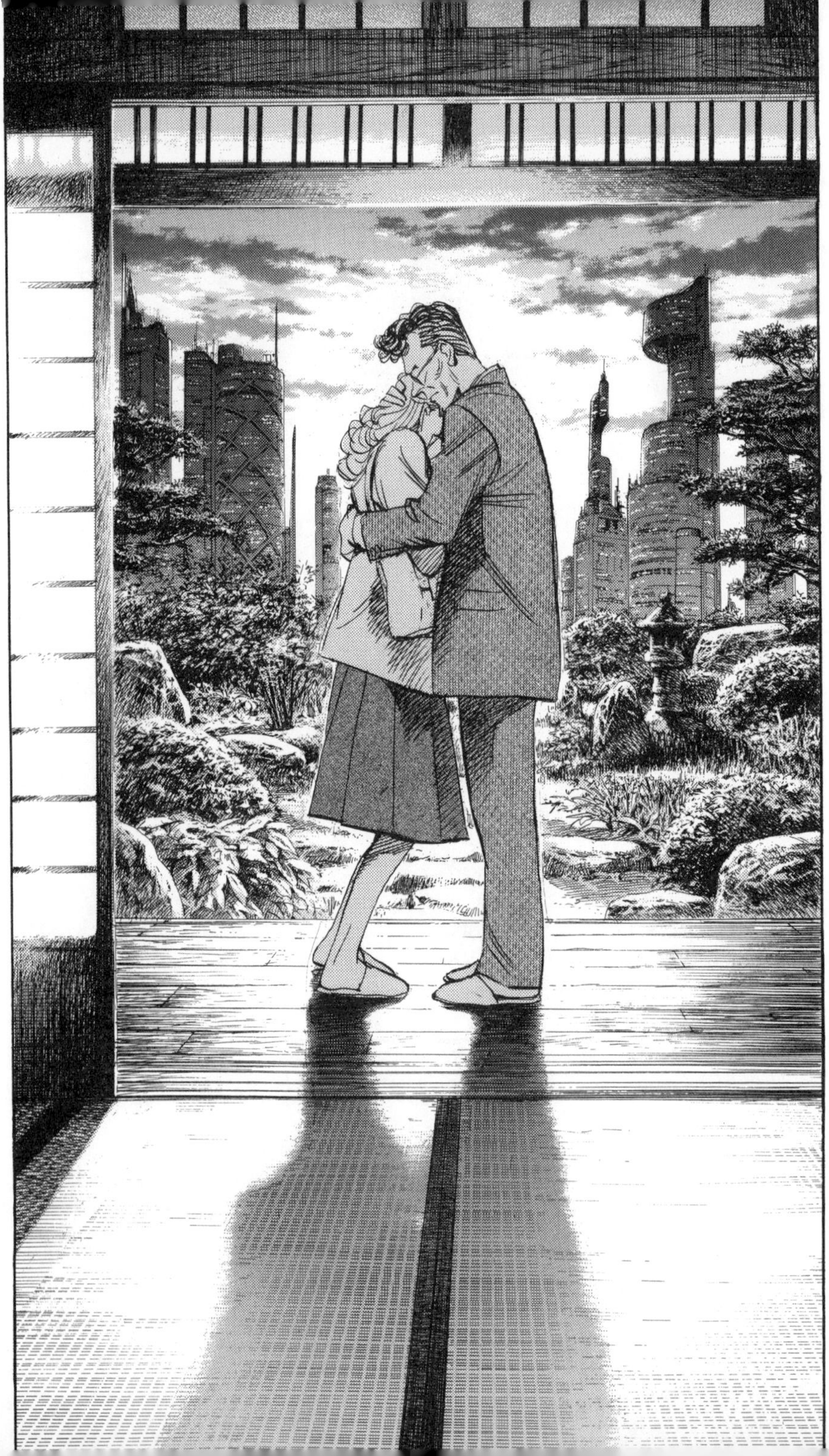

POSTSCRIPT

Gorot Yamada, Essayist and Critic

Old guys like me, born in the Showa era (1926–1989), have the bad habit of discussing generational differences a lot, but when it comes to *Pluto*, this is unavoidable. Naoki Urasawa, the manga artist who created *Pluto*, was born in 1960. He has said that "The Greatest Robot on Earth" episode of *Astro Boy* was his starting point for manga, and in *Pluto* he has tried to bring this episode back to life in a modern format. So *Pluto* has a special significance for those of us from the same generation as Urasawa, such as I who was born in 1958—namely for those of us who were raised as "20th century boys" during Japan's period of high economic growth who have now ended up becoming "21st century middle-aged men."

Astro Boy was serialized in manga format for eighteen years starting in 1951, and "The Greatest Robot on Earth," which appeared in 1964 in the manga magazine *Monthly Shonen*, was one of the most popular episodes in the series. This was the same year that Japan went wild over the Tokyo Olympics, and its creator, none other than the "god of manga" Osamu Tezuka, has said that this time period was when "the work was most enjoyable" for him. The episode was originally titled "The Greatest Robot in History," and the year after it appeared in manga format it was also broadcast as an episode of the *Astro Boy* animated TV series and published as a Kappa Comics paperback compilation. In serializing *Pluto* on a monthly basis in a magazine and issuing the deluxe paperbacks in the same format as the old Kappa Comics, Urasawa and his producer Takashi Nagasaki (born in 1956) are clearly trying to vicariously experience, along with their readers, the manner in which the original was put out into the world.

Members of my generation encountered this classic *Astro Boy* episode just as we became aware of the world around us. We were raised in the exciting era of *Astro Boy* and *Tetsujin 28*, *Godzilla* and *Ultraman*, the bullet train and Apollo 11. This was the time of baseball heroes like Oh and Nagashima, pro wrestlers like Baba and Inoki, and the student movement and Woodstock. You could say that we were the generation that most innocently believed in science, heroes, revolution and rock and roll. But the 1970 Osaka World's Fair—which was supposed to usher in a new decade, one later called *gin iro no mirai* or "a silver future" (coined by writer Toshio Okada who was born 1958)—symbolized an end to this happy dream. Just when we were reaching puberty, we found that in reality science was devolving into pollution, heroes into celebrities, rock and roll into business, and revolution into terror. Most of our contemporaries woke up from the dream and became adults; the rest of us continued to flee reality and became otaku.

As we approached middle age and began to question what we were doing in life, Urasawa created *20th Century Boys*—an appeal for us to regain the view of the future that we had once believed in. And this also helps explain why Urasawa next challenged himself with *Pluto*. This series is far more than a simple remake of an old manga classic. To me, it feels like a manifesto from Urasawa, a plea to his contemporaries to follow him as he revives the source of his childhood dreams.

Pluto can of course be read purely as a manga, for it is entertainment bar none. In the story, the characters are caught up in a series of strange and mysterious incidents. While trying to solve a mystery, they find that forgotten memories are revived and that they may have some responsibility for what has happened. Using the framework for suspense that he previously established with *Monster* and *20th Century Boys*, in *Pluto* Urasawa recreates the original *Astro Boy* story by cleverly weaving in themes from various episodes of the *Astro Boy* series and references to Osamu Tezuka's entire canon. I can only describe my impression of what Urasawa has done as one of amazement, for he demonstrates an extraordinary ability to exploit the depth and density of 21st century seinen manga styles and to depict things that Tezuka could not include or was forced to only hint at in the shonen manga format of the sixties. For example, I find myself particularly fond of the episode in the first volume of *Pluto* titled "North No. 2." The agonizingly beautiful last scene, it seems to me, is one that could only have been created by Urasawa. It will surely go down in manga history as a classic.

There is no trade-off in *Pluto* between scenes of beauty and cruel destruction, as there was in the original *Astro Boy*. That's even true of the scene in this volume where Gesicht is destroyed. And I should also mention that the *ero kawaii* (erotic cute) sequence in the original, where Uran went after *Pluto* wearing nothing more than Atom's short pants, has been transformed into a very straightforward and "nice" sequence in the second volume of Urasawa's version. In other words, we can say that *Pluto* thus far has shown considerably less cruelty and eroticism than the original *Astro Boy* story. And if we read *Pluto* as a manifesto by Urasawa targeted at his contemporaries, this may even be one of its minor weaknesses.

The cruelty and eroticism in Osamu Tezuka's work is sometimes referred to as evidence of his so-called dark side and treated as taboo. But in reality, these qualities were also one of Tezuka's greatest strengths as a children's author. Depictions of cruelty or eroticism, if done poorly, can indeed be harmful, but in the hands of a skilled author they can conversely work as a vaccine, to help young readers develop a resistance to what might otherwise harm them. Tezuka himself recognized these same two aspects in the greatness of Walt Disney, whom he idealized as his mentor, and warned against falling into the trap of emphasizing a cheap humanism simply to placate critics.*

It is impossible to discuss *Astro Boy* without considering the cruelty Tezuka depicted. Atom was created as a surrogate for a real boy who had been killed. After being treated cruelly by his creator he was sold to the circus and then later made to work to satisfy the whims of humans. He was discriminated against because he was a "mere robot." And despite being betrayed over and over again by humans, he continued to believe in them and to fight for them until he broke down.

At the same time, the almost painfully cruel aspects of the *Astro Boy* story were also the source of its hope and optimism. At the end of the episode on which *Pluto* is based, Atom says, "I still believe robots'll all become friends someday and never ever fight each other again..." Although Atom had no real grounds for making such an optimistic statement, it made readers of my generation feel a great sense of hope, because we had just been shown the outrageous and cruel fate of robots, and it had made anger, horror and sadness well up in us as a result.

It is true. Completely negative emotions can create perfect hope. And I'm sure that Urasawa is more than aware of this. In future pages of *Pluto*, probably after Atom has been revived, the story will meet its moment of truth. And then the question will be whether Urasawa will be able to surpass Tezuka, the "God of Manga" who personally witnessed the bombing of Osaka during World War II. The question will be whether he can depict cruelty in a way that injects a bias into the emotions of the sleeping souls of 21st century middle-aged men. Will he be able to make them wake up and revive a sense of hope in an era when people have ceased dreaming about the future?

I am convinced that Urasawa can pull this off. I have no proof, of course, but as Tatsuro Yamashita (born in 1953) sang in his famous song, "No matter how adult we may become, we will always be the children of Atom." As a contemporary of Urasawa and as a fan, I am in a similar position to Konchi from *20th Century Boys*—I'm not an integral part of it, but I desperately want him to succeed.

*See the article titled "Walt Disney: manga eiga no ōja" [Walt Disney, the King of Cartoons], in the June 15, 1973, edition of the *Asahi Journal*.

Atom no Ko ©1991 by Smile Publishers Inc.

The late Osamu Tezuka, a manga artist for whom I have the utmost respect, created the series *Astro Boy*. This timeless classic has been read by countless numbers of fans from when it was first created in the fifties to now. As a child, "The Greatest Robot on Earth" story arc from *Astro Boy* was the first manga I ever read that really moved me and inspired me to become a manga artist. With *Pluto* I've attempted to infuse that story with a fresh new spirit. I hope you enjoy it.

NAOKI URASAWA

Manga wouldn't exist without Osamu Tezuka. He is the Leonardo da Vinci, the Goethe, the Dostoevsky of the manga world. Naoki Urasawa and I have always felt that his achievements and work must not be allowed to fade away. Tezuka wrote that Atom, the main character of his most representative work *Astro Boy*, was born in 2003. This was the same year that we re-made "The Greatest Robot on Earth" story arc from the *Astro Boy* series. Who was Osamu Tezuka and what was his message? For those of you readers who are interested in *Pluto*, I highly recommend you read it alongside Tezuka's original work.

TAKASHI NAGASAKI

PLUTO: URASAWA × TEZUKA
VOLUME 6
VIZ SIGNATURE EDITION

BY Naoki Urasawa & Osamu Tezuka
CO-AUTHORED WITH Takashi Nagasaki
WITH THE COOPERATION OF Tezuka Productions

TRANSLATION Jared Cook & Frederik L. Schodt
TOUCH-UP & LETTERING James Gaubatz
COVER ART DIRECTION Kazuo Umino
LOGO & COVER DESIGN Mikiyo Kobayashi & Bay Bridge Studio
VIZ SIGNATURE EDITION DESIGNER Courtney Utt
EDITOR Andy Nakatani

VP, PRODUCTION Alvin Lu
VP, PUBLISHING LICENSING Rika Inouye
VP, SALES & PRODUCT MARKETING Gonzalo Ferreyra
VP, CREATIVE Linda Espinosa
PUBLISHER Hyoe Narita

Published by VIZ Media, LLC
P.O. Box 77010
San Francisco, CA 94107

10 9 8 7 6 5 4 3 2 1
First printing, November 2009

www.viz.com   www.vizsignature.com

ASTRO BOY

Osamu Tezuka's iconic *Astro Boy* series was a truly groundbreaking work about a loveable boy robot that would pave the way for all manga and anime to follow. Tezuka created the manga in 1951 and in January of 1963 adapted it to become the first weekly animated TV series ever to be broadcast in Japan. In September of that same year, it became the first animated TV series from Japan to hit the airwaves in the United States. The series and its title character were originally known in Japan as *Tetsuwan Atom*, which translates to "mighty Atom" – or for the more literally minded, "iron-arm Atom" – but was released in the U.S. as *Astro Boy*. Decades later, in 2000, Dark Horse Comics brought the manga for the first time to English readers, also under the title *Astro Boy*.

Within the context of the story for this English edition of *Pluto: Urasawa × Tezuka*, the precocious boy robot will be referred to as "Atom" in the manner in which he has been known and loved in Japan for over fifty years. Elsewhere, such as in the end matter, the series will be referred to as *Astro Boy* as it has been known outside of Japan since 1963.